Megabit
Data Communications
A Guide For Professionals

Henry H. Stair, II

John T. Powers, Jr.

PRENTICE HALL
Englewood Cliffs, N.J. 07632

Library of Congress-in-Publication Data

Stair, Henry H. [date]
    Megabit data communications: a guide for professionals / Henry H.
Stair, II, John T. Powers, Jr.
        p. cm.

    ISBN 0-13-573569-6
    1. Data transmission systems.   I. Powers, John T., [date].
II. Title.
TK5105. S72   1990
621.382—dc20   89-15617
                                                     CIP

Editorial/production supervision and
    interior design: Fred Dahl and Rose Kernan
Cover design: Wanda Lubelska
Manufacturing buyer: Mary Ann Gloriande

1990 by Prentice-Hall, Inc.
A Division of Simon & Schuster
Englewood Cliffs, New Jersey 07632

This book can be made available to businesses
and organizations at a special discount when
orderd in large quantities. For more information
contact:

    Prentice- Hall, Inc.
    Special Sales and Markets
    College Division
    Englewood Cliffs, N.J. 07632

Printed in the United States of America
10 9 8 7 6 5 4 3 2 1

ISBN 0-13-573569-6

Prentice-Hall International (UK) Limited, *London*
Prentice-Hall of Australia Pty. Limited, *Sydney*
Prentice-Hall Canada Inc., *Toronto*
Prentice-Hall Hispanoamericana, S.A., *Mexico*
Prentice-Hall of India Private Limited, *New Delhi*
Prentice-Hall of Japan, Inc., *Tokyo*
Simon & Schuster Asia Pte. Ltd., *Singapore*
Editora Prentice-Hall do Brasil, Ltda., *Rio de Janeiro*

Contents

CHAPTER 5
T-Carrier Systems, 103

CHAPTER 6
Digital Interface Units, 135

CHAPTER 7
Digital Synchronization, 169

CHAPTER 8
Common Carrier Digital Services, 206

CHAPTER 9
Satellite Technology, 227

CHAPTER 10
Fiber Optic Technology, 258

CHAPTER 11
Private Digital Services, 280

CHAPTER 12
Time Division Multiplexers, 301

CHAPTER 13
Multivendor Integration, 350

CHAPTER 14
Integrated Services Digital Networks, 372

Figures

Preface

This book results from our reflecting on the data communications business and seeing the surprising difficulty which even simple tasks require. It became apparent to us that information needed to plan, specify, engineer, and install high-speed facilities is spread thinly over a variety of sources, some so obscure that finding them is a skill in its own right. Divestiture has compounded this problem, so that telecommunications professionals are often at the mercy of sales people for vital information on interfaces, compatibility, and standards.

The collection and publication of this information, regardless of its merit as detective work, would normally be useful to a limited audience as a reference. We sense, however, a strong need for the understanding of the historical and technical context surrounding today's digital communications technology, hence the tutorial nature of the book. A surprising number of "warts" on the design of today's digital transmission systems make sense only in a historical perspective. Our goal will be reached if you appreciate not only the what, but the how and the why of the raw information needed by today's network designers and their managers.

We should also say a few words about what you won't find here. There is no information on prices, delivery or vendor performance for the products and services described. Such information would be instantly obsolete in today's fast-paced and competitive environment. In the interest of preserving the value of this book, we have strictly limited our scope to technical matters of engineering interest. Similarly, we have limited our predictions about the future of products, services, and standards to an engineering and systems integration context.

We hope you have as much fun reading this book as we did researching and writing it. Telecommunications is one of today's most dynamic and promising professional fields. Understanding it is a challenge, but we hope you will find it an opportunity as well.

Jack Powers
Pete Stair

Acknowledgments

In acknowledging the assistance we have received in the preparation of this book, the authors wish first to express their thanks to the IBM Corporation, its people, its managers and its executives. Without their cooperation, this book could never have been written. In particular, we would like to extend our sincere appreciation to Norm Pass and Joan Weiss for their continued support throughout the project.

Equal gratitude goes to our technical reviewers at IBM, Bud Porter and Dick Wood, who spent endless hours critiquing and questioning. While the authors remain completely responsible for all errors and omissions, Bud and Woody have given us all their very best.

We next extend our thanks to Ms. Leslie Morton at AT&T Bell Laboratories, and Mr. Frank Phillips at MCI Communications for their knowledge, help, and encouragement. There are many other people who have given freely of their time, direction and comments; we regret that we cannot name them individually.

And last in order but first in our lives, to our families who endure with us.

ACCUNET® and DATAPHONE® and SLC® are registered trademarks of AT&T Communications.

NetView® and NetView/PC® are registered trademarks of the IBM Corp., PARADYNE® is a registered trademark of Paradyne Corporation.

Introduction

Data communications speeds from its telephone adolescence. Analog technology is dying and digital would be king. Megabit techniques compete to capture an exploding market. MIS managers and computer professionals struggle with massive gaps in knowledge. They search for and cannot find a technical book to guide them. We offer you that guide.

Accelerating Pace of Digital Communications

The book is about data communications, where both the medium and the message are digital. A guide book through the modern jungle of communications, the book is the first to describe real applications of megabit speed digital transmission technologies, products and services. Showing readers "What It Does," it also explains "How It Works."

Written in cross-country electronic collaboration by two of IBM's leading internal data network managers, the book describes today's major Megabit digital transmission networks as they are actually being planned, designed, installed and operated. It is directed at Management Information Systems (MIS) Managers, that is, computer, data center, and telecommunications managers and their professional planners, engineers and designers.

Migration from Analog Technologies

Beginning with a concise history and physics of telegraphy, this book will relate early data protocols and the challenges imposed by increasing communication speed. The history and current high-speed application of misunderstood terms such as **mark**, **space**, **break**, **baud**, **bandwidth**, and so on are clarified.

This book follows digital technology development through Telex and TWX, and voice technology innovation through voice channel banks and T-Carriers. The origins of AT&T's DATAPHONE™ Digital Service are shown, followed by a description of the evolution of multiplexing techniques and products of greater and greater speed.

Rapid Growth of Digital Offerings

Introduction and growth of T-Carrier services and related hardware are described, along with their variations and the resulting problems of standards and compatibility. At the end of the introductory part of the book is a description of the awkward mating dance of voice/data integration and the birth of ISDN (Integrated Services Digital Networks).

Here begin our travels into today's unfolding world of megabit data networks. Real examples, techniques and approaches are detailed. Practical methods are emphasized continuously for professionals who must cope with the selection, integration, and operation of complex technologies.

High-speed Digital Communications

The breakup of the Bell System in the United States provides users with an ever-widening circle of services and options. New service vendors join traditional carriers, such as AT&T, to offer new speeds, capabilities and functions. Explaining these services in generic terms, this book will expand your understanding by the use of examples. " How it works" covers digital data services, T-Carriers, terrestrial and satellite services.

New concepts in digital equipment introduce new methods of interfacing and new kinds of interface units. Relating all the pieces brings us to digital timing and synchronization where national and international clocks vie for greater accuracy. Timing interconnections between networks and equipment call for clearer comprehension of digital synchronization. The inner workings of digital communications lead to a review of public and private network services, operations, and techniques.

The Impact of Fiber Optics

Perhaps no technology has ever gone so quickly from laboratory curiosity to full operation as fiber optics. The move toward lightwave transmission and away from copper and radio accelerates an already rapid shift from analog to digital. Concepts of fiber optics and lightwave transmission combine with previous ideas to expand our knowledge. We follow these concepts into examinations of fiber systems and services.

Time Division Multiplexers

Compensating for the mismatch of service speeds and data communications equipment capabilities, time division multiplexers have become vehicles to migrate multiple applications onto digital services. Intelligent network processors compete with each other to "run" voice, data, and video networks. Deriving from early channel banks, these "resource managers" form a whole new class of equipment needing significant user understanding and involvement.

The Multivendor Environment

Once data communications managers ordered from a limited menu of end-to-end circuit services and went back to the already complex issues of front-end processors and software. Today's environment calls for specification, integration, operation and management of equipment and services from diverse sources. Managing this complexity requires new ways of doing business; this section of the book examines the challenges and some suggested techniques.

Getting Ready for ISDN

Integrated Services Digital Networks (ISDN) are more than grist for popular articles and standards committees. This "next wave" in communications is real and is expanding rapidly. Building on the base of material in earlier chapters, we outline ISDN as the final migration from separated analog communications services into a wholly digital world. New kinds of services and applications, offered by ISDN, are moving toward reality. A sound understanding of "how it works" completes our tour through the modern jungle of communications.

CHAPTER 1

Digital Communications

Chapter Overview

It is perhaps ironic that the term "digital" has come to mean the very latest in electronic technology for storing and transmitting information, from documents and images to stereophonic music. The roots of digital transmission extend back into the eighteenth century and early experiments with electricity, flowering with the development of practical telegraph systems in the nineteenth century. Like those of today, these systems were truly electronic, digital, and serial in nature; studying them is an excellent introduction to concepts underlying the design of more modern systems and the terminology used to describe them.

Telegraphy: The Foundation of Digital Telecommunications

History

It was well-known in the late eighteenth century that electricity could travel over wires. It was apparent that this effect could be used to carry signals, but detecting those signals at the receiving end in a convenient and reliable way was a major problem. Electrostatically generated (or **static**) electricity was used in experimental signaling systems as early as 1774, when Georges LeSage demonstrated a system over a short distance in France that used 24 wires, one for each of 24 possible symbols. Signals were detected at the receiving end by the deflection of one of 24 pith balls, each suspended by a string near the end of a corresponding wire. A similar system was used by Don Francisco Salva to send messages between Madrid and Aranjuez, Spain. These cumbersome and impractical systems served to stimulate interest and further experimentation, but were not of much use beyond that.

The term **telegraph** means "writing at a distance" and it is a fitting name for the transmission of written messages. The first practical signaling system to be called a telegraph was not electronic, but a relay semaphore system invented by Chappe in 1792. Chappe's system extended over hundreds of miles and used relay stations up to 10 miles apart. The system had 92 distinct signals, each of which corresponded to a number.

Messages were encoded at the source and transmitted from station to station as numbers, then decoded into text at the last station on the line. Even though it was useful only in the daytime and in good weather, Napoleon made very effective use of this system to control his empire. The value of rapid communications in human affairs was demonstrated beyond doubt.

Discovery of the battery by Volta in 1799 made available a much more consistent and easily handled source of electricity for experimentation. Experiments using batteries with frog legs as detectors took place as early as 1800. Salva used such a system to signal over a short distance in that year, and was the first to note electrical interference from the atmosphere.

The basis for a practical detector of electrical signals became available in 1819, when Hans Oersted discovered the magnetic effect of current through a conductor using a compass needle. That this effect could be multiplied by winding the conductor into a coil around an iron core was discovered by William Sturgeon, who built the first electromagnet in 1825. Progress followed rapidly in electrical research after that, with George Ohm discovering his famous law in 1827. Ohm's law stated the relationship between voltage, resistance, and current and enabled experimenters to accurately predict any one of these given the other two.

Joseph Henry demonstrated an electromagnetic telegraph in 1831, and Morse began working in this area about the same time. Cooke and Wheatstone built the first practical telegraph along a British railway line in 1838, using a compass needle detector. Morse's work was publicly demonstrated in 1844 over a line between Baltimore and Washington, D.C., a distance of 41 miles. This immensely successful public demonstration was a landmark occasion in the history of telecommunications, and Morse's designs and code became an international standard for over a century.

Physics of Early Telegraph Systems

Telegraph pioneers were the first people to have to deal in a practical way with the problems of transmitting electrical signals over long distances. A brief discussion of the most important electrical phenomena affecting their attempts provides an instructive insight into the basic physics of data transmission.

Electrical information transmission, by its very nature, involves the propagation of electromagnetic waves of unpredictable (if they were totally predictable, they would carry no information) characteristics. Telecommunications engineering involves a rather different emphasis on the various aspects of the physics of electromagnetic systems than, for example, power engineering. The activity and body of knowledge that specializes in the physics and mathematics of such systems is called **information theory.**

Electrical effects of principal interest for information transmission are resistance, capacitance, and inductance. All of these, to some extent, affect the rate at which information can be carried over a metallic conductor. A fourth electromagnetic phenomenon, the speed of light, becomes of interest over very long distances and at transmission rates.

Resistance is the simplest and easiest to deal with of the major electrical effects. It is the characteristic of conductors such as cables that requires the expenditure of energy to transmit an electrical current. This energy is dissipated as heat, and is the principle behind electrical heating devices such as toasters and ovens. The unit of resistance is the ohm; a household toaster operates with a resistance in the range of 10-20 ohms. The current (or number of electrons flowing per unit time) through a conductor is limited by the resistance, and is described by the simple formula:

$$I = \frac{E}{R}$$

where I is the current (in amperes), E is the voltage (in volts), and R is the resistance (in ohms). This rule is called **Ohm's Law,** and allows the calculation of any one of the three quantities where the other two are known. Resistance increases with the length of a conductor such as a wire and decreases with increased diameter.[1] Resistance is analogous to friction in mechanical systems.

Capacitance is a very important electrical characteristic, and it often is a limiting factor on the rate at which signals can be sent on a cable. One of the first electrical phenomena to be observed, capacitance is the tendency of matter to acquire and hold an electric charge. A charged capacitor is a reservoir of potential energy, and gives a kind of "memory" to an electrical circuit which can alter its operation over time. The unit of capacitance is the **farad**. A farad is much too large to be useful in communications systems, so smaller units like the **microfarad** (one millionth of a farad) are used. Devices with capacitance of up to a few thousand microfarads are common in modern electronic equipment. We will examine capacitance further under the section entitled "The Challenge of Speed." A mechanical analog of a **capacitor** (device with capacitance) is a spring, because it stores energy in proportion to the force applied. In this case, the force is electromotive, and is measured in volts.

Inductance is a magnetic effect that tends to oppose changes in the current through a conductor. Current flow through a conductor creates a magnetic field; this field has no effect on a steady current flow, but creates an electric field in the opposite direction to that of the existing current when it is increased and in the same direction when current is decreased. Because inductance tends to preserve the current flow in opposition to change, it can be compared to mass in a mechanical system. The unit of inductance is the **henry;** values of microhenrys (millionths of a henry) and millihenrys (thousandths of a henry) are common for parts used in electronic telecommunications hardware.

These effects combine according to well-defined rules that define the response of an electrical system to various time-varying stimuli such as digitized messages. An electrical system can be as simple as a single cable between two pieces of equipment or as complex as the worldwide telecommunications network. The same principles apply to all. The most complex can be understood by means of stepwise decomposition into simpler systems.

Early telegraph pioneers building long lines over land dealt mostly with the effects of resistance, which could be overcome (up to a point) simply by raising the battery voltage. Their main challenge was constructing and maintaining lines that would withstand the assault of the elements (especially lightning) and the attentions of the occasional thief who stole the wire to sell it for scrap metal. Where the length of a line was truly limited by resistance, repeater stations could be used to take messages from one line and place them on another.

---

[1] Effective resistance also varies with frequency for alternating currents, due to "skin effect," the tendency of high-frequency current to flow mostly in the outer parts of a conductor, but this is of interest mainly to telephone and radio engineers and may be ignored in telegraphy.

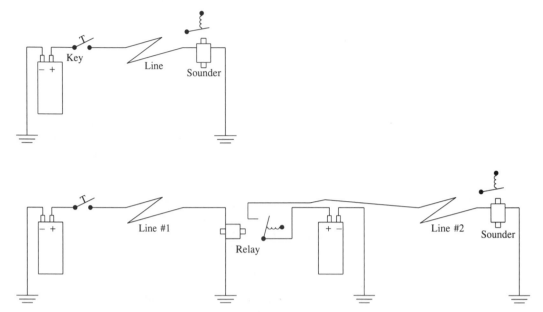

FIGURE 1.1. Diagram of Simplex Electromagnetic Telegraph. (a) Single simplex link; (b) Two simplex links joined by repeater.

A **repeater** could be a human operator who copied an incoming message on one line and tapped it out on another, or it could be automatic. The automatic repeater, invented by Joseph Henry in 1831, made possible land lines of any desired length. Figure 1.1 shows a schematic diagram of a **simplex** (one-way) telegraph and then the same telegraph extended by the use of a repeater. The repeater was essentially an electromagnetically operated telegraph key. The receiving electromagnet, instead of merely making clicks for the operator to hear or operating a recording pen, was mechanically connected to a pair of switch contacts controlling the next telegraph line, replacing the manually operated key. The concept of a repeater is an important one in data transmission and finds application in many modern variations.

Builders of submarine telegraph cables had a more difficult time fighting undesired electrical effects, as we will see shortly. Capacitance was a much more important factor with these lines, due to the design of the cable and its environment. Unable to place repeaters under water, the designers of early submarine cables had to deal with both capacitance and resistance effects for the entire length of the line. These effects limited transmission speed to between 10 and 50 words (50-250 characters) per minute.

Operation of Morse's Telegraph

Morse's original telegraph, patented in 1840, used the receiving electromagnet to move a pen onto a moving strip of paper thereby recording the message permanently. The pen fell into disuse after operators found that they could decode the message from the sound

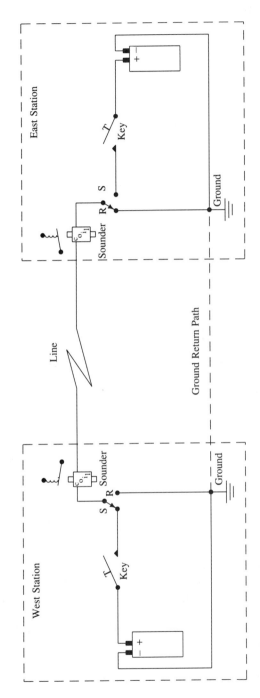

FIGURE 1.2. Simplified Diagram of Morse's Half-duplex Telegraph System.

of the mechanism alone, but the original design has left us with terminology which is still widely used. A **mark** was what the pen left on the moving paper strip, and became synonymous with the current on condition of the line which caused it. Since the paper still moved while the current was off, that line condition became associated with the blank **space** between marks. Short pulses produced small marks, or dots, on the strip and long ones produced elongated marks called dashes.

Figure 1.2 on page 5 is a simplified diagram of how Morse actually connected batteries, keys, and electromagnets to both ends of a line so that they could operate in a half-duplex (one way at a time) mode. Each station had a switch (usually part of the telegraph key, but shown separately here) which places the station in either "send" or "receive" mode; here the West station is shown in "send" and the East station in "receive" modes. When East's key is up (not pressed), the line is in the spacing condition (no current flowing) and a spring holds East's iron sounder away from its magnet.

Pressing West's key puts the line in the **marking** (current on) condition, and causes East's sounder to move toward its magnet, making a sound when it completes its travel. A similar sound is made when the key is released, returning the line to **spacing** (current off). In this way, the sounder at the East station follows the motion of West's key, making sounds which the Eastern operator interprets as dots and dashes.

When West is finished sending, both operators reverse their mode switches, and West has a chance to hear what East has to say. This mode reversal has the effect that the line is controlled by the Eastern key. Note that the line current always flows through both magnets, so that both operators hear all signals sent on the line. This arrangement was continued with teleprinters because it provided local copy at the sending end by recording all messages sent. Another advantage was that if the line was broken, it was apparent to either end as soon as transmitting was attempted. It also allowed the receiving end to interrupt the sender, simply by changing briefly to the "send" mode thus causing the sender's electromagnet to stop operating. The term **break**, meaning for a long spacing condition intended to interrupt the sender, remains in direct use today and has analogs in other signaling systems.

Time and Space Division

While it became common that telegraph systems used short and long on/off signals over a single wire, it is important that we remember that other choices were possible. The Morse code was designed for use over a **binary** (i.e., two-state) channel built from a single wire with a **ground** (literally, the earth) as return. This choice was based on the cost of erecting and maintaining long lines, a consideration which remains important today. Other systems which used several wires at the same time were tried, but were not economically feasible over long distances. The use of two- or three-state signals in a serial manner is still standard practice for long distance transmission, but over shorter distances (for example, within a computer system) the use of several simultaneous signal paths (in parallel) is common in order to achieve greater speed. Computer channels commonly transfer data over eight or more signal paths at a time, allowing at least an eightfold gain in speed over the same serially used medium.

The characteristic of information that allows the substitution of time for space, and vice versa, is a fundamental one. Just as a multiple lane highway accommodates more traffic than a single lane, we can rearrange information so that more of it is sent per unit of time where space allows. **Time division** is the technique of transmitting the parts of a message in a **serial** (sequential) manner over a single channel; **space division** is the combination of these two for simultaneous transmission over multiple parallel paths. Modern telecommunications systems make frequent use of the time-space equivalence, a concept which will recur frequently in this book.

Systems which have only two states, such as current on and current off, are called **binary** in their operation. Their transmission capacity is often expressed in terms of binary digits, or bits per second (abbreviated bit/s). A **bit** is exactly that amount of information required to answer a "yes or no" question where both answers are of equal probability. For binary communications systems, the number of signals sent per unit time and the number of bits sent per unit time are the same. Systems with more than two signaling states are possible, and for these the 1-to-1 relationship between signals per second and bits per second does not hold. The term **baud** is used for signals per second but is often mistakenly used as a synonym for bits per second. For example, a device which transmits, via time division, 300 signals per second with each signal using space division to carry four bits has a transmission capacity of 1,200 bits per second at 300 baud.

Protocols and Codes

A **protocol** is a procedure which, when followed by all parties involved, helps minimize confusion or decrease uncertainty. Anyone who has ever listened to a busy Citizen's Band radio channel can appreciate how effective operation depends on cooperation and a common understanding of the rules. Failure to follow the rules usually results in confusion and frustration. For telegraph and other digital communications systems, a properly designed and executed protocol permits the following:

- *Effective use of shared resources, such as channels:* With early telegraph systems such as those described in Figure 1.1 on page 4, a single line was used for transmission in both directions, but at different times. Such operation was called **half-duplex.** Protocol dictated in what condition the line was left when neither end was sending, how conflicts were resolved when both ends wanted to send at the same time, and how one end could interrupt the other in an emergency.

- *Accurate separation of transmissions into the proper units:* With the telegraph, the units of interest were letters, words, sentences, and messages. Protocol permitted these to be distinguished reliably.

- *Effective recovery from errors and malfunctions:* Human errors and mechanical failures disturb the operation of all kinds of communications systems frequently. When each party knows what to expect from the other when such exceptions occur, normal operation can be resumed much more quickly.

A **code** is a way of representing a set of symbols so that they may be transmitted efficiently over a particular channel. Codes are designed taking into account the characteristics of both the messages to be transmitted and of the channel at hand.

Morse code is both a protocol and a code. The protocol portion of Morse's design consists of the following rules:

1. When the channel is idle, it is left in the spacing (current off) condition.

2. The fundamental unit of transmission is the **dot,** a short interval during which the transmitter places the channel in the marking (current on) condition.

3. Upon returning the line to the spacing condition, it is left there for at least the duration of a dot.

4. Symbols are formed from combinations of dots and dashes, where a **dash** is a marking condition three times the duration of a dot. The number of dots and/or dashes varies from symbol to symbol.

5. Symbols are separated from each other by a spacing condition of duration equal to that of three dots.

6. Words are separated from each other by a spacing condition seven dots in duration.

Note that the duration of a dot, the fundamental timing unit, is not specified. In fact, it varied with the ability of the operators. Once chosen, however, it must be kept approximately the same in order for the receiver to correctly receive the coded characters.

The code portion of Morse's system consists of the assignment of combinations of dots and dashes to the symbols to be transmitted. The collection of symbols in the set is called an **alphabet,** and Morse's consisted of the 26 English letters, the digits zero through nine, and 19 punctuation marks and special symbols.

Synchronism

Transmission protocols are commonly divided into two categories: **asynchronous** (i.e., not synchronous) and **synchronous.** Morse telegraphy is an example of the former, which is better adapted to human characteristics and limitations. Synchronous systems require that the sender and receiver(s) share the same timing, like oarsmen on a crew boat; where this is feasible, they offer the opportunity to transmit information with less overhead (i.e., time spent on signaling that is not directly productive) than with asynchronous systems.

Asynchronous protocols, such as Morse's, carry timing information along with the data; the timing information is self-contained. The individual symbols of Morse code may be sent, once the length of a dot is known, independently of each other without confusion. The ability to accommodate a variable separation between characters is a useful characteristic in systems which are operated by humans, as with keyboards.

When timing information is provided from a source independent of the message itself, the transmission protocol is called synchronous. Synchronous systems were attempted even before Morse, but with little success. One such attempt by Chappe (of semaphore fame) and his brother is instructive: he constructed a dial similar to a clock face, on which the alphabet was written. He rotated a pointer on the dial and struck a frying pan to signal to his brother (who was watching it with a telescope) when the next letter of the message was indicated by the pointer. It failed because the delay due to the speed of sound was so much longer than that of the speed of light that his brother wrote down the wrong letters. Later designs, relying on spring-driven clockwork to advance matching pointers at opposite ends of a line with electromagnets in order to indicate the selected character, worked better but suffered from an inability to build clocks which were accurately matched in speed. Synchronism is described in depth in Chapter 7.

Start-stop Timing

Early in telegraphic history, attempts were made to mechanize the transmission and reception processes, in the hope of gaining higher and more consistent speeds and reduce the training required of operators. Morse code is an unequal length code (symbols vary in the time required to transmit them) in which the most frequently used symbols are assigned the shortest codes. This characteristic increases the difficulty of designing mechanical equipment to send and receive it, which led to its eventual replacement in mechanical systems by codes in which all symbols are of equal length. In order to minimize synchronization problems while maintaining the useful characteristic that the space between characters may vary without constraint, the time for transmission of each symbol (character) was fixed and divided into the following intervals:

1. A start interval which indicated that a character transmission had begun (this was indicated by a marking condition on the line, and the Morse convention of spacing for idle was preserved).
2. Several (five became the standard number, later eight) intervals of equal length, called **code elements**, during which the character code was transmitted using combinations of marks and spaces.
3. A stop interval during which the mechanism could reset in preparation for the next character.

This protocol, called **start-stop,** derived from the names of the intervals that bounded (or **framed**) each character, had the desired asynchronous property. Characters could be sent one after the other at full speed, or pauses of any duration could separate them. Since the time interval over which the sending and receiving mechanisms needed to remain in step was so short (only one character time) and started anew with each character, timing tolerances were quite attainable with the mechanical technology of the 1800s.

The terms asynchronous and start-stop are often used interchangeably, but this is misleading. Start-stop is a communications protocol that is asynchronous on a character basis (i.e., the sender may begin sending a character at any time following the stop interval of the previous character) and synchronous on a code element basis (fixed time intervals separate the elements of a character). Start-stop protocol is still in common use today, especially at low speeds where the information transmitted is originated or read by humans or equipment under direct human control.

The Medium and The Message: The Challenge of Speed

Telegraph company managers, under constant pressure to increase the return on a large capital investment, were understandably interested in increasing the number of messages that could be transmitted simultaneously on a line and/or the speed at which they were transmitted. This led to inventions like Edison's **quadruplex telegraph** of 1874, which permitted two simultaneous messages in each direction over a single pair of wires. The physical laws which limit the speed of information transmission are examined in more detail here, with illustrative examples.

"DC" Telegraph Systems

Morse's telegraph and later systems which operated a receiving electromagnet using a battery power source are called **direct current** or DC systems, but this term is misleading. Starting or interrupting current flow (regardless of the power source) introduces electrical effects characteristic of **alternating current** systems, and requires much more complex analysis than that of Ohm's law where capacitance and/or inductance are present. The following table compares typical values of resistance and capacitance for open wire pairs of the type used along railroad right-of-way with those of early trans-Atlantic cables:

	Resistance *(ohms/mile)*	*Capacitance* *(microfarad/mile)*
Open Wire Pairs	25–50	< .085
Submarine Cable	3.1–4.3	0.35–.42

A major factor affecting the operation of early submarine cables is that it was not possible to place repeaters along the way. Thus, the almost 3,000 mile 1869 cable between the United States and France had a total resistance of over 8,000 ohms and a capacitance of over 1,000 microfarads. One effect of both of these rather large values would have been that the cable would take a considerable time to "charge up" to an applied voltage. A measure of this effect is a quantity called the time constant, which is calculated as the product of the resistance in ohms and the capacitance in farads. The time constant is the time required for a circuit to reach 63% of an applied voltage, and is .8 seconds for the values given. Even with an ideal instrument at the receiving end, the transmission rate would be very slow.

We can draw an approximate equivalent circuit to the cable, which is shown in Figure 1.3, in which the sum of all the resistors is 4,000 ohms and the total capacitance is 1,000 microfarads.

The slowness with which the cable charges and discharges has the effect that brief signals such as the four dots of the Morse letter "H" are spread out over time and overlap. Such distortion might cause four dots to resemble a long dash instead. This effect can be partially overcome by transmitting voltage *reversals* instead of on-off pulses. Transmitting reversals is called **double-current** or **balanced** operation, and is easily accomplished using a two-way key with two batteries and a receiver sensitive to current direction. It speeds the charging and discharging process by adding the electromotive force of the reversed battery to that of the normal discharge. Morse code with double current transmission uses current in one direction for a dot and current in the reverse direction for a dash; dots and dashes may then be of the same duration. Figure 1.4 on page 12 shows received double current Morse signals recorded by a kind of recording oscillograph called a **siphon recorder.** The siphon recorder was an extremely sensitive magnetic receiver which plotted the received current on a moving paper tape.

Double current systems have three states (+ current, − current, and no current).

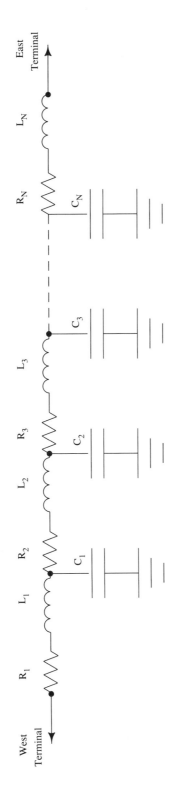

West Terminal

East Terminal

R_1 L_1 R_2 L_2 R_3 L_3 R_N L_N

C_1 C_2 C_3 C_N

Resistance : Sum of $R_1 + R_2 + R_3 + \dots + R_N > 8{,}000$ Ohms

Inductance : Sum of $L_1 + L_2 + L_3 + \dots + L_N$ (Unknown)

Capacitance : Sum of $C_1 + C_2 + C_3 + \dots + C_N > 1{,}000$ μfd.

FIGURE 1.3. Electrical Circuit Equivalent to the 1869 U.S.—France Submarine Cable.

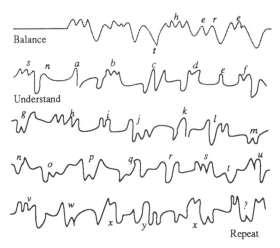

FIGURE 1.4. Double-current Morse Code. These waveforms of the Morse alphabet were received on a siphon recorder. Peaks are dots and valleys are dashes. (Fig. 59 from page 605 of Submarine Telegraphs, by Bright, 1898.)

Three-state systems are called **ternary** by information theorists. Ternary systems such as double-current telegraphs where the polarity is of only passing interest (i.e., the reverse of the previous current) are called **pseudo-ternary** systems (ternary in fact but binary in usage). Pseudo-ternary systems are in widespread use today for theoretical reasons which will be explained in detail in later chapters.

Carrier Systems

Invention of the telephone (Bell and Gray, circa. 1876) brought the attention of engineers and scientists to the transmission of information that was truly continuous in nature and brought about the design of systems to encode, transmit, and decode it. Now commonly called **analog** transmission (because an alternating current, electrical signal follows the information transmitted), telephone channels soon became adapted to telegraph use. Because telegraph signal voltages do not vary continuously like those of voice, they were poorly suited to transmission over voice channels. To say that telephone channels wouldn't pass DC pulses would be an an oversimplification, but a useful one.

A technique called **modulation** was devised so that information which varied over a few states could be carried on systems adapted for continuously varying signals like voice. Modulation varied some characteristic of an alternating current (typically **frequency,** the rate at which it alternates) with the binary telegraph signal, providing continuously varying signals suitable for voice-type transmission. At the receiving end, the reverse process (called **demodulation**) converted the analog signal to binary form. Using this method and a type of space division called **frequency division multiplexing,** it was possible to derive 12 and later 24 50-baud teleprinter channels from a single voice channel. Similar techniques were used over radio channels, allowing economical transmission to and from ships at sea.

Bandwidth vs. Bits per Second

Bandwidth is a measure of the amount of the electromagnetic spectrum used to transmit a signal. It is the difference between the lower and upper frequencies used, and applies to all transmission systems, whether they use a carrier or not. The unit of bandwidth is the **hertz,** or cycle per second, also used for frequency. The efficiency of modulation systems is often expressed as the ratio of bit rate to bandwidth; all other considerations equal, the greater the quotient, the better. Other considerations include error rate and reliability. Typically, a voice channel occupies 4,000 hertz of which about 15% (the first and last 300 hertz) are undisturbed "no man's land". Modern modem designs are delivering at least 9,600 bits/s on switched voice network connections. This represents an efficiency of 2.8 bits/sec. per hertz of bandwidth, not a small achievement using a system designed and optimized for the human voice.

Having begun with the manual DC telegraph, telecommunications technology progressed to more automatic telegraph systems and transmission of the human voice, subjects treated in the following chapter. We will see how the the challenges of voice transmission brought a new level of understanding of the theory of information transmission, which provided the basis for the return to all-digital designs.

CHAPTER 2

Digital Technology

Chapter Overview

This chapter completes the historical section of this book and the story of the telegraph with a description of the teleprinter systems still in use today, followed by the development of the telephone and of analog transmission. Finally, we will examine the evolution of digital systems designed to carry voice and their adaptation to data transmission. We will return later to the theme of mixed voice and data in Chapter 3, *Digital Services* and again in Chapter 14, *Integrated Services Digital Networks.*

Record (Non-voice) Communications Technology

Teleprinters

The basic design for the modern **teleprinter** (teletypewriter) was invented in 1874 by Emile Baudot of the French Telegraph Service. Its five element start-stop code structure is his; however, the International Telegraph Alphabet #2 shown in Figure 2.1 on page 15, often called **Baudot Code,** is really a descendant of the one he developed.

The first practical teleprinters in widespread use were designed by Morton and Krum in 1902. These partners formed the Morkrum Company in 1907, which later came to be known as the Teletype Corporation (1925) and was sold to the American Telephone & Telegraph Co. in 1930. The Baudot design was refined to a high state of mechanical art by Morton and Krum and their successors, a tribute to the imagination and skill of those for whom the main electronic design components were batteries, switches, and magnets.

The early teleprinters consisted of separated transmitter and receiver sections, which could be operated independently. The five element code, still in use over much of the world, has $2^5 = 32$ combinations, not enough for letters, digits, and punctuation. This problem was solved by dividing the symbols into two groups called "Letters" and "Figures" similar to the upper and lower case sets of a typewriter. Code combinations were assigned

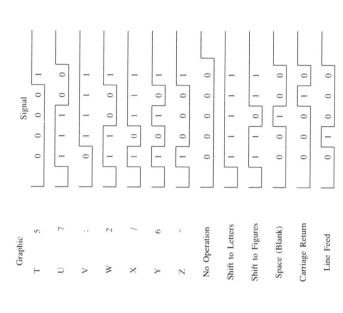

FIGURE 2.1. International Telegraph Alphabet #2.

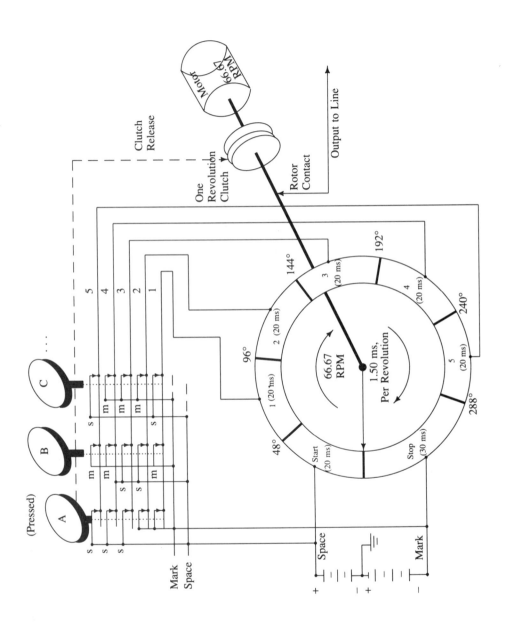

FIGURE 2.2.(a). A Simplified Baudot Teleprinter Keyboard Transmitter.

which would select one set and leave it selected until instructed otherwise. The letters set includes the 26 capital letters A through Z. The figures set includes the digits 0 through 9 and several special symbols and punctuation marks. Six combinations are independent of the letters/figures grouping, and have the following meanings:

- 00000 (No Operation): This code is a single character delay.
- 00010 (Carriage Return): This code caused the next character to be printed at the left edge of the paper. Note that it did not include advancing the paper to the next line.
- 00100 (Space): This code prints a blank (the space between words).
- 01000 (Line Feed): This code advances the paper one line. It is often used following a carriage return, but may be used alone. The horizontal printing position is not changed.
- 11011 (Figures): The codes following this one will be printed using characters from the "figures" set. The printer remains in this mode until a "letters" code is received. Receiving a "figures" code while in the figures mode has no effect, except for the time to transmit the redundant code.
- 11111 (Letters): Codes following this one are printed from the "letters" set. The printer remains in this mode until a "figures" code is received. Receiving a "letters" code while in the letters mode has no effect, except for the time to transmit the redundant code.

Baudot teleprinter signaling is of the start-stop type described in Chapter 1 with a start signal of the same length (20 milliseconds, or 20 thousandths of a second) as a code element, a five element code, and a stop signal one and one-half times as long as a code element. A complete character, including start and stop signals, is transmitted in 150 milliseconds (ms.), corresponding to a character rate of 6.67 characters per second (66.67 words per minute at six characters per word).

In telegraph terminology, these systems used a signaling rate of 50 baud, where the **baud** is defined as the reciprocal of the duration of the shortest signal element (1/.020 = 50).

Teleprinters have improved in design and speed over the years, and the latest designs are almost entirely electronic. Introduction of the (seven element) American Standard Code for Information Interchange (ASCII) in 1963 made the teleprinter much more of an office machine by enriching the character set and providing for many new formatting functions. Today, the ASCII code and speeds of at least 100 words per minute (equivalent to 10 characters per second) are common for teleprinters in the United States.

THE BAUDOT TRANSMITTER

Figure 2.2(a) on page 16 shows a much simplified diagram of a Baudot keyboard transmitter. The function of the transmitter is to select the five code elements corresponding to the key pressed and present them sequentially to the line following a start and followed by a stop signal. The start signal is a space 20 ms. in duration; the stop signal is a mark 30 ms. long. The transmitter contains a distributor much like that of an automobile which connects the line sequentially to seven signal sources in a single rotation. These signal sources are a 20 ms. space (start signal), five code elements of 20 ms. each, and a 30 ms. mark (stop signal), in that order. In the idle condition, the transmitter's motor is running but a single revolution clutch prevents the distributor from rotating; the distributor rotor rests at the end of the stop signal, sending a constant mark. Pressing any key releases the clutch for

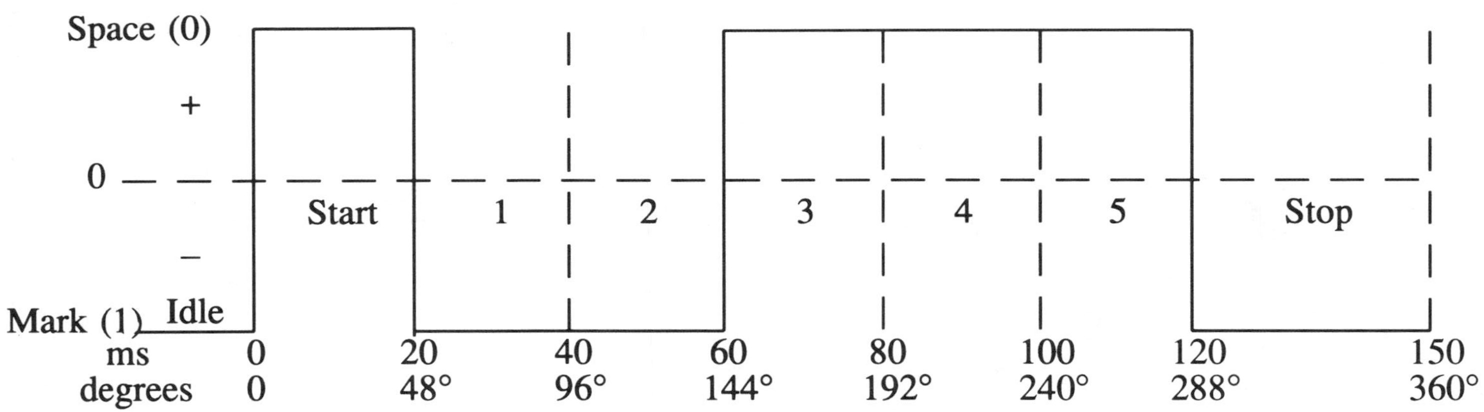

Space (0)

+

0

Mark (1) Idle
ms   0   20   40   60   80   100 120 150
degrees   0   48° 96° 144° 192° 240° 288° 360°

Start 1   2   3   4   5   Stop

FIGURE 2.2(b). Line Signal for Letter "A" (Int'l Alphabet #2).

18

a single revolution, transmitting the code elements selected by the switches under the key following a start and followed by a stop. The transmitted signal is plotted in Figure 2.2(b) on page 18 as a function of time.

The original teleprinter transmitters used mechanical, rather than electrical, means to encode the character to be transmitted; levers and cams, rather than switch contacts, were the basis for what is essentially a parallel-to-serial converter: a device to deliver the five code elements selected all at once (in parallel) to a channel capable of delivering them one at a time, with appropriate timing.

THE BAUDOT RECEIVER

The Baudot teleprinter receiver, too complex mechanically for detailed description here, contains a single revolution clutch like the one in the transmitter. The receiver's clutch is triggered by the start signal from the transmitter's distributor, setting in motion a series of cams and levers that sample the position of the receiving magnet during five 20 ms. intervals following the start signal. Five mechanical latches remember the state of the line during their respective code element times and present the information all at once to a decoding mechanism at the beginning of the stop time. The decoding mechanism selects the character to be printed using this information and the state of a mechanical Letters/Figures latch which remembers the last Letters/Figures selection code received. Some printers were too slow to print the character during the stop signal interval, and so were designed to print one character while receiving the next one.

The teleprinter receiver is essentially a serial-to-parallel converter which assembles the sequential code elements of a character and interprets them either to print a character or take some related action such as returning the carriage or selecting the set (case) from which the following characters will be printed.

The Telex Network

Following the developments of Morton and Krum in the United States and similar progress by Creed in England and others, the teleprinter received wide acceptance by commercial and government communications organizations. In 1915, the Associated Press chose the Morkrum system for the electronic distribution of news and the British Post Office began a public telegram service using Creed products in 1927.

As the advantages of communicating via teleprinter (speed, written record, unattended reception) became known and the International Alphabet #2 became a widely accepted standard, switched public teleprinter services were introduced in Europe. Known as TELEX, these services provided the customer with a Baudot teleprinter and the ability to connect it to any other customer's machine and transmit messages at will. The Telex network outside the USA spread so quickly and became so established that it was actually a barrier to the introduction of the telephone. Switching was manual at first, with the originator of a message sending the address of the destination to a human operator, who set up the connection. Later, systems that switched calls automatically using keyboard input or digits dialed on a telephone-type rotary dial replaced the human operators in many countries.

In the USA, the Western Union Corporation is the original and current provider of Telex service, which has been considerably enhanced with the introduction of computer technology. Modern Telex service offers conveniences such as access to electronic news services and automatic storage of messages for later delivery to busy destinations.

TWX

The American Telephone & Telegraph Co. began a manually switched teleprinter service similar to Telex in the United States in 1931, calling it Teletypewriter Exchange Service, or TWX. This service grew to 60,000 subscriber terminals by 1962. AT&T found that the direct current telegraph circuits (which were incompatible with much voice transmission hardware) and manual switching were growing problems in a network designed around voice transmission and direct distance dialing. It was decided to move the TWX service to the voice network using a device called a **modem** (MODulator-DEModulator) to convert the direct current telegraph signals to continuous, alternating currents at the point where they entered the voice network and do the reverse at the destination. Using this technique, a teleprinter call would travel through the telephone network just like a voice call, a great improvement in convenience and economy. AT&T converted 60,000 TWX subscriber terminals to modems and the direct-distance dial (**DDD**) network over the Labor Day weekend of 1962; this was the first large scale use of the switched telephone network for non-voice purposes, and it was so successful that the technique was copied widely for data communications thereafter. The Western Electric 101 series modems used in the DDD version of TWX were the predecessors of the 103 series later used for customer-provided terminals that became popular with time-shared computing systems of the late 1960s and 1970s.

TWX was sold to Western Union in 1971, and was renamed "Telex II." Western Union proceeded to integrate the two services to minimize interworking problems and capitalize on the greater connectivity that resulted from the acquisition of TWX.

Message (Voice) Communications Technology

The story of the introduction of the telephone and its growth is a peculiarly American one, not duplicated in other countries with any similarity. This difference is only partly due to the American fondness for private enterprise. Enthusiastic government sponsorship of telegraph service and its monopoly thereof became the rule in Europe. The European telecommunications bureaucracy was at first unready and unwilling to accept the telephone, and the results of that reluctance have left many countries with telephone service considerably behind that available in the United States.

The Telephone

Alexander Graham Bell first accomplished electrical transmission of an alternating current representing sound in 1875 while working on a way to send several telegraph signals on the same line using frequency separation (that dream was not realized until the advent of the electronic filter in 1917). Bell and his assistant Watson were quick to analyze the 1876 (partly accidental) result of speaking via a device designed to carry several sound frequencies at the same time.

A patent application for "improvement in telegraphy" was filed by Bell in February of 1876 and granted in March of that year. Bell filed for a patent on an electromagnetic telephone on January 15, 1877 and it was granted on January 30. Bell and his partners, Hubbard and Sanders, offered the electromagnetic telephone patent to Western Union for $100,000 at that time and the offer was rejected; we can only speculate on the result of its acceptance by a business steeped in the technology and lore of the telegraph.

On July 9, 1877, the Bell Telephone Company was incorporated in Massachusetts, replacing the Bell-Hubbard-Sanders partnership. It was reorganized as the American Bell Company in 1880. This company leased telephone instruments to customers who were expected to install their own lines. The difference in prices for residential and business customers dates back to that time, when a pair of telephones could be had for $20 per year if used "for social purposes" and $40 per year for business.

At first, telephones were used on a point-to-point basis, but the advantage of any-to-any connectivity soon became obvious. A burglar alarm contractor named E. T. Holmes started offering telephone service to his alarm customers over existing alarm lines in May, 1877. By August, only three months later, he had over 700 telephone customers in Boston and a central office, operated by young boys, allowed any customer to call any other. The telephone was immensely successful and this rapid growth continued. Lines connecting exchanges and cities soon sprang up. By 1884, lines were in operation from New York City to Albany, Boston, Philadelphia, and Washington.

The American Bell Company's business soon outgrew its maximum permitted capitalization, and in 1885, the American Telephone & Telegraph Co., a wholly owned subsidiary of American Bell, was incorporated in New York with the purpose of building long lines. In 1888, the Western Electric Company of Chicago was purchased and became a supplier of parts and equipment to the Bell System. AT&T grew into the parent company and system coordinator for the Bell System, a role it held until its breakup in 1985. The Bell System included many operating companies along with Bell Telephone Laboratories, the Teletype Corporation, and Western Electric.

The orderly and rapid growth of the telephone industry in the United States under the leadership (and, to a great degree, the ownership) of AT&T is a direct result of policies and practices established very early in its history by Bell's partner Hubbard and his successors. The concept of the telephone business as a service, with the provider responsible for the integrity and performance of the entire network, was a major reason for the high level of quality and wide availability of telephone service in the United States.

American Bell recognized very early the value of research and development; an Engineering Department was established in 1881. As the business grew, other engineering groups were formed or acquired, one of them from Western Electric. In 1907, these groups were combined at the Western Electric plant on West Street in New York City, the seed for what became Bell Telephone Laboratories in 1925. The role of Bell Labs in the development of modern technology would be hard to underestimate, and is not limited to telecommunications. Among the many important developments by Bell Labs are the sound motion picture (1926), television transmission (1927) coaxial cable (1929), a pioneering electro-mechanical computer (1937), the transistor (1947), the first theory of information (1948), and microwave satellite communications (1962).

Telephone Transmission

While the same laws of physics apply to all kinds of information transmission, emphasis varies with the technology in use. By 1900, telegraph transmission engineering was well understood; however, the same could not be said for the telephone. Telegraph transmission over long distances was aided by the availability of the repeater, the ability to switch relatively large amounts of power, and alternating current signal components quite low in frequency. Telephone transmission involves small alternating currents that vary continuously with the sound pressure of the speaker's voice and at frequencies much higher that those important in telegraph transmission. In addition, the basis for a telephone repeater, a suitable vacuum tube amplifier, was not available until 1912. Until the first transcontinental telephone call in 1915, the growth of the telephone industry can be said to have been **transmission-limited** (telephones were numerous and popular, but didn't reach far enough).

Early telephone circuits were designed like telegraph lines (a single conductor line with an earth (ground) return). Improved service was gained by using by a pair of wires for each circuit, especially for long lines like the ones connecting central offices; elimination of the common ground return path greatly reduced the interference between calls and from noise sources such as lightning.

The first big breakthrough in telephone transmission theory came in 1887 with the work of Heaviside, who developed the mathematics of **alternating currents.** Heaviside's theory predicted that the addition of inductance to telephone lines would help compensate for **attenuation** (signal loss) and **distortion** (non-uniform response) due to line capacitance, and was first applied in 1899. This development led to doubling the distance of telephone conversations carried on open wire lines and tripling it in cables.

The invention of the **triode vacuum tube** by DeForest in 1907 led to telephone repeaters first tested across the width of the United States in 1914. Prior to that, the longest possible telephone call in the United States was from New York City to Denver, a distance of 1826 miles. Transcontinental service was inaugurated with an historic call between Alexander Graham Bell in New York and Thomas Watson in January of 1915. The vacuum tube amplifier was particularly useful for circuits carried on multi-pair cable, which has greater loss than open wire lines, even when inductance (in the form of **loading coils**) is added.

Carrier systems, first demonstrated in 1914, used the ability of the vacuum tube to generate an alternating current which could be used to "carry" a voice signal at a frequency other than its natural one. This technique, called **frequency translation,** multiplied the capacity of a pair of wires because several signals could be carried at different frequencies, a savings called **pair gain.** Both frequency division and time division became heavily used techniques in mining more and more return on the capital investment in telephone cable plant. The technique of using a single pair of wires or other medium to carry several signals is called **multiplexing.**

FREQUENCY DIVISION MULTIPLEXING

Transmission systems which represent voice signals as continuously varying quantities such as voltage or current are called **analog** in nature. The term is chosen because the transmitted signal, no matter what its form or carrier frequency, attempts to follow the variations of the talker's voice faithfully and continuously. The transmitted signal is an analog of the original, and if all goes well, what the receiver hears is not much different from what was transmitted. Until the 1960s, all carrier systems were both analog and frequency division in nature.

The vacuum tube, in several roles, was the basis for the Bell System's C-Carrier system of the 1920s, which added three voice channels to an open wire voice line. This system served through the years of the Great Depression, after which more capacity was required.

Analog carrier system development took two different directions. One followed the route of carrying more and more channels on existing media (open wire lines and bundled cable pairs) and the other explored new media altogether. Among the new media were coaxial cable (invented in 1929 and first used commercially in 1941) and microwave radio (first used for telecommunications in 1948).

Developments in the carrier systems area reflected increasing economies of scale as the costs of right-of-way, buildings, towers, etc. increased and the price of electronics decreased over the years. Over the history of analog carrier systems through 1975 (when 500 million voice circuit-miles were in service), the per-channel cost decreased by a factor of almost 1,000. Many circuit miles of both coaxial and radio analog carrier are still in use today.

Coaxial Cable Transmission Systems. Coaxial cable consists of a single center conductor in the exact center of, and insulated from, a metal tube or similar circular conducting structure such as circularly braided wire. Such cables can carry signals at very high frequencies and can be bundled together without mutual interference, making them ideal for use with analog multiplex systems. Those used for telephone transmission use a center wire conductor suspended in a relatively large metal tube by ceramic discs; the insulation between the two is mainly air.

The first coaxial transmission system to span the United States from coast to coast was AT&T's L1, introduced in 1940. This system had a capacity of 600 channels per pair of coaxial tubes (one tube in each direction) and used repeaters spaced at eight mile intervals. Three pairs of tubes were used in each direction (with two spares) to give a route capacity of 1800 voice circuits. Following coaxial systems were called L3, L4, and L5 and had capacities of 1860, 3600, and 10,800 channels per tube pair and repeater spacings of four, two, and one mile, respectively. The L5 system, introduced in 1973, was used with a 22-tube cable, giving an aggregate capacity of 108,000 channels with two tubes reserved as spares.

Microwave Radio Transmission Systems. Frequency translation could be used to multiplex large numbers of channels on the super high (above 3,000 megahertz) radio frequencies achieved with the development of radar during World War II. These frequencies corresponded to radio wavelengths of 100 centimeters and less, a part of the electromagnetic spectrum called **microwave.** Such signals travel along straight lines much like light, and can be transmitted and received using antennas that are highly directional. The directional nature of the signal travel permits re-use of carrier frequencies within relatively small geographic areas. Because of the curvature of the Earth, long-haul transmission involves building repeaters on towers spaced up to about 30 miles apart.

The first experimental long distance microwave telephone and television transmission was demonstrated between New York and Boston in 1947, using seven tower-to-tower links to cover the 220 miles and a carrier frequency of four gigahertz (thousand megahertz). Commercial service over this path began in 1948; coast-to-coast U.S. TV service via microwave began in September, 1951, using AT&T's TD2 radio system. By the late 1950s, the TH1 system started to supplant the TD2, using a six gigahertz carrier, offering up to 29,000 voice channels between repeaters.

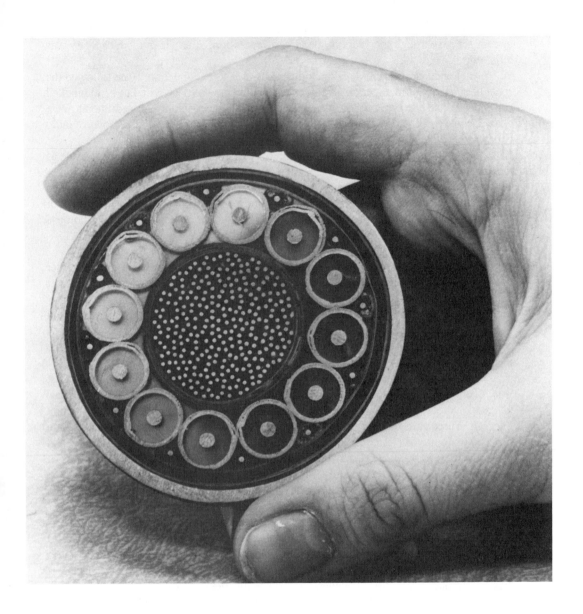

FIGURE 2.3. Cross-sectional View—Coaxial Cable. Reprinted with permission from the *AT&T Bell Laboratories RECORD,* Copyright 1975 AT&T.

Undersea Cable Transmission Systems. Carrier transmission techniques were applied to undersea cables as early as 1931, when Havana and Key West were linked using a variation of the AT&T C-Carrier system described above. This was replaced in 1950 with a 36-channel system using two cables (one for each direction of transmission) which had vacuum tube repeaters powered over the cable from shore about 40 miles apart. This design was so successful that it was copied in a trans-Atlantic version in 1956. Subsequent developments in the terminal equipment increased the capacity to 48 channels, later increased further by eliminating the transmission of silent intervals (called **time-assigned speech interpolation**) in each direction.

Improved submarine telephone cable systems combined transmission in both directions on the same cable, improved quality, and increased even further the channel capacity. The (1976) "SG" undersea cable system carries 4,000 telephone channels between the United States and France on a single cable.

TIME DIVISION MULTIPLEXING

Certain characteristics of analog transmission became increasingly important as the number of repeaters between the ends of a telephone connection grew. These were noise and distortion, unavoidable characteristics of the amplifiers and media used to carry telephone conversations. Negative feedback amplification and combinations of resistance, inductance, and capacitance (called **equalizers**) designed to compensate for distortion on channels helped greatly in limiting the distortion of voice signals, but noise could not be avoided entirely. Noise is an inevitable result of electronic activity, and it is both introduced and amplified by every repeater of a channel. Accumulated noise over many repeaters can make a channel useless, and the number of repeaters along a route is an important consideration in the design of both switched and point-to-point links.

Telegraph channels also suffer from both noise and distortion, but the non-continuous nature of telegraph signals greatly simplifies the job of repeating signals correctly. In the case of bipolar, or double current, transmission, it is a **binary** (two-valued) decision about any incoming signal for a repeater. Telegraph repeaters decide whether the received signal is a mark or a space. The exact value of the received signal is not otherwise important. In systems designed with sufficiently good ratios of signal to noise, it can be shown that noise will not accumulate if it is below the error threshold of each repeater on a link.

These characteristics of telegraph transmission were not lost on telephone engineers, and the result was a digital transmission system called **T-Carrier.** Digital transmission was not practical until both analog and digital electronics decreased greatly in cost and the transistor offered great gains in space, power, and maintenance efficiency.

The T1 Carrier System was introduced by AT&T in 1962 to interconnect metropolitan central offices. It was the first widespread use of the combination of time division multiplexing and digital coding of voice signals, and provided 24 voice channels on two wire pairs (one in each direction). The theory of information provided the basis for its operation: an analog signal can be measured periodically (a process called **sampling**) and then completely reconstructed if the sampling operation takes place at a repetition rate at least twice that of the highest frequency to be transmitted. This means that if we examine a voice signal (for which the highest frequency components of interest are 4,000 hertz) at a rate of 8,000 times per second, we can reconstruct the original signal completely from only the information in the samples.

T1 samples each of 24 channels at an 8,000 sample/second rate. Each analog sample was coded as seven binary digits (**bits**) using a process called **quantization.** Using seven bits offered $2^7 = 128$ discrete values with which the analog signal could be represented. To these seven bits, an additional bit was added for signaling on/off hook information, resulting in a data stream of $8,000 \times 8 = 64,000$ bits per second, per channel. The data for each of 24 channels was sent, in turn, followed by a single bit for synchronization; this grouping of data is called a **frame** and was $(24 \times 8) + 1 = 193$ bits in length. Since 8,000 frames per second were required to send a sample of each channel at that rate, the data rate over the line is therefore $(8,000 \times 193) = 1,544,000$ bits per second.

The ends of a T1 link at which 24 voice channels are converted to and from a digital format are called **channel banks.** The economics of channel banks are such that a great deal of the hardware must be shared, rather than replicated on a per-channel basis; the T1 design achieved this goal.

The unassisted range of the original T1 channel bank was slightly more than a mile. T1 repeaters were used to extend this range, and were installed in manholes at about 6,000 foot intervals; spans of up to 50 miles were permitted with the original design. The repeaters were often located in manholes under city streets and were powered over the line. Later designs, based on operating experience, allowed much longer spans; the principal differences in design from the original were for easier fault diagnosis over longer distances.

T1 technology was the basis for the first high-speed data transmission service that was digital from end to end. In 1971, AT&T offered the type 306A data set which provided a point-to-point data service at 1,344,000 bits per second over distances up to 50 miles. The 306 was relatively efficient (over five times better than modems at the time) in terms of bits per second, per voice channel displaced. According to this figure of merit, it delivered 56,000 bits per second for each of the 24 voice channels that could have used the same T1. The difference between the customer's data rate of 1,344,000 bit/s and the T1 rate of 1,544,000 bit/s was accounted for by framing bits which were unavailable for data (8,000 bit/s) and a single "one" bit stuffed into each voice channel to guarantee sufficient "one" bits to maintain timing (24 channels $\times$ 8,000 samples/sec.= 192,000 bit/s).

Applications of T1 with the 306A included high-speed digital facsimile systems and direct computer-to-computer links for backup and database transfer. Additional multiplexing equipment could be used to split the 306 capacity into a number of lower speed channels, replacing numerous voice channels and modems with a substantial reduction in cost. T-Carrier systems are more fully described in Chapters 4 and 5.

Telephone Switching

MANUAL SWITCHING

Originally, telephone switching was performed by a human switchboard operator who responded to the customer's taking the phone off the hook with the question "Number, please?" Calls between customers of the same central office could usually be completed by this operator, but calls between offices required the services of an operator at each switching point. Long-distance calls often took many minutes to set up; it was not unusual to request a call to a distant party in advance and have the operator call back when the call was ready. Manual switching is still used in parts of the world.

Automatic switching was introduced in 1892 in LaPorte, Indiana by a disgruntled undertaker named Almon B. Strowger. Strowger invented the rotary dial and the central office switch it controlled because he believed that the local telephone operators were unfairly diverting calls to his competition, causing a loss of business; he solved the problem by buying the local telephone company and eliminating the role of human operators for local calls.

Strowger's design, called **step-by-step** switching, used a rotary dial on the customer's instrument to produce pulses which controlled a magnet-operated ratchet switch at the central office. Later refinements of the system used switches of the type shown in Figure 2.4 on this page. The dial pulses cause the wiper arm, held away from the contact assembly, to drop vertically to the level selected; one level per dial pulse. The pause between digits (not unlike the stop interval in teleprinter codes), slightly longer than the time between pulses, indicates to the switch that the current digit is complete. For all digits but the last one of the called number, the wiper arm is then advanced automatically until a set of contacts is reached which provide an unoccupied path to the next level of the switching system. The process is repeated until the last digit is pulsed, for which both the vertical and horizontal motion of the switch are controlled by the caller's dial. The last two digits select one of 100 possible called lines.

Step-by-step switching equipment has a large number of moving parts and contacts which are prone to producing noise when subject to vibration; for these reasons, they require a great deal of maintenance and tend to produce noise in the calls that pass through them.

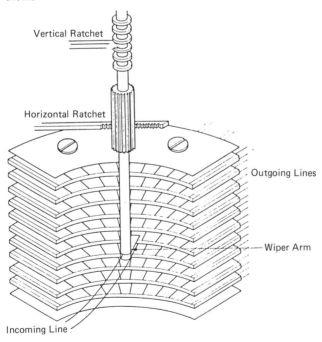

Vertical Ratchet

Horizontal Ratchet

Outgoing Lines

Wiper Arm

Incoming Line

FIGURE 2.4. Stepping Switch. This step-by-step switch is descended from an original design by Almon B. Strowger in 1892.

A more modern electromechanical switching system is called the **crossbar** type and is organized quite differently. Using a technique called **common control,** a single high speed control unit is presented with the called number after the number has been accumulated in a storage unit called a **register.** The control unit, also electromechanical in design, determines a path through the system based on the resources available at the time and operates latching magnets of a series of grid-like switching arrays, typically arranged in units of 10 rows and 20 columns. Once this is complete, the common control unit is freed to process another call. Common control allows the time sharing of complex decision-making logic by a large number of lines and concurrent calls, and allows easier modification for new services because all the decision logic is centralized in one place, rather than distributed throughout the system. The flexibility gained by common control allowed the introduction of direct-distance dialing in the United States in 1951. Crossbar switching arrays are quieter, faster, and require less maintenance than step-by-step systems.

ELECTRONIC SWITCHING

Modern switching systems still use common control, but with a stored program computer rather than hard-wired logic making the decisions. This approach allows an immense degree of flexibility and makes possible such services as call forwarding and abbreviated dialing. Called **stored program control,** it also permits automatic testing of lines to subscribers and between offices, greatly decreasing maintenance costs. Stored program control may be used with either electromechanical or all-electronic switching; currently, both variations are in use.

AT&T's number one Electronic Switching System (#1 ESS), designed for use in local central offices of up to 100,000 lines, uses a stored program computer for common control of a large array of magnetic reed switches called **ferreeds.** Each ferreed consists of a pair of contacts sealed in a glass tube filled with nitrogen and surrounded by an electromagnet. The control program operates the switch (closing the contacts) by turning on a current through the electromagnet; switching action is quite fast, just a few hundred millionths of a second. The #1ESS has all the advantages of the crossbar system described above; in addition, it is much faster, more flexible, and less expensive to maintain.

AT&T's #4ESS is an all-electronic system in which there are no moving parts in the switching paths. It is designed for toll offices (central offices which interconnect only other central offices) for which interoffice lines are digital (e.g., T1). Stored program control routes the time-separated samples of voice signals much like railroad cars in a switchyard in which all the cars are always moving. A combination of time division, space division, and temporary storage is used to separate eight-bit digital voice samples from time slots on incoming lines and place them in the selected time slots on outgoing lines. The all-digital operation completely eliminates **crosstalk** (interference between nearby channels) and introduces no noise or distortion because the signals need not be converted to analog form to travel through the switch. It also facilitates transmission of non-voice digital signals such as data, digitized video, facsimile, and so on. Finally, the all-electronic design is more compact and requires less power than systems with electromechanical crosspoints.

COMMON CHANNEL INTEROFFICE SIGNALING (CCIS)

Where calls must travel through more than one central office switch, it is necessary to transmit the called number and call status (on or off hook) from the originating switch to all others involved in the call. Dialed digits and on/off hook status are called **addressing**

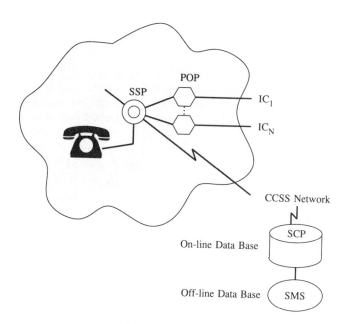

BOC 800-Service customers can specify any number of conditions — time of day, day of week, special holiday, or location of caller — for any number of interexchange carriers. For each 800 call, the service switching point (SSP) queries the service control point (SCP) for routing information, using the common-channel signaling network (CCS). Special packet switches called signal transfer points switch the calls through the signaling network. The SCP locates the customer-specified routing information and transmits it back to the SSP using the CCS network, The SSP then completes the call, routing it to the carrier specified Intra-LATA or InterLATA. For interexchange carriers, the SSP routes the call via the carrier's point of presence (POP).

Note : IC = InterLATA Carrier

FIGURE 2.5. Intelligent Network Architecture for BOC 800 Service. Diagram from page 4 of BellCoRe Exchange Magazine for July/August 1986 "Intelligent Network Architecture For BOC 800 Service." (Reprinted with permission from Bell Communications Research EXCHANGE, Copyright 1986.)

and **supervisory** information, respectively, and prior to 1976 these were always passed over the same voice path as the call, typically using tones. Called **in-band signaling,** this technique required that every line (called a **trunk**) between switches be provided with equipment to transmit and receive tone signals at both ends. It also left open the possibility of customer fraud and interference with network operation, because a caller could, with a device which became known as a **blue box** or **MF box,** generate the same multi-frequency signals. These disadvantages were overcome and a great deal of flexibility gained by gathering all the addressing and supervisory signals associated with the group of lines (called a **trunk group**) between a pair of switches and transmitting them over a special data link reserved for this purpose.

CCIS introduces a digital network for signaling and supervisory data that overlays the voice paths between switches. Operating at 2,400 bits per second with 28-bit (20 data and eight checking) messages which contain the address of the destination switch, the CCIS network is faster and more economical than in-band signaling. The improvement in speed offered faster call setup to the caller and more efficient use of trunks to the telephone companies. Its major advantage, however, is flexibility. It can be used by stored program controlled switches to exchange new and useful kinds of messages with each other and with more conventional computers used for collecting billing information and providing data base services. Bell Communications Research, a development and standards company owned by the Bell Operating Companies (BOCs) has developed a flexible system for routing toll-free calls called "BOC 800 Service" using this approach; the major parts of this are shown in Figure 2.5. Since a telephone number need no longer be tied to a certain physical line, it is possible to route calls to different destinations based on variables such as the location of the caller or the time of day.

The CCIS/stored program control concept is carried much further with the integrated services digital networks now taking shape. These are described in Chapter 14.

The digital revolution in telephone transmission occurred, fortunately, just in time to serve the growing need for data transmission between computers. That story is the subject of Chapter 3.

Digital Services

Chapter Overview

Telecommunications history develops some curious anomalies. The 1960s found data engineers developing devices to make data appear as voice, while voice engineers developed digital data-like devices for voice signals. The anomaly grew in the 1970s as modems, converting data to voice-range tones, were attached to telephone systems which increasingly turned tones back into bits. The two technologies have continued in tandem into the present, amidst confusion to both voice and data users. This chapter reveals how digital technologies, first seen in Chapter 2, were offered as "digital services." On a parallel track, the data community developed techniques, such as high bit rate analog modems to operate over the voice network, increasingly based on digital T-Carriers.

Digital T-Carrier systems, described below and expanded in Chapter 5, formed the foundations of AT&T's DATAPHONE® Digital Service. Installations of voice T-Carriers spread across the nation, forming the base for a truly digital end-to-end connection. Following the announcement, more "digital cities" were added and service became widely available to data users. Then came early high capacity (or T1) services and true megabit data communications was born. Unfortunately, it became a reality before many users were really ready for it. The period of consolidation in the early 1980s has been followed by a feast of offerings. Now, many other carriers offer digital services similar to DATAPHONE® Digital Services. For descriptive purposes, the term DDS will be used to mean conceptual digital data services; specific offerings will take their actual names.

This chapter traces parallel digital voice and data developments during the early days of DDS. Moving on to megabit and higher services, the chapter outlines the introduction of many features common today in high-speed data (and digital voice) communications. Full details of the services, features and functions will come later. Chapter 3 provides a history and with it, hopefully, an understanding upon which to build details. A discussion of voice/data integration follows, leading to the birth of Integrated Services Digital Networks (ISDN), more fully described in Chapter 14.

Data Communications on Analog Services

Telegraph, inherently digital in nature, begot teleprinters, but voice telephony developed a new technique in communications: **the analog channel.** Analog channels simultaneously carried a wide range of frequency tones, sufficient to distinguish individual human voices. Limited by the range of early telephone transmitters (mouthpiece microphones), voice channels soon standardized on a range of frequencies (bandwidth) from about 300 hertz (cycles per second) on the low end to about 3,300 hertz (Hz) at the high end. This meant any tone (or voice) frequency between 300 hertz and 3,300 Hz passed through from telephone to telephone. While significantly less than the range (or bandwidth) of the human ear, almost all voice components or overtones carry through. The 4,000 hertz telephone voice channel became the medium for all communications except telegraph and teletype.

Early ventures into data communications coped with analog voice channels, as digital services lay far in the future. Early data transmission emulated analog signals normally found in this voice telephony world. Beginning with two shifting frequency tones for one and zero, called **frequency shift keying** (FSK), data communications MODulator-DEModulator (MODEM) units extended useable transmission speeds by forming more exotic modulation methods.

Modulation, most simply explained, adds two signals together electrically forming a new signal which may be more easily transmitted. Early radio stations modulated (added) voice and music signals to radio signals in simple **amplitude modulation** (AM). Later, a more exotic technique added the voice and music to radio signals by modulating the radio signal's frequency in a method called **frequency modulation** (FM). Data transmission over the telephone system, followed these approaches with the modems. By changing not only amplitude and the frequency, but also the phase of the tone, faster digital signals could be sent over an analog voice channel. Needs for higher data speeds then came together with needs for more copper cable capacity between telephone offices. These needs brought about new **multiplexing** solutions to provide both greater speed and more efficient use of cables: analog **frequency division multiplexing** (FDM) and digital **time division multiplexing** (TDM).

Multiplexing differs from modulation only in how it is used. In FDM, many (multi) signals are modulated together on a single carrier. In TDM, many (multi) bit streams are combined together into a single bit rate running at or faster than the sum of the individual bit rates. Modulation alters a signal away from its original (or baseband) frequency range to a new frequency range to make it easier to send. Multiplexing takes many signals and combines them using modulation or other combining techniques.

Multiplexing (carrying multiple calls on a single facility) started with a need for more telephone cable. Voice calls had been carried for many years on **local loops** from homes and businesses (subscribers) to central offices on single copper wire pairs. Calls between telephone central offices also used copper pairs, but as demands for service grew, many more pairs were needed. To reduce costs for adding new pairs between offices, systems developed to achieve **pair-gain.** If two copper pairs, one for each direction, had been needed for a call between telephone central offices, and 12 calls could be sent by the new system on the same two pairs, the pair-gain was 12. Multiplexing the 12 calls, starting with FDM techniques, originated the twin concepts of channel banks and channel groups.

The first widely used multiplexing of several calls on one pair placed 12 calls together and coined the term **group;** it continues today to mean 12 channels of telephony. Electronic equipment units which combine the 12 channels into groups take the name **channel banks,** and are banks or racks of equipment rather than depository-type money banks. Multiplexing and modulation combined to place many calls on new, higher frequency for transmission. AT&T's first channel bank multiplexed or combined twelve 4,000 Hz voice channels together and the result occupied 48,000 Hz. This A-type channel bank actually outputted a frequency range from 60,000 to 108,000 Hz and this signal was carried to the next telephone office on another new facility called a carrier.

As needs and facilities grew, so did analog FDM channel bank and carrier families. Just as channels combined to form groups, groups combined to form **supergroups,** and supergroups combined to form **mastergroups.** While FDM group technology originated to handle voice calls, data was not ignored. Data communications needs were met at each level of the FDM **hierarchy.** Low-speed data signals, up to 2,400 bit/s and converted to frequencies by modems, became channels; medium speed data signals to 50,000 bit/s became group-band signals and higher speeds to about 250,000 bit/s became supergroup signals. Much of the world's existing telephone network uses analog FDM techniques, but TDM methods, developed for voice signals, now form the building blocks for newer digital networks and services.

Digital Services Origins

Digital telephone services originated, not for data, but for voice, with the introduction of digital voice channel banks. Digital channel banks converted voice conversations to binary bits for transmission. These channel banks came about as yet another way to save copper wire pairs between telephone offices. As cities grew and demand for telephone services expanded, cable tunnels filled between telephone offices. FDM pair-gain techniques were well developed when solid state devices, such as early transistors, offered ways to make digital conversions from analog voice signals. It was simply another very good way to put more calls on a single pair of copper wires.

FDM technologies originated the concept of carriers and techniques for carrying multiple calls. Individual copper cables had long offered more frequency range or bandwidth than was needed for single voice conversations. FDM used electronic oscillators and modulators to place each conversation into successively higher sections of the bandwidth. Combined groups of voice channels were then sent together over **wideband** carriers on the cable pairs. At the far end, each channel was derived and placed back in the **baseband** or original voice frequency range. These methods were called carrier systems as they carried many conversations simultaneously over a single copper pair. It was natural, following AT&T practice, to call the megabit-speed digital Carrier T; it was the next letter in a line of previous carrier systems, such as analog N and L Carriers. **Time division multiplexing** or TDM arrived as a new technology, but built upon concepts developed in FDM.

Analog FDM systems originated the group, or 12-voice channel concept. Digital systems advanced the concept with the **digroup,** two sets of 12 channels or 24 channels. **D-type** channel banks became the telephone office device to convert a digroup of analog calls into digital bits. At the next office (the other end of the T1 carrier), another channel bank converted the bits back into normal analog voice conversations. The process operated in both directions to provide full duplex or simultaneous bi-directional service. Early T1 systems operated up to 50 miles on ordinary copper cables, with digital repeaters about every mile. Repeaters reformed and squared-up the digital pulses sent from the voice digitizers.

Methods chosen to digitize voice calls derived from a desire to maintain high (or toll) quality of the conversation. These methods, details and specific terminology will be examined more closely in Chapter 5. Here, it is important to recognize the voice origins and design choices of what has become the cornerstone of digital communications. Most channel banks in use today follow concepts from early D-type banks. Called by newer names, such as D3, D4 and D5, channel banks set the bit arrangements to form a consistent set of architectures. In the United States and Canada, the architecture is referred to as the North American Hierarchy. In Europe, concepts remain identical, but structure differs.

European T1 also developed from digital channels representing a voice conversation, but Europe combined 30 channels instead of 24 and European T1 became 2,048,000 bit/s. Europe called the equipment **PCM multiplex,** while North America used the term **channel bank.**

Digital Channel Banks

The North American Digital Hierarchy traces its ancestry to early channel banks and original T1 carrier systems. D-type channel banks still use 64 kbit/s to encode a voice conversation, and this remains the lowest common speed in the voice hierarchy. Twenty-four 64 kbit/s channels combine to form T1 bit streams, the next level in the scheme. Higher speeds in the hierarchy are formed by combining T1s also using time division multiplexing methods.

If 64 kbit/s channels form the bricks of digital structures, time division multiplexing (TDM) becomes the structural steel. TDM techniques, first found commercially in early channel banks, now form the skeleton of almost all digital communications. The most fundamental concept in megabit digital communications, TDM is simple to understand, though often complex to implement.

Returning to digital voice origins, TDM can be comprehended through an analysis of early channel banks. Each voice conversation came to the channel bank on two wires (two more may be used to carry the other direction of speech). The conversation is first sampled or quantized 8,000 times each second, a rate selected by information theory to capture the highest bandwidth of the approximately 4,000 hertz (bandwidth) voice channel. This means electronically sampling the analog value of the instantaneous voltage of a voice signal. This sampled value, represented as **pulse amplitude modulation** (PAM), is a voltage pulse whose height or amplitude represents the analog voltage amplitude of the conversation channel at the instant of digitization.

The PAM pulse from each channel is then sequentially converted to eight binary bits representing the PAM pulse's height. Conversion follows an approach called **pulse code modulation** (PCM) which selects a PAM pulse from each channel and converts it to a true digital value. Eight PCM bits, each coded to "one" or "zero" when added together in a specially weighted binary arithmetic, equal the PAM pulse height. As the PCM coder selects one channel at a time for conversion, and makes eight bits from each pulse, the

FIGURE 3.1. D4 Digital Channel Bank. (Photo courtesy of AT&T.)

resulting output operates eight times faster than the original quantizing rate of 8,000 times per second. Eight times 8,000 yields 64,000 or 64 kbit/s (kilobits per second) leading to a shorthand expression for the process, 64 K PCM.

This method of selecting bits, first from one information channel, then the next, and sending them serially across a line forms time division multiplexing. Time, divided in equal increments, allocates slots for the binary value of each information channel to be sent at a combined high rate of speed. To undo the process at the far end, a method must be found to locate the bits belonging to each channel. This method is called **framing.** At the completion of each cycle of 24 channels, a bit position is reserved for the framing process and the group of information bits, with the frame bit added, is called a **frame.**

When the 192 (eight times 24) bits from all 24 channels are sent, a 193rd bit of the framing is sent and the process repeats. A sampling rate of 8,000 times per second, means that 192 plus one bits will go out 8,000 times each second. A simple calculation of 193 (bits) times 8,000 (times per second) yields 1,544,000 bits per second. Another way of calculating gives 24 channels times 64 kbit/s equaling 1,536,000 bit/s. The framing bit position (one bit) times 8,000 times per second yields 8,000 bit/s. 1,536,000 bit/s added to 8,000 bit/s again gives 1,544,000 bit/s. This final TDM digital stream of binary pulses is called DS-1 or T1. European T1, combining 30 voice channels, yields 2,048,000 bit/s. The European scheme builds 30 channels of digitized voice (with slightly different digitizing rules) and then adds 64,000 bit/s to combine signaling for each of the channels and another 64,000 of framing information. The result of 32 times 64,000 produces 2,048,000 bit/s.

Following conventions started in the voice digitization process for DS-1, each 64 kbit/s channel is called DS-0, or the level below the DS-1. This allocation of channels in eight bit groups within the DS-1 stream is called D4 or DS-1 type channelization format and can easily be confused with D4 type framing format. While the two formats relate in

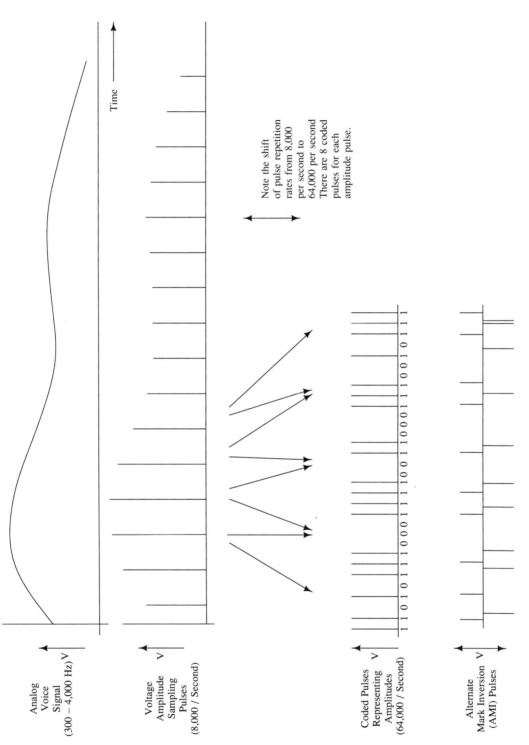

FIGURE 3.2. Digital Sampling and Quantizing of Voice Signals.

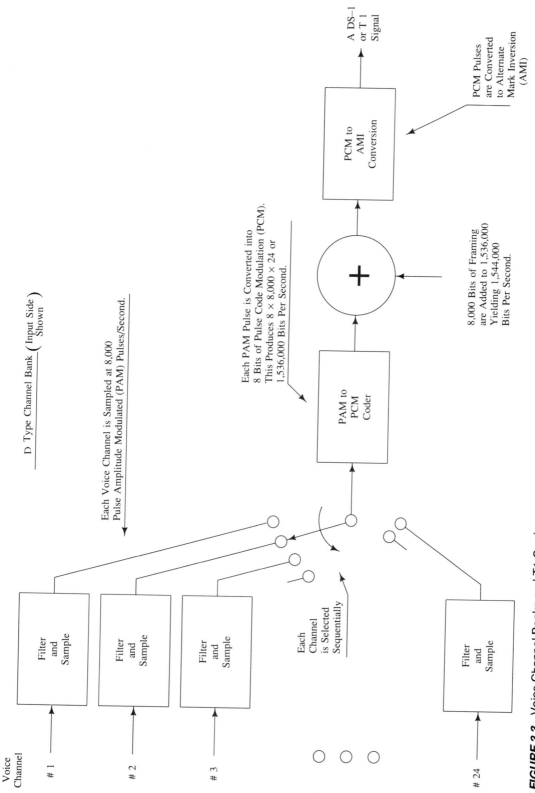

FIGURE 3.3. Voice Channel Banks and T1 Carriers.

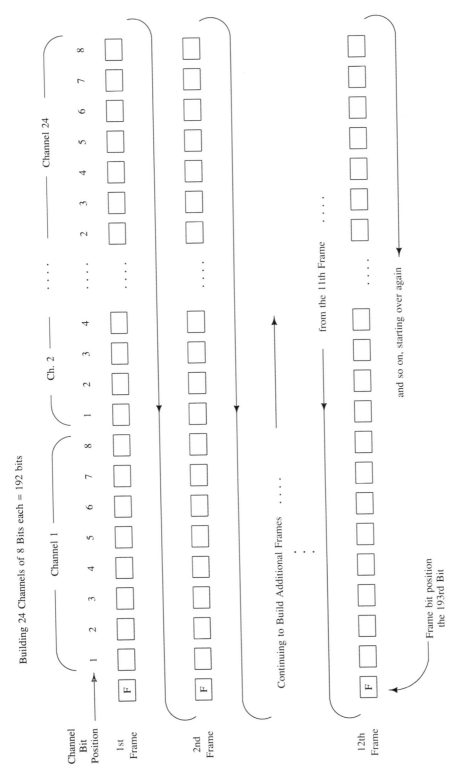

FIGURE 3.4. D4 Framing and Channelization.

voice channel bank operation, other DS-1 producing devices exist which produce only the D4 type framing format, but do not use DS-1 type channelization format. **Format** becomes the confusing noun.

D4 type channelization format refers strictly to the allocation and placement of the eight bit groups inside the 192-bit frame. D4 type framing format refers strictly to the content of the 193rd framing bit position. In ordinary D4 type framing format, the frame bit position contains a repeating 12 bit pattern, 100011011100. This, and this alone, can be called D4 type framing format. Twelve frames, of 193 bits each, take the name **superframe,** containing 2,316 bits. The superframe concept permits the far end channel bank to "find," or "synchronize to," the original channel positions by locking onto the repeating 12 bit framing pattern. An advanced type of framing called **extended superframe** (ESF) will be explained later in the chapter.

Format, then, becomes the most confusing term in the T-Carrier field. To reduce this confusion, only the terms **framing** and **channelization** will be used from now on in this text.

The first channel banks, running at 1,544,000 bit/s, generated their own transmitted timing at each end and recovered the timing from the received DS-1 stream at the other end. As more and more telephone systems moved to digital technology, central timing and synchronization became necessary. Channel banks, large digital voice telephone switches and digital multiplexers began to take timing from a central source. (Timing and synchronization are covered in Chapter 7.) This prepared the path for true national end-to-end digital data service.

Analog Modems and Digital Services

Analog modems, the workhorses of data communications, continued parallel development during the digitization of the voice telephone network. Seeking higher speeds and more reliable operation for computer-to-computer links, engineers turned to more exotic modulation techniques. Underlying their search is a fundamental truth of the world's telephone networks: limited bandwidth. Since the early days of telephony, a standard bandwidth for voice services has been about 3,000 hertz or cycles per second. Origins of this limit trace back to the carbon microphone, developed by Thomas Edison in the 1870s.

While the human ear can recognize tones above 15,000 hertz, the carbon microphone and telephone networks limit transmitted frequencies to about 4,000 hertz. For normal voice communications, this limited bandwidth (range of frequencies) works well; people communicate easily, voices are recognized. The limit, however, imposes constraints on data modem designers. When digital data converts to sounds, the sounds must fall within the available bandwidth. For practical purposes, this means only signals between 300 hertz and 3,300 hertz can be sent, and other technical limits of the telephone network must be met.

Limits of this type stimulate and challenge engineers, and they continue to meet the challenge. Within this limited bandwidth, modems are now available for data rates approaching 20,000 bit/s. A useful rule of thumb to compare advances in modem technology is the simple division of data rate by bandwidth. That is, a 2,400 bit/s modem operating over a 3,300 hertz (Hz) bandwidth yields, by division, 0.73 bits/Hz. Similarly, a modem running at 14,400 bit/s on the same bandwidth gives 4.36 bits/Hz. The measure is simply how many bits can be squeezed into each cycle per second of bandwidth. As the ratio rises above 1.0, more exotic approaches must be found.

Claude Shannon, in his classic 1948 paper, proposed a theory describing the limits of information transport in the presence of noise. In a real telephone network environment, noise will keep the ratio of bits/Hz from rising beyond about 10.0. Current **trellis** modulation techniques approach the Shannon limits on normal analog telephone bandwidths. Now, however, digitization of the telephone network comes into play. When the carrier no longer provides an analog end-to-end channel, analog to digital conversion and digital transmission affect the modem's ability to send and receive data. Here both technologies require closer examination for true compatibility.

D-type voice channel banks, using 64 K PCM, take a full 4,000 Hz in the analog-to-digital conversion and offer reduced noise through pure digital network connections. Combinations of high-bit rate modems and D-type channel banks, although involving multiple digital-to-analog and analog-to-digital conversions, may not impact each other. Other voice digitization approaches, however, may warrant closer examination when combined with current exotic modem approaches. **Continuously variable slope detection (CVSD)**, **adaptive differential pulse code modulation** (ADPCM) and other multiplexing techniques utilize fewer bits to encode each voice channel. While voice quality may be shown to be equal or nearly equal to 64 K PCM, the effects of these conversion approaches on high-bit-rate modems is not clear.

Newer digital voice coding methods, particularly ADPCM, may not be visible to a user as they are often implemented in the inner reaches of a voice network. As these techniques become more popular within carrier and private voice networks, user awareness must increase when high-bit-rate modems are involved. The configuration under discussion is shown in the figure below.

Examining the Figure 3.5, bits from the originating digital source are first converted to analog voice frequency tones. The analog signal carries information to the first voice frequency analog-to-digital conversion device, where it is digitized into bits of a different form. These bits flow through the digital network to a far-end voice reconversion unit. Here, analog signals are re-created and sent to the far-end modem for yet another conversion to bits. The far-end modem interprets the analog content and generates the original data bits. The process, of course, also operates in the reverse direction.

Figure 3.5 shows a simple case of a single set of A-to-D and D-to-A conversions. In real world networks, however, the possibility of multiple conversions exists. At each conversion, the quantizing noise, or the error introduced by making digital decisions from analog signals, accumulates. At some point, perhaps four conversions, the quantizing noise introduces bit errors and the end-to-end process degrades. Many modem designs compensate for these, and other, error possibilities by down-shifting or automatically reducing speed in the presence of increasing errors. **Line conditioning** by the signal carrier offers an alternative. Line conditioning, discussed in Chapter 8, assures users of certain transmission parameters to optimize data throughput and many types of conditioning are offered. Modem manufacturers specify conditioning requirements for each of their modem types, but the user retains responsibility for overall performance.

While this process appears clumsy, it works well as long as assumptions about bandwidth, frequency and other criteria are consistent between analog modem and digital telephone designers, and A-to-D conversions are limited. When, however, one set of designers changes criteria, a simpler scheme to carry the bits may be superior. Digitization

41

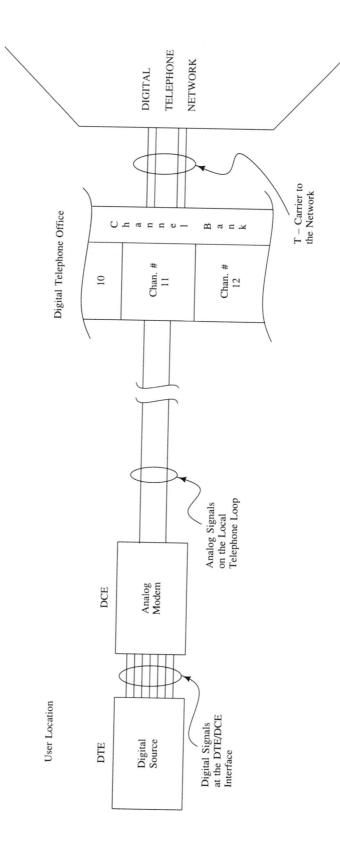

FIGURE 3.5. Analog Modems in Digital Voice Networks.

of the voice communications network paved a smooth path for this simpler, digital data service communications offering.

DATAPHONE® Digital Services

In 1974, AT&T announced DATAPHONE® Digital Services. Building from the increasing digitization of the voice network, AT&T could provide digital end-to-end connections where facilities existed. Channel banks, using 64,000 bit/s for conversation, permitted up to 56,000 bit/s for data. Digital data services offered common computer data speeds of 2,400, 4,800, 9,600 bit/s on "pure" digital facilities. A new higher speed of 56,000 bit/s was provided as a natural extension of D-type channel banks and T1 technology. The services, limited by available facilities, were offered where digital capabilities were ready for the data service. These were called the **digital cities.**

Digital Cities

Digital cities needed access to a national digital network through digital connections like T-Carriers and needed the equipment, local facilities and skills to make it work and keep it working. The early list of digital cities included many major metropolitan areas of the United States and promised expansion to many more. As the years have passed, the promise has been fulfilled. As this is written, over 100 cities of the country have local and long haul DDS capability from many local and long-distance carriers. DDS has become a major and superior service offering for digital data communications and 56,000 bit/s offers new ranges of applications. The original modem-type data speeds of 2,400, 4,800, 9,600 bit/s services remain in place.

Modem-speed DDS Services

The lower three speeds in DDS compete with analog modem services from both AT&T and other manufacturers. Prices for DDS service are higher than equivalent speed-leased voice circuits used for data, but quality and reliability are better. Service objectives are quoted for service availability and error rates and users find end-to-end performance superior. Digital end-to-end services offer reduced errors by their digital nature. Errors do not accumulate as they do in analog systems and error performance no longer depends on modem performance. Users have a choice of price and transmission quality for data for the first time. Leased analog voice circuits can be conditioned or electronically adjusted for data, but DDS is digital and needs no conditioning. At these speeds, analog modems and leased analog voice circuits vie for the attention and business of the data communications professional. Data communications has again been recognized in the world of voice networks. Beyond recognition, data communications now had its own high-speed service, 56,000 bit/s.

56,000 bit/s Services

Before DDS, FDM wideband services gave data users capabilities for higher speeds. These wideband services derived from the utilization of multiple analog voice channels or groups. Group-band modem remains a term from this period of data communications. Although expensive, wideband was the only choice for high-speed computer-to-computer data transmission. This was agreeable to computer professionals in the mid-1970s, as bulk data transmission formed most high-speed data communications needs. High-speed interactive terminal sessions from remote host computers waited for the future. Computer processes were largely batch, as computer work was done by entering a job and waiting for the computer to produce or output the results.

DDS services allowed **remote job entry** (RJE) and **remote job output** (RJO) to be handled at greater distances and at greater speeds. But another opportunity beckoned with 56 K DDS: fast, remote interactive computing.

With terminals attached to host computers, users found new freedom and productivity in direct interaction with applications programs. Data, programs and jobs could be entered from the terminal and results seen quickly. Response time and turn-around time became new measures of computer productivity. Response time directly affected an information worker's output (and productivity). Response time definitions vary depending on the size of an expected response and on the type of a particular application, but generally "faster is better." Turn around time (the time to complete job output in screen or print form) was now measured in number of job completions or **turns** per day. Local terminals connected directly to the host by high-speed coaxial cables showed the best results, but what about remotes? Remote terminals, connected by low-speed analog modems, slowed productivity when compared to local results. DDS services at 56,000 bit/s came to the rescue. Where costs could be justified on productivity, 56,000 bit/s remote terminals performed almost as well as local terminals. RJE and RJO terminals speeded turn-around time at the now available higher speeds.

High-speed digital data communications, founded on T-Carriers and DATA-PHONE® Digital Services, opened a door to the future. Through that door, came even higher speed data communications services.

T1 Digital Data Services

In the late 1970s, user awareness and equipment availability for T1 speed carrier services combined with ever-increasing demands for speed in data communications. Private systems based on T1 equipment and newly developed data time division multiplexing units appeared for local and short-distance needs. These early private systems, used locally to distribute computer data with T1s, proved both reliable and cost effective. Offering speeds not then available from the carriers, users set up private circuits well above 56 kbit/s for applications like **computer aided design** and **computer aided manufacturing (CAD/CAM)**. Users began requesting the carriers to offer longer distance T1 services.

Telephone Common Carrier T1 offerings had been available on a special basis, but costs for special arrangements and installation were high. Only a few large data users had extended their private systems with carrier services. Then AT&T announced 1.544 Mbit/s Digital Service, opening an era of long-distance megabit data communications. Satellite T1 services, such as (then) Satellite Business Systems were offered and users previously limited to 56 kbit/s DDS now examined the benefits of T1. Manufacturers with established positions in modems and statistical multiplexers announced T1 data TDMs. The "big pipes" had arrived.

The "Big Pipes"

Carrier-provided megabit-speed digital service offered T1 fixed circuits directly from a user's computer center to remote facilities. Users bought data TDMs to combine numbers of 56 kbit/s and lower speed circuits onto 1,544,000 bit/s point-to-point links. Users with several large facilities found T1 services could **aggregate** these many circuits onto the big pipe. Costs were lower for high volume data users and the quality of the digital circuits proved an added bonus. Reliability and low error rates attracted many new users to the T1 arena. Maintenance proved no more difficult, and in many cases easier, than banks of modems and numbers of analog voice lines.

The big pipes were really 1,544,000 bit/s leased circuits with few restrictions on frame, channelization or content. AT&T described the technical details of the offering in a Bell System Technical Reference (PUB 41451, May 1977). Two services, available in the first offering, used either 1,344,000 without signal constraints or 1,544,000 with signal limitations. At 1,544,000, the publication specified constraints on pulse density and dotting (long periods of alternating "ones " and "zeros"). Pulse density constraints listed were similar to those in the latest AT&T document (PUB 62411, October 1985) and concerned maximum numbers of "zeros".

Numbers of "zeros" had to be limited, as the timing rate for the service was specified at 1.544 Mbit/s ± 100 bit/s, and timing was carried or imbedded in the transmitted data stream. Chapters 4 and 5 will detail the form of the actual signal on the link; here note that binary "zeros" presented no pulse on the link. This required that the customer either offered no more than 15 consecutive "zeros" to the link, or accepted the 1.344 Mbit/s option. This lower speed option located a Western Electric 306-type data set at the user interface. (Digital interfaces will be described fully in the next chapter.) The 306-type data set reserved the 200,000 bit/s difference to preserve pulse density on the link while giving the user a channel without density constraints. The 306-type data set was described in a separate AT&T publication (PUB 41304) entitled, "Wideband Data Set 306-Type Interface Specification." PUB 41451 contained information on the 1.544 Mbit/s service.

The document detailed interface specifications at the customer side of the (then) AT&T provided **551A channel service unit** (CSU). Data TDM manufacturers, following the recommendations of AT&T's PUB 41451, offered units which connected directly to the CSU. A user could order a circuit from AT&T, a pair of TDM units and, with two manufacturer supplied cables, take full use of a megabit pipe. As an example, data TDMs could aggregate up to 24 channels of 56 kbit/s, 140 channels of 9,600 or nearly 500 channels of 2,400 bit/s on a single T1. Existing statistical multiplexers worked well with the newer TDMs and could multiply the circuit count even higher. While the early data TDMs reserved several hundred kilobits for overhead and other purposes, the remaining bandwidth more than met most user needs.

In addition to bandwidth, the new service described quality and availability objectives. While carefully stating that the new objectives were preliminary and were "not to be construed as minimum performance guarantees" (PUB 41451, MAY 1977), they offered users a benchmark. The quality objective of 95% error-free seconds and the availability objective at least 99.7 % came as good "new news" to users accustomed to analog circuits.

The bonus of objectives and higher speeds stimulated users to explore applications previously unavailable to them. **Computer aided design** (CAD) and **computer aided manufacturing** (CAM) required extremely high data rates between CAD/CAM display terminals and their host computers. This had meant locating the terminals in the same building or on the same campus as the computer hosts and bringing remote users to the terminals. With data TDMs capable of running circuits up to 500,000 or 750,000 bit/s, these high data rate applications could support CAD/CAM terminals at remote locations.

Remote text-oriented terminals, funneled over lower speed analog circuits, could now attach directly to local computers used as terminal **front ends.** These front end machines could then remotely connect with one or more 56 kbit/s links to a larger applications host at a central site. Terminal response time from this arrangement dropped significantly and terminal user productivity improved. These computer-to-computer network links benefited from improved error rates and higher speeds offered by the data TDMs and the T1s. Larger blocks of data could be sent with reduced worry about errors and multiple retransmissions. Users, carriers, and TDM manufacturers continued to expand T1 services and applications.

As first offered in the late 1970s, 1,544 Mbit/s Digital Service utilized a type **551A Western Electric channel service unit** (CSU). A CSU provided a direct interface for customer connection as part of the offering. Later legal divestiture of services separated the CSU and made it **customer premises equipment** or CPE to be supplied by the users. The telephone carrier supplied CSU derived power from the telephone company central office in much the same manner as voice telephone instruments receive power. This **line powering** permitted the network functions of the CSU to proceed independently of power at a user's location.

Beyond powering, CSU functions included capability to regenerate the incoming signal from the telephone line, to recover timing information and regenerate the customer's outbound signal. In addition, the CSU provided circuitry for network test and fault location. As explained in more detail later in Chapter 4, the signals from the customer equipment and the telephone line took a **bipolar** pulse form, where "ones" were positive or negative three volt pulses and "zeros" were the absence of pulses. As this absence could continue too long, the "zeros" constraint mentioned above could cause the CSU to insert a "one" pulse whenever the CSU detected a long "zero" string. The CSU altered the customer's outbound signal stream when the average "ones" density dropped too low and a 16 "zero" string was detected. As the far-end CSU was not aware of this alteration, errors could result in the customer data stream.

T1 CPE designers, aware of this error possibility, developed equipment which inserted "ones" sufficiently often to avoid bit stream alterations by the CSU. Voice channel banks had been designed with sufficient "ones" density under all conditions to prevent CSU bit stream alteration. In data TDMs, "ones" were inserted sufficiently often prior to transmission to the 551A CSU. These inserted ones subtracted from the full 1.544 Mbit/s rate, but usually provided at least 1.344 Mbit/s for customer data aggregation. Where the "ones" bit density could not be guaranteed by the end use CPE, the 306-type data set was placed between the customer equipment and the 551A.

The 306-type data set connected to the customer's data equipment and provided many modem-like functions, in addition to meeting the bit density constraints of the T1 service. To accomplish this, the data set took charge of timing both the 1.544 Mbit/s T1 line and the timing of the customer equipment. It offered both timing and data leads to the user equipment and clocked the outbound user data into storage buffers at a rate of 1.344 Mbit/s. Adding bit density pulses to meet the network needs, it then clocked out the user data and the **stuff bits** (explained in Chapter 5), at 1.544 Mbit/s. At the far end, these stuff bits were removed by the 306 and customer data was presented without constraint.

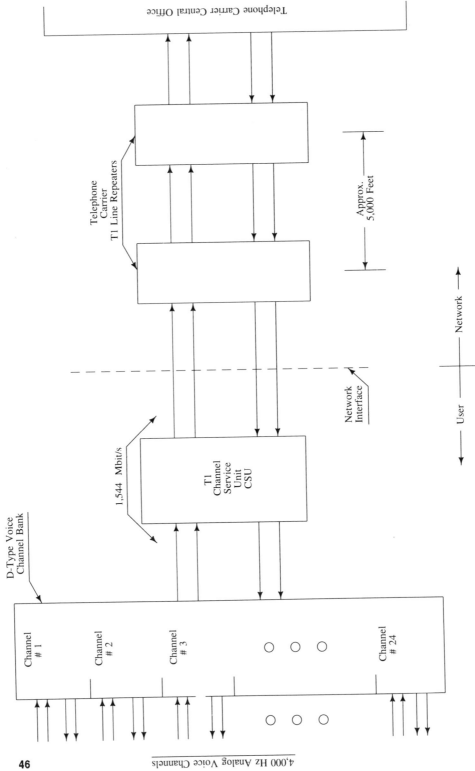

FIGURE 3.6. T1 and 551A CSU Network Connections.

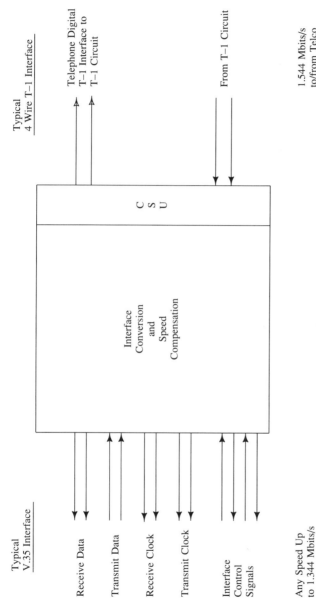

FIGURE 3.7. 306-type Data Set Connections to T1 Service. © Electronic Industries Association. Reprinted with Permission.

47

As T1 service grew in popularity and application, AT&T filed new tariffs and published newer descriptions of the service. Equipment manufacturers continued developments and sales of T1 user equipment for both voice and data applications grew.

High-capacity Terrestrial Service

AT&T Tariff Number 270, filed in 1982, as **high-capacity terrestrial service,** offered even more attractive T1 pricing and provided additional features. The reference publication (PUB 41451) was updated and re-issued with a January 1983 date. While the name altered to high capacity terrestrial service, few other key requirements changed. One changed requirement concerned framing. Remembering the the discussion of D4 framing earlier in this chapter, the new document required customer equipment to supply D4 framing bits. A two-year conversion period to alter existing non-complying equipment allowed users and manufacturers a migration path to the requirement.

Although voice channel bank units already supplied D4 framing (and channelization), few T1 data communications multiplexers supplied the frame bits. The conversion period, which actually lasted three years, ended in 1986 when D4 framing became mandatory on AT&T Communications T1 circuits. By that time all T1 data multiplexer manufacturers offered D4 framing, although only some of them offered D4 channelization on their inter-unit T1s. As D4 framing became consistent, AT&T introduced a new concept—**extended framing**—to improve maintainability of the circuits.

The new concept, introduced earlier in a compatibility bulletin, indicated that AT&T was moving beyond D4 framing to something more advanced. The term then used, F_e (say F, sub E), stood for **extended framing format** and added two new functions to the framing bits. F_e was renamed **extended superframe format** (ESF) in 1984, and will be described in more detail in Chapter 5. The superframe described above, originating in digital channel banks, contained 12 frames of 193 bits. To capture additional function, the superframe was extended to contain 24 frames of 193 bits. By extending the superframe, 24 bits became available at the framing bit position and careful rearrangement of the bits isolated two new functions. D4 framing bits had passed through the circuit at 8,000 bits per second and this rate contained the new functions.

Framing was reduced to a 2,000 bit/s function and required one quarter, or six of the 24 bits. Error checking, the first of the two new functions, also took 6 bits. The remaining 12 bits from the 24 bit extended superframe formed a data link or communications channel operating only within the 193rd bit pattern. Since the data link used the remaining half of the 24 bits (and 8,000 bit/s capacity) it ran at 4,000 bit/s. Considering that most personal computers communicate at 300, 1200 or 2400 bit/s, this 4,000 bit/s data link could carry considerable information. The data link, using **high-level data link control** (HDLC) protocol, contained separate error checking as an **HDLC frame check sequence.**

The error checking function, called **CRC-6** after **cyclic redundancy check** using 6 bits, offered abilities to indicate errors within the T1 stream without subtracting capacity from the 24 channels of 64 kbit/s (1,536,000). The function could not correct errors or indicate how many errors in a superframe, but recorded simply that one or more errors had occurred. As previously offered, T1 could not indicate errors without consuming bandwidth; now error detection was contained within the framing.

Framing, previously a 12-bit pattern, reduced to a six-bit pattern and exposed the risk of false framing, or locking onto a non-frame customer data pattern. Avoiding this was simply a matter of using the CRC-6 along with the six-bit **framing pattern sequence**

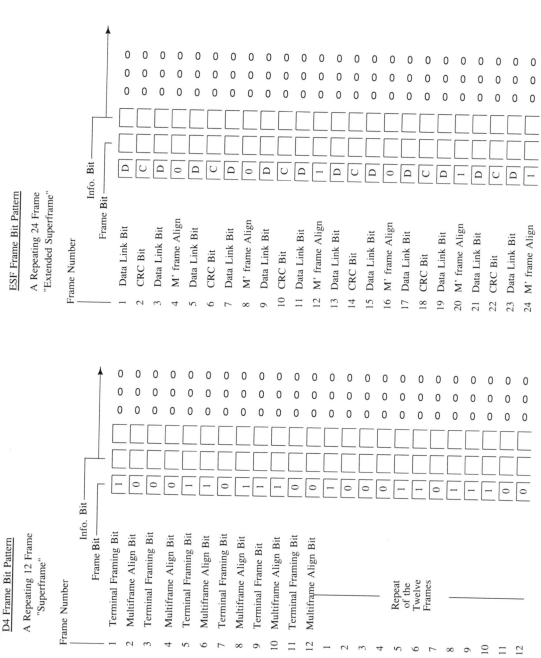

D4 Frame Bit Pattern

A Repeating 12 Frame "Superframe"

Frame Number	Frame Bit	Info. Bit
1	Terminal Framing Bit	1
2	Multiframe Align Bit	0
3	Terminal Framing Bit	0
4	Multiframe Align Bit	0
5	Terminal Framing Bit	1
6	Multiframe Align Bit	1
7	Terminal Framing Bit	0
8	Multiframe Align Bit	1
9	Terminal Frame Bit	1
10	Multiframe Align Bit	1
11	Terminal Framing Bit	0
12	Multiframe Align Bit	0

Repeat of the Twelve Frames

1	1
2	0
3	0
4	0
5	1
6	1
7	0
8	1
9	1
10	1
11	0
12	0

ESF Frame Bit Pattern

A Repeating 24 Frame "Extended Superframe"

Frame Number	Frame Bit	Info. Bit
1	Data Link Bit	D
2	CRC Bit	C
3	Data Link Bit	D
4	M' frame Align	0
5	Data Link Bit	D
6	CRC Bit	C
7	Data Link Bit	D
8	M' frame Align	0
9	Data Link Bit	D
10	CRC Bit	C
11	Data Link Bit	D
12	M' frame Align	1
13	Data Link Bit	D
14	CRC Bit	C
15	Data Link Bit	D
16	M' frame Align	0
17	Data Link Bit	D
18	CRC Bit	C
19	Data Link Bit	D
20	M' frame Align	1
21	Data Link Bit	D
22	CRC Bit	C
23	Data Link Bit	D
24	M' frame Align	1

FIGURE 3.8. Framing, CRC-6 and Data Link in ESF (F_e) Framing.

(FPS). If the FPS appeared correct, but the CRC indicated errors, the FPS could be false and a search should continue to find another FPS without CRC errors. Stated another way, if the FPS were false, the probability of calculating a valid CRC from really random bits was extremely small. These two new functions, while still in a proposed future, promised additional power for T1.

Another promising development unveiled during this period was a **clear channel** capability permitting unrestricted "ones" and "zeros" in a customer T1 data stream. This proposal, identified as B8ZS, suggested the use of **bipolar violations** (BPV) as a method of signalling long "zeros" strings without loss of synchronization. Bipolar violations, described more fully in Chapter 4, originally were measured as incorrectly received T1 pulses. As network equipment became more reliable, a bipolar violation pattern intentionally inserted in the stream, could indicate eight "zeros" of customer data. The **bipolar with eight zero substitution** (B8ZS) pulse pattern, substituted by customer equipment and sent across the T1 link, was removed at the other end and the original eight "zeros" replaced.

With clear channel, error checking, superior framing, and a data link, T1 entered the mid-1980s ready for new and expanded services.

ACCUNET® T1.5 Service

In the mid-1980s AT&T Communications pulled together several digital services under the name ACCUNET®, and continued to expand the services and functions available under the new name. What had started as 1.544 Mbit/s Digital Service was now to be called ACCUNET® T1.5 Service.

Deregulation and divestiture had, by now, divided telephone geography into **local access and transport areas** (LATAs) and had separated services. Three separate concepts, now involved in all telecommunications, split T1 offerings. Channel service units, once part of the carrier offering, became **customer premises equipment** (CPE). T1 connections from the user premises to a long haul carrier's office were local access channels, generally the province of the user or the local (or intra-LATA) telephone carrier. Long-distance T1 connections fell to inter-LATA carriers, such as, AT&T Communications, MCI Communications, or LIS Sprint.

As CSUs came under customer control, a demarcation between the network lines and the CSU came into being. Called the **network interface** (NI), it formed yet another interface between services, circuits and equipment. The network interface (NI) will receive a more complete treatment in Chapters 4 and 6.

Starting from the NI, ACCUNET® T1.5 Service took T1 into this new era with offerings to accommodate various methods of access. AT&T Communications would coordinate provisioning (that is, ordering, assuring installation, and test) or would supply only T1 circuits between **AT&T central offices** (CO). Customers could coordinate or even provide their own access to the AT&T CO. T1 access possibilities are examined in depth in Chapter 5. New or expanded services and functions flowed from the ACCUNET® designers, opening multiple options for its use (such as multiplexing and network cross-connect reconfiguration).

Network Digital Cross-connect Concepts

Network digital cross-connect concepts refer to methods of selecting out individual digital DS-0 voice or data channels with a device capable of locating each channel on a T1. After locating the channel, the device can route that DS-0 channel to another T1. The

51

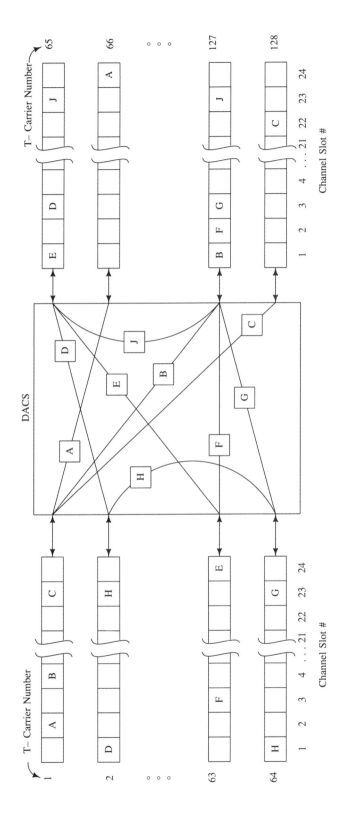

FIGURE 3.9. Channel Slot Switching in a DACS.

device does not demultiplex the *channel* for external use or access, but separates (demultiplexes) and buffers the *bits* from the channel and inserts them into an available **channel slot** of another T1. Common industry terminology calls this device a **digital access cross-connect system** or DACS.

Observe in the figure above that the individual channels from one location route to other T1s connected to the DACS. Clearly, a DACS only handles up to 24 channels on any T1, but routing may be made to any other T1. Think of the DACS as a large digital equivalent of a patch panel with every channel represented. The DACS "patches" or cross-connects, the DS-0 data or conversation channel to a channel slot. One type of DACS unit used by AT&T handles up to 1,524 cross-connections among up to 3,048 individual channels. This permits up to 127 T1 lines containing 24 channels each to exchange their channels under the direction of the DACS processor. Additional channels are available to the DACS for test access.

Operation of the DACS actually involves separating the bits from each individual channel and placing them in a parallel buffer ready for assignment, or cross-connect, to another channel slot on another T1. The process completes when the bits, again serialized, are sent out as a channel on the new T1. Buffering input streams to await placement in an outbound stream involves some delay, but this rarely exceeds several frames. As a T1 frame occurs every 125 microsecond, signal delay through a DACS device is usually small relative to normal transmission delays. (It usually takes over 30 or 40 milliseconds for a digital signal to cross the United States terrestrially.) The DACS, primarily designed to pair inbound and outbound channels for full duplex or simultaneous bi-directional operation, can also function as a digital bridge or conferencing facility. In addition, broadcast capability can send out voice or data channels simultaneously which originate on a single channel. Broadcast capability permits true broadcast of voice or data to many outbound channels or multipoint broadcast of outbound data for polling many data stations.

The DACS function allows bridging, broadcast or rapid reconfiguration of a large number of individual channels without needing to return the bits to analog form. Prior to DACS, reconversion to analog and physical patching or rewiring were required to perform the same function. When controlled from some external position or via separate command circuits, channels may be routed at a customer's discretion. Most implementations interpose a checking facility between the customer's remote reconfiguration orders and the actual commands to the DACS. This prevents incorrect commands or commands inadvertently directing the wrong cross-connections.

A DACS switch located at a long-distance carrier's central office, and directed remotely by a customer, becomes a method to reconfigure the routing of the customer's network. This is the concept behind **customer controlled reconfiguration** (CCR). Commands issued at a customer's CCR terminal are executed within a very few minutes at the carrier's DACS units. More details about this service function may be found in Chapter 8, but specifics about current implementations and specifications of customer controlled reconfiguration should be obtained from exchange carriers (local telephone companies) and long-distance telecommunications carriers.

Satellite T-Carriers

Emphasis has been focused on terrestrial T1 services, but another important implementation of T-Carriers comes from the sky. Satellite megabit digital services offer several unique advantages unavailable on land circuits. Among these are very high signal quality and true broadcast capability. Quality, as measured by bit error rate, can be significantly higher due to the simplified path of the signals. From a satellite earth station, the signal goes directly to the satellite and returns to another earth station. As long as the path is clear, **bit error rates** (BER) well below one error in 10,000,000 can be achieved. This is usually expressed as 1×10^{-7} (say: 1 in 10 to the minus 7th). The low error rates offer abilities to send large blocks of data without fear of multiple retransmissions. Satellite circuits perform extremely well for this type of bulk data transport.

Broadcast applications, perhaps the best-known feature of satellite services, need little explanation in these pages. However, an important variation from typical broadcast services, such as home entertainment, is T1 digital broadcast. Delivery of a digital T1 signal permits extension of the circuit from the earth station on local T1 facilities. While this may seem no different from analog broadcast and CATV distribution, digital T1 holds a unique advantage in the area of security. Digital signals may be coded or encrypted by highly secure digital means. Data, voice, or video signals sent by T1 and encrypted at source, may be broadcast to many locations with little fear of interception. Satellite data quality will possibly degrade twice each year due to solar effects. At times in the spring and again in the fall, the sun aligns with the satellite and the earth station for a few minutes. This may result in temporary signal degradation due to an increase in thermal noise as seen by the earth stations receivers. Satellites also remain exposed to strong illegal signals which may temporarily blind the satellite's transponder receiver.

Data security and information privacy gain emphasis with every published penetration. Industrial and international espionage are considered real threats to information transport. Digital encryption, in contrast to analog scrambling, is considered highly secure and has become the preferred transmission security method of both government and industry. Using digital encryption methods developed for point-to-point terrestrial circuits, broadcast T1 can be secured from source to destination. Interception of either the satellite signal or the terrestrial extension will not compromise the information. Chapter 9 is devoted entirely to satellite technology.

Other Digital Data Satellite Services

While the satellite services so far described bring up images of giant "dishes" behind chain link fences, small dish services also offer high-speed digital data services. Called **small aperture earth station** (SAES) services, they use **very small aperture terminals** (VSAT)—and other names relating to antennas under three meters (about 10 feet)—by placing these small antennas on building roofs and utility yards. The operation of these services, while not widely different in concept, can be quite different in application. In particular, small aperture earth station service types offer much lower priced services and quicker installation times, but sometimes at the cost of data rate. SAES and VSAT technologies are improving rapidly and the very high-data rates of more traditional digital services may soon become more widely available.

VSAT systems often use a large traditional antenna and central system to receive and transmit to the smaller dishes. The larger antenna transmits greater effective power to the satellite transponder and may operate at higher speeds from the central system to the VSAT than the small antenna system is able to return. While this may seem to be a drawback, applications involving distribution of large amounts of information to many points take advantage of the true broadcast nature of VSAT systems. In these applications, information flow from the many small distributed points may be only short inquiries or updates. The main bulk of information flows from the main system outward, and can be as diverse as stock market information to sales literature or insurance policies. With small computer systems available at the many end locations, this high-speed data flow may be sorted and managed. Readers interested in multipoint VSAT services should contact the many firms now offering small earth station data services. In addition, international high-speed digital data satellite services are available and several firms currently offer international connections up to and including T1. Those interested in international satellite digital services should make direct contact with carriers offering these services.

As satellite technology extends into the future, and earth stations shrink in size and cost, megabit data communications will reach for greater speeds of the T-Carriers at T2, T3 and higher.

T1C, T1G, T2, T3 and Higher T-Carriers

Continuing the search for pair-gain, telephone technologists introduced T1C in 1975. Like its parent T1, T1C digitized voice channels onto a serial digital stream, but carried twice as many conversations. T1C handled 48 voice channels from a D4 channel bank using the same methods found in D3 banks and T1. D4 channel banks offered several options and could operate as two D3 banks, each producing a T1 or DS-1 stream. They could also develop a DS-1C stream at 3,152,000 bit/s. Since twice 1,544,000 is 3,088,000, there seem to be some bits missing. The missing 64 kbit/s are taken to separate the two groups of 24 channels and frame the T1C. While T1C proved useful to the voice communications community, data communications ignored the new speed and continued to use T1. Higher speeds beckoned for data and voice and their new friend, digital video.

Video signals had developed in an analog world and resided there long after voice and data had begun their move to digital methods. Hesitation came from cost: digitizing a video (or television) signal produced at least 12,000,000 bit/s using normal approaches. This rate consumed too much bandwidth and was far too costly for practical use. Using TV studio quality equipment, each color video develops a six MHz signal which is carried well by traditional analog cables and satellites. Digitizing video demanded new techniques. They arrived in the mid-1970s and have dramatically improved since in both cost and capability. They all involve digital signal compression.

Digital compression takes advantage of a common fact in communications. Much of the time, channels are not really full to capacity, but send redundant or duplicate information or none at all. In video, think of the background in a news or comedy: small or infrequent changes. If this nearly static information were sent only once, and again only when it changed, bandwidth requirements would significantly shrink. The task is easy to describe, but quite hard to achieve. Video signals stayed analog until digital microprocessor technology developed compression capabilities. Doing mind-boggling calculations to compare digitized TV frames (or static pictures), video compression devices first reduced the six MHz to 3,152,000 bit/s or T1C.

T1C proved, however, not an end for compression, but a beginning. Video compression quickly moved down to T1 for a single video signal. Now, compression units place two, full motion, near studio quality, color video signals on a T1 or 1,544,000 bit/s. Available compression units running as slowly as 56,000 bit/s offer "good" picture quality. Currently, two videos to a T1 is common using 768,000 bit/s, but compression designers continue to develop better and faster methods for video. Meanwhile, digital networks for voice and data reach for ever higher speeds.

In 1985, AT&T Bell Laboratories described T1G as carrying 96 voice channels and streaming at 3,221,000 bit/s for distances up to 200 miles. T1G-Carriers use new digital line signal techniques to code four T1 streams into a more efficient transmission. T1C had used 3,152,000 bit/s and T1G uses the same circuit engineering. What started as one conversation or low-speed data signal over two pairs of copper wires became, in 1985, 96 voice calls or 96 channels of 56,000 bit/s data. While T1G is not a tariffed or offered service of a carrier, the technology will be used between telephone offices to carry customer digital voice, data, and video signals. These techniques may become available to private network users to achieve their own pair-gain, or as an alternate way to send T2.

T2-Carriers, older than T1G, formed the original second layer in the North American Hierarchy of T-Carriers. Designed to combine four T1s, T2 used special cables to carry the 6,312,000 bit/s DS-2 signal. Understanding T-Carrier hierarchy begins at T2 with the concept of T-Carrier multiplexing. T1 signals, from the earliest days, ran like analog modems in their timing. Each was its own timing source. Unless linked to some other service, such as a digital telephone switch or DACS, T1s did not have to conform to a single clock source. As many T1s thread through the telephone network, methods for multiplexing them in groups to higher speeds were forced to allow independent timing. M12 multiplexers did just that with a scheme called **bit stuffing.**

T-Carrier multiplexers, also called **muldems** for MULtiplexer/DEMultiplexer, perform bit stuffing and take their designations from position in the hierarchy. If a multiplexer or muldem, takes several T1s and makes a T2, it is an M12. M12s take four T1s and combine them into a single serial bit stream, running slightly faster than four times 1,544,000 bit/s due to bit stuffing. This slightly faster rate adds 136,000 bits interspersed with bits from each T1. The added bits accomplish two very important tasks critical to framing and timing. A simple explanation, to be expanded in Chapter 5, shows how this works.

T1s remain in timing rate specification from 1,543,925 bit/s to 1,544,075 bit/s, that is, 1,544,000 ± 75 bit/s. If all four of the T1s coming to an M12 are running at the slow limit, the resulting combination will be 6,157,000 bit/s. Bit stuffing adds "one" bits to the outbound DS-2 stream to make it appear that all four are running fast. Other added bits show where the stuffed bits are added. At the demultiplex end, the stuffed bits are removed, and each T1 resumes its slow rate. Now if one T1 speeds up, fewer "one" bits are added and then removed at the far end. Using this method, each of the incoming T1s may range over its speed specification without losing bits; the M12 will compensate and deliver a T1 at the far end at the same rate or speed. If all four incoming T1s run at their upper limit, no extra "ones" will be added or removed. Nothing is really stuffed, but room is left to use "ones" or "zeros" to compensate for incoming speed variations. The same process occurs in an M23 or T2 to T3 multiplexer.

T3-Carriers operate at 44,736,000 bit/s deriving their speed from the same multiplexer methods. Called M13 multiplexers, they first set up seven T2 streams and then combine them into a T3. Thus, a T3 is composed of seven T2s, each of which combine four T1s. Bit rates again add framing and stuffing bits to allow decomposition or demultiplexing at the far end of the T3 link or span. An early application of T3-Carriers was in digital microwave radios which could compact the 44,736,000 bit/s into a radio channel. Limits on the radios, set by FCC regulation on frequency sharing, permitted sufficient bandwidth for the T3-Carrier. In addition to carriers, the FCC authorized private commercial companies to operate these radios, and very high-speed private digital systems began. Chapter 11 expands on these radios and other systems used by private companies for megabit services.

When several T2 systems were connected in tandem or serial fashion, some T1s passed from end-to-end and some stopped part way. This intermediate stopping uses the term **drop and insert**. Drop and insert is a concept of breaking down the higher speed carrier at a middle point and "dropping" or "inserting" one or more lower speed carriers. This drop and insert concept, shown below, forms a basis for larger networks by permitting more than two ends to a network. Individual lower speed carriers originate and terminate at points other than the ends, and the higher speed carrier still runs at or near full capacity.

T-Carrier concepts do not limit the upper bounds of digital capacity. While standards for T4, T5 and higher speeds are still under discussion, they will come in the near future. Fiber optic systems, detailed in Chapter 10, currently use speeds in the T3 range and higher speeds are envisaged. The hierarchy remains open ended and will capture technology advances without disruption. Standards continue development to reach a fast moving transmission upper limit. One message is clear, T-Carriers light the way to our digital communications future. While fixed T-Carriers form the structure of future digital transmission, switched T-Carriers may offer advantageous shared pathways through transmission networks.

T2 and T3-Carrier Services

T1 digital services have become commonly available throughout nearly all of the United States, but higher speed user services await the completion of fiber optic facilities to their cities. A T3 offering, called **ACCUNET® T45 Service,** is spreading rapidly as AT&T completes additional fiber optic systems. T45 is currently available as either a direct T3 connection at 44.736 Mbit/s conforming to North American Hierarchy DS3 cross-connect and framing or as a grouping of individual T1 streams using extended superframe format framing. T45 service is intended for very large customers who require the capacity of multiple T1s between their facilities. T45 tariffed prices, at the time of this writing, become attractive for users with fewer than 10 T1s over significant distances. Access to AT&T central offices may be either at conforming T1 or T3 rates and the T45 service is carried on AT&T's ever expanding fiber optic network. Other long-distance carriers have followed with T3 offerings of their own and fiber optic consortiums, described more fully in Chapter 10, also provide T3 services. Full details on T3 service availability, specifications and costs should be obtained from the vendors.

T2 services, operating at 6.312 Mbit/s, are less common, but are available in some areas of the country from local telephone companies. Details on these services is scarce at this writing, but users are encouraged to inquire of the carriers if their needs encompass T2. Another alternative may be found in switched high-speed services.

Switched T-Carriers

DACS type technologies for switching DS-0 channels in a T1, are also coming on the market for switching T1 and higher speeds. Concepts stay the same, but speeds increase. Newer and faster switches perform any-to-any switching from user T1 circuits. Circuits needed for short times of hours or days (think of conferences or trade shows) "dial" T1s like a telephone line. Data, video or groups of digital voice channels, with fixed access to the switch, may request capacity from larger trunks. While costs for T1 and higher carrier

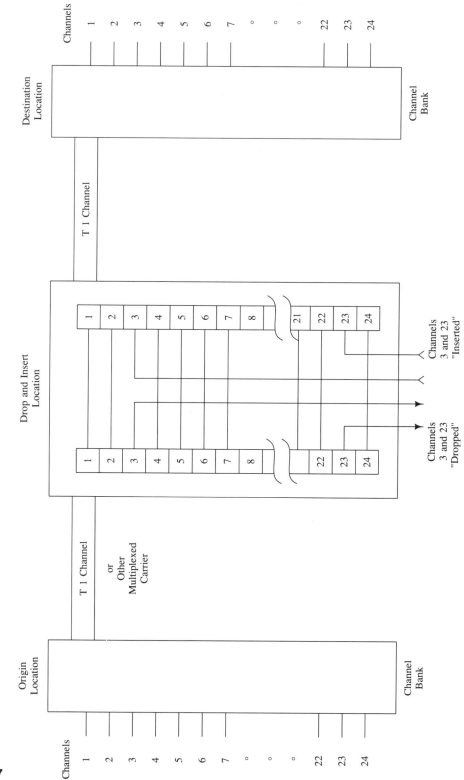

FIGURE 3.10. Drop and Insert in Digital Carriers.

capacity continue to drop, they are not small. Switching requires permanent circuits from a user to the switch, but charges for the switched section, like a long-distance telephone call, are by the minute or hour. Switched service concepts from common carriers can be found, in outline form, in Chapter 8.

Beyond temporary use for conferences, significant applications of switched T-Carriers can be found in backup of leased facilities. Fixed or permanent T-Carriers used for critical business applications, like electronic money transfer, cannot afford outages. Outages, however, occur in the best designed and maintained systems. Protection against total outage can be arranged through use of additional, diversely routed, T-Carriers to a switch. Switches, invoked by telephone or remote terminal command, can temporarily replace broken circuits until repairs are completed. This continuity of transmission adds only the small costs of switch access lines, yet provides backup of crucial circuits in critical times.

Megabit and high-speed digital services lead toward a digital future, but what happens in that future to voice communications? Where does the old analog telephone belong and what will happen to business and residential services as we know them today? Will digitization stop at the telephone office? When will voice and data (and video?) come together? Voice/data integration history and concepts may reveal a bit of the future.

Voice/Data Integration

Voice and data have been integrated in carrier transmission for many years, but discussions about full integration approaches and methods have just begun in earnest. Integration history must be grasped and this discussion partitioned to see what is really going on. This section looks at the history of voice/data integration and divides the argument into manageable pieces. Concepts and directions come together as current reality and forecast the next step in integration—Integrated Services Digital Networks (ISDN).

Integration History

As the first chapter has already told us, electrical communications started in the form of data in early telegraphy after Samuel Morse's 1840 patent. By 1851 telegraph had crossed the English Channel and in 1866 successfully crossed the Atlantic ocean. Telegraphy continued expansion and dominated long-distance communications well into the twentieth century. After Bell's 1876 patent, first local, then long-distance communications moved inexorably toward voice. By the time computers began their need for true data communications, voice technologies dominated the world's networks. World standards for voice telecommunications, established after World War II, set norms for speech instruments, dialing and transmission. Data transmission started inside those voice norms and travelled over the networks as a series of non-musical tones, emulating the characteristics of voice telephony.

While the digital conversion of the telephone network, described above, moved voice telephony toward the bit-oriented world of data, the process of making data sound like voice expanded for personal and home computers. And here lies the true driving force for integration. The real driver can be found in the nature of the telephone local loop.

The telephone network, as currently operated, leads outward from an increasingly digital central system to individual businesses and homes. The last segment of the system, from the local telephone office, to home and business, has always been a pair of copper wires called the **local loop.** The local loop plant, or all the copper wires and cables radiating from a local telephone office, form a huge investment. Using huge banks of batteries (not unlike car batteries) at the telephone office, the local telephone loop and telephone instruments operate using essentially the same analog methods as they did early in the century. Methods of dialing (signaling) have largely changed from dial pulses to tones, but a telephone instrument still converts voice energy to a varying (analog) electric current to be sent to the local office. Often called POTS, for **plain old telephone service,** analog technologies still form an immense part of telephone networks. At local offices, voice is increasingly converted to a digital bit stream for transmission through the network. But at the far-end office, reconversion to analog current must be done to send the voice the "last mile."

Digital technologies have produced digital computers, digital **private branch exchanges** (PBX), and digital telephones to business offices along with personal computers to homes. Services connecting these digital devices will remain analog until some way is found to convert the analog local loop. Larger businesses, beginning to **bypass** the local telephone company's wires with digital technologies, must still cope with analog last miles to their smaller offices. Residences, still uniformly analog, must buy modems if they wish to communicate data. The entire system must continue to cope with analog signals for the local loop. Although existing and cost effective digital techniques exist at the central networks, analog is still the rule in the last mile. Digital voice, data, and video opportunities for homes and businesses must funnel through the analog loop plant.

Even the loop, itself, becomes digital as it approaches the "very last mile." T1 based subscriber loop systems, such as the **AT&T SLC® 96 Subscriber Loop-Carrier** carry digital signals to points near groups of homes. Each carrier system supports up to 96 individual telephone loops, while using only a few actual copper pairs back to the central office. The final leg to the home or business remains analog, although the wires themselves run well below their bandwidth capacity. Digital signals approach their final destination, but have not quite reached it.

Communications history, like any history, has its revolutions and major turning points. Conversion of local loops and telephone instruments from analog to digital is not the simple rallying cry of a revolution. But revolution and turning point it is. History may later choose better names, but for now, voice/data integration and Integrated Services Digital Network (ISDN) must do.

Simply stated, voice/data integration concepts demand the conversion of local loops from analog to digital, and ISDN becomes the conceptual vehicle.

Integration Concepts

Voice/data integration concepts may be viewed from five primary outlooks, end-instruments, local loops, switching, networks, and services. Each outlook presents differing opportunities, but none will succeed widely without the rest. And none will happen at all without a clear migration path from current methods of data and telephony. As each develops ways to accomplish new and exciting tasks, each must continue to support those homes and businesses choosing to stay with existing tasks. Existing tasks include POTS, slow-speed analog data modems, and a host of devices, such as facsimile (FAX) machines, which represent the "installed base" of products and services. The installed base, from pay phones to burglar alarms, must be given time, perhaps many years, before it is prepared for digital conversion. End-instruments represent a large content of the existing tasks, but also offer the largest opportunity for new methods and services.

Integration of an end-instrument begins when a single digital instrument simultaneously handles both voice and data. Integrated digital instruments are already widely available for businesses buying or leasing digital PBXs. Integrated instruments range from digital telephones with data ports on the back, to complete voice/data units with handsets, keyboards and video screens. Conceptually, these desk-top units allow users full voice telephone capability while using a personal computer connected to a local or remote computer. Concepts of end-instrument integration include independent signaling for voice and data calls. For example, a user, working at the keyboard display, may make and receive voice calls, put a terminal session on hold and exchange digital data on a screen with a voice caller. The user may then reconnect the original session and move new data to another computer session or another user.

Two users might wish to access a single data service and simultaneously review and change data from the service while discussing the data by voice. Several terminal sessions might proceed on the same screen, while a conference call is set up by telephone. Not the least of the new opportunities would be simultaneous, but independent, use of voice and data on different instruments in a single residence or office. Anyone needing the telephone while a personal computer is on-line over a single analog telephone line will appreciate this application.

Varieties of new end-instruments can be envisioned if data, voice and signaling can operate independently. On a single digital line to the local telephone company, several household members or business associates will use differing services and multiple devices may "share" the single connection. Groups of personal or desk-top computers or data devices may themselves automatically contend for access to differing data services, while increased ranges of voice telephone services continue uninterrupted. The single, digital, local loop offers capabilities to do it all.

Integrated, or digital, local loops offer both challenges and opportunities. The first challenge jumps out—to convert some users to digital services—while retaining abilities to handle the imbedded base of plain old telephone service (POTS) customers. Many businesses and homes will see no need for new services and techniques for many years. Conversion of the local loop to digital must address these customers and this is indeed a challenge. Similar challenges, however, have been met already. When tone dialing was introduced, users were slow to move to the faster signaling method, and many subscribers still use rotary dial telephones. Local telephone companies found ways to handle both types on the same line and the migration to tone dialing proceeded. Now the challenge concerns simultaneous use by analog and digital devices and the problem becomes more difficult. Can a subscriber operate both analog and digital end-instruments on the same local loop? How can the user signal or send switching information into the networks?

Earlier in this chapter we have described a digital network conversion already well underway. This conversion concerned digital transmission and digital switching, but much work remains to handle signaling. The existing network combines both in-band and out-of-band signaling. In-band signaling uses the same information bandwidth for both information flow and network instructions. An over-simplified example shows a user with a pushbutton telephone sending instructions to a distant service using the voice connection to carry the tones. The tones move through the network in the voice band. Out-of-band signaling may find several differing methods to carry the signaling.

Out-of-band signaling does not use the bandwidth intended for information, but has its own channel or bandwidth. The concept of a separate channel for signaling or dialing instructions gains significant importance in digital networks due to another concept, transparency. When signaling is carried in the information bandwidth, a risk exists that the information itself may be interpreted as signaling. Tone combinations or special data characters must either be reserved for signaling or their probability must be so low that the risk is small. When restrictions are placed on the information content, transparency, or the ability to send any combination of things, is lost. However small the risk, if information signals intrude into signaling, unpredictable things will happen and, in a complex digital network, this may not be acceptable. Out-of-band signaling offers many more ways to prevent information accidents. Full transparency and accident prevention become critical as new voice and digital services join the integrated world.

Integrated Services—New Services

While simultaneous voice, data and perhaps video over a single digital local loop solves many problems, new and unique opportunities will promote full digital services. These new services, the "Services" or "S" part of ISDN, may alter the world in ways similar to the impacts of television, jet aircraft, video-cassette recorders (VCR) and the compact disc (CD). Ordinary activities, such as going to the bank, will become home or office business. Scheduling personal entertainment from cable television, receiving selected sections of the morning newspaper and handling investments will be done on the telephone line. Schooling patterns and training of all types will increase their out-of-school content. Utility meter reading and bill paying will become automatic.

Perhaps the most exciting and promising activities involve work habits. Much has been forecast about altered work routines through the use of computing power, but little has been said about why it is happening slowly. Social and inertial reasons aside, experienced information workers find home terminals slow and unresponsive. The inability to use voice, data, and video together limits the usefulness of remote work. Interaction with superiors, peers, and subordinates is missing. While voice/data integration and ISDN solve none of these problems directly, they offer means toward solution. When capacity and services come together at reasonable cost, movement will begin in earnest.

Widespread and inexpensive digital communications in a community may stimulate satellite offices and the general dispersion of, at least, information workers. If we can see each other and exchange data while talking, business patterns will begin to change. When business patterns change, societal patterns are not far behind. Stimulation of services, business and personal, will be triggered by the new availability of digital bandwidth.

Movement toward the forecasts of the futurists will require more than digital local loops, but digital local loops and services will initiate the communications future. First, a few hurdles must be cleared.

Integration of voice and data, available in many business offices through digital PBXs and **local area networks** (LAN), does not yet cover very small businesses or residences. The analog telephone and the slow-speed modem exclude each other on a single telephone line. Terminals must either time share the telephone line or connect to a dedicated line. Within a campus or business building, technologies vie for connection to the voice network and a variety of computer data services. Digital telephones and digital PBXs must either stop at their borders or connect digitally to the local or long-distance network.

Signaling must conform to standards built on an analog network base. As the network begins migration toward newer forms of digital signaling, analog subscribers continue their needs for connection and services. New standards for digital signaling must gain acceptance from telephone and PBX manufacturers. A standards structure must first be built and agreed upon. Movement will then accelerate toward a full digital communications future.

The Birth of ISDN

In the late 1970s, concepts of voice and data integration began to surface in the technical journals. Integration by digitization of voice at the telephone instrument seemed economically viable as electronic chip costs plummeted. But, while computer terminals appeared in many universities and large corporations, general use of data terminals was viewed as years away. If voice was the main thing to be switched and carried through the electronic networks, why integrate to handle data devices? Digitization of the voice transmission network, as related above, stopped at the long-lines or toll telephone office. Analog voice telephones did the job, were rugged and inexpensive; why consider changing? Pervasive data terminals in homes and small offices were still science fiction. Then, as often happens in history, an unexpected development in computing gave the voice telephone world reason to move toward the new all-digital goal.

In the early 1980s, micro computers became personal and office computers, beginning an explosive growth and acceptance; sales by micro and personal computer makers skyrocketed. Suddenly, small offices and homes entered the data business and soon wanted communications. Existing public computer networks strained to keep up with demand for new connections. Computer bulletin boards sprang up everywhere as both hobbyists and businesses found needs to send and receive data over the telephone network. New slow-speed analog modems came out as rapidly as personal computer magazines. Technical journal articles arguing for voice/data integration were pulled out and re-read. They advocated a digital telephone instrument which used digital local loops and various networks to switch and connect both voice and micro computer over the same lines and at the same time.

Telephone architects, computer designers and network engineers were ready and many proposals came forward to integrate voice and data networks. Local area network manufacturers had several solutions, PBX and computer makers had others, and the world's telephone engineers had many solutions. Integration raced toward multiple incompatible solutions and chaos. Then came Integrated Services Digital Networks (ISDN) and debate on a common solution began.

In 1984, ISDN received a significant boost toward realization when the eighth plenary assembly of the International Telegraph and Telephone Consultative Committee met in Malaga and Torremolinos in Spain. The CCITT (the order of the letters comes from the committee's French name) adopted a series of Recommendations on ISDN. Called the "I-series" and first published in the 1985 "Red Books" by the International Telecommunication Union (CCITT's parent organization), the recommendations formed the first strong base for the future of integration. The CCITT's work set a departure point for the world's manufacturers and carriers.

Building on existing signaling systems and on T-Carrier technologies, ISDN brings legitimacy to both concepts and directions of integration. Full digitization, integration and high-speed data, offered by ISDN, will alter not only communications techniques, but may well alter fundamental philosophies and approaches throughout telecommunications. Chapter 14 will be devoted entirely to Integrated Services Digital Networks, but first much ground must be covered on high-speed digital concepts, systems, offerings, units, and interfaces.

CHAPTER 4

Digital Interfaces

Chapter Overview

Digital technologies and carrier services enable effective communications when successfully interconnected, but success truly depends on interface compatibility. A comprehensive understanding of digital interfaces is needed to assure that every unit in a complex system will attach properly. Interface standards help, yet something is missing. An unspoken truth in data communications is known by all systems integrators: not all real interfaces exactly meet the standard or meet it in the same way.

Moving to build more complete knowledge, this chapter views digital interfaces through different glasses. An imaginary interface is created and divided into parts to build an understanding useful on real interfaces. Parts of this conceptual interface are then combined for concerted operation. Building from this idealized knowledge, current high-speed data interfaces are put under the glasses. The CCITT V.35 interface has become a world standard for speeds above 19.2 kbit/s. The superior, but neglected, EIA RS-449 has recently been supplanted by EIA-530; these two and their electrical support standards EIA-422 and 423 work well into the megabit region. The North American T-Carrier hierarchy and European digital level interfaces provide for connections at 1.544 megabits and 2.048 megabits and higher, reaching speeds approaching the gigabit (1,000 megabit) range.

Upon close examination, each group yields not only its standard, but displays how equipment designers modify and add function in their specific implementations. With the foundations of the conceptual interface and each standard firmly rooted, techniques are described to adapt to the variations and achieve the original goal of successful interconnection. The chapter concludes with further suggestions directed to the interface and systems integrator. Here we discuss methods, approaches and tricks-of-the-trade needed to make complex sets of equipment and services actually work together the first time.

Interface Functions and Standards

Digital data systems take shape when pieces of data communications equipment (**units** or **boxes**) are connected together; the digital interface is the mechanical meeting of the boxes' electrical signals. These electrical signals coming from boxes of different manufacturers must carry uniform meanings for the communication systems to function; their connection must be simple and self-evident. Mechanical connectors must mate. Interfaces are standardized and built to make these things happen.

Standards for interfaces start life as agreements by governments, manufacturers, and carriers who meet to set the standards. These associations propose, debate, vote, and finally issue the standards as documents with cryptic designations, such as **RS-232-D, V.35** or **G.703** which bear no relationship to speed, function, or application. Other *de facto* standards begin as agreements within an industry or by adoption from a single carrier or manufacturer. Much has been printed about standards, usually in consuming detail but without benefit of the standard's quite simple underlying concepts.

Knowledge about low-speed data communications standards, such as the recently revised EIA-232-D, has spread widely with the advent of personal computer communications. But megabit speed interfaces and standards are harder to find and much harder to interpret. Many of these higher speed interfaces are still undergoing changes as industries and carriers adopt new applications and solve new problems. However, they all build upon slower and better known interfaces. The concepts remain the same, only the speeds increase to confound the integrator.

In this chapter, interfaces are described first as concepts: to de-mystify and build understanding. Then, old and new real standards and implemented interfaces are detailed with notes on implementation differences. Techniques to adapt to the differences and to integrate complex data communications systems conclude the chapter.

An interface comes into being when one piece of equipment must meet another, usually at a connector. Real interfaces exist as plugs, sockets and cables. A well-defined interface includes electrical and mechanical information permitting both makers and users to send and receive signals without error. Implied here is the ability for an innocent user to hook different maker's boxes together and expect error-free communications. Questions arise when the interface is not well-defined. Will a standard cable connect to both boxes? What is a standard cable? If the cable is turned end-for-end, will it still work? Which connector is male and which female? Are all of the possible wires connected or only some of the standard signals? Does the interface standard answer these questions or does it create more questions? Interface standards specify correct voltage ranges, timing and signal meanings; they should specify connector types and sexes. Only the newest standards describe connectors and pin assignments. Most standards do not mention connectors; cables are left to the user. Here lies the first of many pitfalls to trap the unwary.

Each standard intends to cover the possibilities, but unanticipated applications, new technologies and complex combinations develop. People differ and so do implementations. Older standards leave unassigned connector pins in their lists, and these tempt designers to add enhanced functions. A standard may not tell the user which box will have the male plug and which will have the female. Connector pins and connector shells both have male/female designations. Unconnected electrical lines may cause false signals from ambient electrical noise. Differences arise, systems fail to integrate, and the standards cannot provide a map away from the trouble. The systems integrator needs more than a standard;

the user wants knowledge and the territory must be mapped. The conceptual interface introduces that broad map.

The Conceptual Interface

Cookbooks yield the best results in the hands of knowledgeable and experienced cooks. Comprehension becomes the key to proper application and utilization in communications, as well as in cooking. Conceptual understanding of communications interfaces must come before detailed descriptions. The concepts introduced here apply to all communications interfaces in data, digital voice, or video. Grasping the concepts now will simplify the use and application of the standards described later in this chapter. Extra time spent on these concepts will pay rewards many-fold in the real business of getting complex communications systems to work.

To ease understanding of the concepts, the interface problem will first be divided into several smaller, more easily handled parts. The task to be achieved by the interface is the error free transfer of information from one box to another. Accomplishing this task, the conceptual parts will work together, but for now, consider each part separately. The conceptual interface is concerned with meanings; physical, mechanical and electrical aspects will be detailed later as each real interface is examined.

Look first at the functions to be done at the interface. Data to be communicated is prepared by terminals, computers, and communications devices. This preparation converts words, numbers, graphics and pictures into serial or sequential streams of bits for transmission. The preparation equipment needs to move the serial stream onto a communications line or medium. This requires a unit to convert the bits from the data equipment into a form used by the communications media. Two units must exchange the serial data and they meet at an **interface.** It is this interface which is studied in conceptual form.

Data signals, timing signals and **control signals** are the primary parts of the conceptual interface. The parts convey information between two conceptual equipment types. These three parts will be treated individually over the next few pages, followed by a combined explanation showing the parts in concert. Later, high-speed T-Carrier interfaces will be described showing not only how the parts combine, but detailing how the parts may exist on the same signal lines.

Conceptual Equipment Types

Data communications interface standards use the term **data terminal equipment** (DTE) to describe the end units beyond and outside the communications media. The abbreviation for data terminal equipment, DTE, will be used throughout this chapter. It will be our reference for units, such as terminals and computer communications controllers which ultimately generate, use, switch, store or process digital data.

Data carrier equipment (DCE) is used to describe the equipment which actually does the work of sending the information "over the wires." The abbreviation for data carrier equipment, DCE, will be used to show the actual carrier driving units. Here the DCE equipment manages and drives the process of moving the data from here to there.

The DTE and DCE conventions are so useful that they will be employed continuously here. How these units actually use the information or drive the wires, fibers, or radios is the business of engineers designing their systems. Here, the concern is delivering correct signals across a standard interface between DTE and DCE. In the current deregulated and divested environment, other names have begun to appear. **Data service units (DSU),** **channel service units (CSU), office repeaters, regenerators, muldems** and **multiplexers** are discussed with alarming and often mistaken familiarity. When the concepts of the DTE/DCE interface are fully grasped, exploration of this newer territory can begin.

Data Signals

The information transfer part of the conceptual model is clearly first; this is the real thing to be communicated. In the conceptual interface, these signals exist as "transmitted" and "received" data. Remember, of course, that some equipment transmits only, as in public address systems. Similarly, some units receive only, as do FM or TV receivers. In these special cases, nothing is changed; one set of signals is merely missing. In the conceptual descriptions below, both transmitted and received signals are covered.

The past tense, transmitted, is used here to aid understanding. Most real interface descriptions and standards list the signals as **transmit** and **receive.** Past tense shows intent and completed action as well as naming the signals. This re-naming will be helpful when the next conceptual part, timing, is presented. Data signal direction is the first concept to comprehend and remember.

Signal direction for transmitted data in our conceptual model always flows from DTE to DCE, that is, from the terminal toward the carrier. Received data flows from the DCE to the DTE, or from the carrier toward the terminal or communications controller. Notice that the DTE's transmitted data at one end is the other DTE's received signal, and the flow from right to left is quite independent of the opposite flow. Confusion over this simple point has stalled many complex communications paths. Figure 4.1 should reinforce this concept.

Another confusion to watch for: many manufacturers of DCE equipment use terms derived from analog telephone usage such as line and equipment. Unfortunately for systems people, not everyone uses the terms in the same way. Here the terms will always be used to denote the carrier side of the DCE (line) and the terminal (DTE) side of the DCE (Equipment). The carrier network, with its **network circuit terminating equipment,** is under the control of the carrier. This additional interface between the DCE and the NCTE will be described in Chapter 6, where the concepts covered will be expanded to show interaction with the high-speed digital networks.

If the transmitted and received data can flow at the same instant in time, the communication is called **full duplex.** If the flow alternates in time, first received, then transmitted, it is called **half duplex.** Communications operating only in one direction at all times is called **simplex.** Internationally, even these terms cause trouble; across the Atlantic, they become **duplex, simplex,** and **broadcast,** respectively. Beyond English, full and careful explanations in several languages may be needed to impart true meaning. Caution and patience must be exercised when communications cross language borders.

The data flow in either direction consists of a serial stream of "ones" and "zeros." The DTE equipment assembles and interprets this data into **characters** or **bytes** or some form of **frames** or **non-coded data.** How this is done depends on how the DTE is designed to work. In slower speed links used by simple terminals and personal computers, the start-stop protocol and the ASCII character set are interpreted from the bit stream. At higher speeds, different protocols and code sets are employed to interpret the data. Non-coded or graphic picture data may be transferred without a code set, but will still require a protocol. The

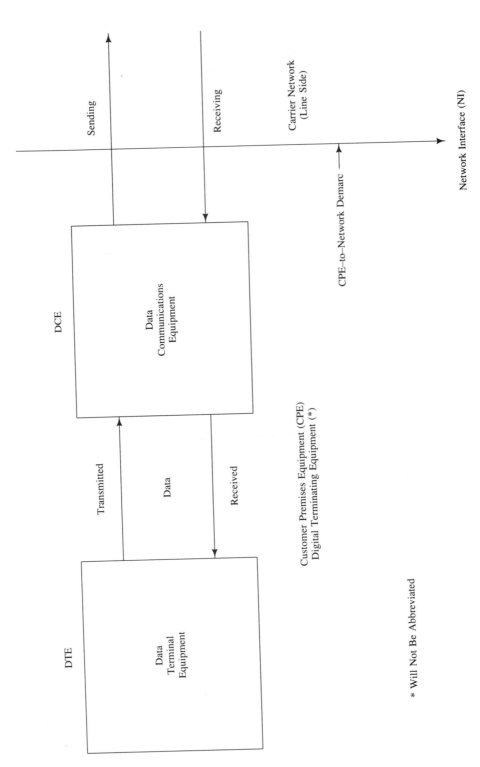

FIGURE 4.1. Data Equipment Types and Interfaces. © Electronic Industries Association. Reprinted with Permission.

protocol is an agreement on where the data starts, where it stops and additional identifying parameters about the data.

The major difference between character protocols and link protocols exists in how the boundaries are set. In character protocols, the character or code set must be sized (usually five to nine bits) and the characters defined before the bits are sent or received. As certain control characters are designated to perform control functions, they must be known in advance. The defined size of the characters becomes the boundary for the protocol. Examples are the ASCII code set in start-stop protocol and ASCII or EBCDIC code sets for **binary synchronous** (BSC) protocols.

In link protocols, such as SDLC or HDLC, the information is contained between single reserved characters called **flags.** The flags are not permitted to exist anywhere in the information, control, or error checking parts of the data. The flags act as the boundaries for the transmitted and received data frames. Within the boundaries of the frame, bit groups are defined to carry addressing, control, information and error-checking. The information portion inside the frame can be variable in length and may carry non-coded or non-character data.

At the interface, the electrical voltage or current level must fall into one of two states. A range of voltages (or currents) is set to interpret a "mark" or a "one"; another range is set to mean a "space" or a "zero." Any voltage outside the two defined ranges is an error condition and should not exist except when moving from one state to the other. If you overload an interface, that is, if too much resistance "loads" an interface signal line, the voltages may become marginal and create errors or may move too slowly from one state to another. If the movement is too slow, the electrical level may be wrong when the timing signals cause sampling and an erroneous bit may be generated.

The data signals across the conceptual interface exert no control over "when" or "how" the data is transferred. These lines carry the bits for data (or digital voice or video) under joint control of the DTE and DCE. How they decide when and how to move data is the subject of the control part of the conceptual interface. Before examining control, the timing portion of the interface has to be detailed. The timing discussion is limited to synchronous communications; asynchronous communication is rarely used at higher speeds.

Timing Signals

In a digital world, signals are either "one" or "zero", "up" or "down." In addition, the signals are "up" or "down" for only a discrete length of time. Since the signal is only valid (i.e., accurate or correct) for a limited length of time, the conceptual interface must be told when to look for validity. The data signal is examined or sampled at—and only at—a time indicated by the timing. This is the sole function of the timing part of the interface. For both the transmitted data and the received data signals, a separate timing signal is provided by the interface. Received signal timing will be described first.

Timing signals are always a steady stream of alternating "ones" and "zeros" used to examine the data signals for validity. The conceptual interface is illustrated by Figure 4.2. Notice that the DCE supplies the timing for both the transmitted and received data signals. The DCE may obtain its clock signal through an external timing signal connection, but it will always tell the DTE when to provide each transmitted bit. Similarly, the DCE will always tell the DTE when each received bit is valid. The signal arrows in Figure 4.2

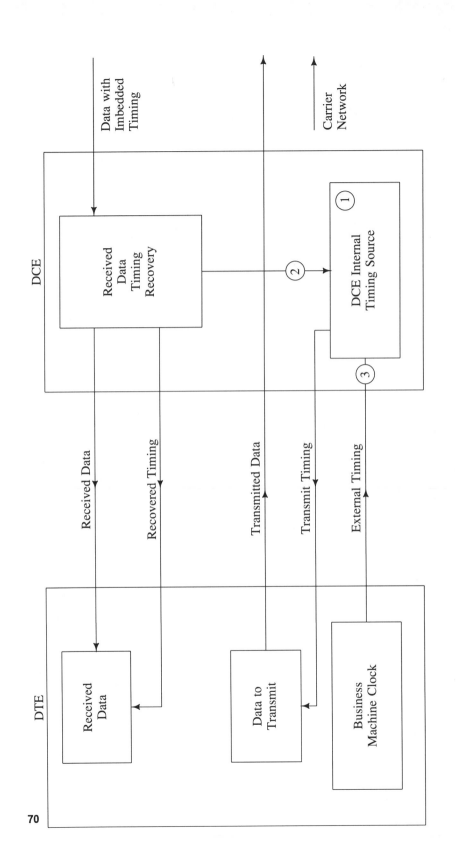

70

* Timing must be set to one of the three:
① Internal, ② Recovered, or ③ External

FIGURE 4.2. DTE to DCE Timing Choices.

indicate each direction; the timing from the transmitted side of each flow controls the entire flow in that direction.

Carriers of digital information do not carry the timing signal separately; it is "imbedded" with the data on the carrier. Explained another way, a single electrical or optical signal combines or imbeds both the data and the timing. Imbedded timing uses each pulse twice: first as a bit of information, then as a reference for timing. Usually, the front edges of pulses indicate where timing should start. This front edge, captured by timing recovery circuits, maintains the beat of the timing. Pulses are not always present in random bit strings, and the recovery circuits must coast along at the last timing rate until new pulses arrive to resynchronize the beat. If the incoming pulse edges do not arrive where expected by the recovery circuits, **jitter** may have been introduced by network equipment. Jitter complicates the job of the recovery circuits and can lead to errors, not in the data bits, but in when they are sampled.

At the receiving DCE, the timing is stripped or extracted by the DCE's timing recovery electronics and supplied to the interface on signal lines separate from the data signals. The use of the past tense, received, is a memory aid for understanding this extracted sense of the data and timing. The DCE does not create or originate the timing signal for the received data in any interface, real or conceptual. Timing for the received bit stream is almost always carried or imbedded on the received network signal or pulse stream.

The timing always originates at the transmitting DCE. Sometimes the DCE itself creates this timing from an internal clock; sometimes it accepts the timing from an external clocking source across the interface. This choice is made at the time of installation, and is dependent on the configuration of the total system. Three choices are possible: the first and simplest is internal timing set by switches, straps (small, moveable plugs or jumper wires on printed circuit cards), or software options. The second possibility is external timing where the clock signal is obtained from a unit outside the DCE, such as a DTE or **station clock.** The third possibility is either called **received timing** or **loop timing.** In this case, the timing signal extracted by the DCE from the incoming received carrier signal is turned back to the transmitted side of the DCE to assure that both the received and transmitted signals are clocked at the exact same rate.

In a simple point-to-point communications path, the timing may be different on the two directions of the path. Here, each DCE may be set to internal for its transmitted signals. The originating DTE is always given transmitted signal timing and produces its transmitted data in time with this DCE clock. At each of the ends, the received timing is recovered from the carrier signal and supplied with the received data to its DTE. Communications paths set-up this way offer little complexity and timing is not a serious concern.

As more complex sub-systems are connected, however, timing becomes a major concern. Now the decision must be made to select a single clock, at least for each direction. In most cases a single-clocking signal must be used for both or all directions, and all units must be set to respond to this timing. It is not obvious why this must be done. An example will illustrate the point. When two simple point-to-point links are connected, the received clock from one must become the transmitted clock for the other at the middle. If this is not the arrangement, the data passing between the two DCEs may be lost or garbled by being sampled at the wrong time.

To accomplish this common timing, the received clock from one link's DCE is supplied to the external transmitted timing input of the other link. This ensures that the received and transmitted information transferred between links is clocked at the same rate. In this example, each direction may still be at a different rate, as long as the transfer rate

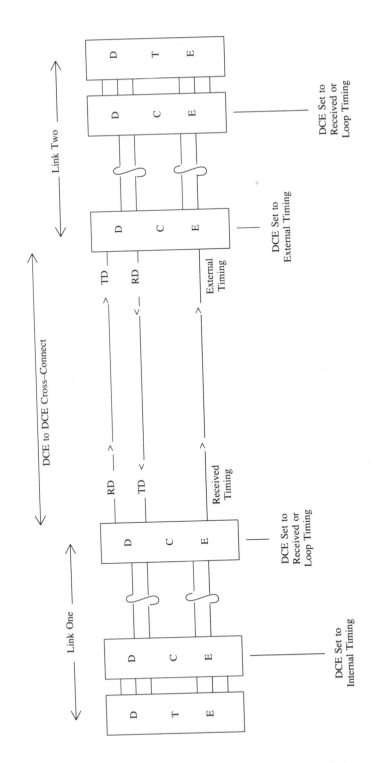

FIGURE 4.3. Two Point-to-Point Links Interconnected with Timing.

between links is the same in each direction. As more and more links are interconnected, common clocking becomes both mandatory and more complex. This subject will be covered more detail in Chapter 7.

Control Signals

Control signals exchange status information between the DCE and the DTE. Each informs the other of its readiness to send or receive data to or from the far end. Almost all DCEs provide and use the control or status signals, but many DTEs use and offer only a partial set. Highlighting this, the control signals in the conceptual interface divide into primary and secondary groups. The primary signals are nearly universal in application and really state each unit's readiness to receive and send. The secondary group concerns functions less often needed in regular communications.

PRIMARY CONTROL SIGNALS

The primary set contains five signals: **data terminal ready** (DTR), **data set** (or DCE) **ready** (DSR), **request to send** (RTS), **clear to send** (CTS), and **data carrier detect** (DCD). The two **ready** signals usually indicate only that the unit providing the signal has power and is turned on. The unit receiving the signal accepts this control signal as evidence of readiness. More complex DTEs will provide DTR only after actual readiness has been established. It is safe to assume that the DTR and DSR signals mean only that power is applied, the switch is on and the cable is installed. **Request to send** and **clear to send** are the control signals used to initiate sending.

Request to send (RTS) from the DTE and its response from the DCE, **clear to send,** (CTS) are most useful when a master DTE/DCE combination uses a single communications circuit to talk to more than one subordinate DCE/DTE. The signals then tell which subordinate pair has permission to send. This arrangement is called **multidrop.** In a typical multidrop configuration of units, a master DTE/DCE may send at any time and will address each subordinate DTE/DCE in turn. This addressing is called **polling.** The addressed DTE may then raise or activate the RTS signal to indicate to the DCE that it wishes to send a response. The DCE, when ready, will return the CTS signal to the DTE and transmitting will begin.

When the DTE completes sending, the RTS signal is lowered and the DCE removes its carrier or tone from the shared communications line. If a delay exists between the DTE's RTS and the DCE's CTS, it is called **turn-around time** after the time taken to turn the line around from one pair to the next. If a fault causes the subordinate DTE/DCE to continue sending after it should have stopped, the communications line will not be available to the next addressed pair. This condition is called **streaming** and may require manual intervention to shut down the offending DCE.

When two DTE/DCEs communicate point-to-point, the RTS/CTS function is not really necessary, unless the communication is half duplex. Many DTEs, however, still initiate each transmission by activating RTS and waiting for CTS. If the communications circuit is full duplex and ready for the transmission, time may be lost waiting for the return CTS signal. Many DCEs permit several options in the methods used to return CTS. CTS may be returned immediately, may be delayed a fixed number of milliseconds, or may depend on some far-end action to be taken. Maximum throughput of data on full duplex circuits is achieved when the CTS signal is returned immediately after sensing RTS.

The last of the five primary control signals, **data carrier detect** (DCD), is very important to slower speed analog circuits and modems. Higher speed digital facilities transmit bits instead of tones and the notion of carrier loses importance. This signal can also cause significant delays in high-speed digital circuits. In its original form, the signal was intended to indicate to the DTE when the circuit or the far end DCE had failed. The DTE then warned operators or programs to take corrective action. In digital circuits, momentary short error bursts are not uncommon. If these short bursts cause **carrier detect** alarms or interrupts, operators or programs may begin taking unneeded corrective actions. DCD requires special attention in a digital network at higher speeds.

SECONDARY CONTROL SIGNALS

The secondary control signal group contains signals less often used in higher speed digital communications which are not included in the conceptual interface. They are discussed, briefly, in the individual standards later in this chapter. Before leaving, however, two of the secondary control signals—test and loopback—demand mention.

With the increasing use of microprocessors in DCEs, test and loopback functions permit various analysis functions to be performed under software control by the DTE. The test control signal usually indicates that the DCE is in TEST mode rather than data transmission mode. That is, data signals sent to and received from the DCE are not from the far end DTE, but are directly from the DCEs. These data signals pertain to the health of the DCEs or the communications circuit.

Loopback control signals permit the DTE to cause a signal turnaround (or loopback) either at the near end DCE or far end DCE. Data may then be sent into the near end DCE and into the circuit at the far end DCE to segment the circuit for problem or quality analysis. The conceptual interface includes **local loopback** (LL) and **remote loopback** (RL). **Local loopback**, when activated by the DTE, causes the transmitted data to be returned by the near end DCE as received data.

Remote loopback causes the data to be returned from the far end or remote DCE, including a full round trip on the communications circuit. By first activating local loopback, data may be sent to the near end or local DCE and examined on return for accuracy (or even existence). Then the process may be repeated using remote loopback. A fault in the near end DCE will be indicated by failure of the first test; a failure during the second test might show a fault in the circuit or the far end DCE. Finally, test data may exchanged under program control between the DTEs to all units and the complete circuit. This process is called **segmenting**.

Now the conceptual interface is ready to operate to move serial data streams from DTE across to DCE and onto the communications line. First DTR and DSR signals exchange between units indicating readiness to start. A coordinated operation for a data exchange then begins with RTS from the first DTE. The first DCE responds with CTS informing the DTE that all is ready to initiate data transfer. Timing is already flowing from DCE to DTE to clock the data bits. Transmitted data now flows across the conceptual interface toward the DCE which conditions the data bits and sends them across the media. At the far end or second site, the bits have come into the second DCE and are presented with received timing to the second DTE as received data. Note that two conceptual interfaces act in the example, one at the first or near end and the second at the far end.

The conceptual interface is complete. Data, timing and control signals will now be

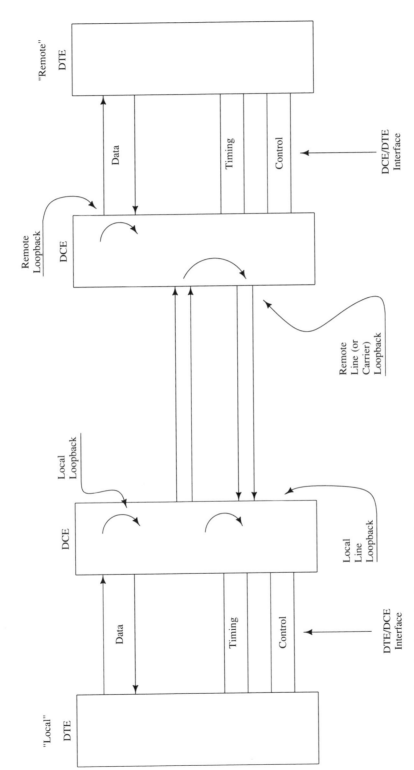

75

FIGURE 4.4. Loopbacks in the Conceptual Interface.

detailed for several real interfaces: the CCITT V.35 Digital Interface, the EIA 422/423/449/530 family of digital interfaces and the DS-1 level of T-Carrier interfaces.

V.35 Digital Interface

The CCITT (The International Telegraph and Telephone Consultative Committee) released recommendation V.35 in 1968 and has since amended it several times. An interface recommendation designed for wideband modem data transmission in an analog world, it has gained acceptance for many high-speed digital services.

V.35 (say: Vee-DOT-thirty-five) was intended for data communications only at 40.8 kbit/s in specific equipment and carrier sets. It became, through default, the most common high-speed interface for data communications in the 1970s and early 1980s. Today, it is the most important data communications interface for use between 19.2 kbit/s and two Mbit/s. The importance comes from the "balanced" nature of this interface.

The concept of balanced electrical signals becomes important to understanding the capabilities of V.35 and other high-speed interfaces. In earlier interfaces, such as EIA-232-D (formerly RS-232-C), individual signals each passed on a single wire and connector pin, and the return currents for all passed through one signal ground. When electrical circuits are arranged this way, it is called **single-ended.** Single-ended means that all data, timing, and control return currents pass through the same signal ground wire and connector pins and can interfere with each other at higher speeds and longer cable distances. In a balanced electrical circuit, each signal has its own return current path on its own wire and pin, thus reducing or preventing interference. Electrical signal driver and receiver circuits for this balanced method are also called **differential circuits.** Appendix II to recommendation V.35 specifies the electrical characteristics for V.35 balanced signals.

In the V.35 interface, data and timing signals are carried on balanced circuits, while control signals utilize single-ended circuits. Since control signals operate much more slowly, this arrangement causes little objectionable interference. Balancing the data and timing signals permit V.35 to operate at speeds higher than anticipated in the original standard.

CCITT recommendation V.35 contains most of the signals described previously in the conceptual interface. Only a ground or common return for the single-ended signals is added. Thus, descriptions and operations of the conceptual interface apply directly to the V.35 digital interface. See the Figure 4.5 for a list of the interface signals actually described in CCITT recommendation V.35. In the table, ϕ indicates balanced signals (see above), all other signals follow CCITT recommendation V.28, similar to EIA-232-D.

Although no specific connector is mentioned in the original V.35 standard (the signals are assigned circuit numbers), there is a standard connector for V.35: ISO 2593. The problem is that no one has ever heard of ISO 2593 and in practice, this 34-pin rectangular specified in ISO 2593 has become accepted with many differing pin configurations. CCITT V.35 recommendation provides data, timing, and control signals as shown in the diagram in Figure 4.6. The recommendation circuit numbers are shown beside the pins in parentheses. Notice that data and timing signals each use two pins in the connector for a balanced implementation.

The data and timing signals operate as detailed in the conceptual interface, and although recommendation V.35 does not offer **external timing,** most real interfaces do. For these balanced signals, a binary zero or a space condition exists when the voltage on the

NUMBER	FUNCTION
102	Signal ground or common return
103 φ	Transmitted data
104 φ	Received data
105	Request to send
106	Ready for sending
107	Data set ready
109	Data channel receive line signal detector
114 φ	Transmitter signal element timing
115 φ	Receiver signal element timing

φ indicates a balanced circuit.

FIGURE 4.5. CCITT recommendation V.35 Interchange Circuits. Reprinted from CCITT Red Book, Volume VIII—Fascicle VIII.1 V.35 by permission.

"A" pin is greater (more positive) than the voltage on the "B" pin. A binary one or mark condition exists when the reverse is true. The voltage, small relative to EIA-232, is specified at 0.55 Volts, plus or minus 20 %; that is: 0.44 volts to 0.66 volts when terminated or loaded into a 100 ohm circuit.

For the control signals, a control on condition exists when the signal is positive with respect to the signal ground. Another CCITT standard, V.28, describes the voltages for these single-ended signals, which are similar to EIA-232 levels. A control OFF condition

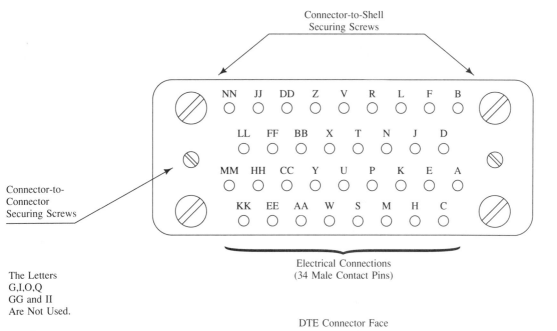

The Letters
G,I,O,Q
GG and II
Are Not Used.

FIGURE 4.6. V.35 Connector and Signal Connections.

exists when the level is negative. Control signals defined in recommendation V.35 include DSR, RTS, CTS (called **ready for sending**), and DCD (called **data channel receive line signal detector**). No DTR is defined and no secondary control signals are defined, although common practice differs. Although no direct EIA equivalent exists, products and services in the United States increasingly use V.35 for high-speed services. A few of those products and services are described to show actual implementations.

V.35 Implementations

Two real product examples focus on V.35 as used in current product implementations. One DTE and one DCE indicate, in practice, what has been described in concept. Many examples could be chosen from current offerings, but the point is to explain, not to list or endorse products or services. Common practice in V.35 implementations puts the male pin connectors on both cable ends and places the female pin connectors on the unit interfaces.

The DTE selected is IBM's 3745 Communication Controller. Offering a wide array of interfaces to various media, its V.35 interface supplies 56 kbit/s and 256 kbit/s digital communications. The terminology used by IBM for this interface is **line interface coupler type 3** (LIC3) and provides "A DCE interface meeting the CCITT V.35 recommendation (256 kbps maximum)."

As described[1] in IBM's Original Equipment Manufacturer's Information manual (Publication Number SA33-0099), the V.35 interface contains the following interchange circuits:

Connector Pin	CCITT Number	Signal From	Sent To	IBM Descriptive Names for Interchange Circuits
B	102	—	—	Signal Ground
P	103 *	DTE	DCE	+Transmit Data (A)
S	103 *	DTE	DCE	−Transmit Data (B)
R	104 *	DCE	DTE	+Receive Data (A)
T	104 *	DCE	DTE	−Receive Data (B)
C	105	DTE	DCE	Request to Send
D	106	DCE	DTE	Ready for Sending
E	107	DCE	DTE	Connect Data Terminal
H	108	DTE	DCE	Data Terminal Ready
F	109	DCE	DTE	Carrier Detect
Y	114 *	DCE	DTE	+Transmit Clock (A)
AA or a	114 *	DCE	DTE	−Transmit Clock (B)
V	115 *	DCE	DTE	+Receive Clock (A)
X	115 *	DCE	DTE	−Receive Clock (B)

* indicates a balanced circuit.

FIGURE 4.7. IBM 3745 LIC3 V.35 Interchange Circuits and Connections.

[1]Reprinted by permission from IBM 3745 Communication Controller Mod 1 & 2, Original Equipment Manufacturer'© Information © 1983, 1985 by International Business Machines Corporation.

Note the presence of pin H, data terminal ready, which is beyond those circuit numbers defined in the V.35 standard. Also observe the absence of **external signal element timing** (or external clocking). External signal element timing (SCTE) cannot be easily used with DDS type services. Chapters 6 and 7 will further detail the technical reasons why the DDS-type service must be clocked or timed by the network.

Where private circuits or facilities are used, however, it may be desirable to clock the DCE from the interface. Many **limited distance modems** (LDM), data sets or data distributors using the V.35 interface offer the option of external timing. When provided, current industry practice (and ISO 2593) established pins U and W for the balanced external timing signals. Extending network timed circuits via LDMS mandates external timing of the LDM cross-connected, as shown in Figure 4.3 on page 72.

The IBM 3745 DTE V.35 interface, and the PARADYNE® V.35 interface shown in Figure 4.8, are as close to "pure" V.35 as any real implementations can be. Other real implementations will add to the standard, always with useful functions, but the additions may or may not be uniform. Industry practice has defined a number of circuits in this manner, and the most common will be listed with ISO 2593 in the following V.35 adaptations section.

The DCE selected to demonstrate V.35 interfacing is the PARADYNE® Corporation Digital Data Service Basic Service Unit (BSU), Model 3056. Service Unit (DSU) for connection to fixed (not switched) digital 2.4, 4.8, 9.6 and 56 Kbit/s transmission services. As described in PARADYNE's® Document Number 3000-A1-GN31-10, Digital Data System Data Service, Basic Service Unit, Installation and Operation Manual, dated February 1987, the interchange circuits are provided as shown in Figure 4.8.

Note the additions of pin A (protective ground), Pin H (data terminal ready), and pins U and W (external TX signal element timing). While these signals are defined by CCITT, and listed in ISO 2593, they do not appear in CCITT V.35. PARADYNE® also includes pin BB (test or external alarm), pin DD (transmitter loopback), pin EE (test control or external alarm), pin MM (test mode), and pin NN (external control). None of these pins appear in V.35. They do appear in ISO 2593, but sometimes under different designations. This is not a criticism of IBM, PARADYNE®, CCITT or ISO; it is an example of the confusion present in apparently compatible interfaces.

Any number of actual V.35 interface examples could now be shown, but the reader is advised to seek out equipment planned or in use for particular installations. By studying specifics, the presence or absence of non-standard circuits will provide the best school for interface integration. The keys to remember in interface study are the function or what the signal does, the direction or which units sends and which receives, and the level of standardization. Standardization level tells the source and consistency of an interface circuit, National or International Standard, Industry Standard, Industry Group Standard, or manufacturer unique. Clearly, the more standard a circuit is, the less difficult it will be to integrate a system of units coming from multiple manufacturers and service providers.

V.35 Adaptations

When the DTE's cables connect directly to the DCE, adaptations are usually unnecessary. This would be the case if the example IBM DTE were connected to the example PARADYNE® DCE. When, however, other equipment for patching, switching or monitoring interposes between the two, adaptations may be needed. Adaptation first requires understanding, then specification, installation, and test. Understanding built from the

Connector Pin	CCITT No.	V. 35 Designation	PARADYNE® Signal Description
A	AA	101	Protective (Frame) Ground
B	AB	102	Signal Ground
C	CA	105	Request-to-Send (RS)
D	CB	106	Clear-to-Send (CS)
E	CC	107	Data Set Ready (DSR)
F	CF	109	Receive Carrier Detected (CD)
H	CD	108.2	Data Terminal Ready (DTR)
P	BA(A)	103	Transmit Data (TD)
R	BB(A)	104	Receive Data (RD)
S	BA(B)	103	Transmit Data (TD)
T	BB(B)	104	Receive Data (RD)
U	DA(A)	113	External TX Signal Element Timing
V	DD(A)	115	Receiver Signal Element Timing
W	DA(B)	113	External TX Signal Element Timing
X	DD(B)	115	Receiver Signal Element Timing
Y	DB(A)	114	Transmitter Signal Element Timing
AA	DB(B)	114	Transmitter Signal Element Timing
BB	—	—	*RT Test Control or External Alarm 0
DD	—	—	Transmitter Loopback
EE	—	—	*RDL Test Control or External Alarm 1
MM	—	—	Test Mode (TM)
NN	—	—	External Control

*Strap selectable

FIGURE 4.8. PARADYNE® 34-pin DTE Connector Interface Definitions. Reprinted by permission.

conceptual interface guides the systems integrator on the correct path. Study of each supplied interface quickly identifies signals which connect without trouble. Unique or special signals then need study, and perhaps adaptation, in the form of special cables or requirements placed on unit manufacturers.

Adaptation begins with the listing of provided interface signals from each unit to be interconnected. The list may be a pencil sketch or a formal drawing, but it must show every wire in each interface. With the sketch, missing and extra signals become obvious and adaptation starts. Extra signals sent by a unit are judged critical or unimportant to the system under design. Sending unimportant signals across an interface rarely impacts a system, but critical extra circuits must be received and handled. Special interface boxes or cables, designed to route the signals to functional receivers, must be added to the sketch for later implementation. Missing signals must be handled in the same manner.

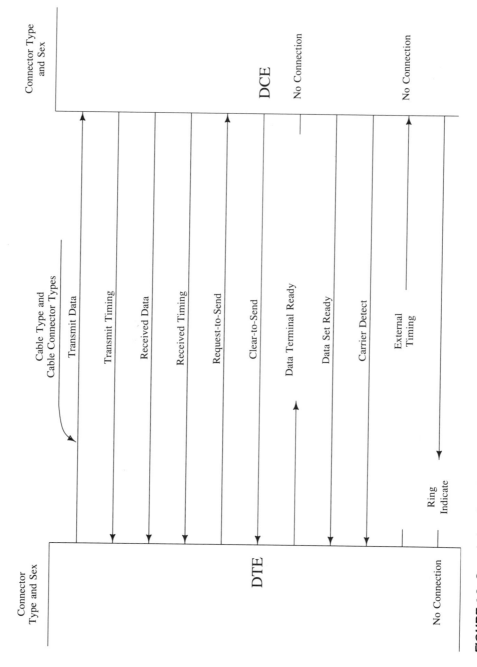

FIGURE 4.9. Sample Interface Signal Connection Sketch.

Connector Pin	CCITT Number	Signal From	Sent To	Function
A	—	—	—	Protective Ground
B	102	—	—	Signal Ground
P	103	DTE	DCE	Transmitted Data A-Wire
S	103	DTE	DCE	Transmitted Data B-Wire
R	104	DCE	DTE	Received Data A-Wire
T	104	DCE	DTE	Received Data B-Wire
C	105	DTE	DCE	Request to Send
D	106	DCE	DTE	Ready for Sending
E	107	DCE	DTE	Data Set Ready
H *	—	DTE	DCE	Data Terminal Ready
F	109	DCE	DTE	Received Line Signal Detector
Y	114	DCE	DTE	Transmitter Signal Element Timing A-Wire
AA	114	DCE	DTE	Transmitter Signal Element Timing B-Wire
V	115	DCE	DTE	Receiver Signal Element Timing A-Wire
X	115	DCE	DTE	Receiver Signal Element Timing B-Wire
U *	113	DTE	DCE	Transmitter Signal Element Timing A-Wire
W *	113	DTE	DCE	Transmitter Signal Element Timing B-Wire
J *	125	DCE	DTE	Calling Indicator
L *	141	DTE	DCE	Local Loopback
N *	140	DTE	DCE	Loopback/Maintenance Test
NN *	142	DCE	DTE	Test Indicator

*Those pins marked with an * are specified in ISO 2593 but are not included in CCITT V.35.

FIGURE 4.10. ISO 2593 Assignment of Pin Numbers. Reprinted by permission.

Signals expected by the receiving side must appear and adaptation supplies them. Since nothing sends these signals, ON and OFF will not arrive. At the receiving side, a choice is made and the signal is forced either ON or OFF by connecting the receiver wires to a permanent voltage or ground. A cautionary note: do not overload voltage sources on the sending or receiving side by connecting too many receiver circuit loads; spread them around and then test them for proper action. The concluding section of this chapter includes guidance on testing interface circuits.

Some guidelines from common industry practice will help on V.35. Of the 34 pins in common practice (and ISO 2593) in the V.35 connector, only 22 are assigned in common use. Figure 4.10 lists circuits from the almost unknown ISO 2593 specification for V.35. While no one unit may contain all the circuits shown, the list offers a standard checklist to begin the study of a specific interface. As data communications expands and changes, the list may need corrections and additions. Each user should note the additions and changes important to an installation. Signals indicated with two pin assignments are balanced; those with one pin assignment are single-ended.

Occasionally, manufacturers assign additional functions to the unused pins, and caution must be followed when connecting these additional signals. V.35 cables may carry only the standard defined signals, may carry only the signals used by the manufacturer, or may fully populate all 34 wires between the 34-pin connectors. When interconnecting these additional functions, special cables may need to be designed to assure that the functions are connected to the correct pins. Here, as elsewhere in data communications, good practice dictates the design and use of symmetrical cables. More can be found on complex interconnections and symmetrical cables at the end of this chapter.

EIA-530 Digital Interface Family

The Electronic Industries Association (EIA) Standard, EIA-232, has been in use as a DTE to DCE digital (or serial binary) interface since the 1960s. EIA-232 has become the most widely known and used DTE/DCE interface in the world through its application to personal computer communications. (The shift from RS- to EIA prefixes was made in the early 1980s "to provide more positive identification of the source of the Standard.") Although some EIA standards still carry an RS-designation, we will generally use EIA- in this text and will drop the suffix letter where it is unnecessary. Exact and current information about standards and their latest revision (or suffix) level should always be obtained from the relevant standards organizations.

In early 1987, the Electronic Industries Association published ANSI/EIA-232-D and ANSI/EIA-530 as complimentary standards. (The ANSI part refers to the American National Standards Institute.) Both of these EIA standards significantly affect the definition and application of high-speed communications interfaces. For those unfamiliar with EIA-530, this standard augments the older (and sadly under-utilized) EIA-449 connector standard by allowing high-speed electrical signals from EIA-422/3 to appear in a standard 25-pin (DB-25) connector familiar to the users of EIA-232. The EIA-530 connector and pin assignment set takes the 25 most needed high-speed signal lines from EIA-422 and implements them in a standard 25-pin connector. No longer is the 37-pin connector of EIA-449 the only choice for speeds above 20 kbit/s; now physical designs using the old 25-pin connector may be upgraded to meet the needs of a high-speed digital world.

This revised pair of standards now divides the DTE/DCE interface into speeds below 20 kbit/s (EIA-232-D) and above 20 kbit/s (EIA-530 and EIA 422/3) and use an identical 25-pin connector. Although pin assignments differ due to the unbalanced nature of low-speed interfaces (EIA-232) and the balanced nature of high-speed interfaces (EIA-422/3), they both use a common 25-pin mechanical connector familiar to data communications users from EIA-232. Before detailing EIA-530, a little history is needed on this family of interfaces.

In the early 1980s, explosive growth in the use of personal computers made EIA-232 the most widely used DTE/DCE interface of all time. It had long been recognized, however, that EIA-232 could not cope with speeds higher than 20 kbit/s or interface cable lengths over 50 feet (15 meters). To meet this need for higher communications speeds and greater cable distances, the EIA released a family of new standards in 1977 and 1978.

These were:

EIA-422-A—Electrical characteristics of balanced voltage digital interface circuits.

RS-423-A—Electrical characteristics of unbalanced voltage digital interface circuits.

RS-449—General purpose 37-position and nine-position interface for data terminal equipment and data circuit-terminating equipment employing serial binary data interchange.

Expanding a little more on the names, EIA-422 and RS-423 described only the nature of the interface electrical signals, balanced or unbalanced, without reference to their function. RS-449 described the function of the interface, the limitations placed on speeds and cable distances, and specific signal function details. It also, for the first time, described mechanical details of the connectors recommended as standard. As any of the three numbers were used to refer to the group of standards, some confusion existed in the applications and specification of this most useful family.

The family offered a complete and well defined interface with only two undefined or spare connections in the main 37-pin connector. This reduced the risk unique pin assignments by manufacturers and maintained consistency between equipment. However, few products were offered with RS-449 as the primary interface, and it became clear that this superior interface would never achieve wide acceptance. The release of EIA-530 should correct the problem of the interface connector and EIA-530 should become the interface of choice for speeds above 20 kbit/s. It is recommended that copies of the EIA-422, 423 and 530 be obtained from the Electronics Industries Association at the address listed at the end of this chapter. The simple definitions and complete descriptions provide excellent reference material for communications professionals and for basic understanding of interfaces.

Following the lead of RS-449, EIA-530 updates many functions provided in EIA-232 and offers definitions and descriptions for many others. The EIA-530 family continues to define connector mechanical and physical specifications. In addition, the sex of the connectors for the DCE (female contacts and a male shell) and the DTE (male contacts and a female shell) are defined. RS-449 defined two connectors, a narrow 37-pin and a narrow nine-pin connector, both from the same family as the familiar 25-pin connector. The 37-pin connector carried all necessary signals for the first or primary channel; the nine-pin connector was specified for secondary channel applications. As secondary channels are rarely used at higher speeds, the nine-pin connector was almost never implemented. Those interested in more complete understanding of the 37- and nine-pin connectors and secondary channels should refer to the RS-449 document. We will now focus attention only on EIA-530 and its supporting electrical interfaces: EIA-422 and EIA-423.

The real power of the EIA-530 high-speed standards family comes from the definitions of the electrical signal standards, EIA-422 and EIA-423. These standards expand on the application of balanced signal electronics by recommending full electrical specifications for electronic drivers (signal generators) and signal receivers.

As in V.35, two types of signals are found in EIA 530: balanced electrical signals are called category I and unbalanced signals category II. Category I generating and receiving electronics should follow the balanced circuit recommendations of EIA-422 and provide individual pairs of wires for each signal. Only three signals are classified as category II, and all three concern only testing and test control. All category I circuits require balanced signal generators, individual wire and connector pin pairs and balanced signal receivers. The circuits and their categories are detailed in Figure 4.11.

EIA-530 Pin	Category	Circuit Mnemonic	Interchange Points	Signal From	Sent To	Circuit Name
1	-	SHIELD	-	-	-	Interconnecting cable shield
7	-	AB	C-C'	-	-	Signal Ground
2 14	I	BA	A-A' B-B'	DTE	DCE	Transmitted Data
3 16	I	BB	A-A' B-B'	DCE	DTE	Received Data
24 11	I	DA	A-A' B-B'	DTE	DCE	Transmit Signal Element Timing (DTE Source)
15 12	I	DB	A-A' B-B'	DCE	DTE	Transmit Signal Element Timing (DCE Source)
17 9	I	DD	A-A' B-B'	DCE	DTE	Receiver Signal Element Timing (DCE Source)
4 19	I	CA	A-A' B-B'	DTE	DCE	Request to Send
5 13	I	CB	A-A' B-B'	DCE	DTE	Clear to Send
6 22	I	CC	A-A' B-B'	DCE	DTE	DCE Ready
20 23	I	CD	A-A' B-B'	DTE	DCE	DTE Ready
8 10	I	CF	A-A' B-B'	DCE	DTE	Received Line Signal Detector
18	II	LL	-	DTE	DCE	Local Loopback
21	II	RL	-	DTE	DCE	Remote Loopback
25	II	TM	-	DCE	DTE	Test Mode

FIGURE 4.11. EIA-530—25-position Connector Interchange Circuits. Reprinted by permission.

Following our earlier approach, the signals above are grouped by data, timing and control. The interchange points column refers to EIA-422 balanced circuits; the interchange point letters (A-A' and B-B') designate electrical specifics. The letters A and B refer to signal generators, A' and B' are the loads or receivers. Binary "1" (or the MARK or OFF state) is indicated across the interface when the A generator point is negative with respect to the B point by at least 2.0 volts. Binary "0" (or SPACE or ON) is signalled when A is positive with respect to B. Voltage minimums and maximums, load resistances and many other specifics can be found in EIA-422. Thus, A A' means the connection of the

A-type signals from generator to signal receiver and B-B' indicates connection of the B-type signals.

While RS-449 carried many additional signals, EIA-530 carries those which the working groups decided were necessary and sufficient. In picking those signals and pins for the standard, a mechanical and manufacturing problem has been solved but a new problem for integrators and users has been created. Older mechanical designs which used 25-pin connectors may now be adapted for higher speeds, but users may not always know which is EIA-232 and which EIA-530. Pin assignments are completely different and voltage levels from EIA-232 may possibly damage receivers from EIA-530. In addition, cables designed for low-speed applications with EIA-232 may not be suitable for EIA-530 speeds or applications. More will be said about this under EIA-530 implementations and adaptations. The few problems should not, however, detract from this fine new standard.

EIA-530 offers the opportunity to consolidate to a new and attractive interface. As we have already seen, V.35 served to fill the gap for higher speeds but was never intended for its current range of uses and applications. As we write, few pieces of real-world equipment have been announced to use EIA-530, but we anticipate wide acceptance of the standard. With that in mind, we will go on to treat this interface as a viable and commonly used standard.

Like its predecessor, EIA-530 includes complete mechanical drawings for both the male and female connectors and pins; it also suggests minimum mounting spacing and finger clearances. Experienced communications planners and installers will recognize the benefit of these mechanical mounting recommendations. Not infrequently, plugs are too large to mount to sockets or sockets are built too close together for easy attachment. Plugs in EIA-530 are given envelope dimensions to prevent tight and potentially damaging cable bending or finger injury during installation.

While EIA-530 defines all of the available pins in the 25-pin connector, the standard permits partial implementations under certain applications. The next section outlines these applications and tells where the partial implementations are permitted.

EIA-530 Implementations

EIA-530 has not yet been selected by many manufacturers as a primary interface. For this reason, no specific DTEs or DCEs will be examined. Rather, the standard itself will be viewed showing mandatory and optional signal implementations. Here the user must peer deeply into each real unit's interface to see what is present and what is missing. The missing or optionally omitted signals of one device may not exactly match with the optionally included signals of another unit.

The options complicate the application of this otherwise excellent standard. Where an optional signal expected by one unit is not supplied by its mate, adaptations will be needed. Discussion of adaptations will follow this section, and a clear understanding of the mandatory and optional signals will be needed. The standard defines four configurations for application of the standard and indicates which signals are mandatory or optional; the standard describes all configurations. For present purposes, two configurations will be studied. The chosen set includes most common potential applications of the EIA-530 family.

The four configurations are: **send/receive**, **send-only**, **receive-only**, and **data-and-timing-only**. Clearly the most usual is send/receive; that is, alternate or simultaneous sending and receiving. Send-only and receive-only are very special cases beyond the scope of this section, but are recommended for independent study. Data-and-timing-only will be viewed as an important subset showing that an extremely limited implementation of the standard is still "standard."

The data-and-timing-only configuration may be built with only three of the fourteen signal functions supplied. They are, not surprisingly, **signal ground, send and receive data** (BA and BB). If the data is synchronous, two additional signal functions, send timing and receive timing must appear. If DTE sourced transmit timing (DA), or external timing to the DCE appears, it is optional. This is the minimum set of signals which can be called EIA-530 and only eleven wires are used in a 25-pin connector. If a unit supplying this standard interface were attached to a unit employing a fully implemented send/receive configuration, the many missing functions could cause distinct problems. Configurations are different, but without close scrutiny, both devices meet EIA-530.

A more common real configuration example is send/receive. For the send/receive configuration, required or mandatory signals are:

- Signal ground (AB);
- Transmitted data (BA);
- Received data (BB);
- Request to send (CA);
- Clear to send (CB);
- DCE ready (CC);
- Received line signal detector (CF); and
- Test mode (TM);

For synchronous operation, the two timing signals (DB and DD) are mandatory; for switched operation, DTE ready (CD) is required. All other signals are optional, although the standard requires unused optional control signals to be powered ON or OFF by dummy generators or voltage levels. The standard also suggests that optional signal generators must be prepared to find this signal "open" or unterminated at the other end. Each signal, mandatory or optional, is individually defined in the standard and full details are given on the expected interactions of signals.

Standard EIA-530 concludes with recommendations and explanatory notes for alternate use of communications service, for line signals and for dummy generators. Expected functioning and signal behavior during testing is covered quite completely. The final section defines terms in a useful glossary and a table shows how to interconnect EIA-530 equipment with older RS-449 units.

A few words should be added on the electrical parts of the family. EIA-422 and EIA-423 challenge the reader more than EIA-530. Here, detailed electrical design criteria and test measurement methods vie with schematics, holding the interest only of dedicated circuit designers. For the data communications professional, each standard's brief appendix should suffice. These sections contain specifications and limits for interconnecting cables. EIA-422, the balanced signal standard, offers a "conservative guide" to cable length versus data speed. Based on normal twisted pair cables of 24 AWG (wire size) copper cable, EIA-422 recommends maximum cable lengths of 1,200 meters or nearly 4,000 feet for speeds under 90,000 bits per second. Above 90,000 bit/s, the maximum recommended length decreases to 15 meters (almost 50 feet) at 10,000,000 bits per second (10 megabits).

These high speeds result from the balanced nature of the signals recommended by this standard. Lower speeds are found in EIA-423.

Standard EIA-423, while dwelling on the electrical design basis of the interface, pictures a series of example interconnections between balanced signal receivers and unbalanced signal generators. The appendix again recommends cable lengths for various data speeds. The chart asks more intellectual effort than EIA-422, but gives up some very useful limits upon study. Unbalanced circuits severely limit data speeds when compared to balanced circuits, but this standard must be used when EIA-232 signals drive the EIA-530 interface. Hopefully, this will rarely happen. If required, Industrial Electronics Bulletin 12, *Application Notes on interconnection between Interface Circuits using EIA-449 and EIA-232* shows how the interface circuits may be attached using EIA-423. While EIA-530 is not mentioned, the concepts remain the same. This bulletin should also be obtained from the EIA by anyone designing cross-standard integration.

EIA-530 Adaptations

As one of the most recent standards in data communications, EIA-530 requires fewer adaptations if the complete standard is implemented. As noted above, however, partial implementations are available due to the optional nature of many signal functions. Here, as in V.35, adaptations may become necessary. The approach described above for V.35 may be followed for EIA-530, but with more difficulty. More decisions about more functions and a great deal of research into each unit's interface begin the adaptation effort.

Perhaps the fastest method is **Occam's Razor.** William of Occam, a fourteenth century philosopher, taught analysis through reduction of assumptions. For data communications interfaces, this means starting with the data interface lines, following with the timing lines and adapting only for the really necessary remaining signals. Overdesign in adaptation can both slow the process and overly complicate the result.

Following the order of the conceptual interface, data is adapted first, then timing and finally control. Ground and common signals must, of course, be connected in the proper manner. It will be also suggested later that loopback control signals receive special preference in interconnection adaptation. The rest of the control signals may be set to fixed ON or OFF voltage levels through clever connection to already fixed signal levels or dummy generators. The guidance of EIA-530 in this area is quite specific and very useful.

Another consideration is circuit speed. Data signals take center stage in interfacing and the interface is often named for the data signal's speed, (i.e., a 56 kbit/s circuit). Remember that the data and timing signals operate at 56,000 bits per second. Control signals, however, operate at a fraction of the actual data speed. That is, when transmitting and receiving data at 56,000 bits per second, control signals such as **local loopback** (LL) will operate no faster than one or two times per second and only in maintenance periods. While the standard sets category I (balanced electronic drivers to balanced electronic receivers over 20 kbit/s) for the data, many control signals may be successfully operated as category II (unbalanced electronic drivers to common ground balanced receivers).

Following the process suggested for V.35 adaptations, each unit interface is fully diagramed, and the interface between two mating units is compared. Missing and extra signals are identified. In EIA-530, each signal on each side of the interface must be understood. Is the signal driver balanced or single-ended? Does the signal receiver meet EIA-530's requirement to be balanced? Once answered for this interface connection, adaptations suitable for each answer are found either in the standard or in simple cable designs. Since EIA-530 specifies connector sex completely for DTE's (male pins) and DCE's (female sockets), direct DTE to DCE connections proceed with the standard cables.

If other units such as manual or remote control patching or monitoring units lie between DCE and DTE in the signal path, connector sex again becomes an issue. EIA-530 recognizes this possibility, and diagrams an interconnection between DTE and DCE with intermediate equipment. Now our sketch expands to include the extra equipment at each DTE to DCE interface, and each signal traces its way through all the equipment. Here equipment design differences will jump out of the sketches to identify extra and missing signals and connector sex. If male to male cables must be designed, symmetry should be observed. More is said about complex interconnections and symmetrical cables at the end of this chapter.

Another question arises about the interposing equipment. Does it pass the signals without electronics, or does it actually contain electronic receivers and drivers? In the electronic case the sketches must expand again to reveal signal categories and balanced or unbalanced types. The unit in the middle becomes a strange hybrid, neither DCE or DTE but possessing some qualities from both. It must be examined as if it were both DTE and DCE. Stated another way, it appears as a DTE to the DCE and a DCE to the DTE.

Samples of the diagrams or sketches described here and for V.35 appear at the end of this chapter in the section on interface integration. Sample sketches are generic; that is, each refers to an artificial interface which is neither V.35 or EIA-530. The sketches illustrate an integration process valid for any data communications interface and lead the planner, engineer or implementer toward a solution method.

T-Carrier Interfaces

T-Carrier services, introduced in Chapter 3, use digital interfaces which differ from the conceptual interface in several important ways. Until now, interface descriptions have focused strictly between the DCE and DTE. The actual interface to the carrier service from the DCE has not been of concern. As T-Carrier services are put under the glasses, interest shifts to that interface. AT&T calls this place the **network interface** (NI) and an older set of terminology applies. For various historical and regulatory reasons, the interface to the *network* is specified by FCC Rules (part 68 of the FCC Rules and Regulations) and by tariffs filed with the FCC by the carriers. Internationally, T-Carrier standards are issued by the CCITT in the "G-series" recommendations on digital networks. CCITT recognizes both the North American 1,544,000 bit/s and the European 2,048,000 bit/s T1s. Explanations of the differences and similarities of these two digital carriers and their respective hierarchies will be found in Chapter 5.

Because of regulatory and international standards processes, the interfaces are simpler, easier to understand and also less subject to manufacturer interpretation. While minor variations happen from time to time, the interfaces remain remarkably stable at the physical and electrical levels. As this section examines only these physical, electrical and function characteristics, the descriptions, implementations and adaptations will be brief. The next chapter delves more deeply into the actual operations and higher level functions of these very high-speed digital streams.

A new confusion enters here, however, as the telephone industry has chosen to call the equipment on the user side of the NI by the name "DTE." This is *NOT* the **data terminal equipment** from data communications standards, but **digital terminating equip-**

ment and describes functions found in both data DTEs and data DCEs. More complete information on this form of digital terminating equipment will be found in Chapter 6 on interface units. Throughout this text, the term DTE will continue to mean data terminal equipment as found in data communications standards. The telephone industry term, digital terminating equipment, will always be spelled out. Caution is advised when reading reference publications to avoid confusing these two similar terms.

T1 Standards

Chapter 3 outlined the origins of the T1 or DS-1 rate carrier systems. Following the convention started in that chapter, T1 will serve as the overall descriptive term for DS-1 signal streams or those operating at 1,544,000 (or 2,048,000) bit/s. The timing or clocking source for this digital stream of bits is omitted here and covered at length in Chapter 7. While a more exact name for the T1 interface is DSX-1, which derives from the T1 or DS-1 rate cross-connect, this chapter concentrates on T1 equipment and the T1 interface available to users and integrators. The interface remains the same wherever located in the network, but it holds the interest of users only at the network interface. To retain consistency with earlier high-speed interfaces, the term T1 interface will be used for the DSX-1, the CSU to DSU interface, and the interface to the network interface (NI).

Several new concepts are introduced with the T1 interface. All previous data standards concerned rectangular binary electrical pulses, that is, a "one" of a certain voltage and a "zero" of another voltage. Any third voltage level was interpreted as an invalid signal. At the T1 interface, a third level of zero volts is the normal "zero" level and "one" may be either a positive or negative voltage. Where previous signals were **unipolar**, either up or down, T1 uses bipolar pulses of either up, down or zero. The two are compared in Figure 4.12.

In bipolar, "one" pulses alternate, first up, then down, while "zero" pulses remain at the zero voltage level. A second new concept, the **bipolar violation** (BPV), occurs when two "one" pulses do not alternate, that is, they appear sequentially in the same voltage direction. Originally considered an error condition, carefully arranged BPVs have become a method of indicating long "zero" streams. This method is called B8ZS for **bipolar with eight zero substitution.** B8ZS is an arrangement to adapt for long "zero" streams in the original data and is described in the next chapter on T-Carriers.

Reflecting on Figure 4.12, it can be seen that a large number of "zeros" produce no pulses at all. Since the timing is imbedded in the pulses along with the data, a lack of pulses risks losing the timing information. B8ZS is one method currently chosen by AT&T and shown in CCITT G.703 to provide clear channel capability, or unrestricted "zeros" flow, while continuing to supply pulses to the network. Other methods are under discussion by other manufacturers and carriers to provide a clear channel capability. B8ZS and the other methods have a single goal, to allow large numbers of "zeros" without restriction and still carry timing information across the links. Clear channel means the ability of the link to carry any combination of bits without restriction. Without this ability, manufacturers and carriers must impose bit or pulse density restrictions to maintain timing recovery. Without B8ZS, many carriers require that no more than 15 "zeros" be transmitted sequentially. A more complex formula for transmitted pulses is found in the AT&T technical reference for ACCUNET® T1.5 services, PUB 62411.

Transmitted data pulses are sent into the carrier's network at the NI on two wires across the interface, and the network supplies the received data pulses on two other wires to

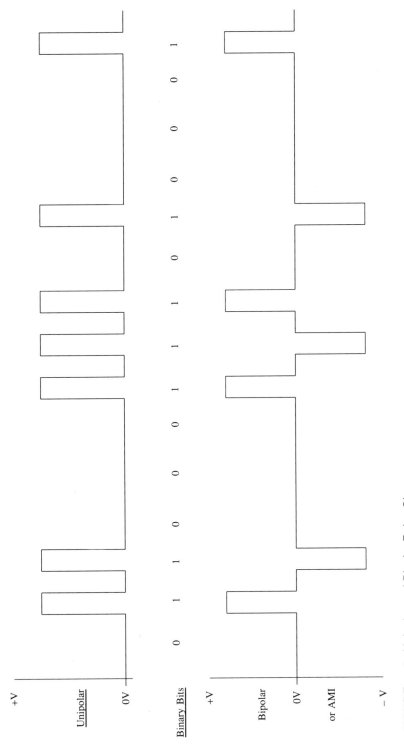

FIGURE 4.12. Unipolar and Bipolar Pulse Shapes.

the devices at the user's site. Timing and control signals are imbedded in the transmitted data and received data streams. Connecting to these four wires at the network customer or user site, a pair of units provide the DCE function introduced in the conceptual interface.

The first of the two, the **channel service unit** (CSU) connects to the four wires coming from the carrier facility or carrier equipment. The second unit, a **data service unit,** connects the DTE to the CSU.

A DSU may offer the interface types studied above, such as V.35 or EIA-530, to the DTE. As shown above, the interface between the CSU and the DSU will contain, as a minimum, the two transmitted data wires and the two received data wires. It may contain several additional control leads or wires, but may not provide the timing or control signals detailed in the conceptual interface. As will be seen in voice channel banks, video CODECS and data time division multiplexers, the DSU function is often imbedded with these units and only the CSU retains its external existence.

The functions of the CSU are manifold. First is the protection of the carrier's network from harm induced by faults or failures in the DSU or DTE. Protection is mandated by the Federal Communications Commission under Part 68 of the FCC's Rules and Regulations. The CSU also electronically shapes and powers the transmitted data pulses to acceptable voltage levels for transmission into the carrier's network at the NI. On the received data side, the CSU regenerates the signal coming from the carrier's wires and develops a standard level signal for the DSU. A third function is the generation and recognition of test and condition signals into and from the network. With the introduction of **extended superframe format** or ESF (detailed later) by AT&T, the CSU takes on many error statistic collection tasks (collecting information over time about the number of errors) for use by the network.

Another new concept, line powering, derives from the need to collect error statistics. Other tasks required of the CSU also mandate the continuous powering of this unit by the service provider. Anyone who notices that telephones usually work during local power failures will recognize line powering. As home telephones are powered by a DC voltage sent on the voice wires from the telephone central office to the instrument, CSUs are powered in a similar arrangement. This powering assures the network provider that critical functions of the CSU continue whether or not local power is available. The usual power supplied by the service provider is a DC current of 60 or 140 milliamperes. The current, originating at the provider's offices, arrives on the data wires in a method called **simplex.** One side of the current supply is connected by isolating transformers on the transmitted side, with the return current on the received side. The DC current is again isolated in the CSU by transformers and supplies the critical functions.

Critical functions include signal regeneration, alarms, **keep alive** signals and loopback command recognition. All these functions will be seen in greater detail in Chapter 6 on interface units. Of interest to the interface is the presence of the DC simplex current on wires where only data pulses were expected.

Data pulses, specified only for the output or transmitted direction, must be, in general, between 2.70 and 3.30 volts, positive or negative, for the "ones" pulses. More complete and comprehensive specifications for the pulses may be found in CCITT recommendation G.703, or in carrier's references, such as AT&T PUB 62411. In United States interfaces, any CSU registered under Part 68 of the FCC Rules and Regulations can be expected to meet the full requirements. On the received data side, however, the situation is not as firm. Here, the pulses arrive from the **last line repeater** (LLR) in the serving carrier's network where the specifications apply. Wiring distances from that last line repeater to the

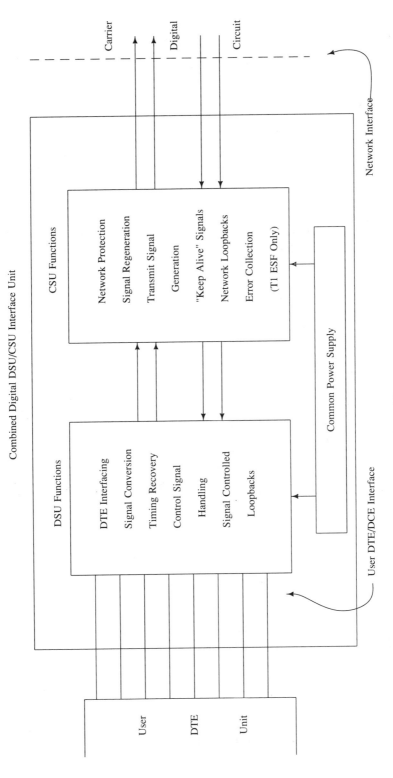

FIGURE 4.13. CSU and DSU Functions at the Network Interface (NI).

user's CSU vary, and assistance from the carrier may be needed to assure proper pulse levels at the CSU.

Proper pulse levels may be adjusted for distance by using **line build out** (LBO) attenuators or level reducers at the LLR or the user's CSU. LBOs may also be called **pads** or **attenuator pads.** At both the CSU and the carrier's LLR, receiver circuitry accepts pulses over a much wider range down from the 3.30 volts, permitting just a few LBOs to adapt for various distances. Both carriers and CSU manufacturers supply the technical information necessary to select proper LBOs for a given physical installation.

Physical connectors for T1 interface range from simple telephone wire blocks to a proposed ISDN telephone-type modular jack. The most common connector for T1 inter-faces is a 15-pin D shell similar to the 25-pin EIA-232 and EIA-530 connectors. Some references recommend use of the 15-pin D shell International Standards Organization (ISO) 4903 interface connector. While all of these connectors are similar, exact pin-outs and lead assignments should be carefully checked for consistency. At most of these connectors, **send data** (transmitted) is assigned to pin one (for the tip) and pin nine (for the ring), and **receive data** (received) is pin three (for the tip) and pin eleven (for the ring). In the recommended ISDN mini-modular connector, pin eight is **transmit** (tip), pin one is **transmit** (ring), pin five is **receive** (tip), and pin four is **receive** (ring). In the 15-pin connector, AT&T recommends pins two and four be reserved for "network use." The remaining pins in both connectors are not used, and few special functions have been adopted by industry for the empty pins.

The **tip** and **ring** naming convention for T1 data signals comes straight from tele-phone industry history dating back to early switchboards. On those boards, each voice line was presented by a jack and was accessed with a plug. Since the plug had a tip connection and ring (or metal band near the tip) and a shell or sleeve for the electrical body of the plug, the circuit names of tip, ring and sleeve (shield) were adopted. That convention comes untouched into the world of megabit data and identifies the individual wires in the T1 interface carrying the data signals and the DC simplex powering current.

DC powering current appears on both send data tip and ring, with the return current appearing on the receive data tip and ring. Using both wires for current offers half the DC resistance; the DC separates from the signals at the isolation transformer in the CSU. This form of powering, explained in greater detail in Chapter 6, is illustrated in Figure 4.14.

T1 Implementations

T1 interfaces are recommended internationally by the CCITT, and in the United States by several standards bodies. As they all work toward the same goal—interoperability of T1 services—the interface implementations do not significantly differ. The Exchange Carrier Standards Association (ECSA), an association of wireline exchange carriers, has established an advisory committee and a T1 standards committee. (This T1 committee was named for Telecommunications under the American National Standards Institute coding scheme for committees and is not the same as the T1 carrier thus far described.) The various ECSA T1 technical subcommittees do, however, work on standards recommendations for T-Carriers and will continue to produce new and revised recommendations. Their work will continue to refine digital (and analog) standards. Some options as LBOs and bit rate tolerances may vary in a given unit, but there exists great uniformity for this T1 interface. Interface details are available from all of these sources. For the easiest reference, T-Carrier interfaces are described in both the CCITT "G-series" book available from the United

95

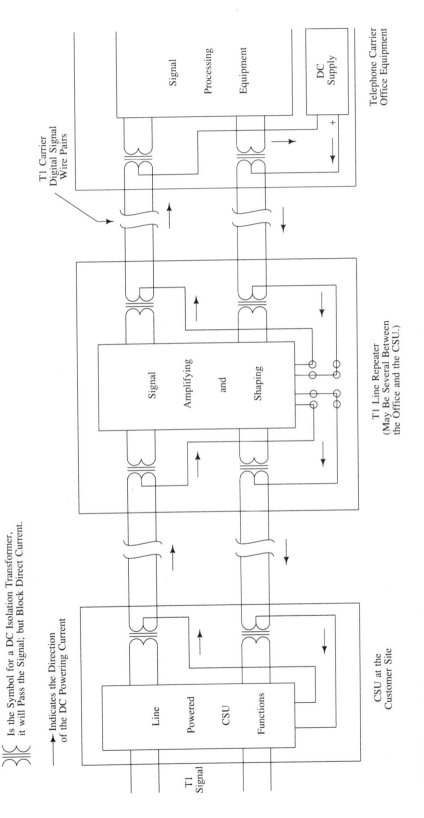

FIGURE 4.14. DC Powering in T1 Interfaces.

Nations Bookstore in New York City and in AT&T Publications available from the AT&T publications center.

Technical references show various physical implementations for the T1 interface, while the electrical interfaces retain consistency. Individual manufacturers describe their T1 interfaces in varying levels of detail. Some list only "T1 interface," while others offer many pages of information on the interface and the options available. As most installations can be planned with minimum distances between the DSU (or DSU function) and the CSU, the details are unneeded. The CSU to NI interface works out between the CSU and the carrier's termination. More often the implementation involves a problem of physical connection. One side may offer the recommended 15-pin D-type connector and the other may have a telephone style wire block. Adaptations for these problems follow.

T1 Adaptations

T1 interface adaptation falls into three simple areas: first, the **physical interconnection**; second, the **test access**; and finally, **line build outs** (LBO). The first two are often solved together through the use of T1 patch panels, or their electronic equivalent: **digital access and cross-connect** (DACS) units. LBOs are explained in the next chapter. Patch panels force a user to organize all interfaces to a common point, offer monitor, test and patch-around capabilities, and solve the physical problem by making it common to all equipment. Patch panels, specifically designed for T1, bring all transmitted and received signal wire pairs to a common physical point through custom site wiring provided by the user or a contractor. The panels then offer jack access for inserting test or monitoring equipment and permit rerouting of individual signal pairs to spare or alternate equipment. Alternate equipment routing through patch panels may be used in some installations to segment problems by substituting known working equipment (from a trouble free circuit) for suspected equipment.

Patch panels exist for both the older style 310-type jacks and plugs as well as the newer mini-310 (also called **bantam**) jacks and plugs. Both are in common use, but test equipment increasingly supports the newer, smaller style mini-310. Standardization of user patch panels permits one style throughout, and mini-310 style is the authors' choice for new patch panel installations.

Without patch panels, suspected equipment must have connectors removed, often with the aid of tools, and may lead to potential damage of cables and connectors. The use of test equipment to verify good operation of a unit or circuit also requires removal of connectors. Patch panels justify themselves in valuable time saved on the first serious trouble-shoot. Chapter 13 delves more deeply into recommendations for multivendor installations. Patch panels, test equipment, and other practical techniques for installation, integration, acceptance and trouble shooting will be found there.

For larger networks, DACS permit the same capabilities, but with some additional advantages. A DACS allows electronically directed patching, switching and monitoring. DACS units and their operation will be explained in greater detail in Chapter 5.

At speeds higher than T1, interface definitions continue to develop. T1C, T2 and T3 Interfaces are described in the latest CCITT "G-series" recommendations and will not be repeated here. Work continues on these standards primarily by the CCITT and ECSA's T1 technical subcommittees, particularly T1X1, carrier-to-carrier interfaces. Reports of their activities appear regularly in data communications and telecommunications publications.

This completes the overview of three high-speed data communications interfaces. Other, higher speed, interfaces will come into view as data communications reaches for ever higher rates. T3 interfaces, already in use by carriers and now standardized by the CCITT, are emerging into private network use and these and other interfaces will demand study. The conceptual interface and the three real interfaces examined here form a strong base for understanding new interfaces as they develop. One additional section leads the reader to the new territory of interface integration.

Interface Integration

What is interface integration and who is the interface integrator? In complex communications systems, the integrator is a planner, programmer, engineer or technician who must make things work together the first time and without error. The integrator is often a member of a team planning a new or revised installation to get it to a working state. This working state must be verified as a benchmark for later problem evaluation. Too many complex systems are brought to apparently working conditions without complete verification or acceptance. Specification acceptance and verification mandate understanding not only each component in a complex system, but also how the system's components work together across their mutual interfaces.

Successful complex systems exhibit two primary characteristics: long, satisfactory working periods and short, uncomplicated problem determination and repair times. Problem determination in complex systems warrants its own study. Here, interface integration focuses on initial installations and the assurance that everything was "once working."

In problem determination, the known working units and circuits must be sorted from the suspect. Only if units and circuits are known to be working at original acceptance can the sorting be accomplished quickly and with certainty. A question is raised several times in this text: "Is it broke or did it ever really work?" Integration answers the question before it is asked by assuring that working is a proven normal state and anything else is probably "broke."

When differing units must connect to form a communications system, the interface integrator must perform some "magic" to assure the initial working status. The information listed above about concepts and several interfaces will guide the integrator toward a class of solution, but ultimately the integrator must understand, plan, design and install the components and the adaptations. The integrator's job is more a state of mind than a skill; a state of mind which can be achieved by anyone understanding the overview, function, and interfaces of the units in the system.

An integrator starts with the overview of the system. A simple set of DTEs connected to a single set of DCEs with little complexity may be integrated with a wave of the hand and a straight set of cables. If the system becomes more complex and involves subtle clocking, switching, monitoring and fallback systems, the integrator needs tools to perform the magic. Simple tools often set the stage for the magic. Diagraming or sketching the total collection of the units to be integrated, and detailing each inter-unit interface point, begins the understanding.

This simple overview sketch illustrates the meeting points of differing equipment and permits identification of critical interface concerns. Usually, differing equipment from one vendor should interconnect easily; even here, however, interface integration approaches should be followed. Expanding the diagram at each interface with data flows, timing sources, directions, and control connections will quickly show where more detail is needed. Expanded sketches highlight interface questions and inconsistencies. Each expanded sketch guides the integrator to the right questions to be asked of equipment vendors and carriers. While the answers sometimes add new questions, the process converges toward both a firm understanding of the total system and knowledge useful in later problem analysis.

Then comes function. What is the complete communications system and, perhaps, the total system required to do? When must it do it? What if it doesn't? What alternatives exist to perform the function? A functional example may help refine the questions.

If one pay telephone instrument in a group of pay telephone instruments fails, it may be safe to assume little function is lost if it is repaired quickly. If a critical fire station radio-telephone fails, major difficulties and perhaps great destruction may result, independent of the speed of repair. Thus the function related questions plus those pertaining to the specifics of the installation must be asked. The answers will begin to uncover sensitive sections of the system and what needs to be provided in the event of a failure or multiple failures. Each unit's failure characteristics, identified at diagram time, outline a map for alternate means to provide function and quickly perform problem analysis.

The outline sketch showing the system overview and function reveals many answers to the functional questions and directs the integrator toward the rest. (See Figure 4.15.)

Now the interfaces of the several sub-systems can be studied for integration. What functions exist in the units which will supply the system? What functions are missing? Can additional units such as monitors or switches be used to supply the function? Expanded sketches may reveal the redundant, conflicting and missing functions. If not, perhaps the sketch needs further expansion. Now special cable and optioning requirements can be found. Before jumping to special cables as a fix, unit options may yield a solution. Most units offer option selections by switch, strap, or program settings. The expanded sketch provides a place to list the settings and compare similar actions from different boxes.

Choices made here by the integrator determine the workability and maintainability of the system of components and the choices must be consciously made. Timing sources for the components must be determined and the effects of source failure examined. Alternate timing sources and fallbacks can be conceived and evaluated. Each control lead, observed for function and necessity, is sourced, terminated or fixed. Many control functions appear for certain configurations and are unnecessary for others. Use Occam's Razor again to eliminate useless function. Follow the "keep it simple" rule wherever and whenever possible.

Control functions may be used as indicators without use for control. A DCD line from a DCE may not be appropriate for a given DTE, but may show on a patch panel lamp to indicate DCE and incoming circuit working to the operators. A consistent approach must be followed throughout the system; trouble shooting speeds when people at opposite ends of a circuit see the same indications for the same condition.

Careful study of unit manuals, coupled with vendor and carrier consultation could give an option solution. Only after that fails should special cable designs be tried. Special cables, while solving interface problems quickly, are time-bombs. As installations grow more complex and people change assignments, details of special cabling begin to disappear. Cables changed during maintenance or unit substitution may find themselves on the shelf or hanging as spares. Since they are special, later use may cause untraceable problems and long unexplained outages.

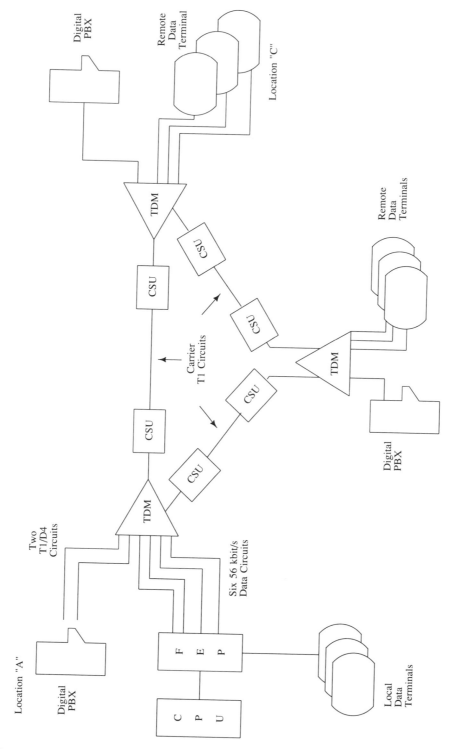

FIGURE 4.15. Example Integration Sketch Diagram.

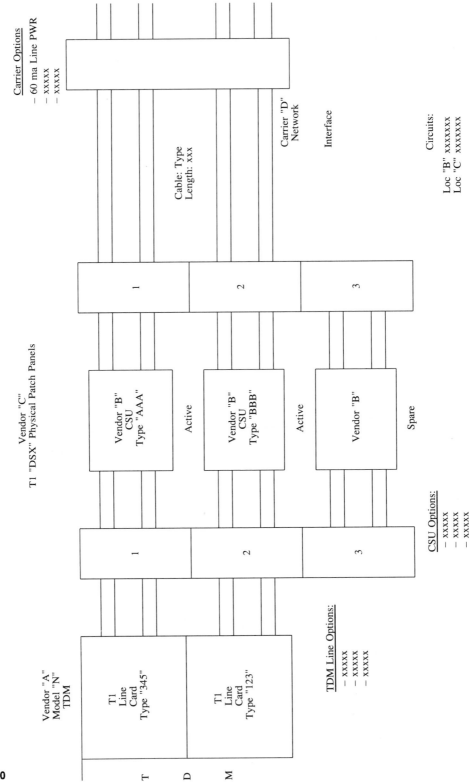

FIGURE 4.16. Example Interface and Option Sketch Diagram.

While most installations cannot avoid special cables completely, uniform and easy to understand marking techniques will prevent later problems. One common approach marks all unique cables and their connectors with bright colors and complete descriptions to warn of their nature and prevent inadvertent or improper use.

Software and firmware programs in DTEs connected to the system may interpret control signals in different ways. Early consultation with programmers and specialists about their side of an interface solves many problems before they erupt. Thorough reviews of control signal actions and reactions prevent unanticipated hardware/software collisions. Software parameters should be recorded alongside other hardware options and adaptations on the interface sketches.

Whatever adaptations evolve, the systems diagrams and interface sketches are completed with all cables and options shown. The next step is review. Self-reviews, peer reviews, and vendor reviews of the systems outlines and expanded interface sketches are invaluable. All of us are liable to overlook our own errors even when careful self-reviews are done. Faulty assumptions about unit functions may be exposed by vendor reviews and peer reviews force the integrator to articulate design choices.

After the interface choices are made and installed, they must be tested. Often, more may be learned about how systems operate when they are stressed or intentionally disrupted. Interface verification must be performed at installation time and it must be complete. Installation interface testing and acceptance training often work well together. Systems diagrams and sketches provide the training material as well as test documents. This form of training of new people, or people inexperienced on the new system, is doubly valuable.

By working through a methodical process of testing, complete hands-on education can be gained for later systems support. The systems outline and the detail sketches frame the testing. Each critical function from the design must be exercised. Interface cables are disconnected and breakout or signal test boxes are inserted into the interface. Critical leads from the detail sketches are broken, or fixed high or low, and system results are observed. If all functions are correct, this portion of the acceptance test is recorded as "once worked." These documents later form the base of maintenance documentation along with the systems outlines and interface diagrams.

The completed overview, function, interface and test sketches have built the foundation of system documentation, which later permits a host of necessary activities. Sketches and documents smooth systems training of new people, and guide problem determination. Documentation, often a painful and much delayed process, builds easily from early systems and interface sketches. Readability and accuracy of the sketches and diagrams hold the key to future usefulness.

A working installation of a new complex system offers a secure reward to the integrator. Knowing a system is working and knowing why it is working give a feeling of true accomplishment. For this system, the integrator has done the job and done it well.

Where to Write for Standards

Standards are published for sale by each of the organizations listed below. Reference books containing these standards are also available from technical bookstores, data communications consultants, and by mail order through advertisements in major technical journals. Addresses for the following standards organizations were current at the time of this writing.

CCITT Recommendations

CCITT recommendations are available in the United States from the United Nations Bookstore. The United Nations Bookstore will accept mail orders, but indicates that the orders must be prepaid. The standards bear costs similar to quality technical and professional books; contact the bookstore for lists and current prices.

United Nations Bookstore
Room GA 32B
New York, NY 10017

You may also wish to contact The International Telegraph and Telephone Consultative Committee (CCITT) directly:

CCITT
C/O Union International des Telecommunications (ITU)
Place des Nations
1211 Geneve 20, SWITZERLAND

EIA Standards

Recommended standards from the Electronic Industries Association (EIA) may be ordered from the EIA. These standards are also described and detailed in many technical books on data communications. You may contact the EIA for current prices and ordering procedures.

Electronic Industries Association
2001 Eye Street, N. W.
Washington, D. C. 20006

Carrier Publications

Communications carriers issue technical publications, many of which are available for sale. You may contact representatives of the carrier to learn how to obtain copies of catalogs and the available publications.

CHAPTER 5

T-Carrier Systems

Chapter Overview

High-speed digital data communications grew from digital voice technologies of the 1960s. T1 digital voice carrier systems, developed for transmission between telephone central offices, spread throughout the telephone network, building DATAPHONE® Digital Services in the 1970s. Higher level T-Carriers, multiplexing T1s together, added capacity for both voice and data to the network. T-Carriers offered true digital interconnection across the nation. Users are now involved with both the carriers and with their own private systems for T-Carriers and a knowledge and understanding of T-Carrier systems and components is needed. This chapter develops background, knowledge and understanding of T-Carriers, T-Carrier hierarchies, and how T-Carriers operate. T-Carrier interface concepts, already outlined in Chapter 4, will be extended by a discussion of interface units in the next chapter. The focus here concerns concepts and fundamentals of T-Carriers.

   With earlier analog technologies, data communication professionals monitored circuits between data centers with analog techniques and test equipment. Digital data and digital techniques stopped at the DCE. Digital circuit technologies, combined with divided network and equipment responsibilities, now force digital understanding of what is happening in "the network." Digital data transmission and ISDN will require knowledge of the structures and operations of digital networks. Private networks and **bypass** connections to long haul carriers make the need for digital knowledge imperative. Network framing, channelization, signaling and line signals must be understood as part of the total communications system. The material below traces beginnings of T-Carriers through current use and outlines expected developments in the Megabit digital field.

T1 Carrier Structure

T1 carriers came into the telephone network to carry 24 digitized voice channels at 1.544 Mbit/s on copper pairs by using time division multiplexing D1 and D2 channel banks. Digital channel bank development continued, producing the D3 bank and with it, stable telephone industry standards and practices. Voice digitization at 64,000 bit/s per channel from the D1 remains in effect in current implementations, but channel order has changed. Current hardwired D4 and the newer software driven D5 channel banks continue the D3 standards. D3 framing and D3 channelization, often called D4, form the base layer for the digital network in North America. European telecommunications developed similar techniques for voice digitization paralleling North America, but extended the channel count to 30, yielding 2,048,000 bit/s. CCITT "G-series" recommendations now describe both the "North American" and the "European" standards. The text below concentrates on North American implementations of T-Carrier, but concepts remain the same for both. As we move well into the megabit range, brevity in terminology shortens—1,544,000 bit/s becomes 1.544 Mbit/s, 2,048,000 bit/s becomes 2.048 Mbit/s, and so on.

D3/D4 T1 Framing

A confusion between D3 and D4 terminology causes concern until differences are understood. D3 standards strictly mean a frame of 24 channels, sampled (digitized) in sequential order, multiplexed into a 1.536 Mbit/s signal, then combined with an 8,000 bit/s framing pattern yielding 1.544 Mbit/s. Each channel uses eight bits, with the most significant (highest binary weighting) bit first. This gives 192 bit positions (24 times eight); the single framing bit position totals to 193 bit positions in a single frame of 24 channels. The 193 bit pattern repeats at the channel sampling rate of 8,000 times per second, producing 1.544 Mbit/s. This may be easily verified on a calculator. Figure 5.1 illustrates the D3 frame and channel concept.

Developed later, D4 channel banks extend the T1 approach to a T1C carrier, combining 48 voice channels. The T1C rate combines two T1 streams to give 3.088 Mbit/s, adds 64,000 bit/s of T1C specific framing, and runs at 3.152 Mbit/s. To assure compatibility with, and migration from, existing T1 carriers and D3 banks, D4 banks offer several modes of operation including a D3 mode. In **mode 3,** as the D3 mode is called, the D4 unit operates as two independent D3 channel banks, each combining 24 channels into separate T1 streams. Much digital T-Carrier and channel bank literature describes T1 streams as D4 framed and D4 channelized, and in D4-mode 3, this is correct. Other literature calls it T1/D3 and this is also correct. Most of the industry uses T1/D4 to describe 24 channel operation and the authors will follow that usage; that is, T1/D4 in this text will mean T1 with D4-mode 3 operation, compatible with T1/D3.

The other modes of D4 utilize the channel bank at T1C and T2; Mode 1 communicates between two D4 banks at T1C and Mode 2 communicates between a D4 (Mode 2) and an M1C digital muldem or multiplexer. Mode 4 combines two D4 banks, producing 4 T1 streams which multiplex together to form a T2 stream running at 6.312 Mbit/s. Digital muldems or multiplexers will be explained just after this section on T1 carriers.

T1 Carrier Systems

The T1 carrier system, fundamental to the study of all T-Carriers, entered the telephone system in 1962. Structurally, current T1 systems differ little from those early systems. Systems as new as T1G, carrying 96 voice (or data) channels, follow conventions and engineering techniques put in place for T1 and its successors. For this reason, we begin

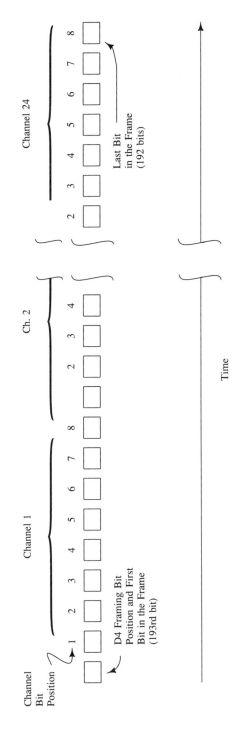

FIGURE 5.1. Simplified D3 Frame and Channel Composition.

with a very detailed look at T1; ideas and concepts found here will reappear many times. First, a look at the driving factors which produced the concepts and the carrier.

Solid state electronics, using individual transistors, came into its own in the late 1950s. Device and manufacturing costs were falling rapidly and transistor reliabilities promised extremely long times between failures. Early applications of the new devices followed traditional analog design paths, but by 1960, solid state proved itself in cost-effective digital design. Digitization of previous analog strongholds accelerated and bits replaced analog levels throughout the electronics industry. Stimulated, perhaps, by a rapid expansion in digital computer applications, voice transmission began its move to digital.

Sampling analog signals and producing digital values, already well along in the process instrument field, appeared a natural application for voice. Two problems had to be solved—analog-to-digital conversion and the transmission of the digital values over existing cables. The first, A-to-D conversion, followed theoretical sampling techniques. Nyquist predicted the method in 1928, and a sampling rate of 8,000 samples per second was picked using 4,000 Hz as the needed bandwidth. Voice signal sampling was produced as **pulse amplitude modulation** (PAM), and was then altered to **pulse code modulation** (PCM) for multiplexing and transmission. Current PCM techniques continue at 8,000 samples per second and actual voice encoding follows certain encoding law standards. For those interested in the voice encoding law standards, CCITT recommendation G.711 describes two current PCM methods. For data communications purposes, two key facts suffice: 8,000 bits (samples) per second and eight bits per sample. The digital bit stream now needed a transmission method.

Digital transmission over the copper cables required newer techniques. Wire cable pairs offer significantly more bandwidth than needed for 4,000 Hz voice conversations, but bandwidth is not unlimited. To carry pulses faster than a megabit, ordinary rectangular pulses of "up for ones" and "down for zeros" could not be used reliably over the desired distances. A bipolar pulse technique called **alternate mark inversion** (AMI), produced zero volts for a "zero" bit and alternating positive and negative voltage pulses for "ones." Bipolar AMI solved several problems in transmission; it consumed less bandwidth, did not unbalance the pair and provided a method for errored pulse detection. Oversimplified, pair unbalance results when too many ones slowly shift the nominal voltage on a circuit. AMI balanced the line and offered a new way to recognize bit errors. Received "ones" which did not alternate violated the bipolar rules, and **bipolar violations** (BPV) could indicate errors. This 1.544 Mbit/s AMI pulse train or stream takes the designation DS-1 for its digital nature, its pulse shape and its speed. That is, DS-1 names it as the digital signal at the first level of the North American hierarchy.

T1 or DS-1 signal transmission between telephone central offices accomplishes the original purpose of carrying more conversations on existing copper pairs. In analog circuits, copper pairs use **load** or inductance coils to compensate for cable capacitance, and these are removed for T1 digital signals. On long cable runs, digital **repeaters** with signal shaping amplifiers (regenerators), replace the loading coils in manholes and on overhead wire poles. Repeaters take central office DC battery power from the T1 signal pairs in the same way CSUs are line powered (Chapter 4). On a given inter-office T1 line, called a **span line,** several repeaters may be needed to restore the digital pulse shape.

After passing over several thousand feet of ordinary telephone cable, AMI pulse shapes degrade and require recovery and reshaping. The reshaped AMI pulses out of each repeater drive the next section of the span, and since span section lengths differ, **line build**

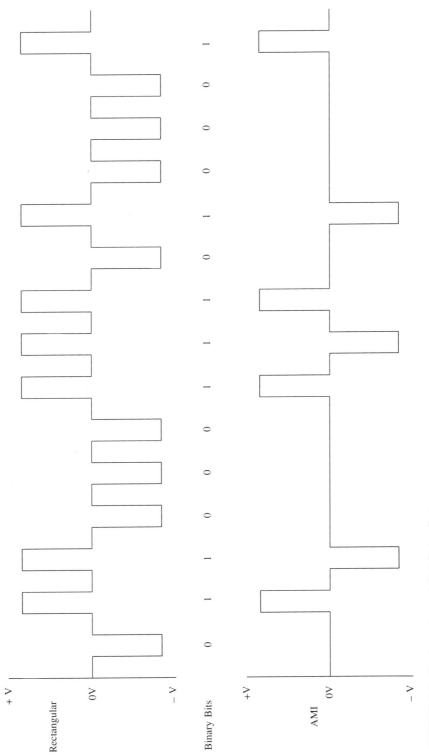

FIGURE 5.2. Rectangular and AMI Pulse Patterns.

108

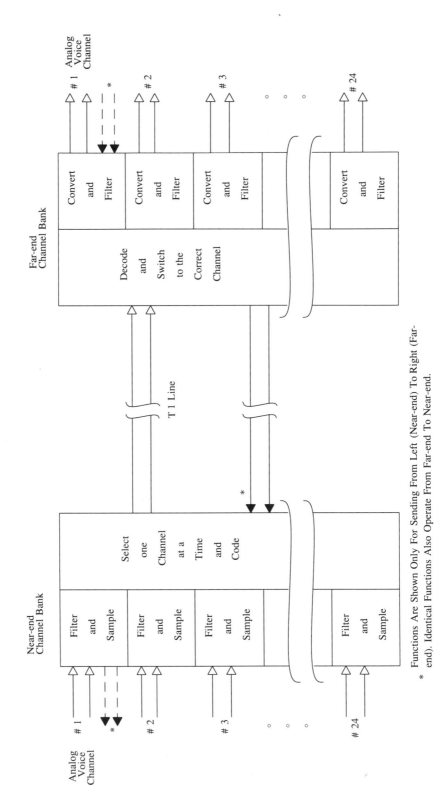

FIGURE 5.3. Example of D4 Channel Banks.

Functions Are Shown Only For Sending From Left (Near-end) To Right (Far-end). Identical Functions Also Operate From Far-end To Near-end.

out (LBO) components compensate. Each repeater amplifier creates larger than needed output pulses and LBOs reduce the pulses to match section lengths. One of several optional LBOs matches expected section length, with long sections using straight, or non-attenuating LBOs. After the end of the span, locally powered office repeaters may connect to another span or may terminate in a far-end channel bank for conversion back to analog.

T1/D4 Framing and Channelization

Voice signals, now digitized and transmitted, need conversion back to analog at the far end. Digital bit streams convert easily back to analog once the right set of bits are chosen. The problem is finding them. A serial stream of "ones" and "zeros" needs a reference; the 193rd frame bit position from the channel bank marks that point. The receiving channel bank's frame detector searches the bit stream for a specific superframe pattern in the 193rd position. A superframe combines 12 frames of 193 bits each, producing the T1/D4 superframe pattern of:

$$1\,0\,0\,0\,1\,1\,0\,1\,1\,1\,0\,0$$

At the receiving channel bank, the DS-1 pulse train enters a frame detector to find the frame pattern. Twelve 193rd bit positions from the incoming train, starting at a random bit, are examined for the T1/D4 superframe pattern. Since a random match may be found, the detector checks multiple times. If the frame pattern keeps changing, the frame detector shifts over one bit and looks again until the superframe pattern locks in. Once locked-in, channels sequentially digitized by the near end channel bank line up for D-to-A conversion at the far end. Each frame bit shown above actually begins the frame of 24 channels and precedes the eight bits from channel one. Presented graphically, the serial bit stream finds channel slots for decoding to analog. Slots represent channel positions from the originating bank and must align before channel use. The process acts independently in each direction between banks, but both directions must lock in before channels become available for use.

All proceeds well unless bit errors happen on T1 transmission between banks. If a short error burst occurs, the frame may not be disturbed and will pick up the beat after the burst. Errored bits decode to a voice channel as noise or remain errored on a data channel. With long error bursts or broken lines, the channel bank will electronically declare an error condition and **busy-out** the connected voice channels to prevent their further use. When the trouble clears, frame detection which had continued searching, re-establishes the channels. Channels used for switched circuits become available again for new connections, and fixed circuits are reconnected. Passing of switching signals between banks, accomplished by using or **robbing** certain bits is covered later in this chapter.

Channelization determines where the bits from each channel belong. Following the framing bit position, eight bits from each channel sequence through the frame. Leading the stream, after the frame bit position, is the most significant bit of the first channel. The most significant bit takes its name from its value. In any binary system, each bit carries a weight, just as the decimal system. In decimal, numbers in the order XYZ 0 take weights as X= hundreds, Y = tens, and Z = units or ones. In binary, rules follow the same pattern. A binary set of four bits, VXYZ, carries weights as V = eights, X = fours, Y = twos, and Z = units or ones. In this example, V carries the heaviest weight of eight. Another way of looking at this

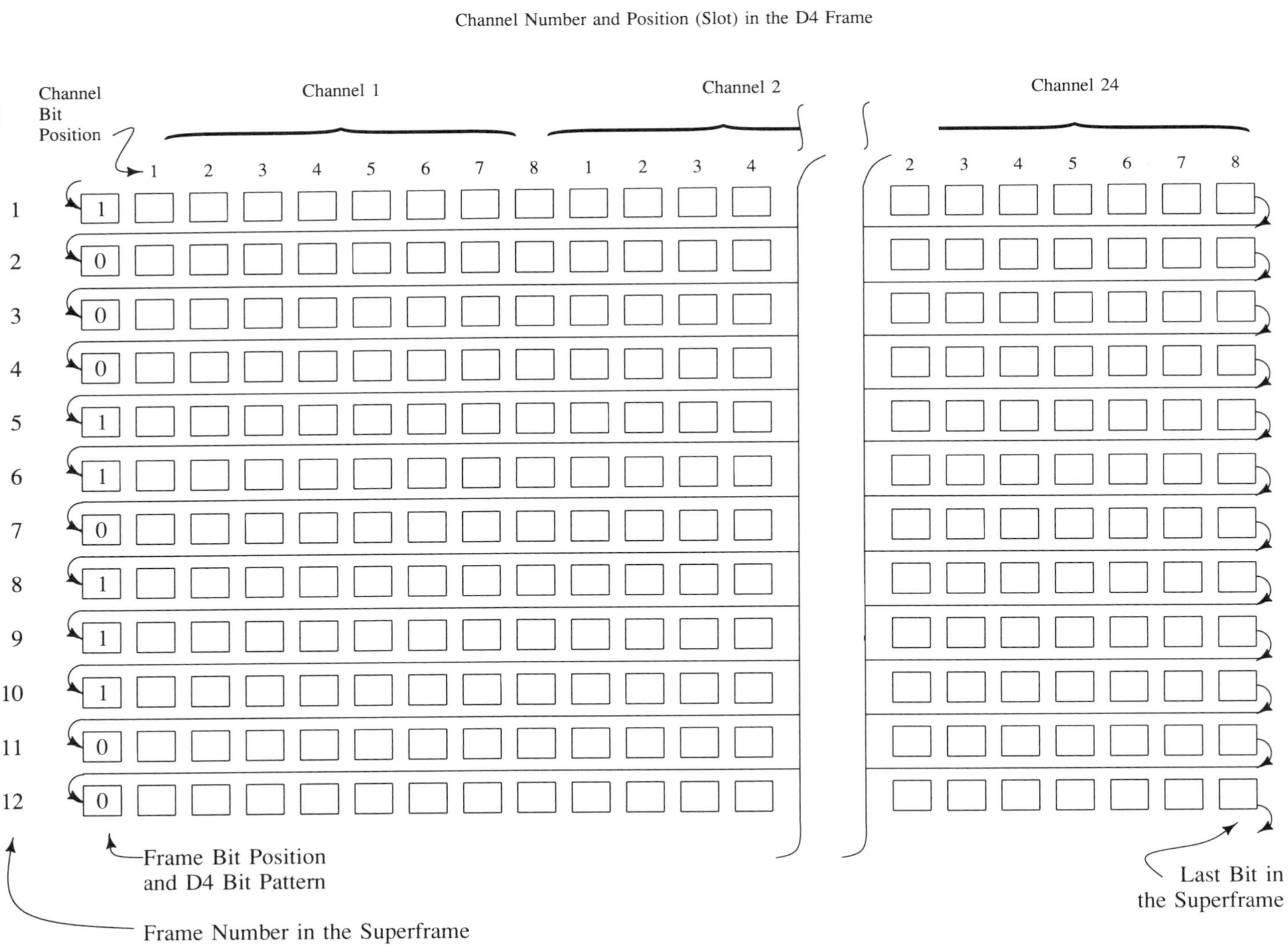

Channel Number and Position (Slot) in the D4 Frame

FIGURE 5.4. T1/D4 Superframe and D4 Channel Slots.

would multiply the value in the position by its weight and add up the result. Decimal and binary examples would be:

DECIMAL		BINARY		BINARY	
3254.0		1111		1010	
3000	+	8	+	8	+
200	+	4	+	0	+
50	+	2	+	2	+
4	+ 3254	1	= 15	0	= 10

In the examples above, decimal three and binary eight take the most significant weight or are at the most significant position. In digital channel banks, the first bit after the frame position is the highest weighted or most significant bit of that channel. That makes the eighth bit following the frame bit, the least significant bit. If the value of this bit changes, it has the least affect on the voice signal. Emphasis on this concept may appear too great, but knowledge of bit position and weight becomes key to understanding signaling.

T1/D4 Voice Network Supervision and Signaling

Supervision, in its simplest form in telephone networks, is ON-HOOK or OFF-HOOK, coming down to us from the days when telephones actually had hooks to hang up the ear piece. Off-hook tells the telephone central office that someone wishes to use the telephone and on-hook tell the office they are done. Lines between telephone offices also need this status information to tell if a line is available or in use. T1 carriers and D-type channel banks appear to have no mechanism to send supervision, but the least significant bit of information in digitized voice may be used from time to time without really affecting voice quality. Remember the bit's significance; its occasional loss will cause no harm. Occasionally taking, or robbing, this bit position makes it available for supervision or signaling. Signaling in the telephone network generally means the passing of call-related information, such as the address or number being called.

Bit robbing developed with each generation of channel banks, but the T1/D4 method finds most common use. In T1/D4, the superframe positions not only each channel, but each of the 12 frames. In T1/D4 signaling, the sixth and twelfth frames locate the signaling bits. In the sixth frame, the least significant digitized voice bit turns into signaling bit "A." From the twelfth frame comes the "B" signaling bit. How these bits are actually used in each application becomes the choice of engineers and installers. The key point is the method. On-hook and off-hook, along with dial pulses and busy indications, transit the T1 using the A and B bits robbed from the voice signal. When data flows through T1 carriers and D4 banks, the bit finds another use.

In data applications, T1/D4 requires the assignment of the eighth bit of each (data) channel to a "one." Note that this is not just in the sixth and twelfth frames, but every frame. Most channel bank manufacturers offer special data channel cards for their channel banks which place this eighth bit automatically. Later in this chapter, bit density on T1 carriers focuses on the need for a minimum number of "one" bits. For channel bank data circuit operations, this forced "one" guarantees that density, but slows the overall data rate. A short calculation discloses that the seven bits available for data, running at 8,000 times per second, yield 56,000 bit/s and here lies the origin of DDS 56 kbit/s. Individual channels

Channel Number and Position (Slot) in the D4 Frame

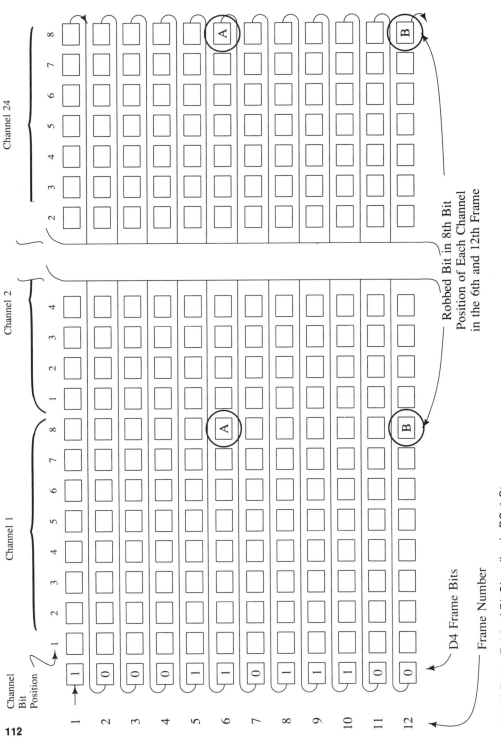

FIGURE 5.5. Robbed Bit Bit Signaling in DS-1 Streams.

between D-type banks run at 64 kbit/s, but only 56 kbit/s can be used for data on a channel. The channel signal stream of 64 kbit/s takes a name below the T1 DS-1 stream and is called DS-0. When 56 kbit/s data flows, the channel sometimes takes the name DS-0A, but it remains a DS-0 with the eighth bit forced to "one."

DS-0 bit streams at 64 kbit/s recur throughout the digital hierarchy, and form the basic unit for switching and routing. DACS devices, already discussed, route DS-0 channels. **Digital private branch exchanges** (PBX) and telephone company digital switches handle DS-0. ISDN "B" or bearer channels are also 64 kbit/s. DS-0 digital streams have become the digital version of the classic 4,000 Hz analog voice channel.

In an analog circuit world, maintenance takes place on individual circuits or groups of circuits. Maintenance information derives from analog characteristics at each point in the network. In digital networks, combined circuits flow together as high-speed bit streams multiplexed with other high-speed bit streams and maintenance information also becomes digital. Separation of network equipment responsibilities adds difficulty, with CPE belonging to the user and network equipment belonging to several carriers on a single DS-1 circuit. Methods to derive service information require altered approaches, and those new approaches must migrate easily from existing installations. In DS-1 digital streams, well-defined DS-0 channels of 64 kbit/s leave little room for new information, yet new information must pass. The maintenance information dilemma begged for creative solutions and a creative solution came forward with **extended superframe format** (ESF).

Extended Superframe Format (ESF) Framing

T1/D4 framing, described above, uses a superframe of 12 frames with a specific bit pattern in the 193rd bit position. This pattern operates at 8,000 bit/s and practice finds it very robust. Robustness describes a systems property of operation under stress, in this case, the presence of line errors. The use of D-type digital channel banks since the 1960s, has shown that 8,000 bit/s of framing are more than needed to assure solid performance. The framing bit pattern specifically reframes or locates correct channel position and locks onto it. After loss of lock, reframing with T1/D4 framing patterns usually occurs less than 50 milliseconds after clean signal returns. A sufficiently robust alternative should retain nearly this speed of reframe, but might make some of the bits available for other purposes, such as maintenance. This robust alternative, proposed first as F_e, (say: Eff sub eee) now takes the name extended superframe format or ESF. CCITT documents call it the 24-frame multiframe, but ESF remains easier to say and will be used here.

The word "extended" in the title offers clues to ESF operation. The previous D4 superframe of 12 frames extends to 24 frames and framing bit positions take new functions and meanings. A D4 superframe consists of 2,316 bits (12 times 193); ESF consists of 4,632 bits (24 times 193). In D4, 12 of the 2,316 bits are frame bits. In ESF, 24 bits are available and ESF divides the bits into three functions: framing, error checking and maintenance communications. Maintenance communications takes 12 bits or half of the available 24 bits; framing and error checking divide the rest with six bits each. Think of the 8,000 bit/s D4 frame as a reference; in D4, all 8,000 bits concern framing. In ESF, 2,000 bit/s form a **cyclic redundancy check** (CRC) code pattern for error checking, 4,000 bit/s form a data link for communications, and 2,000 bit/s find use for framing.

The new frame bit pattern provides the same function as in D4 framing; that is, locating the structure of the channels for correct connection and finding channels six and 12

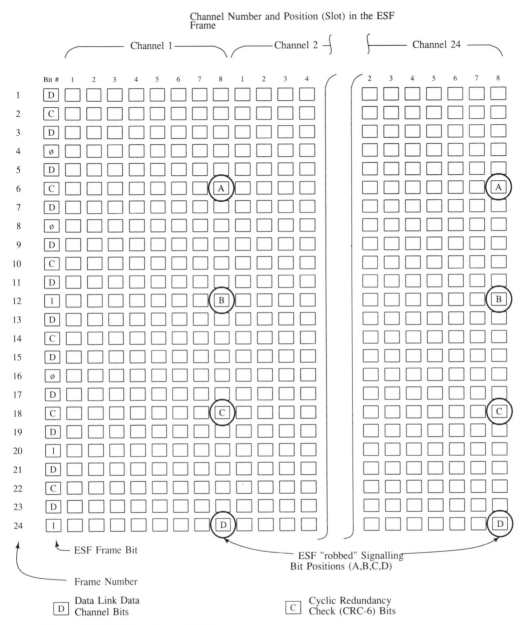

FIGURE 5.6. T1/ESF Framing and Bit Use.

for robbed bit signaling. In addition, as 24 frames now comprise the superframe, possibilities exist for new robbed bit signaling bits in frames 18 and 24. These new signaling bits, called "C" and "D", permit additional signaling states to be sent in band on the channel.

Framing in ESF does not differ greatly from D4 framing, with the exception of the new signaling bit possibilities. Error checking and maintenance communications via the data link are, however, totally new capabilities with T1/ESF.

Previous T1 communications error checking depended on connected end equipment; the channel banks and network transmission equipment relied on bipolar violations for indications of line or equipment errors. ESF offers, for the first time, a means of validating the presence or absence of single bit errors between network points. ESF provides a six-bit cyclic redundancy check pattern inside the ESF pattern. All 4,632 bits of the superframe pass through a CRC-6 pattern generator which calculates six check bits. These six CRC bits carry to the next checking point imbedded in the following superframe. At that checking point, the 4,632 incoming bits of the first superframe again pass through a CRC-6 generator and wait for comparison with the incoming CRC six-bit pattern in the following ESF block. If the two patterns compare equal, there exists a high probability that no individual bit errors occurred in transmission.

The mathematics of error checking offer only a high probability of no errors; specific multiple bit errors can produce the same check pattern as no errors. A high probability of no errors, however, greatly exceeds no error checking at all, and CRC-6 permits continuous (or inband) checking of network transmission facilities. Unless error checking is carried along with the data by inband error checking, testing for errors requires taking a circuit out of service and inserting known test patterns between test equipment. If error conditions clear before the test equipment takes over, the loss of service is wasted. Gradually increasing error conditions on a circuit must wait for hard failure thresholds. Continuous CRC-6 error checking provides continuous monitoring of each circuit and even offers the ability to segment a circuit by comparing error statistics from different segments of the circuit. This allows network maintenance personnel to switch a failing segment to a spare circuit and repair the failing segment. With maintenance communications, many points in the circuit can be interrogated by central points and repair dispatched efficiently to the failing segment.

Maintenance communications uses the data link portion of the ESF pattern. AT&T's preliminary publication (PUB 54016) describes a message protocol, based on packet switching techniques, and a series of commands which conforming **channel service units** (CSU) must meet. These commands permit network maintenance centers to interrogate each CSU status register and to zeroize or reset the registers to zero value. CSUs meeting the requirements of T1/ESF contain digital registers which accumulate statistics about errors and errored seconds, a key parameter measuring the number of seconds containing one or more errors. Additional commands permit initiation and deactivation of CSU loopback functions. More information about the registers, functions and commands will be found in Chapter 6. These many commands, detailed in PUB 54016, concern primarily CSU manufacturers and the AT&T network. Readers wishing to study the commands and their actions at the CSU and in the network should obtain a current copy of PUB 54016 from AT&T.

While T1/ESF represents one direction of T1 carrier systems, and will see a migration from current T1/D4 links, other framing patterns exist on T1. As suggested in the following discussion, other framing patterns exist primarily from data time division multiplexers.

Non-D3 T1 Framing

Devices other than voice channel banks use T1 carriers. In the early 1980s, modem and statistical multiplexer manufacturers extended their devices to meet the new high-speed digital carriers. T1 carriers, at that time did not require any specific framing or channelization and each manufacturer selected a framing and channelization best suited to product needs. Products from the data communications industry used T1 in an unformatted and unframed mode from the carrier's viewpoint. The products frame and channelize their bit streams, but each uses a unique or proprietary pattern. Because of the varying needs of data communications and the many speeds of data channels, framing patterns more complex than D-type channel banks developed. Each manufacturer creates these unique framing patterns to suit the product's architecture, and the length of the total patterns often exceeds the 193 bit frame of channel bank architecture.

These long bit strings meet the electrical standards for DS-1 and contain sufficient "one" bits to meet common carrier requirements. But each unit only works with another of the same type and manufacture. When data TDMs, as they are called, operate in point-to-point configurations over single T1 lines, compatibility with other T1/D4 units is unnecessary. Some manufacturers follow D4 framing patterns from channel banks, but until recently, most data TDMs followed unique framing patterns. Channelization of most data TDMs differs substantially from D-type channel banks for the simple reason that many more channels must be carried. When AT&T notified users and manufacturers that D4 framing would be required, all manufacturers moved to implement D4 framing in their DS-1 streams. This D4 implementation, however, may be in addition to existing, longer and proprietary framing patterns used to synchronize the data TDM's many channels and functions.

Data TDM units use significantly differing framing to cope with much larger channel counts and with needs driven only by data communications. The earliest data TDM units permitted over 50 data channels and carried control signals, such as **request to send** (RTS) and **clear to send** (CTS). Multiplexing of many data channels and data control signals requires more than 192 bits and many data TDM patterns not only run longer than D4 but also contain D4. This means that two independent framing patterns may exist in the same DS-1 stream. While confusing to understand, two independent framing patterns do not confuse the electronics. An outgoing DS-1 stream builds by first channelizing and framing the data channels and then adding a D4 or ESF framing pattern. At the incoming end, the D4 may first be checked and removed, and the remaining pattern checked for the proprietary framing and channelization.

The clearest message from multiple frame patterns concerns what can be attached to what. If a device, such as a data TDM from manufacturer XYZ, connects to one end of a T1 link and contains proprietary framing, then the only device which can be expected to work at the other end is an XYZ data TDM. Further complexities involve different versions and levels with each manufacturer's products, but these must be addressed to each manufacturer. Even when a TDM unit conforms totally to T1/D4 framing and T1/D4 channelization for voice signals, data patterns may be questioned. CCITT and industry standards for framing and channel bit positions are slowly clearing the fog of inter-operability. Until certainty arrives, T1 interconnection of non-D4 channel bank devices should be approached with great care and only after significant study and testing. Even when D4 framing is assured, channelization must be verified.

Other T1 Channelizations

As mentioned earlier, D1 and D2 voice channel banks use 64 kbit/s channelization, but order the channels differently. Some non-voice devices using T1/D4 or T1/ESF framing contain unique channelizations. Many data TDMs maintain their own multichannel assignments and other types of equipment use fewer than 24 channels. T1 video compression devices compact what would otherwise occupy 12,000 Mbit/s for color television signals to a single channel. These video **CODECs** (COder/DECoder) frame on T1/D4 or T1/ESF, but only one video channel, or at most a few channels, fill the entire T1 bit stream. Again, the devices may be safely paired or networked to each other, but may not operate successfully with units of differing level or manufacture.

DS-1 Line Signals

Discussions about T1 and DS-1 signals ultimately get down to the bit level of "ones" and "zeros." Some has been told about the DS-1 interface in Chapter 4 and more will be said in Chapter 6 under T1 interface units. But line signals in DS-1 streams should be studied more closely here as the signals are fundamental to the operation of T1 and higher level T-Carriers. **Alternate mark inversion** (AMI) and the density of "one" bits begin the study. Marks, as opposed to spaces, come to us from the days of telegraph and mean "one" bits in digital carrier systems. Bipolar signals are often called alternate mark inversion or AMI signals after the alternating direction of sequential, although not necessarily contiguous, "one" pulses.

AMI and Bipolar Bit Density

AMI pulses, diagrammed in the figure below, alternate successive "one" bits and present "zero" bits without a pulse. This curious pattern contains a hidden advantage for signal transmission. An all "ones" pattern exhibits alternating pulses in every pulse interval or time slot. With a little visualization, you can see a sine wave outlined by the pulses. The frequency of this sine wave turns out at half of the pulse rate; at 1.544 Mbit/s the sine wave would be 772,000 Hz. This relationship of bits per second to hertz allows the pulse stream to be sent over a facility offering less bandwidth than would be needed with rectangular pulses. Without delving into the mathematics of Fourier, this AMI pulse pattern permits the use of simple media such as copper cable pairs to carry megabits. An additional advantage of this lower (fundamental or lowest contained) frequency concerns crosstalk. **Crosstalk,** or the coupling of signals from one channel to another, increases as frequency increases. With lower fundamental frequencies, AMI also reduces potential crosstalk.

As Figure 5.7 shows, "zeros" code as no pulse at all. A large number of successive "zeros" presents a new problem for receiving and regenerating electronics. Imbedded timing, or timing carried in the pulses themselves, requires at least some pulses. Digitized voice communication solves this problem by presenting at least one pulse in every channel or eight bits. Data communications, sent through D-type channel banks, forces the eighth bit to "one" and also avoids the problem. This, of course, wastes about 13% of the available bandwidth. Other types of T1 devices, however, may produce the forbidden long "zeros" strings. Most T1 carrying systems will not accept the pulseless strings without risking loss of timing synchronization. Channel service units (CSU) may be set to meet carrier require-

Binary Bit Pattern

1 1 1 1 1 1 0 0 0 0 0 0 0 0 0 0 0 0 0 0 0 0 1

Alternate Mark Inversion (AMI) Pulse Pattern

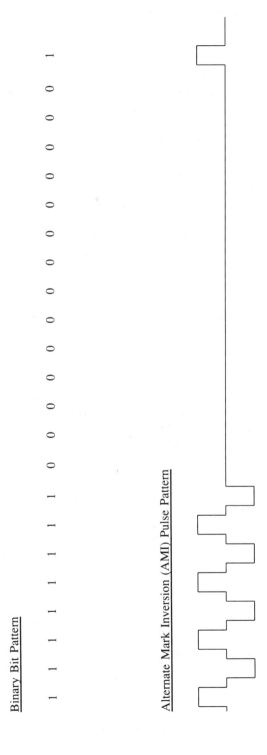

FIGURE 5.7. AMI Pulses and "Ones" Bit Density.

ments by arbitrarily inserting false "ones" when too many "zeros" are detected in the outbound stream.

Current practice and carrier specifications often call for a maximum of 15 successive "zeros" in a DS-1 stream. After the fifteenth "zero", timing begins to drift and later pulses may be lost (errored). To compensate for this limit, equipment generating DS-1 streams will often insert a false "one" bit in about every eight to assure the proper pulse density. Pulse density is really an average over a longer time and some devices do not insert false "ones" until the overall density drops below design point. Other units scramble the DS-1 stream using consistent descrambling methods at the far end of the T1. Both these methods resolve the 15 maximum "zeros" quandary, but either compromise signal quality or bandwidth. Signals compromised by "ones" insertion contain forced errors, and the effect of the errors varies by application. Scrambling DS-1 is probabilistic and may insert errors when less frequent, but possible, patterns develop. Bandwidth approaches take about 200,000 bit/s only for the purpose of "ones" insertion and so the T1 really contains only about 1.344 Mbit/s useful for signal. Neither method yields full bandwidth and error-free operation at the same time. New methods arise to gain full use of the bandwidth and offer error-free channels.

B8ZS and Clear Channel

In the early 1980s, AT&T proposed bipolar with eight zero substitution (B8ZS) to permit any combination of "ones" and "zeros" to be sent without impacting the carrier systems. Clear channel means freedom of combination in the signal, and B8ZS substitutes a fixed pattern of previously illegal bipolar violations to signify eight successive "zeros." At the far end of the T1 line, another B8ZS decoder recognizes the pattern, removes it and returns the original eight "zeros" to the end equipment. A concern with conversion to B8ZS surrounds older equipment which called BPVs errors and removed them from the stream. This older equipment must be modified or replaced to permit B8ZS to pass unmolested through the entire connection.

Several CSU manufacturers offer units which use other methods for "zeros" substitution, but may impact the CSU's ability to operate with newer framing schemes. As networks convert to extended superframe format (ESF) framing, convergence on B8ZS is to be expected in the North American T1 arena. As Integrated Services Digital Networks (ISDN) become available, 64,000 bit/s bearer or "B" channels will require full use of bandwidth. This promotes migration to B8ZS compatible equipment permitting clear channel use of all eight bits. European T1 networks may arrive earlier at clear channel operation through another method called HDB3.

HDB3 Binary Signal Coding

CCITT recommendations offer a high density bipolar three code for "zero" substitution. Substituting every four successive "zeros" with one of two bipolar violation patterns, HDB3 carries the four zeros in substituted marks or "ones." AMI and both "zeros" substitution patterns (B8ZS and HDB3), as shown in Figure 5.8, offer a richness of pulses and also balance the frequency of positive and negative pulses to prevent DC voltage bias on the signal line. DC voltage bias occurs when there are more positive than negative pulses (or vice versa) and the average value of the voltage on the line drifts away from zero volts. This DC drift confuses regenerator electronics and may contribute to bit or pulse decoding

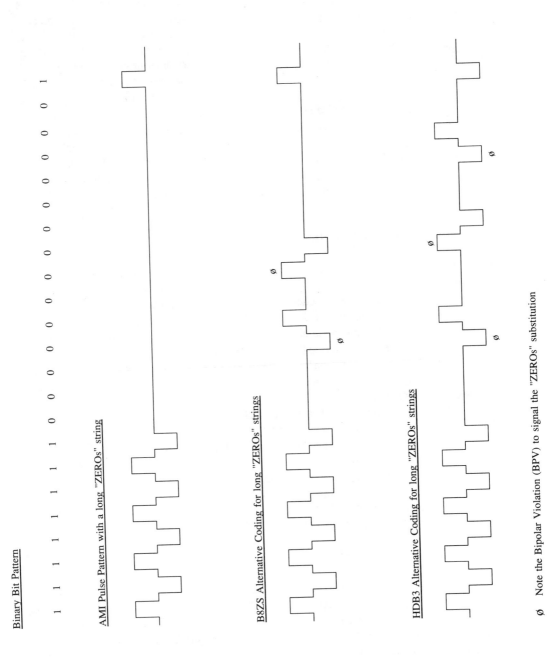

Binary Bit Pattern

1   1   1   1   1   1   1   0   0   0   0   0   0   0   0   0   0   0   0   1

AMI Pulse Pattern with a long "ZEROs" string

B8ZS Alternative Coding for long "ZEROs" strings

HDB3 Alternative Coding for long "ZEROs" strings

Ø   Note the Bipolar Violation (BPV) to signal the "ZEROs" substitution

FIGURE 5.8. AMI, B8ZS and HDB3 Pulse Pattern Comparison.

errors and to **jitter** (a timing problem discussed at length in Chapter 7). While pure AMI will remain with us for some years, B8ZS and HDB3 techniques will migrate steadily into digital networks to make way for clear channels and ISDN.

T1/D4 Error Signals

So far, discussion of DS-1 bit streams concentrated on the normal T1/D4 or T1/ESF frame and channel assignments within the frame. But other signal streams may occur on T1 under abnormal situations. These other signals act to notify connected equipment of faults on the line or in the equipment. Certain signal patterns pass alarm information or control maintenance actions in the equipment. These other signal types fall into two primary groups of alarm and control. Alarm signals take curious names from an uncertain history. Some may have derived from the color of alarm lamps on early equipment, but others just appeared and have stayed in common usage. The first group of alarm signals use colors for names.

A *red alarm* (perhaps named from the red lamp signifying local failure) is a local equipment alarm indicating a sustained framing failure of an incoming network DS-1 signal. A red alarm on equipment connected to a T1 carrier tells us that a number of frame bits or the entire frame pattern of the incoming DS-1 signal has been lost for more than several seconds. The red alarm usually first indicates visually on the equipment detecting the frame failure and then alters the normal outbound DS-1 stream. This responding outbound signal, called a *yellow alarm*, warns the network that the other (incoming) side of the T1 has failed to frame up. Yellow alarm signals in T1/D4 currently take several forms, with the most common being the setting of a bit in every channel to "zero." In T1/ESF, an alternating pattern of eight "ones" and eight "zeros" transits the data link back toward the network to tell of the frame failure.

Frame failure may occur in several ways. A total loss of incoming signal certainly results in a frame failure, but so does a heavily errored but still pulsing line. As T1 carriers nominally operate error free for long periods, the red/yellow alarm scheme indicates a serious problem. Yellow alarms, when recognized by network equipment, permit rapid isolation of circuit and equipment faults by segmenting or separating sections of the circuit. Sectionalizing may be a heavy word, but it represents a physical or conceptual segregating of pieces of a long circuit. With T1/D4, the line must usually be sectionalized by disconnecting the spans or links in the total circuit. With T1/ESF, unit error registers may be examined through data link requests while the line still attempts to operate. Segmenting the circuit may also be initiated by examining test points in the network for arrival of yellow (or other) alarms. Since much of the equipment carrying the digital signal examines the frame pattern, the first unit to return a yellow alarm may be at the end of a failing section. This is illustrated in Figure 5.9.

Another colored alarm found in DS-1 signals is the *blue* or *all ones signal*. This alarm results from a total loss of DS-1 signal entering either network equipment or connected customer T1 generating equipment. A *blue alarm*, also called a *keep-alive signal*, indicates total absence of incoming DS-1 signal. The keep-alive name provides both quick identification of the failure point and a signal to maintain the rest of the circuit in synchronization and operation, that is, keep it alive. Notice in the figure above that the blue signal from the left causes a red alarm at the right, which in turn, sends a return yellow alarm. This alarm scheme, enhanced by T1/ESF segmentation, offers tools for rapid diagnosis and repair of failing circuit sections. As the alarm signals arrive at a user's location and equipment,

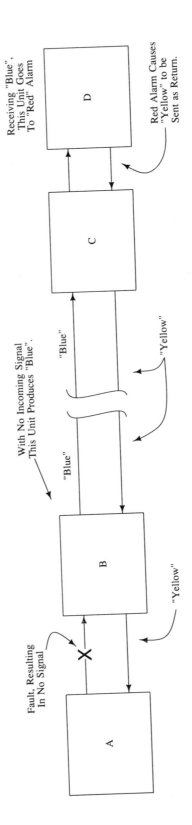

FIGURE 5.9. Alarm Signals and Circuit Segmentation.

opportunities also exist to switch to alternate facilities while awaiting original circuit repair. When a valid DS-1 signal again appears, the blue alarm signal ceases and the regular-framed signal again enters the circuit.

T1/D4 Loopback Signals

The only control signal defined for T1/D4 drives device loopbacks. Loopback, while disruptive to the main signal stream, offers the best method for circuit verification and error segmentation. Channel service units, certified under Part 68 of the Federal Communications Commission, recognize a specific pulse pattern as a command to loopback or return an incoming network signal as an outbound signal. With loopback, end-to-end operation or segment operation may be performed from one end of the circuit or segment. A T1 test signal generator (test set) passes a known bit pattern into the suspect circuit and examines the result returned from the loopback point. If the link operates error free, the test signal returns, without errors. If errors occur, they may be counted and compared to expected or previously measured performance. If no signal or a blue or yellow alarm returns, the link or some of its equipment may have failed or the loopback signal did not get through. In this case, further segmentation, substitution and testing continues until the offending piece is identified and replaced. After replacement, the loopback and testing tries again to validate good operation.

Loopback signals in T1/D4 consist of at least five continuous seconds of a loop-up pattern:

$$...10000100001000...$$

within full, normal D4 framing. The **loop-up signal** arriving at a user CSU from the Network Interface (NI) causes the CSU to loop the network signal back to the outbound side of the NI. Most CSUs will continue to hold the loopback state until reset by a **loop-down command.** The loop-down command, which also runs for a minimum of five seconds, is:

$$...100100100010010...$$

and is also D4 framed. Many T1 test sets will generate these T1/D4 loop-up and loop-down patterns in preparation for transmitting test signals. CSU panel switches also generate the loopback patterns, but a caution is in order when users generate loopback signals into a private or a carrier's network. If a T1/D4 circuit consists only of a CSU at each end and regenerators in the span, the loopback signal from one end will cause loopback at the other end and vice-versa.

In a more complex network, however, advance knowledge and cooperation are needed, as more than one piece of equipment may accept the loopback command. In this case, the loopback and subsequent tests may not tell the whole tale. If the user's loopback causes the first network box to loop-back, then only a short portion of the circuit will be tested. When this test shows error free operation, maintenance personnel are lead off on a false trail. Single-ended testing must assure that the entire circuit responds. Initial acceptance testing, done before production operation, and with personnel at each end, establishes where loopback commands take. Test sets permit manual injection of errors and a process exchanging loopback and injected errors tells how things really operate. CSUs may need options or straps changed to cause this to happen. If a carrier is involved, the carrier's people should be invited to verify the commands and tests. Operation of user CSUs, carrier repeaters and carrier office equipment then sets the baseline for future tests.

Digital Repeaters and Regenerators

Digital repeaters amplify digital signal streams permitting long-distances between digital office equipment. Repeaters revive signals weakened and distorted by normal attenuation due to cable characteristics. The advantage of digital streams for carrying many simultaneous conversations or data connections is lost when the signal drops too low for reliable differentiation between a pulse and no pulse. Engineering sets standard lengths for each type of copper pair cable; repeaters may be in manholes or on poles, but their function remains the same. They recover the low incoming signal (in each direction), derive fresh timing, and shape a more powerful pulse train for transmission to the next point in the overall span. Most designs dictate that T1 wire carrier systems place repeaters and regenerators at intervals, called **repeater sections,** of about a mile on ordinary copper pair cables. Repeater functions consist of four major parts, preamplifiers, regenerators, DC powering and line build-outs.

Line Repeater Functions and Options

Preamplifiers take weakened signals from the cable pair and amplify them to useable levels for timing recovery (regeneration) and output. The preamplifier also separates the signal from any DC power riding on the incoming pair. After amplification, the repeater shapes the pulses to their original AMI, B8ZS or HDB3 form. Since these three schemes really alter only meanings of multiple pulses, the repeater need only square-up the individual pulses and power them for the onward trip. Following the amplification, timing recovery switches the pulses out at the correct timing. Timing recovery uses simple electronic techniques to gate or permit the output pulse when the recovered timing dictates. Timing gating derives from the amplified input pulse train and may involve active and complex electronics or may consist of a few diodes. Here lies the reasoning for keeping any DC signal component (voltage level) on the pulses very low. If a DC level develops in the pulse train, timing recovery may switch at the wrong moment for each outgoing pulse and the error may not be recoverable. DC components which fluctuate alter the timing over short time periods and add jitter to the signal stream.

Jitter is the name for short-term variations in inter-pulse timing and will receive full treatment in Chapter 7, but jitter contributions must be watched at each device in a digital stream to prevent jitter build-up. Even well-designed repeaters may add jitter if the pulse signal stream varies its DC level due to improper balances of positive "ones" and negative "ones", and this is a property of the signal stream and not the repeater or timing regenerator. This jitter producing DC component must not be confused with the DC powering supplied over the same copper pair as the signal.

DC powering of repeaters uses the signal pairs, but sends the power so as not to affect the signal. One side of the powering DC current comes to the repeater using both wires of a pair. That is, one polarity of DC power signal arrives on the westbound signal pair and the other polarity connects to the eastbound pair. The same DC power is present in roughly equal amounts on both wires of the pair and the preamplifier connects to the line with a transformer to isolate the DC power from the signal stream. On the output side of the repeater, another transformer again isolates power from signal. DC power, provided at one or both connected telephone offices, supplies the repeaters between them. Engineering specifies the power strapping at each repeater to pass or loop the power. At one repeater in the span, power from both end offices loops back to those offices providing complete DC current paths for all repeaters in the span. (On short spans, powering may be done completely from one office.) The point selected for this power loop comes from the lengths of the sections in the total inter-office span. Span lengths also determine the line build out.

Line build out does exactly what it says, it builds out additional length to a line. To prevent making field adjustments to repeater signal gains, the concept of line build outs developed. Repeaters, usually designed to work over distances of 6,000 feet, may be used with shorter distances. Repeater design provides enough signal strength to carry 6,000 feet, but may overpower a preamplifier at a shorter distance. Preamplifiers accept a certain range of signal power without distortion, but the range must be held down to keep designs simple and reliable. To compensate, one of several **line build outs** (LBO) or pads may be installed once the repeater section length is known. LBOs or pads may be straps set in the field or small component boards which snap in. An important point to note, LBOs usually are only placed on the outbound or transmit signal to build out short lines. The signal expected at the inbound side preamplifier is thus corrected before leaving on the section length. LBOs offer adjustment to tailor an installation but, once installed, remain constant and stand no risk of field misadjustment. As an LBO only affects the outbound or amplified and shaped signal, there exists only one LBO per line in a line repeater, and it must strapped optioned or installed for the distance toward the next receiving repeater. At the ends of the span, office repeaters terminate the digital carrier.

Office Repeater Functions

Office repeaters function as the interface units between T-Carrier lines (and their line repeaters) and office equipment such as multiplexing and cross-connect units. Office repeaters differ little from line repeaters electrically, but are designed for equipment racks rather than manholes. Powering may be done with telephone type 24 or 48 volt DC batteries or with power supplies from the AC system. When AC powering is used in private systems, the effect of power failures must be assessed. If the repeaters carry signals from other AC powered equipment, the cost of DC batteries may be avoided. If, however, signals must continue through local power failures, battery powering should be used. Battery selection, installation and safety considerations are beyond the scope of this book, but excellent assistance can be readily found from battery vendors. As some batteries may vent danger-ous gasses during charging, design, safety and local jurisdiction code reviews are manda-tory.

Additional functions available with office repeaters include alarms and associated **automatic protection switching** (APS) systems. Alarm and APS systems provide an ability to switch to spare span lines when a single span failure occurs. Switching may be manual through the use of patch panels and cords or may be automatic with APS units.

Automatic protection switches exist throughout both telephone company and private T1 systems to assure continuity of service. Within telephone networks most T1s between telephone offices are protected. This means spare T1 circuits, held in reserve to back up line failures, switch in to carry signals from a failed line. Protection may be arranged on a single spare for every operational T1 circuit, called "one-for-one" protection or, more likely, is accomplished on a "one-for-N" basis. One spare, but working, circuit backs up four, or seven or more signal carrying T1 circuits. Automatic switching to the spare occurs when the APS system detects a failure on the inbound signal stream. The APS switches both outbound and inbound signal streams to the spare carrier and, due to the subsequent failure at the far end, the other APS also switches. Multiple layers of protection can exist when T1s are combined to form higher level T-Carriers in the T-Carrier hierarchy.

North American Hierarchy Multiplexing

Advantages and benefits of T1 digital carriers soon drove engineers to combine T1s into groups for yet more efficient transmission. T1C could group two T1s, T2 systems grouped 4 T1s and T3s combined 28 T1s. To do this, additional digital multiplexing developed. Some engineers use the term **muldem** (MULtiplexer/DEMultiplexer), some use **digital multiplexer,** and most just call it a **MUX.** The terms are generally interchangeable above T1. Terminology for T-Carrier multiplexing simplifies to an "M", followed by the T-Carrier levels into and out of the device. That is, a muldem combining four T1s into one T2 becomes an M12, and a unit combining two T1s into a T1C is an M1C. Similarly, a muldem pulling together seven T2s into a T3 is an M23. Many times, a middle step will be skipped in nomenclature, even though the step is electronically used. An M13 may package an M12 with an M23.

The figure illustrates some possible combinations of the various muldems and T-Carriers built from the basic 24 channels and the T1 (North American) carrier.

Higher T-Carriers exist, but standards for these levels continue in development. The approaches and muldem techniques between levels remain quite consistent, permitting rapid agreement between carriers, makers and users. A study of T1 through T3 structure should ease understanding of yet higher level Ts. This background, then, prepares the path for closer examination of each carrier and the muldem relationships between them. A key ingredient in higher level multiplexing is T1 timing independence; this needs to be understood to cope with the apparent complexities of T2 and T3 multiplexers.

T1 timing independence stems from the many sources of T1 signal streams and the fact that each may run through a single higher level multiplexer. The many sources, options and methods of digital timing forms the entire content of Chapter 7. Here, assume that T1s may operate at rates which, while close to 1.544 Mbit/s, actually exist over a range of speeds. Earlier it was noted that T1s must operate within ±75 bit/s, and this tolerance gives rise to a narrow timing independence. The technical word for this timing situation comes from adding *plesio* (the Greek word for "near"), to the Greek word for time, *chronos*. *Plesiochronous,* to be detailed in Chapter 7, means that two signals run nearly, but not exactly, at the same rate. When more than one T1 arrives at a multiplexer, and each runs at a slightly differing rate, the multiplexer must somehow cope.

The multiplexer copes by assuming each incoming T1 runs at its slowest permissible rate, and by adding or stuffing additional bits to bring it above its fastest permissible rate. T1s running faster then need fewer stuff bits, but all T1s are stuffed up to higher fixed rate. These stuffed fast rate T1s combine in the multiplexer, along with other bits to tell where the stuffed bits were placed. Upon demultiplexing, the stuff bits are removed and the T1s are sent out at their original rate by using elastic buffers. Elastic buffers act to smooth out the rate of the T1 signal which becomes jerky due to stuff bit removal. A full discussion of elastic buffers must wait for Chapter 7, but this preview hopes to explain why higher level

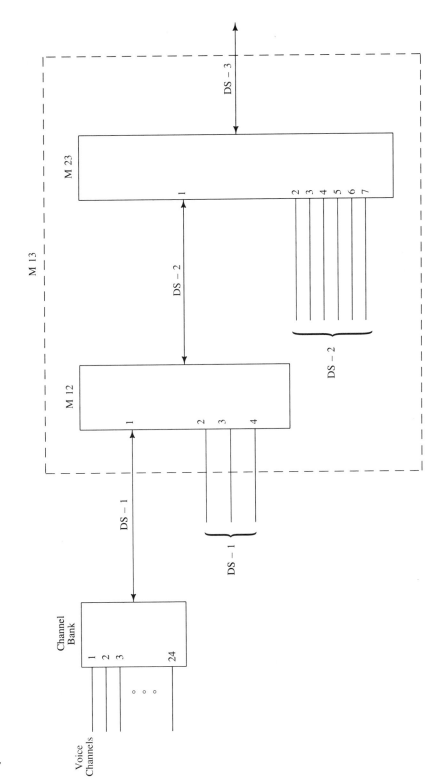

FIGURE 5.10. T-Carrier Combinations (North American Hierarchy).

T-Carrier rates do not match a simple multiplication of the lower speeds. For instance, a T2 operates at 6.312 Mbit/s and this is 136,000 bit/s faster than the four T1 carried by the T2. Similarly a T3, which combines seven T2s, runs 552,000 bit/s faster than the product of 7 and 6.312 Mbit/s. These rate differences make sense only when stuffing and timing independence come into play. Figure 5.11 lists combinations and bit rates for the North American Hierarchy.

The concepts developed from T1 to T2 and T3 and similar concepts found in SYNTRAN and SONET standards (see Chapter 7) will continue the drive toward standards for ever-higher level T-Carriers. Needs and capacities for communications tend to make quantum leaps, but not always together in time. New capacities and the availability of higher speeds drive engineers to develop new devices and applications. This has been called by some the **interstate effect,** paralleling curious phenomenon of traffic jams on newly built super highways. A major new set of applications will arrive with the ready availability of trans-ocean T-Carriers. Here, the differences between European and American T-Carriers must resolve. While the North American Hierarchy built upon a 24 channel T1, the Europeans chose 30 channels for their first level T1 and the result produced two incompatible sets. Before examining methods to connect them, we need to look at the European T-Carrier family.

CCITT and CEPT Hierarchy Multiplexing

CEPT, the European Conference on Post and Telecommunications Administrations, set standards for digitized voice on time division multiplexing based on 30 channels. While differences also exist in signaling and digitizing methods (μ–Law vs. A-law rules for

Carrier Level	Speed Mbit/s	Number of Channels
T1	1.544	24 Voice Channels or 24 56 kbit/s Data Channels
T2	6.312	4 T1 Channels or 96 Voice or 56 kbit/s Channels
T3	44.736	7 T2 Channels or 28 T1 Channels or 672 Voice or 56 kbit/s Data Channels

FIGURE 5.11. North American T-Carrier Speed Relationships.

digitizing voice signals, for example), the basic rate of 64,000 bit/s for the DS-0 equivalent channel is the same. This commonality at the lowest digital level means much to data communications professionals, as 56,000 bit/s channels may be sent from the North American structure to the European. More difficulty exists in routing a terrestrial European 64,000 bit/s data circuit after it reaches North America, but it is not impossible. Several techniques will be covered in Chapter 13, multivendor integration. At the higher level T-Carriers, much work remains. An examination of the CEPT levels exposes the differences. The bridge of conceptual commonality was crossed in 1984, when the CCITT adopted both the North American and CEPT levels in the CCITT "G-series" recommendations. Figure 5.12 compares the North American Hierarchy (and the Japanese variation) with the European CEPT levels.

At its 1984 plenary assembly, the CCITT incorporated both the North American and the CEPT hierarchies in the "G-series" of recommendations. CCITT recommendation G.702 recommends those hierarchical rates already in place as shown in Figure 5.12, and suggests gently that the CEPT hierarchy (2.048 Mbit/s primary level) "... could be a preferred solution ..." for compatibility. Within hierarchy borders, however, both sets of levels will continue for many years. Two factors continue the drive toward compatibility solutions, digital voice and its successor, ISDN. Both 64 kbit/s digital voice and Integrated Services Digital Networks "B" channels use the 64,000 bit/s rate as their fundamental building block. Between hierarchy borders, compatibility solutions focus above the first levels and suggest that three North American T3 (44.736 Mbit/s) carriers would fit within a CEPT fourth level of 139.264 Mbit/s to connect the T-Carriers.

Connecting CCITT and North American T-Carriers

Direct intercontinental interchange of data channels at 56,000 or 64,000 bit/s may be achieved at a cost, but direct T1 interchange between continents presents some problems. One difficulty lies not in the intercontinental link, but in the domestic circuit from that link to its end location. European carriers do not easily provide 1.544 Mbit/s circuits and American carriers do not generally offer 2.048 Mbit/s circuits. Proposals to solve the incompatibility suggest new combinations of multiplexing both North American and European T1s onto the fourth CEPT level of 139.264 Mbit/s. Special multiplexing of this type, called **M34E,** permits three standard North American Standard (NAS) T3s to be combined to a CEPT rate of 139.264 Mbit/s. On the European side a special multiplexer combines 21 CEPT T1s onto the same rate facility. Combinations of these special multiplexers and multiplex systems converters will permit almost all combinations to connect (or pass across) currently incompatible regions. Solutions are underway to simplify the conversion of signaling and voice digitization. For the digital data user, 56 and 64 kbit/s and 1.544 and 2.048 Mbit/s interconnection will be possible through international switching centers which will house the special multiplexers. Local access (to a region) using special speeds may remain more difficult for a little longer.

Digital Cross-connect

Digital cross-connect, introduced in Chapter 3, extends the concept of wired circuit cross-connection to a digital world. Cross-connection still means the wiring of an individual circuit to another at a central point. In an analog environment, circuits arrive on copper

Digital Level	Speed in Mbit/s for the 1.544 Hierarchy	Speed in Mbit/s for the 2.048 Hierarchy
1	1.544	2.048
2	6.312	8.448
3	32.064* 44.736	34.368
4	97.728*	139.264

* Variation used in Japan

FIGURE 5.12. North American T-Carrier and CEPT Digital Levels and Speeds.

pairs and connect to each other physically at connection blocks. Cross-connection completes through circuits from incoming copper to outgoing copper. For example, a leased circuit arriving at one central office cross-connects to an outgoing circuit to continue the routing of the leased circuit. The cross-connection, accomplished by physical wiring, remains fixed until the connection is no longer needed. Physical cross-connections form reliable and semi-permanent routes, but reconfiguration is both labor intensive and slow. When individual circuits arrive, not on copper pairs but imbedded as bits in digital streams, cross-connection needs new methods. Traditional connection means demultiplexing the signal to derive the single circuit and then cross-connecting on physical blocks. After connection, the signal must again be multiplexed back up to a digital carrier. This method inserts noise due to analog to digital conversion and adds significant equipment. Digital cross-connection substitutes electronics for the physical wiring and preserves the entire circuit in its digital form.

Digital Cross-connect Fundamentals

Understanding digital cross-connection fundamentals requires reference to known ideas and will be easier if we use T1 carriers and DS-0 channels. Digital cross-connection, in its simplest form, routes T1 bits instead of circuits, but the bits represent individual DS-0 circuits. Remembering the makeup of a T1 as twenty four D-4 type individual DS-0 channels (circuits), cross-connection collects incoming bits from each channel, places them in buffers and waits to put them in one or more outbound T1s. In most cases, the reverse direction maps channels the same way to the same end points, so that complete end-to-end connections exist. In Figure 5.13, several T1s deliver streams to the cross-connect which separates the individual DS-0 channels logically, and routes or connects them to new channel slots on other T1s. Effectively, the cross-connect unit replaces older physical connections of circuits with virtual equivalents. Note in Figure 5.13 how channel three of the upper incoming T1 (A) connects to channel four of outgoing T1 (D). The connection process, called **time slot interchange** (TSI), works under the control of a central processor, and here lies the first key advantage of the digital cross-connect—programmability. By altering the program instructions to the central processor, channels are relocated through time slot interchange to new connections. This key advantage allows a single operator to re-route many hundreds of circuits using only a keyboard. Alternate maps of the connections may be stored for frequent changes, reconfiguring the configurations rapidly at the unit.

The second key advantage of digital cross-connection jumps out from its name, *digital*. Whether connecting digital data signals or digitized voice signals, the connection stays digital. This advantage may not be as obvious as the ability to program connections from a keyboard or stored memory map, but close examination will reveal it. When T1 carriers first transported voice signals, digitized by D-type channel banks, it was realized that the analog to digital (A-to-D) conversion process added quantizing noise. This quantizing noise results from minute errors introduced by making digital decisions about analog signals. No matter how fine the analog signal is cut, the final digital value differs slightly from the analog reality and this quantizing error remains after re-conversion to analog. If the A-to-D process repeats a number of times, the quantizing noise adds to a point where signal quality degrades. Using 64 kbit/s A-to-D methods, signal quality measurements display serious degradation after about seven conversions. Each A-to-D conversion must, of course, be followed by re-conversion to analog. While seven conversions may not be

likely in smaller networks, large networks may need to pass through multiple cross-connections. By retaining the end-to-end digital nature of the circuits, only the first small amount
of quantizing noise is added. Changes in routing caused by digital cross-connections do not
degrade the signal at all, and the small additional delay in cross-connection buffers does not
differ substantially from buffering in multiple A-to-D conversions.

Digital cross-connections appear in networks in several forms. In the public switched
network, **digital access and cross-connect systems** (DACS) and similar digital cross-connect devices are replacing analog systems. Also, very large digital telephone switches are
being installed in private networks. Newer types of time division multiplexers, discussed at
length in Chapter 12, offer digital cross-connect functions. The common thread, at the T1
level, is the ability to switch, route, or connect individual sub-T1 rate (or sub-rate) channels.
All of these devices may function as described above, retaining digital end-to-end connections, and providing either switched (short duration) or leased (long duration) type circuits.
In addition, many application functions such as multi-point bridging and broadcast are now
handled digitally by these units.

Digital Cross-connect Applications

Bridging and broadcast form the first special applications of digital cross-connect,
but the power offered by such units makes new services and applications possible. In
multipoint bridging, a single circuit arrives at a cross-connection and departs simultaneously on several other circuits to form digital multidrop data connections. The circuits
bridge together at the cross-connect and the user's end equipment DTEs manage polling
and response. In broadcast applications, the single circuit on the input side broadcasts or
sends the same signal to a large number of output circuits. Beyond the similar functions of
bridging and broadcast come new types of applications. If an operator at a terminal can
re-route network lines, then an authorized call to the operator can direct those changes. If
another terminal at a user location sends the change messages to the operator, then the user
gains control of a piece of the network and leased (or private) circuits may be changed as
needed. This form of network reconfiguration, now offered by major telephone carriers,
will be described in Chapter 8. That chapter will deal with carrier services. Exact details
and latest offerings, though, should be obtained from the carriers themselves.

Digital Cross-connect and non-D4 Channelization

While more about proprietary channelization on T-Carriers will be said in Chapter 12
on time division multiplexers, a word about compatibility with digital cross-connect must
be mentioned here. A unit with proprietary channelization would seem to be incompatible
with digital cross-connect switching, but a non-D4 channelized stream may pass through,
as long as D4 (or ESF) framing is present. Passing through may be accomplished if the
cross-connect routes or switches *all* 24 channels and retains the original channel order. That
is, incoming channel one must be assigned to outgoing channel one, channel two to channel
two, and so on. Even if the device's channels do not fall within the eight bit boundaries of
a DS-0, preserving channel order will keep the bits in the right order. If the digital
cross-connect does not disturb the order, or the timing, of the original DS-1 stream, all bits
within the D4 frame should pass successfully. Clearly, manufacturer and carrier agreement
and testing should precede commitment to service with such an arrangement.

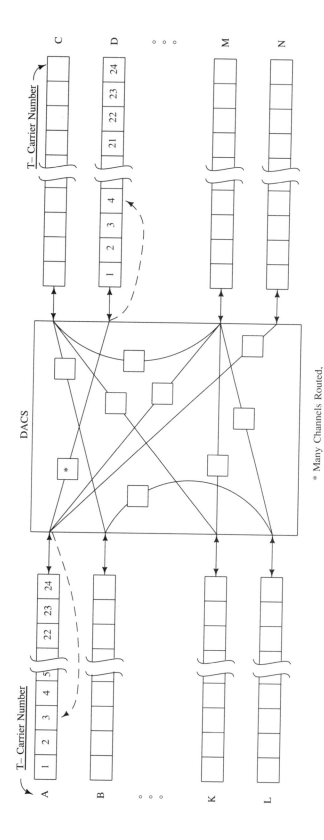

FIGURE 5.13. Digital Cross-connect Routing Example.

This brief overview of T-Carriers builds a basis for further study which is strongly recommended. T-Carriers have become the skeletal structure for digital communications in the next wave of developments. Voice, data and video signals ride today on T-Carriers and the concepts and fundamentals form the bases for Integrated Services Digital Networks (ISDN) covered in Chapter 14. Next we look at digital interface units where MIS and computer data worlds come together with the world of digital telecommunications.

CHAPTER 6

Digital Interface Units

Chapter Overview

After nearly fifty years of regulatory stability, telecommunications in the United States was swept into a new era in the early 1980s. Regulatory changes, anti-trust judgments and competition created a "brave new world." This new world brought the divestiture of AT&T, creation of independent local telephone companies, "equal access," and the separation of services; it also brought complexity to the user. Perhaps nowhere did this new complexity strike harder at data than in digital interface units. Data communications people, once concerned only with interfaces between **data termination equipment** (DTE) and **data communications equipment** (DCE), now faced **network interfaces** (NI), equipment certification, mixed vendor environments and an explosion of terminology. No longer could one "telephone company" supply a circuit and DCEs and take care of it all. Now users could (and for a time had to) buy DCEs and meet the network at a block on the wall. Continuing regulatory changes have eased early confusions, but the new world still requires users to make informed choices in this area of digital interface units. This chapter delves into that brave new world of choice.

In a post-divestiture world of telecommunications, each user needs a greater understanding and a road map to make informed choices. This chapter draws a map and introduces **customer premises equipment** (CPE), the **network interface** (NI), **data service units** (DSU), **channel service units** (CSU), **private digital systems** and **limited distance digital data units.** It also explains digital concepts, operations, new interface points, and terminologies and will show how to make them work together. The chapter also explores digital interface units for both carrier services and for private network use. Digital interface units for **digital data services** (DDS) and for T1 carriers are also detailed and explained. A few comments relate these technical matters to continuing divestiture moves and regulatory changes, but our main concern here is how things work.

Post-divestiture Environment

For many years, telephone company data circuits included both transmission and the equipment needed to translate telephone circuit electronics to data communications interfaces. Users rarely thought of data sets as other than a place where the data circuit met the data equipment. These units had been, for many years, on the user's premises; divestiture brought the name, **customer premises equipment** (CPE), to everyone's notice. CPE still provides the same function, but now comes from many sources and is usually controlled by users, not carriers. With the advent of private transmission circuits and networks, CPE took on a new role—interfacing with user transmission equipment. Bypass, or direct user connections to long-distance carriers, brought needs to understand not only CPE, but what happened in the networks or the bypass. Using current digital CPE requires, at least, a minimal knowledge of the local circuit and equipment at the other end of the wires. First, however, we will examine the nature of the CPE itself.

CPE forms the end-point equipment of a circuit and is found, physically, at a user's building, office, campus or home. In the new world, user selected CPE must provide functions to two parties—users and carriers. Each party places needs on this unit to satisfy function. In digital data communications, well understood DTE/DCE interfaces form the user side of the CPE. Functions at the carrier or network circuit side are not as well understood, but they are federally regulated and open to view. The point where CPE meets the carrier's network circuit takes the name **network interface** (NI) and is usually tariffed and regulated. The reasoning behind this regulation begins with protecting the network and personnel who work on it. Protecting means preventing damaging signals or voltages from appearing on network lines which might harm people working on the lines or equipment attached to the circuits. Additional functions available at the NI may include carrier supplied DC power and requirements for the CPE to recognize and act on network diagnostic signals. A process called **equipment registration** ties together the physical and electrical specifications with protection requirements needed for CPE to meet the NI.

Registration and the Network Interface (NI)

Under current rules of the U.S. Federal Communications Commission (FCC), equipment connecting to public switched analog circuits (normal telephone lines), **digital data services** (DDS), and **local area data channels** (LADC) must be registered. (Local area data channels are leased circuits usually within a single telephone office serving area.) These rules and specifications are contained in Part 68 of the FCC's Rules and Regulations. While most users need never refer to these rules, it is important that users recognize that rules exist and that vendor equipment meet the rules at the network interface. While registration (sometimes called **certification**) has been required for many years on analog telephone equipment, registration for digital data connections began in 1986.

A process called **grandfathering,** or listing of equipment in service prior to a closing date of registration is used in order to allow continued use of older equipment. Registration for new equipment may be done by the equipment vendor or by private testing laboratories who specialize in registration. Another process listed under FCC rules concerns electrical radiation which could cause interference to radio communications. Compliance with these rules, described in Subpart J of Part 15 of the FCC Rules and Regulations, affects radiated energy from equipment in a commercial environment. Protection from interference in a residential environment is not covered, and users may need to "take whatever measures may be required to correct the interference." These measures will usually be at the user's expense.

For network connection, FCC rules Part 68 detail some of the network requirements. Additional requirements come from carrier publications and will be listed later in this chapter. Part 68 of FCC rules also details physical and electrical requirements for other devices connected to a telephone network. The most widely known and used devices are telephones. Specifications required by Part 68 include small modular jacks which "plug in the phone." For standard telephone circuits in the United States, **registered jack number 11** (RJ-11) forms the predominant interface to the telephone wires. Many other RJ-type jacks exist for both voice and data communications and are proposed as connectors for Integrated Services Digital Networks (ISDN). Figure 6.1 shows a sketch of a typical RJ-type connector. RJ-type connectors come in many versions, but most are either six or eight-pins and are either keyed or non-keyed. Figure 6.1 illustrates a keyed eight-pin modular jack and is among those found at the network interface.

The network interface exists as a physical point where a user's wiring meets the carrier's wiring. In connections to carrier services, a carrier's wiring enters a user's facility and terminates at some point short of the user's devices. Users must then continue circuits from the NI, also sometimes called a "demarc," or **demarcation,** to their CPE equipment. This may be as simple as a telephone-type extension cable or may involve significant **inside wiring.** Inside wiring and CPE, in the current regulatory climate, are completely the user's responsibility. This responsibility may, of course, be delegated to others; many companies now offer complete installation and maintenance. Opportunities and variations on this theme will be covered in some detail in Chapter 13 when we discuss multivendor environments. Ultimate responsibility for correct operation of inside circuits and CPE remains, however, with the user.

Private Network Equipment

An old concept flowered about the time of divestiture, that is, the concept of a private network. While private networks have existed for many years using leased circuits from telephone carriers, the connotation today adds a new dimension, namely, private circuit

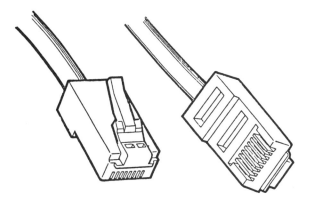

FIGURE 6.1. Typical Registered Jack—RJ-type Connector.

ownership. Privately owned data circuits have existed since the first **null-modem** connected two DTEs back-to-back, but scope and scale are changing. Private networks will
receive full treatment in Chapter 11, but an outline is needed here to permit discussion of
digital interface units.

In scale, private networks now encompass national and international private circuits
derived from higher speed carrier facilities. The rapidly growing use of carrier T1 circuits
for private voice, data, and digitized video illustrates this type of private network. As long
as economies of scale favor this mode of operation, and as long as large volume users need
this capacity, private networks will flourish. Private network scope is changing, too.
Beyond leases for high-speed circuits, users now build transmission facilities. Inexpensive
small microwave transmitters mounted on several rooftops permit rapid and cost-effective
high-speed links between parts of an organization. Larger microwave systems, spanning
hills and rivers, are in use by large corporations to connect their people and computers.
Private fiber optic cable installations are planned, thereby putting companies, colleges, and
governments in the telecommunications business to serve their own needs and reduce their
costs. In this type of private network environment, digital data interface units may take
several very different forms from those used in leased carrier networks; or they may be the
same.

Digital data devices used with public carrier networks must, as said above, meet
regulatory and technical criteria set by carrier or regulatory processes. In wholly private
networks, **data communications equipment** or DCEs may range more widely. If a fiber
cable exists only to connect computers on a campus, it does not make sense to convert all
signals to a common carrier accepted format and speed. A pair of direct computer-channel
to computer-channel fiber optic devices will accomplish the objective and minimize costs.
Local digital DCEs used to drive signals over local inside wiring or private cables need not
meet the more stringent public network specifications. Many requirements imposed by
public carriers concern the ability of network trouble centers to remotely diagnose equipment. If a repair technician can walk to both ends of a circuit in five minutes, such exotic
diagnostic circuitry is unneeded.

If, however, a private network emulates a public network including typical telephone
carrier equipment, then telephone carrier type specifications should be met on the private
circuits. Here is where hard decisions must be made. If we know in advance that a private
network will not grow beyond a certain size, then limited function interface equipment
should be procured. If a network anticipates growth to significant size and scope, initial
DCEs should meet the more stringent requirements. In the material below, we will discuss
both limited function interface units for private networks and full function devices for use
on public lines.

Digital DCE Units

Data communications equipment (DCE) devices for digital services differ significantly from their analog modem cousins. Unlike analog modems, which convert serial
digital bit streams to serial analog tones, digital DCEs convert only the form of digital bit
streams. Why is so much circuitry needed to convert signals from digital to digital?
Understanding the somewhat complex answers to this simple question will uncover many
significant variations from earlier analog DCEs. A few functions remain the same between

digital interface units, DCEs, and analog units; these functions are those used by **data termination equipment** (DTE). We begin with those common functions.

The DTE devices meet our digital interface units (or DCEs) at interfaces described in Chapter 4. These are DTE-to-DCE interfaces, such as V.35 and EIA-530. Data interfaces neither know nor care whether the DCE and the transmission circuit are digital or analog. Across these interfaces, data, control and timing functions must be maintained for DTEs to function. Substitution of digital DCEs for analog DCEs should, at least within limits, be transparent to the DTEs. Data pulses or bit streams such as unipolar serial data pulses are handled by digital units in the same manner as analog units. Control signals, also as described in Chapter 4, perform similar functions. **Data set ready** (DSR) still means power is on in the DCE and **data terminal ready** is still accepted as evidence that the terminal device has power. Some control signals, while appearing to provide similar functions, actually perform slightly different tasks. For example, **received line signal detect** (RLSD) or **carrier detect** (CD) cannot actually detect a carrier where none is used. The function is retained, however, by monitoring continuity of digital pulses from the network and indicating this as RLSD. **Request to send** (RTS) still offers a return **clear to send** (CTS) when the digital interface unit is ready to transmit outbound data signals. Differences show up, however, in the handling of timing signals.

Timing pulses still clock data pulses for transmit and receive, but are usually restricted to network originated clocking. External timing pins may exist at the interface, but timing may really only be used if it originates from the network. Internal timing and external (or **business machine clocking**) usually may not be used on a carrier's digital network circuit. In most cases, digital DCEs will accept received timing as any other DCE device, but will be set to **loop time**; that is, use recovered received network timing for transmit timing. Digital network timing and synchronization occupies all of the next chapter; sources of digital network clocking will be covered. This timing source limitation begins a discussion of things which are not quite common between analog and digital DCEs.

Uncommon functions between analog and digital DCEs concern attachment to a digital network interface (NI). Attachment of digital DCEs to digital local loops requires both new functions and changes in analog functions. When digital services were first introduced with the announcement of DATAPHONE® Digital Services,[1] new functions were separated into two newly named unit types. These new units were **data service units** (DSU) and **channel service units** (CSU). They worked together to offer a traditional DCE function and data interface to user's data terminal or computer communications controller. Together these two units provided all the functions previously found in analog DCEs, but each performed distinct tasks and each was oriented toward its own side of the connection.

A **data service unit** (DSU) pointed toward a user's data device—the **data terminal equipment** or DTE. Notice the word "data" in both unit descriptions. The DSU provided a standard EIA-232 or V.35 data interface to existing customer data terminals or computers.

A **channel service unit or** CSU pointed toward the channel or network digital local loop. The CSU provided needed functions for the new digital local loop or digital channel. The other end of the local loop, at a telephone company local office, usually connected to a device called an **office channel unit** (OCU). With the exception of the local loop, all descriptors on the CSU side use "channel" in their names.

---

[1]Generic digital data services will be abbreviated in this text as DDS. DATAPHONE® Digital Services is a registered trademark of AT&T and will always be spelled out.

This identification using "data" and "channel" helps remind us where each unit functions. Distinctions between DSUs and CSU will remain in our lexicon for many years, as newer applications and higher speeds sometimes use only one of the two. Later in this chapter, T1 CSUs will be detailed and an absence of T1 DSUs will be noted. As we probe DSUs and CSUs for digital network services, remember the direction which each unit faces: data service units toward a user's data devices; channel service units toward a carrier's network digital channels.

Figure 6.2 on page 141 shows how all these pieces fit together in a digital services or DDS network. From the EIA-232 or V.35 interface to a user's DTE to the networks time division multiplexers and T1 carriers, data transmission is all digital. Each unit will be explained in turn.

Combined DSU/CSU units, now the most common units available, will be described following an examination of each unit, but, in concept, individual functions will remain distinct. A question develops because of these two units: what interface exists between them?

Interfaces between DSUs and CSUs may take a form similar to a CSU to network interface. That is, a four-wire connection; one pair for signals to be sent to the network and one pair for received signals. An additional pair may be supplied to carry signal ground and a status indicator. The status indicator, while functioning like data set ready (DSR), may go OFF during network controlled testing. In combined DSU/CSU devices this interface is buried in electronics in the box. The interface concept remains, however, as functional separation between DSUs and CSUs must be retained. In digital data services (DDS), combined DSU/CSU units now dominate. In T-Carrier services, channel service units most often stand alone as interface units between a user's equipment and a network. These T1 CSUs will receive full treatment after the concepts of DSUs, CSUs and combined units are covered for lower speed DDS. We now turn our attention to individual units and functions.

Data Service Unit (DSU) Functions

Data service unit functions follow those originally developed when telephone companies provided fully packaged services. A generic or conceptual DSU must offer a minimum function set to claim the name DSU. This minimum set includes:

- data and timing recovery and conversion;
- Data Communications Equipment (DCE) interfacing;
- DTE/DCE control functions appropriate to the service used; and
- functions needed by the network and CSU.

We will examine each function, beginning with data and timing recovery. Signals coming in over the CSU interface are balanced bipolar pulse trains containing data, timing and control information on a single pair of wires. As a brief reminder, bipolar signals use positive or negative pulses to carry "ones" bits and an absence of pulses to carry "zeros." The "ones" pulses must alternate in polarity, that is, a positive pulse must be followed by a negative pulse even if it is separated by several "zeros." A common term for this type of pulse train remains **alternate mark inversion** or AMI. "Ones" pulses, or marks, which do not alternate in priority are termed **bipolar violations** or BPV. (BPVs, usually avoided in T1 digital services, find use in DDS as network control signals and are discussed in the next

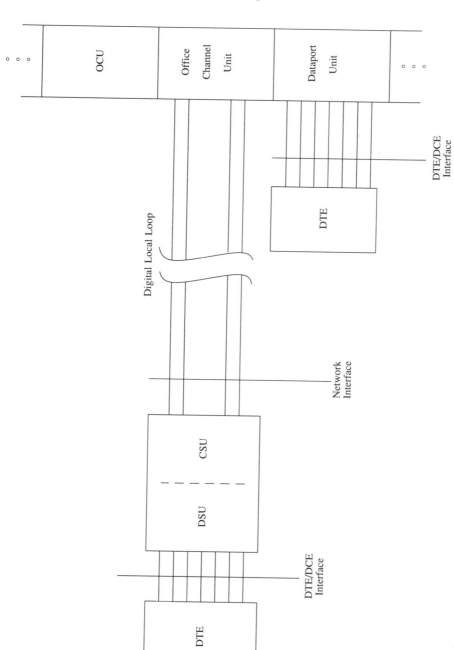

FIGURE 6.2. Units in a Digital Services Network.

section.) AMI rules, detailed fully in the following CSU section, maintain a minimum "ones" density so that a continuous timing reference can be kept.

The DSU uses this incoming pulse train of "ones" to drive a timing recovery circuit. (Remember that "zeros" are non-pulses and cannot carry any timing information.) Recovery circuits may be simple or complex, but they must find, hold and output a consistent timing pulse train signal to an attached DTE. Figure 6.3 on page 143 compares an incoming network (or CSU) received pulse train with derived timing and data signals. Note that the timing signal must continue when no incoming DDS network pulses exist.

Digital data services operate on a single system-wide synchronized clock for both transmit and receive signals. DSU timing recovery derives this system clock and generates timing pulse trains for both **transmit data timing** (TT) and **received data timing** (RT). Timing streams for both appear in Figure 6.3 and relate to the received network pulse train. Timing recovery in DDS becomes somewhat simpler due to DDS "ones" density rules preventing more than six consecutive "zeros," but timing from a network must be recovered and used. The density rules are illustrated later in this chapter in Figure 6.7 on page 153, showing how bits are added to maintain a flow of "ones" bits in digital data services. DDS network timing sources, operations and recovery will be covered in depth in the next chapter dealing with digital synchronization. With timing recovered from an AMI stream, data pulse recovery and conversion may proceed.

Data recovery simply means determining when a "one" or "zero" pulse exists on the incoming signal pair. Circuit complexity may vary, but the job has been simplified by the CSU. In a moment we shall look at CSU functions, and its task of signal regeneration, but to a DSU, it means clean signals. Data conversion takes clean network pulses and alters them electrically into EIA-232 signal levels for 2,400, 4,800 or 9,600 bit/s, or V.35 signal levels for 56,000 bit/s. These two well-known data communications standards encompass most available DDS services. Recovered timing pulses sample incoming signals at precise times, determining "ones" from positive or negative pulses or "zeros" from an absence of pulses. Determinations are made through voltage thresholds set by the DSU. Pulse voltages above certain thresholds determine "ones" and voltages below thresholds become "zeros." Both recovered timing and data signals become ready for interface voltage level conversion and DCE interfacing.

Data communications equipment (DCE) interfacing standards set voltage levels to be offered to a DTE at standard interface connectors. In the reverse direction, that is, data to be transmitted from a DTE, voltage levels from EIA-232 or V.35 interfaces are converted to AMI signals to drive the CSU. Transmit timing of DTE signals derives from recovered incoming timing to maintain network synchronization. DTE interfacing consists primarily of voltage level conversion, mechanical connectors and determining what interface control signals should do. As most control signals (discussed in Chapter 4) came from earlier analog modems, some meanings must change while functions remain roughly the same.

DTE/DCE control functions appropriate to digital services adopt meanings to simulate these older analog functions. An example is **received line signal detect** (RLSD), often called **carrier detect** in earlier communications systems. With analog modems, an actual carrier was present on incoming signal lines when a far end modem transmitted. In digital services, RLSD simulates the functions of carrier detect. That is, data pulses are coming in from a network line; but a distinction must be drawn between incoming "data" pulses and other incoming pulses. DDS services define non-data pulse streams used for DDS network control which may affect operation of DTE control signals. Typical "non-data" pulse streams arriving from network DDS lines maintain timing and indicate ready (control-idle),

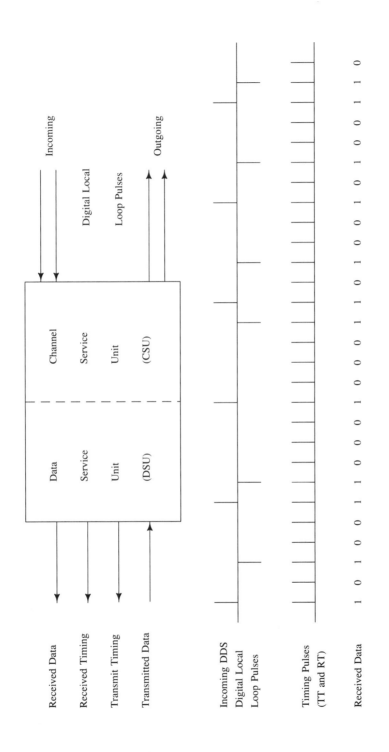

FIGURE 6.3. DDS—AMI, Timing and Data Streams.

"zeros" strings (zero suppression), trouble (out-of-service or out-of-frame) or test conditions (optional loopback). Details of these DDS non-data pulse streams and their affects will be reviewed following needed CSU functions provided by the DSU. Non-data pulse streams, however, affect operation of control signals passed to the attached DTE.

DTE control signals may receive slightly different treatment in digital interface units. **Clear to send** (CTS) may respond directly to a DTE's **request to send** (RTS) or it may be interrupted by network trouble signals. Since interpretation of CTS varies according to both DTE hardware and software, this option must be chosen carefully. As digital networks often respond very quickly to troubles by automatically re-routing digital signals, interruptions of CTS may be very brief. If a DTE interprets a momentary interruption of CTS as a complete failure of communications, operator intervention may be necessary to restart a line which really never failed. Similarly, received line signal detect (RLSD) may switch OFF and ON as the incoming line moves from control-idle to data mode. In some cases, even data set ready (DSR) may be affected by network test signals. Control signal changes should be compared carefully to expected operations which may have been assumed in analog services. Selecting options in DSUs and DTEs should now be coordinated. Some DSU functions must be provided for use by an attached (or combined) CSU.

DSU functions needed by digital service networks and CSUs also differ from analog modems. Two key differences are "carrier" behavior and network command response. Where an analog modem would turn "carrier" ON and OFF to follow a DTE's request to send (RTS) interface signal, a DSU must always produce pulses. In DDS, a DSU must generate **control-idle** pulse patterns for the CSU when RTS is turned OFF by the DTE. Control-idle signals indicate active non-data status to the network. This could be used by the network for **multipoint** (also called multistation) operation of several DSUs on a common channel. Multipoint operation in DDS follows multipoint operation in analog modem networks. In normal multipoint operation, a single master or control point unit may transmit continuously to several remote or secondary units. Secondary units usually transmit only when **polled.** Response to master station polling in analog modem systems involves recognition of the poll (usually by an attached DTE), and transmission by a secondary back to the control point. In digital services, DTEs may still raise RTS, but the DSU must stop sending control-idles and permit the DTE to send real data. The network must then sort out which secondary units sends real data and which control-idles. The network device which does the sorting is a **multipoint junction unit** (MJU).

A multipoint junction unit provides several ways to combine data from multipoint secondary units (or remote stations). A preferred method, which is less sensitive to individual bit errors, forwards to the master station only those data bits from secondary stations not in control-idle mode. When remote DTEs have request to send (RTS) in an OFF condition, digital DSUs send control-idles to the MJU. If all but one secondary unit transmits control-idles, the remaining unit's data bits pass the MJU back to the control or master station. Another, less preferred, method combines all bits arriving from all secondary units at the MJU and sends any "zeros" to the master station. This means all non-polled secondaries must send "ones" or MARKS when not sending data. This mode can be called "mark-hold." Clearly, if a line error turns a "one" into a "zero," the MJU will send the errored "zero" on to the master station. In control-idle mode, line errors could be ignored. Most commercial DSUs offer a choice between mark-hold and control-idle operation. Other control circuits from a user's DTE may also select among several different options.

Digital services networks often include special control bit patterns. Some of the more common will be listed below in the section on office channel units. One code, however, may be used to control DSU loopback from the network. This code, when recognized by the DSU's electronics, causes disconnection of data signals from the DTE interface and return of incoming network data as transmit data. This DSU loopback (also called **remote terminal test**) can confirm operation of most of a DSU's circuitry, as well as operation of the CSU and local loop. In a moment, we will examine another loopback for the CSU alone. Channel Service Unit and network functions now complete our digital interface unit picture for DDS or digital service networks.

Channel Service Unit (CSU) Functions

Facing the network interface from a user's premises, channel service units must meet digital service or DDS network requirements. Under current Federal Communications Commission regulations, CSUs attaching to digital services networks will comply with Part 68 of the FCC's rules either by registration (for newer units) or by grandfathering. The same requirements exist for combined DSU/CSU units which connect directly to digital service networks. FCC rules compliance statements can be found in manufacturer's manuals supplied with each unit. Note that compliance with radio interference protection under Subpart J of Part 15 of the FCC Rules usually exists only for commercial environments. Protection in residential areas becomes the responsibility of each user. Network interface functions provided by CSUs are relatively simple.

The primary functions of a CSU are network testing and electrical isolation of the network from a user's DSU or other CPE. Network-controlled testing permits carrier test centers to remotely set-up and take down loopback tests at the user's premise CSU. Figure 6.9 on page 155 illustrates where these CSU test loopback points exist in digital data service networks. Electrical isolation, usually supplied by electrical transformers, protects the network (and network maintenance personnel) from encountering harmful voltages caused by faults in a user's equipment. Figure 6.4 shows examples of CSU transformer isolation techniques. The electrical transformers prevent DC voltages or low frequency AC voltages, such as the 120-volt power line, from passing between the CSU and the network interface.

CSUs do not usually protect either themselves or attached user equipment from abnormal network fault voltages such as lightning. Lightning protection should be provided on the carrier side of a network interface. On private networks, lightning protection becomes a user's responsibility. After network electrical isolation, responding to network controlled testing is a CSU's most important task.

As in DSU network testing, network-controlled testing allows carriers to verify operation of the CSU and the local loop. The CSU loopback test operates by remote command of a disconnection of the user's DSU data signals and connecting the received network signal to be sent back to the network as transmitted data. The signal passes through most of the CSU's circuitry prior to the loopback function, thus testing not only the local loop but the CSU's electronics. Two methods exist to control this loopback test from the network. The first method involves a concept not previously discussed here—**sealing current.** Sealing current, originating at the carrier's **office channel unit** (OCU), flows through the local loop's two pairs as a simplex DC current. Understanding this operation requires viewing the combination of channel service unit (CSU), digital local loop and office channel unit (OCU) together. Figure 6.5 shows these three pieces interconnected and displays the simplex sealing current flow.

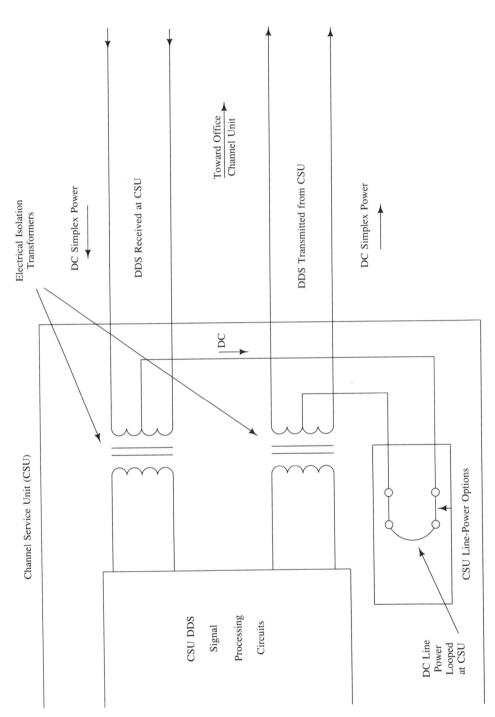

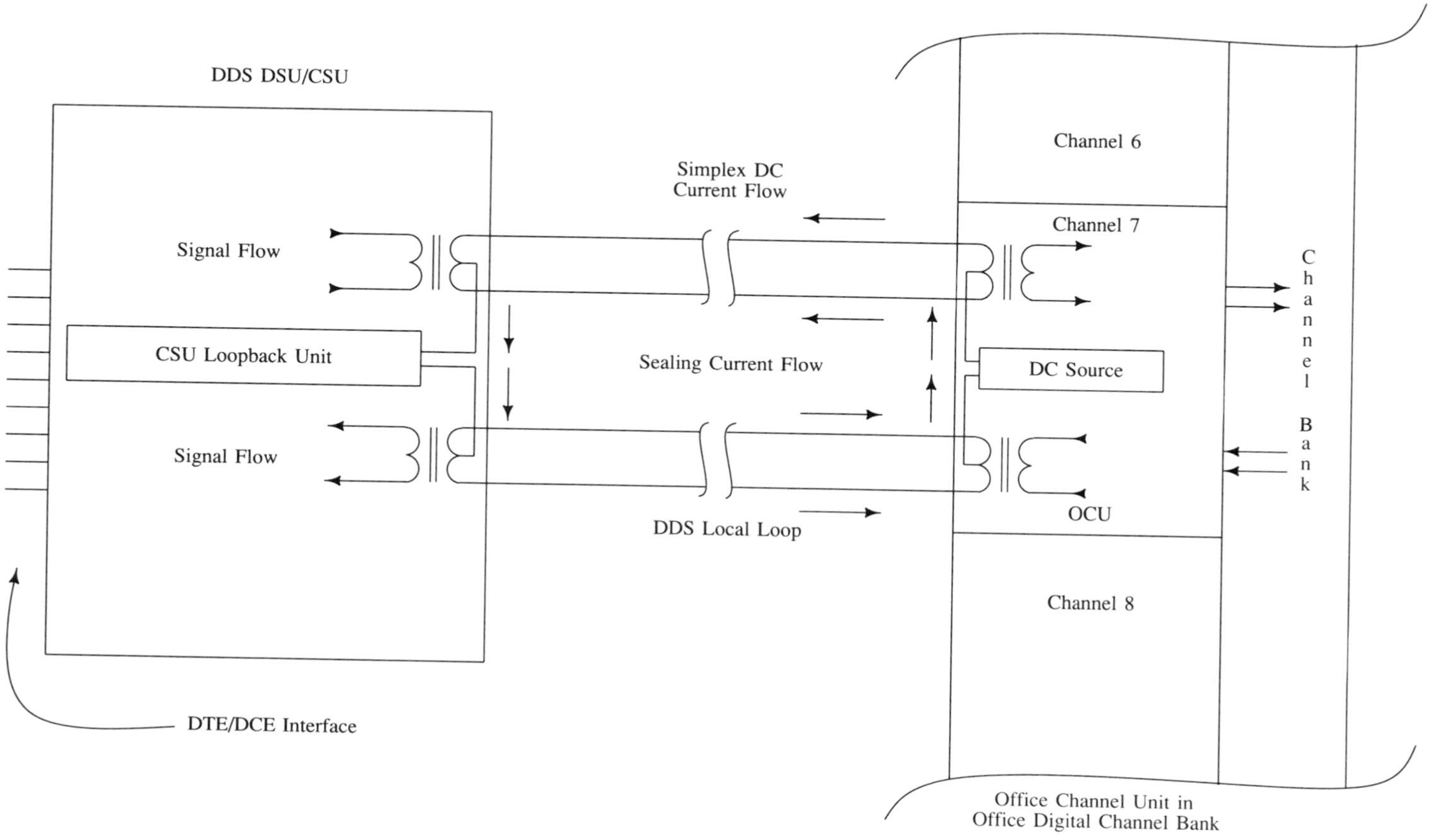

FIGURE 6.5. DDS—CSU, local loop, and OCU Connection

Sealing current, flowing as shown in Figure 6.5, helps to maintain low resistance in the splices and wire junctions of the local loop. Sealing current stays typically between four and 20 milliamperes of direct current (DC). The current also provides a method for network-controlled CSU loopback. When the polarity (current flow direction) of the sealing current reverses, CSU control circuits disconnect user data and set-up a CSU loop back as indicated in Figure 6.5. Carrier network test centers may then insert test signal patterns toward the looped CSU and compare the returned signal. The CSU loop will be held as long as the sealing current stays reversed. When sealing current polarity returns to normal, under control of the OCU, the loop back is taken down and user data returns to the circuit. An important note here for users installing CSUs (or combination CSU/DSUs) concerns correct polarity at installation. Figure 6.5 shows the usual connection to maintain correct sealing current polarity. Sealing current reversal loopback is the primary method, but as in the DSU, control bit patterns exist to cause CSU loopback. Not all CSUs are equipped to recognize CSU loopback bit patterns. Combined DSU/CSU units usually operate DSU loopbacks from control bit patterns and CSU loopback from sealing current reversal arriving on the digital local loop.

Digital Local Loop Requirements

Local loops are copper wire pairs running from telephone central offices to user premises. For normal analog voice telephone use, loops may involve amplifiers, build-out capacitors, bridges to other pairs (bridged taps) and loading coils to assure correct electrical characteristics. The same copper pairs, when used as part of a digital services network, must be corrected to meet digital requirements. A phrase often encountered in DDS is "unloaded," meaning removal of all inductive loading coils. But removing loading coils may not be enough, especially at higher speeds. Bridged taps (places where other wire pairs connect) may cause electrical signal reflections which alter digital bit streams and analog amplifiers may distort bit shapes. Usual practice for digital local loops involves removal of all loading coils, build-out capacitors and repeating amplifiers; bridged taps are either removed or reduced in number or length. In addition, where local voice telephone circuits usually need only one pair of wires, digital services require two pairs—one for transmit pulses and one for receive. Data speed then controls suitability of the loop with lower speeds permitting longer loop distances and smaller wire gauges.

Wire gauge, expressed in AWG for **American wire gauge,** measures wire diameter; diameter and material determine resistance. Most installed local loops in the U.S. range between 26 gauge (small) and 19 gauge (larger), and are made of copper. By comparison, most electrical power wiring in U.S. residences is between 10 and 14 gauge, considerably larger than telephone loop wiring, with considerably less resistance. Resistance, though, does not tell the whole tale. As frequencies rise, capacitance and inductance effects in a cable begin to exact their toll. The combined effect, called **distributed impedance,** works to shrink, round-off, and distort digital pulses. In practice, the **loss,** or combined reduction of signal strength, is expressed in **dB** or deciBels. DeciBels express loss (or gain) in a logarithmic or exponential manner and are used by engineers to specify precisely total gain or loss effects. (For our engineering readers, local loop loss is usually limited to 31dB.) Larger loop wire (smaller gauge numbers) reduces these effects; for each wire gauge and data speed distance limits have been determined. The limits vary somewhat between equipment types, but Figure 6.6 gives example distance ranges for 9.6 and 56 kbit/s DDS with common local loop cable gauges.

Local Loop Wire Size	Range at 9.6 kbit/s	Range at 56 kbit/s
19 gauge	12 to 16 miles	6 to 10 miles
22 gauge	8 to 10 miles	4 to 6 miles
24 gauge	6 to 8 miles	3 to 4 miles
26 gauge	4 to 5 miles	2 to 3 miles

FIGURE 6.6. Typical DDS Local Loop Distance Ranges.

The numbers shown in Figure 6.6 are examples only; actual distance limits for specific equipment and loop types should be obtained from CSU vendors and carriers. Operation beyond these typical limits may also be possible through use of specialized digital repeating amplifiers. Local exchange carriers can assist users in determining the actual equipment needed to provide digital service to the nearest digital telephone central office or DDS serving office. While a few areas of the U.S. do not as yet have digital capabilities, interest in Integrated Services Digital Networks (ISDN) will eventually bring all areas of the country to digital service. One small concern remains for the connection of user CSUs to a local loop, that is, polarity. While Figure 6.5 indicates usual local loop connections by cable colors or RJ-48S pins, not all connections may be the same. Assistance from the carrier will determine the right connections for correct operation. In private networks, users must set standards for their own connections. Note that what is transmitted from a near-end CSU must be the received signal at the far-end. This entails a reversal somewhere in the private local wiring. Carriers provide this reversal automatically within their systems, starting at their office channel units.

Office Channel Unit (OCU) Functions

Digital channel banks, first described in Chapter 3, also may function to terminate digital local loops at telephone offices or in private networks. Reviewed quickly, digital channel banks originally converted analog voice conversations from analog signals to 64 kbit/s digital bit streams. The 64 kbit/s then combined to form T1 streams at 1.544 Mbit/s. The most common channel banks come from the D4-type families and produce compatible D4 framed and D4 channelized bit sequences. These are the DS-1 compatible signals and permit up to 24 channels of analog voice signals to travel as serial digital bit streams. As digital data services entered telephone systems in the 1970s, channel banks took on increasing importance for both voice and digital data. Electronic **cards**, carrying electronics for analog to digital voice conversion could be replaced with loop terminating electronics for digital data. The name given to such DDS cards was office channel unit (OCU). Instead of receiving a single analog voice channel and converting it to digital for T1 transmission, OCUs matched digital local loops at the office, or telephone company, end. Functionally, they "cooperated" with CSUs located at the other end of the loop at a user's premises.

Channel banks of the D4-type offer many differing cards for differing functions. Typically, a channel bank is an empty **nest** prepared to accept cards with these differing functions and using cards containing **common equipment.** Common equipment combines up to 24 channels for one T1 or up to 48 channels for two T1s (1.544 Mbit/s) or a T1C

(3.152 Mbit/s). Common equipment also provides power for all cards in the nest, sources for digital timing and for interfacing T1 or T1C lines, called **spans.** Voice or data cards may then fill the channel bank to capacity. For analog voice channels, at least nine different type of cards exist depending on the type of voice channel. For data, two classes of cards exist. The most usual class accepts digital local loop signals from customer locations. This is the OCU mentioned above; the other class presents a digital data interface connector directly at the channel banks and is called a **dataport** card. Dataport cards offer full data communications equipment (DCE) interfaces such as EIA-232 or CCITT V.35 right at the channel bank. Before examining dataport cards and their applications, office channel unit cards and their functions need to be understood.

Office channel unit (OCU) cards form pairs with channel service units (CSUs). Functions and data speeds expected and generated by CSUs must be provided and accepted by OCUs. CSU and loop functions needed at the OCU are:

- Loop electrical isolation;
- Signal transmission to the loop;
- Signal recovery from the loop;
- Retiming to/from 64 kbit/s;
- Network control code handling;
- Simplex sealing current for the loop; and
- Loopback control of the user's CSU.

Loop electrical isolation takes the same form as it does at a CSU; transformers or electro-optical isolators separate signals from both simplex sealing current and from fault voltages which may occur on the loop. Signal transmission infers conversion of channel bank signals into suitable driving voltages for the local loop with pulses generated at precise moments determined by channel bank timing. Since this timing will be looped by the devices at the far end of the loop, outbound signals should be at the lowest possible jitter. Signal levels in digital data services operate generally at fixed voltage levels depending on data speed. These voltage levels leave both CSUs and OCUs at about ± 2 volts, representing a "one" and less than ± 0.2 volts for a "zero." With fixed voltages leaving the transmitters and varying lengths of local loop reducing the signal, signal recovery becomes the key to successful reception of the bit stream.

Signal recovery in local digital data service loops begins just after electrical isolation. The next function in the bit stream's path is usually an **automatic line build out** (ALBO). To avoid manual adjustment of signal strength over various length local loops, each signal is filtered to remove noise and then enters a device which "standardizes" the signal. **Line build out** (LBO) was, and still is, a method to reduce standard voltage level signals leaving a transmitter. For short distance cables with small losses, an LBO device was added to simulate the longest cable. LBOs were almost always simple resistive networks to reduce or attenuate a signal's voltage level. LBOs of this type find their place at the output of network signal transmitters. Automatic LBOs or ALBOs, however, come into play at the receiving end of a line. An ALBO may be thought of as an automatic volume control, adjusting strong signals down and weak signals up. ALBOs reduce manual measurement and adjustment of loop lengths and signal voltages permitting interchangeability of equipment.

Coming back to OCUs and CSUs, this means each unit will adjust itself to an incoming bit stream's voltage level and provide the correct level for the rest of the signal recovery electronics. Signal recovery from the local loop completes by circuits which actually "decide" when a voltage level is a "one" and when a "zero." Triggering or slicing electronics uses timing already recovered (see Figure 6.3 on page 143) to tell when to measure the filtered output of the ALBO. The resulting bits are either customer data bits or "non-data" DDS control bit patterns. Before detailing "non-data" and control codes, a fundamental function, retiming to/from 64 kbit/s must be reviewed.

In digital channel banks, all channels operate on the network side at 64 kbit/s. This builds, as we saw in detail in Chapter 5, to T1 speeds. But digital data services usually operate at 56 kbit/s and below. The OCU performs this conversion of 56 kbit/s to 64 kbit/s and retimes both signals to "lock" to the network clock as we will see in Chapter 7. A simple way of viewing this conversion involves two patterns of seven and eight bits. An eight bit pattern running at a rate of 8,000 patterns per second produces a bit rate of 64 kbit/s; a seven bit pattern running at the same rate produces only 56 kbit/s. If one of the bits arrives at the OCU from the T1 network at 64 kbit/s and is consumed by the OCU, the remaining bits may be sent to the local loop and user CSU at 56 kbit/s. In fact, this is how it is done. The bit pattern:

$$B_1 \, B_2 \, B_3 \, B_4 \, B_5 \, B_6 \, B_7 \, B_8$$

will be the example pattern used to describe both retiming between 56 kbit/s and 64 kbit/s and to explore DDS control codes. The bit positions above will be referred to as Bit-1, Bit-2, and so on. In normal digital data services, Bit-1 through Bit-8 move together through the network, each in their own slot or position relative to the beginning of the frame. Thus in D4-type channel banks slot 1 comes first followed by slot 2 and so on, until all 24 slots have completed. A framing position bit identifies beginning and end of a frame and the transmission of slots continues.

This byte oriented multiplexing for transmission carries each group of eight bits (Bit-1 through Bit-8) together. It is also called **byte-interleaved** multiplexing and contrasts **bit-interleaved** multiplexing. More will be said about byte- and bit-interleaved multiplexing in Chapter 12 on time division multiplexers. For present purposes, Bit-1 through Bit-8 travel together. We can now examine how the bits are used in DDS for both data and non-data purposes and for retiming or rate conversion.

Retiming may be thought of as a box transmitting and receiving 64 kbit/s signals on the network (or T1) side and 56 kbit/s signals on the local loop side. Bit-8 does much of the work involved in retiming by being examined, then thrown away on signals flowing from the network to the loop. On signals flowing from the loop toward the network, Bit-8 is added by the OCU. Each OCU channel card takes in eight bits at 64 kbit/s from the network, examines and discards Bit-8 and sends the remaining seven (Bit-1 to Bit-7) bits to the user through the loop. Since the two data rates of 56 kbit/s and 64 kbit/s are exactly locked to a single higher speed clock, only one byte need be buffered or held at the OCU to accomplish the retiming or data rate conversion. DDS clocking is covered in more detail in Chapter 7 on digital synchronization. Bit-8 exists, then, only in the network between channel bank OCU cards and does not flow to the user's CSU.

Bit-8 has been assigned, in usual D4-type channel bank services, to tell whether the rest of the bits are data or non-data. When Bit-8 is a "one", the other bits carry user data; when Bit-8 is a "zero", the other bits are examined for network control purposes. With the exception of speeds below 56 kbit/s, where Bit-1 takes on special meanings, Bit-1 to Bit-7 contain user digital data. A special case of user data exists to identify all "zeros." As mentioned in Chapter 5, high-speed digital streams need to maintain a minimum number of consecutive "zeros." While Bit-8 stays at "one" during user data transmission, it does not appear on the local loop. An all "zeros" signal from a user's CSU (or from an OCU) will not supply enough pulses to keep timing in synchronization. Some other code must flow between CSU and OCU when this situation occurs. This special pattern for all "zeros" takes the name **zero-suppression,** or more correctly, **zero-substitution.**

Zero-substitution explains the function more clearly, as nothing is suppressed; another bit pattern substitutes for the "zeros." This pattern involves bipolar violations (BPV). When the rule says that "ones" pulses alternate in polarity, successive "ones" pulses which do not alternate violate the rule. On local loops for digital data services these BPVs become useful to signal control codes and zero-substitution. Figure 6.3 on page 143 shows normal AMI pulses alternating on a digital circuit. Figure 6.7 on page 153 shows how BPVs indicate all "zeros" on the loop between the CSU and the OCU. Remember that Bit-8 remains at "one" during these substitutions as user data is flowing. The flow continues, but the form of the "zeros" has been changed to assure pulses on the line. The substitution between CSU and OCU is removed before the data passes to the user's devices at the other end. That is, an all "zeros" pattern will appear at the other end as all "zeros." Substitution really only occurs between CSU and OCU, "zeros" flow in the network between OCUs. A steady "one" in Bit-8 keeps the density of "ones" in the network.

Note in Figure 6.7 that BPVs in zero-substitution alternate to prevent voltage build-up in a single direction on the line. This alternation also prevents ALBOs from becoming confused about incoming signal levels.

All other conditions on a digital services circuit are non-data and Bit-8 is set to "zero." The OCU must recognize "non-data" control sequences arriving from the network T1 and convert them to correct actions for the loop and user CSU. In the opposite direction, control codes arriving from the CSU (or perhaps no signal at all) need to be communicated to the channel bank common electronics and the network. The most common "non-data" control bit sequences are found in Figure 6.8 on page 154. Bipolar violations are again sent between OCUs and CSUs to identify the various codes. Figure 6.8 shows both the pulse form on the local loop circuit and the Bit-1 through Bit-8 code assignments.

Figure 6.8 shows three loopback codes for testing a digital data services circuit. In digital data service networks carriers often operate one or more test centers with access to user DDS circuits. The loopback codes enable test center personnel to "takeover" a circuit (with user permission) and loop the circuit at many points. With the circuit looped, test pattern signals may be placed on the circuit to isolate a failing or troublesome section. Users may also take their own circuits out of data service and initiate local-only or end-to-end loopback tests to verify operation. Figure 6.9 on page 155 identifies these loopback points in an example DDS circuit. The names used in Figure 6.9 compare exactly to names and codes used in Figure 6.8. Only the DSU loopback command is permitted to pass through most networks allowing users to test end-to-end. DSU loopback commands may also be issued from network test centers.

Loopback command codes generally cause electronic (or mechanical) loopbacks, connecting received data to become transmitted data for return and comparison. The comparison reveals any errors which may have occurred during transmission. The OCU converts the network codes from Figure 6.9 to local loop codes for execution by the DSU. In the case of the CSU loopback, the OCU reverses the sealing current to the CSU. As noted

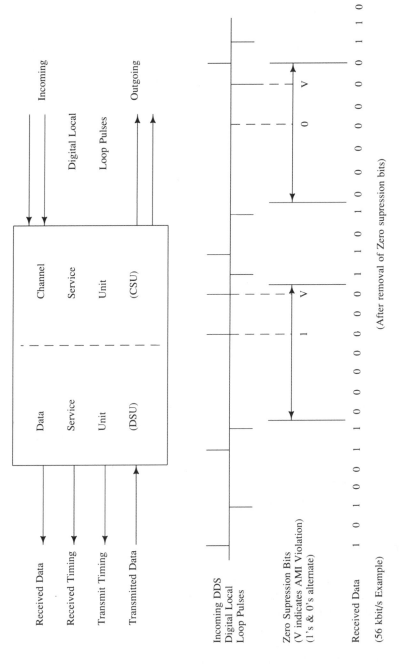

FIGURE 6.7. DDS Zero-substitution BPV Example.

153

Bit Patterns from the OCU to the CSU →	DS–0 Bit Position (64 kbit/s Rate)								Local Loop Bit Position (56 kbit/s Baseband)						
	1	2	3	4	5	6	7	8	1	2	3	4	5	6	7
Normal Service															
Normal Data Pattern	1	D	D	D	D	D	D	D	D	D	D	D	D	D	D
0 Supression Pattern	1	0	0	0	0	0	0	0	0	0	0	0	X	0	V
Network Control															
Control-Idle Pattern	1	1	1	1	1	1	1	0	1	1	1	1	X	0	V
DSU Loopback Pattern	0	0	1	0	1	1	0	0	0	0	1	0	X	0	V
CSU Loopback Pattern	0	0	1	0	1	0	0	0	0	0	1	0	1	0	0
OCU Loopback Pattern	0	0	1	0	1	0	1	0	0	0	1	0	X	0	V
Out-of-Sync* Pattern	0	0	0	1	1	0	1	0	0	0	0	1	X	0	V

D = Any "1" or "0" data bit, V = Bipolar Violation bit,

X = 0 or 1 if # of bits since last V is odd or even, respectively.

* Also called out-of-service

FIGURE 6.8. DDS Control Code Bit Patterns and Codes.

under CSU Functions, reversal of sealing current causes the CSU to enter a loopback condition and stay until the sealing current returns to normal polarity.

Beyond loopback commands, other control codes, listed in Figure 6.8, remain. Control-idle was described earlier in this chapter under DSU Functions; it provides a bit stream when the user has no data to send. This can occur in point-to-point circuits when a user's data terminating equipment (DTE) has turned off request to send (RTS). In multi-point circuits, many DTEs share a common DDS circuit and only one may transmit in a given direction at a time. The others will turn off RTS and their DSUs will generate control-idles. These control-idles carry timing and tell connected units that, at the moment, no user data is flowing.

When network conditions arise preventing user data flow, other signals exist to tell DSUs of the trouble. The most important of these are Out-of-service and Test. **Out-of-service** (OOS) arrives from an OCU to a DSU/CSU to indicate network troubles preventing the flow of user data. Some DSU/CSUs offer an option to turn off Clear to Send if an OOS arrives. This is optional as side effects on DTEs and communications software may prevent its use. Some DTEs and software prefer to deal with data errors or transmission stoppages directly. Abrupt turn-off of CTS may signify that a permanent failure has occurred, requiring manual intervention. This option, sometimes called **circuit assurance,** should be examined carefully in each situation. The other control signal, Test, will usually indicate to

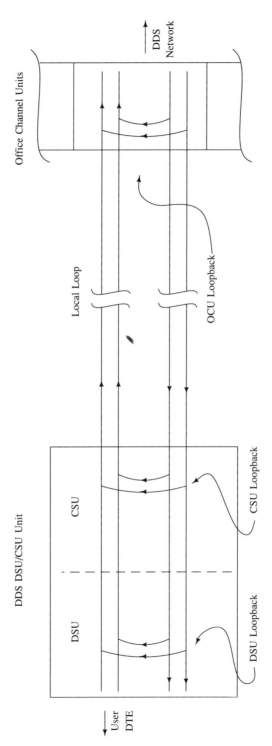

FIGURE 6.9. Example DDS Circuit Showing Loopback Points.

155

the DSU/CSU that a remote test originated by a user or a carrier is in process. Other control signals have been defined and some codes reserved for future definition, but those listed demonstrate the nature and method on OCU and network interaction with DSUs and CSUs.

Combined DSU/CSU Units

Our discussion has isolated DSUs and CSUs into separate functional boxes, but current reality combines them. Most digital data service interface units now available come in one box (or one card for multiple circuit installations). The term data service unit (DSU) is slowly replacing the combined DSU/CSU term. The functions described in the sections above remain in these combined units, and can form a basis for informed choice in these newer units. All units do not necessarily offer all functions listed and individual choices must be made based on real communications applications. Finally, the functions detailed above were limited to fixed or permanent circuits. Another variation in digital data services has arrived in the form of "switched digital data services," allowing user originated connections.

Switched Digital Service Functions

Digital data services originated as leased services, offering users full-time access to point-to-point or point-to-multipoint data connections. Supplementing leased analog voice-grade channels for data communications, DDS offered objectives for availability and quality. They were, however, still full-time, by-the-month type services. Switched (or dial-up) data services continued to use regular voice telephone channels with low-speed modems and were relegated to lower speeds. Currently offered modems for dial-up voice-grade now reach to exceed 19.2 kbit/s on low-noise connections, but speed often varies by the variable nature of the dial-up voice connection. In the public switched networks, quality can often vary widely and data speeds and quality cannot be guaranteed. Availability depends on call duration and on blockage in the network. At busy-hours for the voice networks, busy signals block data as well as voice calls. Several all-digital switched services now permit connections over separate digital data service networks on a demand basis.

AT&T's ACCUNET® Switched 56 Service and **circuit switched digital capability** (CSDC) from Regional Bell Operating Companies merge the capabilities of dial-up voice and digital data services. While these services are limited to certain serving areas, concepts may be examined while the services expand. Currently, the limiting factors lie more within data terminating equipment than in the (CSDC) networks. A digression into low-speed data services helps explain the limits.

As personal computer use spread in the early 1980s, demand for communications access grew quickly. Modems rapidly appeared which combined an ability to meet current voice-grade modem standards while performing traditional voice telephone dial functions. Software followed quickly to support these "smart" modems, combining signaling (dialing) functions with data modem support on a single EIA-232 interface. While the signaling functions are quite limited in terms beyond dial pulsing or tone dialing, these packages offered integrated computing, communications software and "smart" modems. This integration permitted users to pre-program both connection and communications. Higher speed integrated packages are now just beginning to appear, partly due to requirements to support multiple interfaces. While a single protocol exists at the network interface, two interfaces may be needed at the DTE to DCE boundary.

Digital interfaces, described in Chapter 4, are well defined for data communications, but another interface must often be used to provide signaling. This dialing interface, EIA-366, must somehow be combined in the DSU to offer the network a single interface. DSUs offer this possibility by single connections to the CSDC network interface and dual connections to the DTE—CCITT V.35 for data and EIA-366 for signaling. Limits on signaling similar to those at lower speeds also exist at 56 kbit/s CSDC. While the EIA-366 interface can dial telephone number equivalents into the network, such things as far-end and network (fast-busy) busy-signal recognition and DTE software coordinated answer supervision (electrical circuit and communications recognition of an answer) are yet to be provided. Another question to be resolved is local access. In some areas, access to a switched service requires a leased access to the switched service node. This means leasing a standard 56 kbit/s local digital data service circuit to connect to an office capable of switching. The same requirement could exist at any or all of the possible far-end points of the switched connection.

This type of switched service data connection is clearly a precursor to real Integrated Services Digital Networks (ISDN), which we will cover fully in Chapter 14. For now and where available, these services remain increasingly good alternatives to consider for leased circuit back-up and non-regular bulk data transfer.

Error Correction in Digital Services

Digital data services have earned an excellent reputation for meeting their availability and quality objectives. AT&T quotes these objectives for their ACCUNET® and DATAPHONE® Digital Services to be at least 99.5% error-free seconds at 56 kbit/s and better yet at lower data rates. These rates exceed the AT&T and Regional Bell Operating Company objectives for T1 services on which DDS is carried and additional error control is sometimes provided for DDS to meet the quality objectives. Briefly, this is accomplished at speeds below 56 kbit/s by sending multiples of the data bytes in the allotted 64 kbit/s DS-0 channel. For example, at 9.6 kbit/s, the user's data may be repeated five times in each DS-0 channel and a majority vote is taken at the receiving channel bank. At lower DDS speeds, user data is repeated more times, but the majority vote on each five repeats is also used. When error correction is needed at 56 kbit/s, an additional DS-0 channel may be dedicated to a complex polynomial parity error correction scheme. Availability objectives for both T1 and DDS exist in the 99.7% to 99.9% range, and are accomplished largely through "protection" or realtime switching to spare transmission facilities and equipment.

Building on our understanding of digital interface units for carrier networks, we move now to a review of interface units for private digital network systems.

Private Network Digital DCEs

Users build private systems for digital data communications to reduce costs, provide flexibility and control their destinies. Private systems range in size from simple point-to-point single links to systems spanning campuses, high-rises and industrial parks. The full scope of private digital communications systems will be addressed in Chapter 11, but digital interface units play a pivotal role in private systems. Special considerations are needed for private system interface units, and these considerations take form in the outline below. Support functions, expected from carrier or public systems, are the user's responsibility in a private system. Interface unit compatibility and function, no longer mandated by a tariff or carrier, must be assured by the user. Manufacturers, eager to sell their equipment, may not always be aware of complex inter-operability questions raised in private network design or construction. The user may truly be "the court of last resort."

In discussing private systems, we intentionally omit those totally designed around a single vendor's equipment and software. In these cases, the vendor can and will take full responsibility for the proper (or at least specified) operation of the total system. It is only when multiple vendors supply equipment to a user designed network that the user must understand all aspects and take full responsibility for correct operation. A variation called **turn-key**, described in Chapter 13, delegates these tasks to the turn-key vendor but, as in all delegated responsibilities, the user must ultimately be responsible. For these reasons, and several more to be covered in Chapters 11 and 13, users contemplating private network design must understand that the "buck" stops with them. Again, a map of the territory is needed. We begin the map of private systems at limited distance digital units.

Limited-distance Digital Units

For many years, interface units have been offered by manufacturers intended specifically for private use. Key differences between these units and those offered for public or tariffed network use lie in regulation and compatibility. In carrier network use, all devices must meet some network interface at a standard or network determined interface. The specifications for these network interfaces were detailed in our previous discussion. In private use, vendors may offer either greater function or lower cost to perform the same (or nearly the same) function. Public network interfaces must retain the standardizations demanded by size, previous technologies and interconnected complexity. Private network units may venture off in new directions. As a result, limited-distance data units may provide optional features for interconnection or media use not available (or not available yet) in carrier-based units. **Limited-distance data units** (LDM, LADD or LDDM), also called **local area data distributors** or **local area data sets** do the same job as carrier network DSU/CSUs, but may do it less expensively or with added function. Media and distance choices may be greater and response to DTE control signals may differ. They may also do it with radically different speeds and interfaces.

Before outlining the radically different, let us examine some units closer to network standard units. In general, LDDUs mimic functions of their public network cousins—conversion of DTE interfaces to signals which may be sent over distances to other units for re-conversion to other DTEs. In most units, the differences exist in the signals used on the media. If carrier network voltages and speeds need not be met, the LDDU may use proprietary signals and signaling methods between LDDUs. LDDUs specify what media types and sizes can be supported and distances often vary inversely with media loss. That is, larger (or lower attenuation) media permit longer distances between LDDUs. LDDUs are available to support user owned copper wire pairs, coaxial cables and private optical fibers. Some units provide support for several media types by offering internal card or option plug substitution. Typical copper cable oriented LDDUs may support 19- to 26-gauge copper pair cables or 50-ohm to 92-ohm coaxial cables as the local, user owned media. As some LDDUs use proprietary signal methods on the copper cable, vendors should be contacted if the cables are to be shared with other services, such as voice. Some signal methods may induce noise into the voice signals or ringing current on the voice lines may cause noise on the data lines. Beyond media choice, other considerations involve interconnection and timing.

Like carrier based networks, applications of LDDUs force decisions on network topology, that is, point-to-point or point-to-multipoint operation. A simple, but not totally obvious, need in topology concerns the reversal and matching of wires and impedances. These functions come automatically with carrier services, but in private networks must be designed by the user. Figure 6.10 on page 160 shows the simple reversal of wires needed in point-to-point links, along with timing choices.

In point-to-multipoint private networks, an additional problem arises—the **multi-junction unit** (MJU) function. When carriers offer point-to-multipoint services, they include MJUs to match signals, correct overloading of circuits and convert control-idles to non-signals when one unit transmits real data. When users build point-to-multipoint networks, they must provide the MJU function in some fashion. Figure 6.11 on page 161 gives an example of the MJU function in a private network.

Multijunction units perform several necessary tasks in point-to-multipoint connections, but they must be compatible with the LDDUs they connect. For example, if LDDUs produce digital control-idle signals when not transmitting data, the MJU must recognize the control-idle. If another remote unit in the connection begins to transmit data, the MJU must remove control-idles from the data stream returning toward the master unit. If an LDDU turns off all signals toward the MJU when no data comes from its attached DTE, the MJU need merely balance signals toward the master LDDU. If the LDDU system is based on **radio frequency** (RF) **carriers,** the MJU may be a much more complex device which allocates and assigns frequencies. In these more complex limited distance private network schemes, we enter the realm of **local area networks** (LAN). Many excellent texts exist on LANs, and we will not attempt to cover that material here. If the private network is based on a form of LAN, the user should refer to these texts. Timing considerations complete this brief overview of private network interface units.

If the remote LDDUs receive timing from the master LDDU, the connecting network (and the MJU, if present) must pass the timing without adding significant jitter. If the MJU must clock the entire system, its source of timing must be sufficiently stable for the LDDUs and attached DTEs to be derived from some outside stable source, such as a public or carrier network connection. Timing and synchronization topics, discussed in the next chapter, apply equally to carrier and private networks. Concepts covered in Chapter 7 for the timing of digital networks should be applied in the planning and design of private digital networks. Particular concern should be focused on possible later connections to carrier networks which may insist on providing network timing.

Private Extensions of DDS

When private networks grow to include connections to carrier networks, timing must usually be derived from the carrier network. The simplest case of private network interconnection with carrier networks is illustrated in the private extensions of **digital data services** (DDS). Figure 6.12 on page 162 diagrams such a private extension of a DDS circuit.

Figure 6.12 provides an example of a DDS extension and includes a typical **crossover** cable layout. While this particular crossover illustrates one way of connecting data, timing and control signals, manufacturers and carriers should be consulted for specific installations.

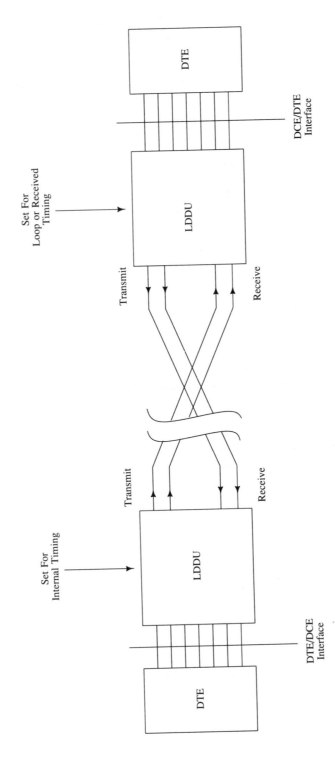

FIGURE 6.10. Private Network LDDU Wiring and Timing.

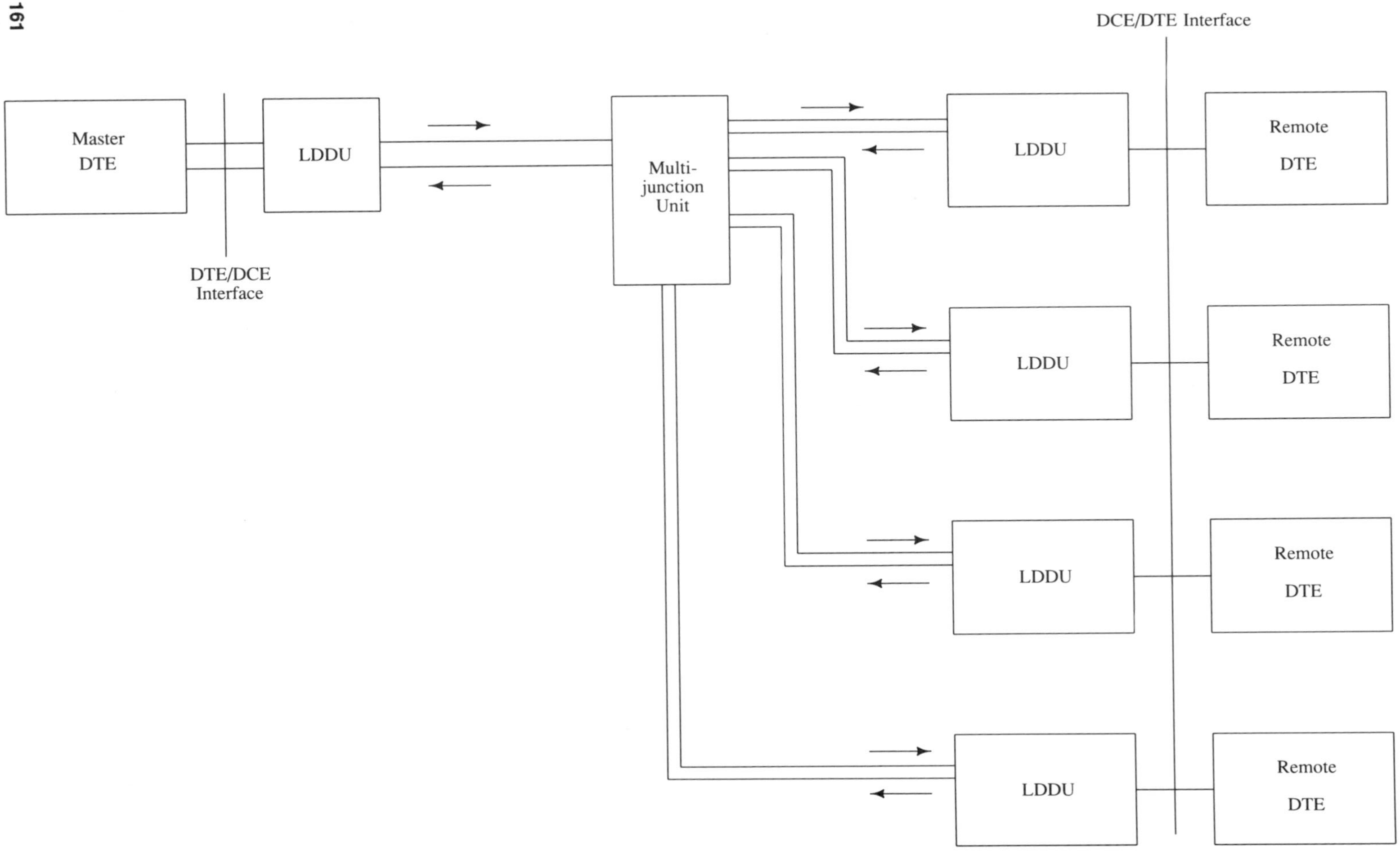

FIGURE 6.11. Multijunction Unit LDDU.

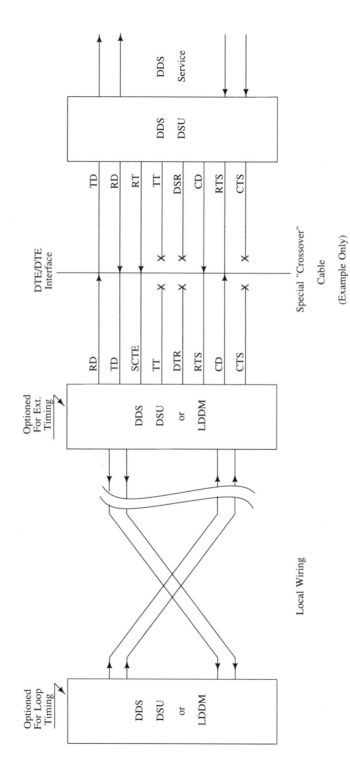

162

FIGURE 6.12. Connection between DDS and Private Network Circuits.

In the example of Figure 6.12, timing received from the DDS network on the DDS DSU's received timing lines is crossed over to the user's LDDU as external timing. At the far end, LDDU timing is returned in the method already described as loop-timing. Data signals are crossed between network DSU and user LDDU as they are both DCEs and their expected DTE interface connection must be simulated. Observe that several of the normal control signals connect strangely to give this needed simulation. Many choices exist for this interface crossover, and our readers are encouraged to sketch several variations and examine the reactions of the connected units to normal and abnormal conditions. Before completing private network interface units, a few words about the use of carrier network qualified DSU/CSUs as private network devices.

DSU/CSUs in Private Networks

Many commercial DSU/CSUs designed to interface to carrier DDS networks are quite capable of operating in user owned networks, simple or complex. If such use is anticipated and supported by device manufacturers, their manuals will often explain how to do it. If no mention is made in unit manuals, the manufacturer may be consulted to obtain more information on private network use of DSU/CSU units. The key points in the use of DSU/CSUs in private networks remain the same as those with LDDUs: media type and size, timing sources and multipoint operation. Several advantages exist for using carrier network type DSU/CSUs in private networks: fewer equipment types, consistent operational procedures, reduced training and fewer spare units. The disadvantages usually involve unit cost as LDDUs traditionally cost less than network qualified DSU/CSUs. This choice then becomes another in the growing list of decisions now required of the user.

T-Carrier Channel Service Units

Prior to AT&T divestiture, T1 channel service units (CSU) were supplied and installed with T1 service by the telephone company. Most of these units were Western Electric 551A CSUs. Divestiture made CSUs the responsibility of the user and many companies have entered the business of supplying T1 CSUs. Combined CSU/DSU units exist for direct T1 connection, and these have become known as **T1 modems.** They provide the combined functions described earlier for attachment of DTEs to T1 facilities. Manufacturers of T1 user devices, such as channel banks, time division multiplexers and T1 video equipment usually offer the T1 DSU function in their boxes, but CSUs remain largely separate units. Figure 6.13 on page 164 illustrates a typical T1 channel service unit.

The truly explosive growth in the use of T1 carriers since 1980 has brought users into a field for which they were little prepared. T-Carriers, as explained in earlier chapters, came not from the world of computer communications but from voice telephony. T-Carrier interfaces did not look like traditional EIA-232 or V.35 interfaces and digital carriers did not act in any familiar ways. Just as users began to become familiar with DDS digital communications concepts and the combination DSU/CSU, the T1 carrier arrived with only a CSU. Its four-wire (two-pair) line side interface looked like its four-wire (two-pair) equipment interface. Users began to question why they needed to spend many hundreds of dollars to convert one AMI bit stream to another AMI bit stream. The answer unfolds through a description of CSU functions.

FIGURE 6.13. Typical T1 Channel Service Unit. (Photo Courtesy of Verilink Corporation.)

T1 CSU Functions

In its simplest form, a T1 channel service unit (CSU) performs the the following functions:

- user T1 signal interface;
- user T1 signal monitoring;
- bipolar violation removal;
- network loopback operation;
- T1 signal repeater functions; and
- CSU powering options.

While the user and network interfaces indeed appear the same T1 bit streams as described in Chapter 4, the CSU's functions add value to both user and network signal streams. Figure 6.14 on page 165 shows the major components of a typical T1 CSU. In a typical T1 CSU, major components may actually plug into overall CSU physical frames or may come built together in a single compact unit.

The user side of a CSU, often erroneously called data terminal equipment, will be referred to here as user interface or user side. The abbreviation DTE, found in CSU literature, does not mean data terminating equipment as we have described it in Chapter 4. This confusion of terms comes from the merging of common digital technologies from differing voice and data origins.

Beginning with the user interface side, T1 signals enter and leave through test jacks whose use may either interrupt or monitor either direction of the T1 stream. Interruption of signals to or from the user equipment will, of course, completely disrupt any communications. Disruption must, however, be done to insert test signals onto the line for diagnosis when line faults are suspected and all non-disruptive test methods have failed to locate the fault. Use of the monitor jacks to connect test equipment does not disrupt user or network

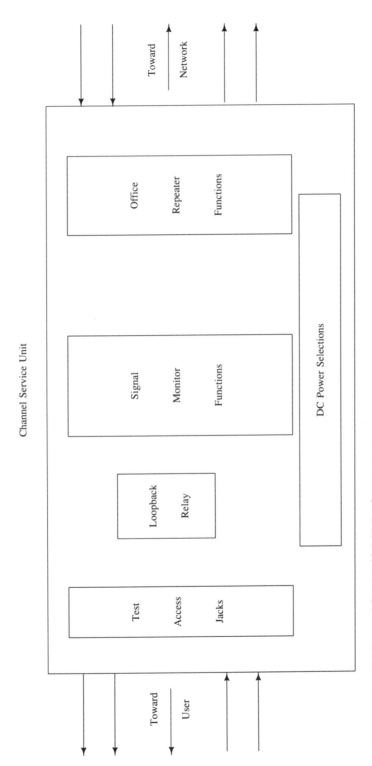

FIGURE 6.14. T1 Channel Service Unit Major Components.

signals. The test equipment must be able to interpret at least some portion, say the D4 framing pattern, of the user bit stream. As more T1 streams convert to extended superframe format (ESF), monitoring may offer significantly greater opportunities for non-disruptive fault location.

Most CSU signal monitor units remove bipolar violations in the AMI stream from the user interface. Additionally, ones density is monitored to indicate whether more than 15 consecutive "zeros" have been sent by the user equipment. Some CSUs offer options to indicate a higher number than 15. Excessive zeros will usually be indicated by a panel lamp on the CSU. Another user signal monitor function substitutes an "all ones" or blue signal toward the network when no signal at all comes in from the user interface. Some CSUs optionally loop incoming network signals in place of the blue signal to prevent network equipment alarms. Another option provides loopback of network signals without bipolar violation removal to assist in fault location. That is, network incoming BPVs are returned to the network on a loopback rather than being removed by the CSU's signal monitor.

Loopback command recognition functions permit remote control of the CSUs loopback. Unlike DDS CSUs, sealing current reversal is not used to cause loopback of a T1 CSU. Loop-up and loop-down commands come from the network in the form of repetitive pulse streams described previously in Chapter 5, under T1/D4 Loopback Signals. As a reminder, loopback signals in T1/D4 consist of at least five continuous seconds of a loop-up pattern:

$$...1\,0\,0\,0\,0\,1\,0\,0\,0\,0\,1\,0\,0\,0...$$

within full, normal D4 framing. This pattern is really a "one," followed by four "zeros." The loop-down command, a "one" followed by two "zeros," also runs for a minimum of five seconds:

$$...1\,0\,0\,1\,0\,0\,1\,0\,0\,1\,0\,0\,1\,0...$$

and is also D4 framed. Many T1 test sets will generate these T1/D4 loop-up and loop-down patterns in preparation for transmitting test signals. These command streams, which are long enough to prevent inadvertent loopbacks, can be issued from network test centers or from far-end CSUs. As many devices in a T1 circuit may recognize these loop-up and loop-down patterns, it is important to work closely with the carrier when using loopbacks. Loopback signals inserted at a CSU may cause loopbacks at unexpected places in the circuit.

Next, the CSU connects to the network interface through an office repeater. Office repeater functions, already mentioned in Chapter 5, include regeneration of the incoming network T1 signal usually with automatic line build out (ALBO) signal level compensation. On the outbound network side, optional signal attenuating pads permit corrections for the distance to the carrier's line repeater. Network line isolation through small transformers and surge protection against lightning or other high voltage line faults also come with office repeater functions. The most complex options of the office repeater involve powering.

Figure 6.15 on page 167 shows a combination of line repeaters and the office repeater of a typical CSU. In the figure, the office repeater is "line powered" from the "span." This means that all power for the CSU comes in on the network signal pairs in a form previously described as simplex powering. T1 circuit powering, however, differs from DDS CSU simplex or sealing current. Figure 6.5 on page 147 illustrated simplex sealing current

167

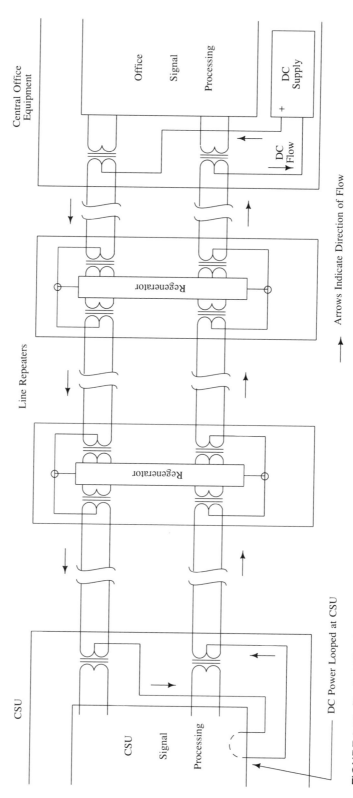

FIGURE 6.15. Typical Simplex Powering of Line Repeaters and CSUs.

flowing to the DDS CSU to maintain low resistance in the loop and to tell the DDS CSU when loopback was commanded. Figure 6.15 illustrates a more complex scheme which not only keeps resistance low on the loop, but may also actually supply power to each connected repeater.

Figure 6.15 seems relatively straightforward and easy to understand. DC battery power from a telephone central office flows through the T1 cable pairs powering both line repeaters and the user's CSU. This unfortunately is the simplest case; local loop CSU powering may take one of many forms. Office repeaters may either supply DC simplex current into the local loop or may receive it from the loop for power as shown in the figure. If an office repeater generates the span current, it may be required to accept −48 volts, +130 volts or some combination (+178 or +260 volts). The office repeater function may then generate a current of 60 milliampere (ma) or 140 ma (less common) into the local loop. This sealing current may then power one or more line repeaters between the user's CSU and the network's office repeater. If the user's CSU takes power from the loop, it may arrive as 60 ma or 140 ma. Clearly, an option strap set wrong may cause damage here. Yet another case becomes more common with the installation of fiber optic cables.

Fiber optic cables offer enormous advantages over copper cables, but cannot deliver sealing or powering current. (Although the FCC no longer requires local telephone companies to supply DC simplex powering current on the metallic local loops, many local companies will continue to supply powering on existing installations.) Where T1 arrives on a fiber, local power must be provided for the CSU. Most desirably, this power should be supplied by batteries to permit network testing even through local (user) power outages. Often, however, the CSU may be the only device needing DC battery power and small DC power supplies connect CSUs to the local AC power line. The CSU is then optioned for −48 volts DC or +130 volts DC. Each of these power options is listed in the vendors documentation, but experienced help should be requested before attempting CSU power option setting. This complex area requires full cooperation between the user, the T1 circuit carrier and the CSU vendor to achieve results.

T1 CSU Optional Features

Beyond the required options for normal CSU operation, many advanced features for network monitoring and testing are supplied by CSU manufacturers. These include test units which can replace signal monitors, external test sets and "clear channel" CSUs for use with user T1 devices which produce unusual T1 bit streams. T1 digital encryption units used to secure data privacy and authenticity will often produce long "zeros" strings which may violate network limits. In Chapter 5, extended superframe format (ESF) was described as an extension of the more well-known T1/D4 framing method. As network carriers convert more of their facilities and circuits to ESF, channel service units will increasingly offer functions to take advantage of the advanced features of this T1 line framing discipline. Channel service unit manufacturers should be contacted directly to learn about these advanced features and options. It becomes apparent that CSUs offer many options for a user to select prior to proper operation. This long list of options confuses many new users and may, on occasion, cause damage to the CSU. We suggest a careful review of all CSU options with the CSU vendor, the T1 equipment vendor and the network T1 carrier prior to actual installation.

CHAPTER 7

Digital Synchronization

Chapter Overview

Synchronization aligns digital data signals with timing signals, and timing signals tell when a data signal's "one" is truly a "one." Synchronization links timing from differing parts of a network into a concerted whole. Perhaps no subject creates more confusion than digital timing and synchronization; certainly digital timing concepts and words about timing intimidate people. But if complex timing can be decomposed into simpler concepts, then fear reduces and comprehension grows. By examining these simpler themes, we hope to extend understanding of how timing works and how it controls the whole of digital communications. Then digital master clocks, timing distribution through networks and timing application will seem less mysterious.

Beginning with the concepts of timing as it transmits and recovers digital bit streams, the chapter goes on to explain where timing comes from and how timing signals move along with digital signals. Master clocks from private sources and major carriers, examined and compared, become watches by which we time our new railroad. Oversized words, such as plesiochronous and homochronous, break down into simple ideas and uncover the mechanics keeping digital signal equipment locked together. Arcane topics of jitter and elastic buffers disclose the inner workings of digital data systems permitting interconnection of private and common carrier networks. T-Carrier timing, long misunderstood, is found to be an extension of techniques first developed in analog modems.

Characteristics of digitally timed data streams differ, however, from older technologies and suggest different tuning for **front-end processors** (FEP). Digital signal error behavior also affects data communications and computer equipment in different ways from earlier analog methods, and this warrants discussion. Many strange behaviors observed in computer digital communications can be traced to analog FEP tuning in the presence of digital services. Digital data services (DDS) and T-Carrier timing and synchronization, once put under the glasses, yield to understanding. Following understanding of these concepts and workings, private system timing schemes and interconnection with carrier services are contemplated. Finally, fallback sources of clocking conclude the chapter.

Timing of Data Signals

Think of an orchestra leader using a baton to signal musicians to play together, and you will understand the beginnings of digital signal timing. A data device, ready to send a "one" or a "zero," needs to be told when to transmit. At the other end of the line, the receiver needs to be told when to sample the voltage or current on the communications line. The baton of our conductor moves up and down to signal these times. Clean rectangular digital bit streams leave a transmitter on the beat, but arrive rounded and deformed after transmission. Sending digital signals into a hostile world is an easier process than recovering them from signal lines; timing recovery forms our major focus. Before discussing recovery, however, timing signals must originate and transmit.

The following discussion covers one of two major areas in data origin signal timing, bit timing and synchronization. The other major area is character or frame synchronization. Bit-sync must come first as bits form the characters or frames. Once bit-sync locks, then bits may be examined for patterns indicating characters or frames. Character-oriented schemes, such as asynchronous (async) or binary synchronous (bisync), first set bit-sync and only then apply character synchronism. Special, reserved characters tell where control, address, and message boundaries exist. Frame-oriented schemes, such as IBM's **synchronous data link control** (SDLC) and CCITT's **high level data link control** (HDLC) move immediately from bit-sync to frame-sync by locating special bit sets called **frames.** Once frames are located, bit content between frames decodes to control, address and information bits. Character and frame synchronization schemes are well described in other places; we shall concentrate on bit synchronization methods and we start with bit transmit timing.

Transmit Timing

Somewhere in each data transmitting unit exists a clock; this clock creates a beat to send the bits. In Chapter 4, timing signals moved across the interfaces from data terminating equipment (DTE) to data communications equipment (DCE) on separated leads or wires. Several choices for driving or using timing signals were illustrated; these become the starting point for this chapter's work. The timing generator, also called a clock, produces a continuous stream of alternating pulses, operating at the desired data transmission rate. That is, at 56,000 bit/s the data signal contains "ones" and "zeros" depending on data content, but the timing signal runs continuously at 56,000 pulses per second. Each pulse of the timing signal clocks out a "one" or a "zero" at its appointed moment. Figure 7.1 illustrates this fundamental timing phenomenon.

Notice that the timing signal runs continuously, or in other words, a positive electrical pulse exists for each potential positive data pulse. If a sending DTE contains a "one" to

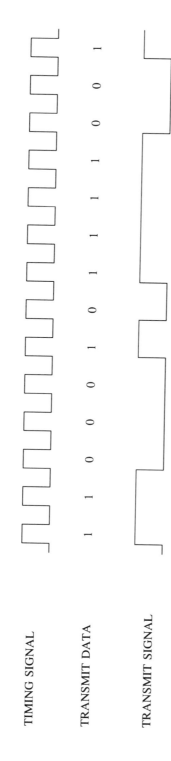

TIMING SIGNAL

TRANSMIT DATA

TRANSMIT SIGNAL

FIGURE 7.1. Transmit Timing and Data Signals.

send, the "one" moves out when told by a timing clock pulse. Each data pulse leaves the DTE at an exact moment dictated by the clock pulse train. The next question asks where our transmit clock originates.

In analog modems used in personal computers and low-speed communications links, a clock exists in each device, and needs no external reference. Each DTE/DCE combination transmit section contains a clock which the data signal follows. Where two DCEs connect by a simple point-to-point link, each DCE may clock data out at its own transmit rate. Whether the clock exists in the DCE (modem clocking) or in the DTE (business machine clocking) does not matter. Each end times out its data signal; if two transmit ends run at slightly differing rates, no data damage results. Bit buffering in DTE devices prevents slight differences from affecting data integrity. Most data messages have finite lengths with a pause following each character and message. An example of this type of timing, found in most simple analog data communications links, permits independent clocks at each end to conduct the data. Here, each modem drives the line rate; data recovery, discussed later, becomes a problem for the receiving modem. Thus, a modem pair really exists as two independent units, with a near-end modem speaking over a long line to a far-end modem— another pair conducting business in the other direction. This form of independent data signal timing may be called **independent** or **non-synchronized timing.**

An important distinction must be understood between two similar words, synchronous and synchronize. Synchronous (and its opposite, asynchronous) timing of data signals talks to the nature of timing, not its source. Synchronous timing is an alternate to asynchronous timing. In asynchronous timing each character stands alone, and timing may run most independently indeed. Each new character starts, appropriately, with a start pulse or bit; each data bit follows at about the right rate. Asynchronous means that each character moves a-synchronously, or without timing reference to the next data character. A little thought reveals that minor variations in speed or rate will not affect a five-, six-, seven- or eight-bit character. A stop bit follows each character to separate it from the next character. Each new character starts the process over again with a new start pulse or bit; even a 10% variation in timing between ends will not affect the result. Thus asynchronous data timing is only approximate and is accomplished by setting clocks to about the same rate. Typical asynchronous speeds might be 1,200 bit/s or 2,400 bit/s; bit timing starts afresh with each character.

Synchronous timing, however, runs continuously assuring that send and receive clocks operate on exactly the same time reference. As timing continues indefinitely, small variations in clocks will eventually cause incorrect bit sampling and data errors. If clocks differ by 1%, about one in every one hundred pulses may be missed. Synchronous timing, then, must assure that sending and receiving clocks run together. This locking of clocks on synchronous links introduces our second word: synchronize. Like soldiers in a battle film, synchronize means setting (and keeping) clocks together. In our simple example link of two DCEs, this synchronization is achieved by recovering transmit clock at the receive end. Recovery will become the single most important concept in synchronization of timing. Once a clock or timing signal is recovered, it may be used to clock or time both received data signals and other transmitted data signals. Synchronized recovery of incoming data will be detailed very shortly.

Thus synchronize and synchronous relate, but differ in application. Synchronous describes how the data clocks out; synchronize tells where the clock comes from. If a clock operates independently, it will be called free-running. If, however, a clock depends on some other source, then the dependence must be examined; this will lead to clock and network synchronization.

Dependent Transmit Timing

Referring again to a simple point-to-point connection (holding the subject of recovery for a moment) transmit clocks may depend or rely on one of several outside sources. This mode of clock synchronization takes the name external timing. External means accepting a clock synchronizing signal from outside the unit containing the transmit clock. A very simple case exists when a DCE takes timing from an attached DTE, as in business machine clocking from a communications front-end processor or communicating control unit. Dependent clocking does not remove the clock from our example DCE, but does force its internal clock to track, follow or lock to an external timing signal. Outside signals for external timing come from at least two different places; each bears examination. The first outside signal is a timing source acting as a local master clock (station clock) or **building integrated timing system** (BITS).

When many units in a single location must operate together, a central source of stable timing may supply timing for all. This single master clock generates an accurate and low jitter timing reference for all attached devices. (Jitter, a complex subject on its own, receives full treatment later in this chapter.) The timing signal from this master feeds each unit; all units lock to its beat. Another way of expressing the connection is that all unit timing slaves to a master clock. The local master, itself. may take yet more accurate timing from some other place in a large network in a hierarchy of timing signals.

The second major source of external timing leads naturally into the subject of recovery. Clock recovery, already outlined in Chapter 5 under regenerators, describes a method of extracting stable timing signals from incoming data bit streams.

Recovering Clocking Signals

Up to now, only transmit timing has been discussed, but what of receive data timing? In asynchronous transmission, independent clocks running at about the correct rate served well. In synchronous data transmission, however, about is no longer good enough. Now timing signals must lock together, and means must be found to detect what timing was used to send the data. This detection is timing recovery from incoming data signals. But data (in bipolar signals) contains both "ones" with pulses and "zeros" with no pulses. If pulses represented both "ones" and "zeros", the job would be easier, but in high-speed data this is not the case. Timing in bipolar streams must be recovered where no pulses exist. Something must keep our beat when no beat arrives and that something is a **clock recovery electrical circuit.** This circuit extracts what timing can be found on an incoming data stream, cleans up jitter (jitter will be covered in the next few pages), and remembers the beat until new pulses arrive.

Extraction of timing from data streams, now possibly rounded and deformed, starts with circuits which decide when a front edge of a pulse rises sufficiently to call it a pulse. At this moment, clock recovery starts a timing pulse feeding it to a remembering part of the circuit. Remembering a clock rate takes a device usually called a **phase locked loop** or **phase locked oscillator** (PLL or PLO). The PLL runs as a free-running timing source unless told to move its frequency or timing rate. Once told to move to a higher (or lower) rate by the extraction circuit, the PLL keeps this new rate for a short time or remembers the new rate. Many excellent books cover the subject of PLLs is consuming detail; for data communications purposes, PLLs exist as tools to remember a clock rate coming in on a data signal. The key to PLLs in timing recovery becomes how long they keep the beat in an absence of new incoming data pulses and what constraints they impose on the data transmitter. While timing recovery involves extraction, PLLs and distribution, the term PLL will be used here to cover all clock recovery functions.

Keeping the beat may be designed into PLLs at a wide range of choices, but choices limit data transmission options. If a PLL keeps the last known rate for a long period, say several seconds, changes in incoming data may be missed. If the PLL only remembers a rate for several pulses, then a "one" following many "zeros" may be missed as our PLL drifts back toward its free-running rate. A design choice must compromise between long and short term data recovery. The choice made many years ago by design engineers could be challenged today, but with little import. The choice suggested for most digital transmission facilities allows up to 15 consecutive "zeros" without a "one." This choice limits the data transmitter. While exact parameters of this design choice involve more than just counting consecutive "zeros," and concern how many "ones" appear in a stream, we shall refer to the design choice under the name "ones" density. Remember that in bipolar bit streams, only "ones" contain pulse energy. As almost all high-speed digital transmission systems use bipolar, this "ones" density issue is fundamental to transmission timing recovery.

"Ones" Density

"Ones" density, oversimplified as no more than 15 consecutive "zeros" which allow clock recovery circuits to coast through periods of about 15 to 30 pulse times. During this coast time, PLLs keep the beat and remain ready to sample new "ones" at an old rate. As arriving pulse rates change slowly, PLLs modify their rates to match or continue timing lock to the incoming pulses. A mechanical analogy may help to understand the function of PLLs. Think of a hoop driven along a path by hitting it with a stick; this hoop continues rolling at a near constant rate as long as the stick is regular. If we fail for some seconds to hit our hoop, it will slow and eventually fall. A PLL will not fall, but will slowly revert to its natural or free-running rate. How far this natural rate drifts from an incoming data rate will determine when sampling errors will begin. As long as incoming data drives the PLL, it will stay with an incoming data rate through short pulse-less intervals. The amount of drift varies also depending on the needed quality of the PLL.

If a PLL exists only to recover a single data stream, quality (and cost) may be just sufficient to do that job. If, however, this PLL must not only recover timing, but supply it to many other devices, it must be more accurate (and expensive). This type of clock recovery device needs several costly additions to function as a clock distributor. Accuracy and stability of the free-running rate in a clock distribution PLL need to be much higher. The PLL must be closer to a desired system frequency; it must be stable at that rate for long periods of time if input lock frequency disappears. In addition to accuracy and stability, other key functions must be present, such as an ability to select from two or more external lock frequencies and to know when to select them. Key to the operation of these more exotic recovery devices is reduction of jitter.

Jitter in Timing Signals

When a pulse arrives at other than an exactly expected time, the variation takes the name **jitter** or **wander.** Jitter concerns short-term variations over a short period and wander describes longer term variations. While no one yet agrees what is short and what is long, the terms describe real problems in a digital world. Jitter contributes to errors causing difficulty in timing signal distribution. Jitter, most simply, is just what it sounds like—a wobble (in time) of what should be exact pulses. The art and science of jitter measurement develops continuously, but a few terms and many approaches exist to reduce jitter in high-speed digital circuits. Illustrated in Figure 7.2, jitter can cause an incoming data pulse to be missed or misinterpreted. As incoming data streams carry timing along, jitter must be controlled and reduced if timing is to be redistributed.

The illustration shows jittered data pulses arriving and being sampled by a non-jittered timing signal train. Imagine, however, that timing derived from that incoming data stream becoming as jittered as the data. To distribute such wobbly timing would severely distort everything it touched. Prior to distribution, jitter must be removed or at least reduced to satisfactory levels. But what are the levels by which we measure jitter and what are the units? For consistency at the many speeds of digital communications, a **unit interval** (UI) has become the most common descriptor of jitter. A unit interval is simply the time from the leading edge of one pulse to the leading edge of the next pulse, assuming a pulse exists. Another way of expressing a UI is one over the pulse rate. For a 56,000 bit/s signal stream, each pulse period, and, therefore, the UI, is 1/56000 or 17.9 microseconds (μsec). At T1, a period (and UI) is 1/1544000, or 0.648 μsec. Jitter can now be expressed in unit intervals and understood as portions (or multiples) of pulse periods.

Without additional electronics, jitter of more than a small portion of a UI would be disastrous. If jitter in timing or data became greater than about half of a pulse period, few incoming pulses could be interpreted correctly. If means existed to recover data pulses separately from timing, then timing could be de-jittered (**jitter-attenuation**), or at least timing jitter could be reduced for further distribution. The PLL would scan over many pulse periods to smooth out jitter, and data pulses could be held for (slightly later) use. The means exist in the form of elastic buffers. Concepts of storing data in buffers goes back to the origins of computers, but elastic buffers work differently.

Elastic Buffers

In discussing digital buffers, the order of input and output to and from a buffer must first be known. Terms drawn from accounting describe buffer actions with simple acronyms used to tell when bits enter and leave. If bits enter and leave in sequence, **first-in first-out** (FIFO) illustrates action. If the most recent bit entering a buffer leaves first, then **last in first-out** (LIFO) describes buffering operation. Note that conversion buffers, such as serial to parallel, are not considered here; only serial-in to serial-out bit streams interest us here. **Elastic buffers** (also called **elastic stores**) operate in a FIFO manner with bits leaving at the same average rate as they enter. With bits entering and leaving at the same average rate, a question arises as to why buffer at all? The answer lies in average rate. If timing pulses and data pulses did not wobble, elastic buffers would be unnecessary for timing purposes. In real world transmission scenarios, however, multiplexing, noise, variations in ambient temperatures and electronic units operating out of specification cause jitter requiring elastic buffers. Also, timing for an incoming data stream may originate elsewhere

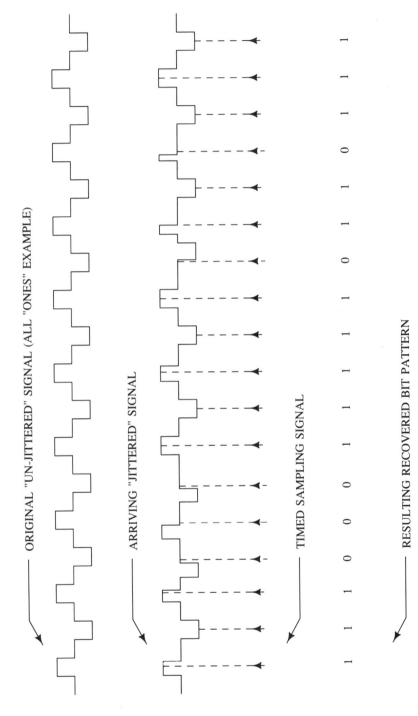

FIGURE 7.2. Jitter in Data and Timing Signals.

in the system. External timing transitions, while running at the same average rate, may not occur at the precise instants needed to capture incoming data.

Given need for these buffers, how do they work to recover jittered data? In Figure 7.3 on page 178, an example elastic buffer with eight-bit slots illustrates one form of operation. Bits enter from the left as they are detected on the incoming signal line. As each bit enters, an electronic pointer moves right to show the position of the first (as yet unremoved) bit in the buffer. As each additional bit enters from the left, all bits in the buffer shift right along with the pointer. A timing extractor PLL also reads the incoming signal line developing a timing pulse train, which runs at the same average rate as the data. A smoothed timing rate has reduced jitter, but without an elastic buffer, it may create errors when reading data pulses entering the buffer faster or slower than the smoothed timing rate. Like an elastic band, this buffer takes up slack, permitting smoothed timing to read out jittered data. This smoothed timing signal, by following the buffer pointer, removes bits from the buffer sending them on to other processing electronics at a smoothed and steady timing rate. As each bit leaves the buffer, the pointer shifts left to mark the newly-elected oldest bit. Entering bits, "ones" or "zeros," shift our pointer right; departing bits shift it left.

The smoothed timing rate may, at any one instant, be a little ahead or behind current data pulses entering the buffer. Consider two data pulses moving into a buffer faster than the smoothed timing signal. As the first enters this buffer, a pointer moves right to mark the position of the oldest bit in the buffer. Before our smoothed timing signal can remove this oldest bit, another bit enters the buffer moving the pointer another position to the right. Similarly, a slower data pulse enters buffering after timing has removed several older pulses. Imagine a buffer pointer sliding back and forth continuously, compensating for variations in incoming data rate. Elastic buffer size in clock recovery circuits gives rise to a unit's ability to tolerate jitter. This is called **jitter-tolerance;** it varies with the speed or frequency of the jitter itself. Slower moving jitter becomes easier to handle than higher frequency jitter; reference books will show jitter masks which are graphs describing jitter-tolerance in UI at various frequencies. (A mask for allowable T1 jitter is shown later in this chapter with a discussion of jitter in T1 signals.) Thus an elastic buffer arrangement operates with a certain jitter-tolerance providing jitter-attenuation.

Output from the buffer, however, runs at a very steady rate indeed reducing jitter in our sample buffer. This process may also be called jitter-attenuation.

The buffer's elastic nature comes from this movement of the pointer, with buffer contents varying continuously depending on timing variations. What happens when too many (or too few) bits enter before removal? A condition called **buffer overflow,** for obvious reasons, results. Overflow (or underflow) of elastic buffers causes slips of data streams forcing restart of an entire synchronization process. Slips, which may originate from excessive jitter or from timing drift between timing systems, become another measure of timing system performance. Slip rate measurements characterize total system performance; carriers set objectives for slip rates when transmission systems interconnect and synchronized network timing is needed.

Synchronized Network Timing

Earlier in this chapter, DTE/DCE clocks were described as capable of operating free-running at differing rates on simple point-to-point circuits. When can this be done and when must timing be synchronized from network sources? While private and some local

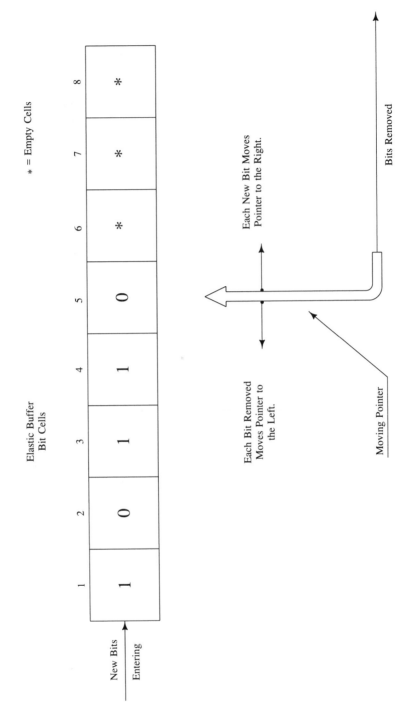

Elastic Buffer
Bit Cells

* = Empty Cells

1	2	3	4	5	6	7	8
1	0	1	1	0	*	*	*

New Bits
Entering

Each New Bit Moves
Pointer to the Right.

Each Bit Removed
Moves Pointer to
the Left.

Moving Pointer

Bits Removed

FIGURE 7.3. Elastic Buffer Example Operation.

individual circuits may operate without concern for network timing, increased complexity of circuit connections moves even simple data networks toward synchronized network timing. Use of leased digital data services (DDS) from carriers usually mandates acceptance of DDS clocking schemes. Interconnection of private networks with carrier networks infers use of network clocks; large digital networks require network-wide timing synchronization. Integration of voice and data signals on common transmission and switching equipment quickly demonstrates a need for a common stable clock. Integrated Services Digital Networks (ISDN) must include provision for consistent and network-wide timing designs.

Shortly, sources available for synchronized network timing will be covered and compared. Before proceeding, however, variations on the timing theme must be understood and some important words explained. Simple digital data communications facilities may start without deep concern for timing sources, but as expansion occurs and additional functions are needed, timing designs may be difficult to retrofit into a network. An underlying understanding of what may be needed as networks expand means that a timing strategy should be part of a network planner's tool kit. As circuits and functions grow, well-defined synchronization strategies phase in to network design. Techniques to cope with differing network and equipment requirements should be understood at the outset and plans prepared. As user needs for very high availability develop, backup circuits and facilities are added to a network, synchronization becomes more complex. The last section of this chapter outlines considerations for developing strategies in complex digital networks. To prepare for those considerations, a somewhat heavy timing vocabulary is needed to permit successful verbal communication of the topics.

System Timing Terminology

Synchronization has been explained as the ability to lock to or follow a timing reference or source, but several characteristics of the source or reference must be known. In addition, various parameters of the equipment to be synchronized need to be defined and understood. Then several types of system timing and the words describing them must be detailed. First we cover timing source characteristics.

For an electronic timing source or clock to be useful in a digital network, timing accuracy and stability specifications are paramount. If a clock must accept external timing from another source, then that acceptance ability must be known. From the elastic buffer material above, these clock specifications drive toward maintaining a network slip rate objective. Accuracy of a digital timing clock reference differs little from accuracy of any clock; that is, how close to real time is it? Stability also relates to clocks by stating the amount of change over a long period of time, but unlike other clocks, a digital reference clock's stability specifies its drift away from the frequency it had when locked to another reference. In hierarchies of clock reference levels used by carriers, lower level clocks lock to higher levels up to the highest level which determines a reference frequency for all clocks in a timing system. When a timing link between higher and lower levels fails, the lower level clock's stability measures its drift away from what used to be the central clock. Finally, each clock specifies over what range it will pull-in to a reference supplied by a higher level master. Thus accuracy, stability and acceptance or pull in range determine the quality of each clock in the system. In the next major section, typical specifications for these three criteria will detail what exists in current clocking technology.

Terminology for digital clocking derives from simple Greek words and, once explained, should reduce further anxiety. Each term refers to some type of timing within a bit stream or digital system; all end with a Greek origin word, *-chronous,* standing for time. While a great many terms are defined, only a few are needed to describe all but the most exotic timing schemes. An examination of Greek origin prefixes helps out here. The six most common terms and their approximate English meanings are:

HETERO—Different

HOMO—Same

ISO—Equal

MESO—Middle

PLESIO—Near

SYN—With

Starting with an old friend, *synchronous* means operation at precisely the same average rate. *Mesochronous* (say: may-sock'-run-us) is used by the CCITT as an alternate word for synchronous. Note that both terms refer to "precisely the same average" rate deriving from somewhat differing source words, namely "with" and "middle." This becomes a caution to users that such things as elastic buffers, as previously described, may be needed. Both terms speak to characteristics of an individual digital signal or a single bit stream, rather than to sources of timing. Contrasting synchronous with asynchronous yields a meaning of having fixed continuous timing, and this is a near-accurate definition.

The next two words also associate similar meanings about the nature of bit streams rather than clock sources, although an inference is made that different clock sources are used. In both these words, two or more signals or bits streams are implied. Thus these words compare timing of similar bit streams or groups of digital signals. *Plesiochronous* (say: plee-zee-ahhk'-run-us) refers to signal rates which, while nominally the same, really differ within narrow limits. Plesiochronous, for example, may refer to several independent signals, each close to 56,000 bit/s, but not exactly the same. The limits usually require signals to be very close to a specified rate, such as 1,544,000 bit/s ± 50 bit/s. In this example, two DS-1 streams operating within limits, but driven from separate clocks, would be plesiochronous signals. *Isochronous* (say: eye-sock'-run-us) also refers to signal rates which do not match exactly. Common practice adds a meaning for independently clocked signals. Some signals, which cannot be locked to a system rate, may be carried at their own isochronous speed by special equipment. In digital systems practice, both these signal types may require bit-stuffing when multiplexed to higher speeds.

Finally, two words describe clocking systems contrasting their sources. *Homochronous* (say: home-ahhk'-run-us) infers a single clocking source. Homochronous speaks of clocks which relate directly and consistently from a single (same) reference. *Heterochronous* (say: het-er-ahhk'-run-us) becomes the opposite of homochronous by defining differing sources or references, that is, clocks which are not able to lock together. It should be clear, at this point, that discussion of timing systems involves some complexity, but that detailing actual meaning can simplify the problems. Understanding timing really involves knowing which clock is the master, how timing is distributed and what systems lock to the master source.

Sources of Timing and Clocking

Clock sources for digital communications exist in almost all data communications equipment, but differ in levels of accuracy and stability. In analog circuits, even at higher speeds, these independent clocks suffice. As each data signal converts from digital to analog for transmission through public or private network lines, synchronization of original timing rides the analog signal. After conversion back to digital at each circuit far-end, this recovered digital timing signal may be used and discarded or may loop time a return circuit. Loop timing merely supplies recovered incoming received timing as an external timing signal for data transmit timing. In analog transmission, no requirement exists for synchronizing or locking multiple circuits together. Analog transmission networks do not use timing signals, at least not in their analog sections. Where conversion to digital occurs inside a transmission network or facility, that timing remains invisible to analog end points. Digital networks and direct digital network connections change all this.

Consider two basic types of synchronous digital connections, plesiochronous and homochronous. In a plesiochronous network attachment, DTE/DCE end equipment must generate and recover timing within a frequency tolerance or limit imposed by carrier or network equipment. In typical point-to-point T1 connections to local or long-distance digital carriers, users must supply timing from their DCEs to the network at 1.544 Mbit/s within 50 or 75 bit/s, plus or minus. This user timing signal rides the carrier network through to far-end user equipment, appearing at close to its original frequency or rate. For example, if a user DCE clocks out data at 1,544,045 bit/s, the network will deliver a far-end data signal at about 1,544,045 bit/s. For plesiochronous operation, network equipment accepts and delivers user data timed at any rate within tolerance limits. If a user's data rate drifts outside the carrier's limits, errors can occur not only in a user's circuit, but may affect the network; it will certainly cause alarms in network equipment. At far-end user equipment, timing from the near end may be used to loop time far-end data transmitting circuits in the user's DCE. Although less often used, an alternate method clocks far-end transmit data from an independent far-end clock. Many private network data T1 connections to public carriers use plesiochronous timing. With DDS services and more advanced T-Carrier services, however, homochronous timing must be accommodated.

Homochronous timing, or network generated master timing, delivers clock signals to *all* user end equipment, and *all* user equipment must be optioned to loop time. That is, all user equipment should use recovered incoming timing to drive all transmit data sent back to the network. Where large numbers of circuits originate, a local master clock arrangement may take clocking from one or more circuits distributing that timing to all user DCE equipment. Circuits used to derive source timing to local master clocks should be selected based on circuit reliability and quality of network timing represented. Circuit reliability becomes a key selection element for obvious reasons, as operation of a master clock depends on this signal. Master or station clocks often accept at least two timing sources. If a master clock accepts more than one timing input, additional feeding circuits should be selected on the same basis as the first. Network derived timing rapidly becomes a preferred method when advanced features or multiple network interconnection enters our picture.

Network derived timing opens an entire field of questions for examination; this will now occupy our study, beginning with a review of the world's digital clocks.

Digital Master Clocks

The story of digital timing starts in the seventeenth century on the Thames River, near London. Greenwich Observatory has been associated with time since 1676 when two great clocks began keeping what is still called **Greenwich Mean Time** (GMT). **Mean time,** produced by clocks, differs from **apparent time** as indicated by sundials. Mean time provides a steady "beat," but may drift as far as 20 minutes from apparent time in any given month. When averaged over 12 months, mean and apparent times come very nearly together. While astronomers need to work with time as seen in the heavens, the rest of us have become quite used to mean time. Dropping the famous Time Ball from a high turret at Greenwich to signal mid-day, mean time, began in 1833. The ball dropped daily signaling the exact hour at 1300 hours (1:00 PM), as navigators were expected to be busy "shooting the sun" at noon. For many years, daily synchronization proved adequate, but railroads soon needed more accurate timing.

In the mid-nineteenth century every city and village kept its own time. While close enough for local use, it was not good enough to keep railroad schedules. The time for standard time arrived. Four time zones were established dividing the U. S. into four time areas. On Sunday, November 18, 1883, a U. S. Naval Observatory noon-time signal was telegraphed across the nation. Differences between some major cities were found to be over 30 minutes! While the nation's railroads and many cities agreed to "railroad time," it was not until the Standard Time Act of 1918 that a national time standard became a reality. Synchronization had been reached down to the minute.

World agreement on timing began in the nineteenth century at an international meeting in Washington. In October 1884, at the International Meridian Conference, 25 nations voted to " . . . to adopt a single prime meridian for all nations." The conference proposed that their governments select Greenwich Observatory for that prime meridian of zero degrees longitude. Of importance to timing, the meeting also adopted a "universal day" beginning at midnight and having 24 hours. Work began to obtain agreement on differences between this day, the astronomical day, the agricultural day and the nautical day.

The development of radio communications permitted exchange of time signals down to the second. Agreement on time in seconds, however, was not an easy task. The earth's rotation of one day is not constant when measured accurately. Tidal friction, irregular orbital fluctuations, polar wobble, and seasonal variations cause minor variations in time. After several attempts at reconciliation between various methods measuring time, the 1967 General Conference on Weights and Measures in Paris resolved that the second be referred to atomic standards. Atomic clocks had progressed to extreme accuracies and the conference agreed to define a second as ". . . the duration of 9,192,631,770 periods of the radiation . . . of the cesium-133 atom." Cesium-beam timing technology had reached accuracies approaching a few microseconds (μsec) per year. From 1919 until the end of 1987, the Bureau International de l'Heure (BIH) in Paris operated as a timekeeper for the world. Beginning in 1988, the International Earth Rotation Service, located outside Paris, coordinates what has become known as **coordinated universal time** (UTC).

UTC has replaced GMT as the world's time standard and all scientific, governmental, and commercial clocks count their time in UTC. In the United States, the National Bureau of Standards and the U. S. Naval Observatory maintain coordinated cesium-beam clocks traceable to coordination from the International Earth Rotation Service in Paris. Government radio stations broadcast these time signals throughout the nation and at sea. When corrections are needed, orders go out that leap seconds be added or subtracted around the world; this compensates the new atomic second for variations in astronomical time. World time is now standardized and coordinated down to the second.

Time standardization using cesium-beam clocks keeps science and navigation together through worldwide consistent time to the second, but what about digital communications? Digital consistencies, better than one part in 10^{-11} needed to lock digital pulse streams, rely on the same cesium-beam technology used in national clocks. These network clocks trace their accuracies to the national clocks, which in turn, trace to UTC coordination.

Network Master Clocks

Network clock sources must operate at greater levels of accuracy and stability than individual circuit sources. With the announcement of AT&T's DATAPHONE® Digital Service, nationwide digital communications clocking began. Today, AT&T's national timing generation and distribution system originates in AT&T's facility at Hillsboro, Missouri, where three cesium-beam timing references are continuously compared to produce an extremely accurate timing source. Originally called the **Bell System Reference Frequency** (BSRF), divestiture caused a name change to **Basic System Reference Frequency** (also BSRF). The BSRF currently acts as a central timing reference for most digital transmission and switching equipment connected to AT&T Communications services. Another cesium-beam timing reference operates from the U. S. Naval Observatory in Washington, DC, and is carried on the U. S. Government's long-range navigation radio system (LORAN). The current navigation system, LORAN-C, supplies reference timing to many carrier and private digital facilities.

Two clocks might, at first, seem to present problems when digital signals from one network clock pass to a network timed from a different clock. The primary cesium-beam clock's accuracy, however, prevents serious problems, as the clocks are frequently checked against LORAN-C as the national reference. Cesium-beam timing generators or clocks operate as primary standards with accuracies greater than one part in 10^{-11} over the life of the clock.

Accuracy numbers in this range are hard to understand; some comparisons may help. Variations between two cesium-beam clocks, drifting at one part in 10^{-11} over approximately 20 years, will move less than seven milliseconds in the 20 years. As the clocks are verified against each other much more frequently, noticeable errors due to primary clock differences will rarely occur. How big are these differences when viewed from a data communications perspective? A difference of one part in 10^{-11} varies a T1 data rate of 1.544 Mbit/s by less than 0.00002 bit/s. Standards groups will continue to examine national clocking strategies and sources, and this will ultimately improve accuracy and interconnection of all national digital networks, but data errors due to differences in primary clock source references should not concern us here. Clock distribution and accuracies below the primary levels form more of a real problem for users and designers of high-speed digital data networks.

Timing Stratum Designations

Clock distribution from the primary reference in the national AT&T Communications system involves four levels or strata. The word **stratum** (strata is the plural) comes from the Latin word for "cover", and simply means layer or level. AT&T Publication 60110 (December 1983) defines requirements for four levels of clocks. Level one, called stratum one, is the cesium-beam primary reference. As primary reference, stratum one forms the highest level of a hierarchy of clocks from which all lower clocks take reference. A valid question asks, why not just synchronize all signals and equipment to a primary reference and forget this stratum business? In a perfect world, without line and equipment failures, this would work well. The real world of reliable communications, however, needs to cope with real world failures of facilities. And so, the strata define lower level (and lower accuracy) clocks which maintain a digital beat in the temporary absence of reference to the primary clock source.

Lower stratum levels connect in a hierarchy to higher levels, eventually connecting to the primary reference. An additional confusion in this hierarchy calls higher (more accurate) levels by lower numbers. Remember that level or stratum 1 is the highest; level or stratum four is the lowest. While another choice of words, such as "accuracy level," might have been easier to remember, stratum level is its name. A phrase, often heard in clocking discussions goes, " . . . traceable to BSRF . . . " meaning that a given local timing system somehow locks onto the stratum hierarchy. That is, it fits into the hierarchy by obtaining its timing from a clock which synchronizes or is locked to another stratum level, preferably higher (more accurate), which ultimately locks to BSRF.

Stratum two clocks, while not as accurate as cesium-beam clocks, require accuracies of greater than ± 1.6 in 10^8, when not locked to stratum one clocks. This accuracy converts to a one second (plus or minus) variation in about two years. In addition to this accuracy, if a fault disconnects the last synchronizing signal from the stratum one clock, a stratum clock two must not drift from the last known frequency faster than one part in 10^{10} per day. When a clock reference signal returns, the stratum two clock must be able to lock or synchronize to that signal within its own accuracy range. Another way of explaining says that a stratum two clock must be capable of locking to any other stratum two or stratum one clock as a reference. And that remains true throughout the hierarchy; each clock level must be capable of locking to its own or a higher (more accurate) level. As we probe more deeply into clock signal distribution, reasons for this rule will become clearer.

At stratum three, accuracies become less stringent and several drift or stability strategies become available. Accuracy requirements for a stratum three clock are ± 4.6 in 10^6 equating to time accuracies of plus or minus one second in about 2.5 days or ± 0.26 bit/s tolerance in a 56,000 data signal. Remember again that this accuracy is worst case and may occur only in the event of complete loss of outside timing reference. Another calibration on accuracy at this level shows that a T1 stream of 1.544 Mbit/s may be clocked at ± 7.1 bit/s by a free-running stratum three clock.

The lowest level, stratum four, needs only an accuracy of ± 32 in 10^6 to qualify. This lowest level clock can hold to within one second for just under nine hours, and within ± 1.8 bit/s at 56,000 bit/s. At T1, a frequency tolerance of ± 50 bit/s can be held.

When a stratum four clock must free-run due to loss of reference, tolerances approach a problem point where errors will occur. If a single data circuit clocks wholly from this stratum four clock, and can operate within tolerances, no clock related errors will be expected. If, however, a circuit must pass to another part of the network where clocking

STRATUM	MIN. ACCURACY	MIN. STABILITY	PULL-IN RANGE
1	± 1 in 10^{-11}	Master Reference	Master Reference
2	± 1.6 in 10^{-8} ⟶ $(\pm .025$ *$)$	1 in 10^{-10}	Should synchronize with a clock accurate to ± 1.6 in 10^{-8}
3	± 4.6 in 10^{-6} ⟶ $(\pm 7.0$ *$)$	± 3.5 in 10^{-9} (some conditions)	Should synchronize with a clock accurate to ± 4.6 in 10^{-6}
4	± 32 in 10^{-6} ⟶ $(\pm 50$ *$)$	N/A	Should synchronize with a clock accurate to ± 32 in 10^{-6}

* = Minimum accuracy relative to T1 at 1,544,000 bit/s.

FIGURE 7.4. Comparison of Clocking Stratum Levels.

remains locked to higher levels, then slip (elastic buffer over- and under-flows) errors will happen at regular intervals. These errors may be reduced, but never eliminated, by properly sizing elastic data buffers. Near the end of this chapter, there will be a discussion of sizing of elastic buffers to compensate for clocking differences. Next, however, distribution of timing signals and strategies for distribution faults will be the focus.

The distribution of timing signals from the primary reference or stratum one clock to lower hierarchical clock levels becomes a subject of study all by itself. Distribution, remember, is complicated by an analysis of possible failures and the provision for back-up linkages "traceable to BSRF," or to some other primary reference.

Timing Signal Distribution

Timing distribution from a primary reference becomes more complex the further from a standard one gets. A timing design, shown in Figure 7.5, illustrates the complexities. The timing scheme describes a typical digital telephone timing design referencing a primary standard, such as BSRF. This example clocking represents a type found in digital data services (DDS) circuits from long-distance carriers.

In Figure 7.5, primary reference clock signals drive from a stratum one clock to several stratum two clocks. Each of those clocks, in turn, supplies reference to lower levels. Note how stratum three clocks receive reference signals from two different stratum two sources, and how stratum fours are fed by several paths. This simple layout shows distribution and how design compensates, in advance, for single circuit or clock failures. In the event that a single stratum two clock fails, all clocks at stratum three and below continue to receive clock "traceable to" our primary reference. This easy design does not really represent the true complexities in a real world design.

A complexity posed by timing distribution considers all possible combinations of failures in a distribution system. Distribution design insists on continuous accurate operation after faults occur, and satisfactory, if degraded, operation until all faults are removed. A straightforward strategy for interconnection of clock levels can be stated simply as: clock reference signals must come from the same stratum or higher under all conditions. Another way of putting it is, a clock must never obtain a reference from a lower level source. This turns out to be easier to say than to implement, for the reason that undesired lower to higher loops become hard to find in complex timing designs. As clock distribution networks expand and interconnect, the possibility of low-to-high loops becomes greater, and greater vigilance is required to identify and remove them.

Figure 7.6 on page 188 depicts a more complex problem and contains a design error. Before revealing the specific error, the reader is encouraged to examine Figure 7.6 for loops which cause lower level clocks to drive higher level clocks. In several failure scenarios, this clock network will produce very strange behaviors.

In Figure 7.6, the stratum one reference point (A) feeds timing down to the lower strata points. Links marked "P" form the primary or first choice timing source for each point and those marked "S" are the secondary synchronization links. As you examine the figure, it will become evident that a break in the primary link between "B" and "C" will cause a potential clock loop (over secondaries) from "G" to "C" to "H" to "G." A failure of the primary link from "D" to "H" will put this loop into operation with unpredictable results

Stratum

1

2

3

4

Primary

Secondary

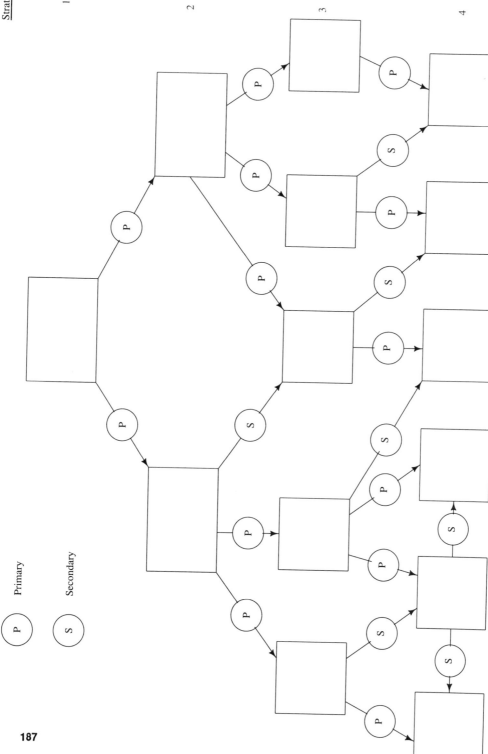

FIGURE 7.5. Typical Clock Distribution in Digital Networks.

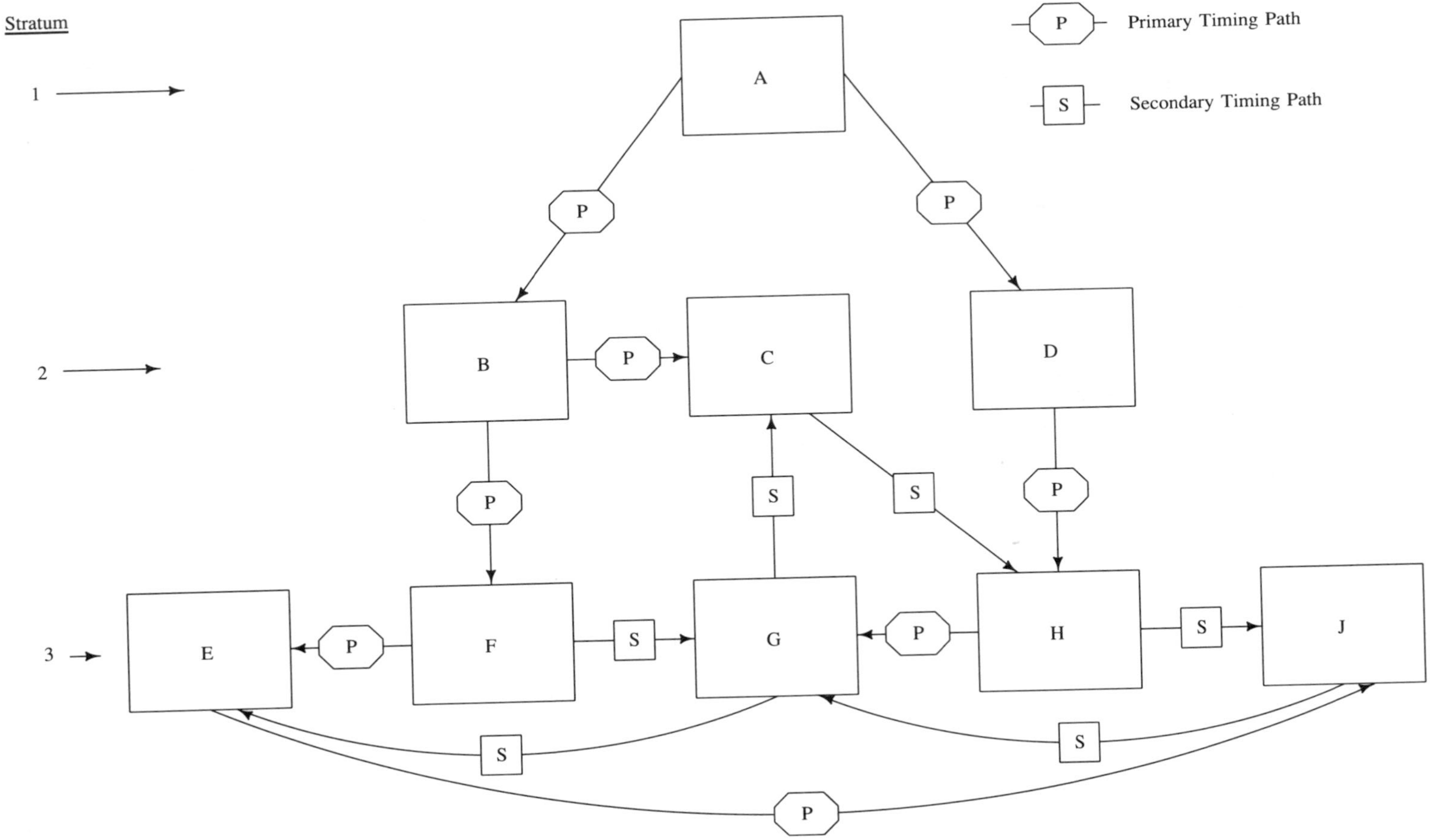

Stratum

1

2

3

P — Primary Timing Path

S — Secondary Timing Path

P Primary Timing Path

S Secondary Timing Path

FIGURE 7.6. Clock Distribution Design (with errors).

to the network. To correct this design, remove the unneeded secondary link from "G" to "C" and reverse the secondary from "F" to "G."

Clocking system designs stemmed from early digital service networks when locking of digital pulse trains became a necessity. AT&T's DATAPHONE® Digital Service described an early scheme for the distribution of national timing.

DDS and Network Clocks

The announcement of DATAPHONE® Digital Service included descriptions of methods for the distribution of the Hillsboro BSRF to the digital communications network. Initial distribution was to be to the St. Louis hub office via a 2.048 megahertz (MHz) analog signal from Hillsboro. Further distribution was to be via 1.544 Mbit/s digital signals. Originally described as master, nodal and local timing supplies, they formed a base for stratum levels to come. Other digital data services (DDS) have usually followed similar schemes for clock distribution.

DDS Clocking Methods

Digital data service clocking systems involve distribution of timing signals imbedded in T1 data streams. After the original 2.048 MHz analog stratum one signal is received at a digital distribution point, called a hub office in telephone terminology, further distribution occurs at 1.544 Mbit/s. At each distribution point several clocks are derived for use in DDS office equipment. Each distribution point should receive timing from at least two sources so that failure in one will not allow the point to free run. Clocking at each point requires two signals—one at 64 kbit/s for bit clocking and one at eight kbit/s for frame or byte clocking. They derive from local office oscillators which lock to equal or higher level (lower stratum) timing sources. The two signals distribute through DDS office equipment in a complex form called a **composite clock signal.**

DDS Composite Signals

The composite clock signal builds from two individual bit rates, providing a single stream to all DDS equipment on a single pair of wires. The eight kbit/s timing signal on the composite clock operates at the frame rate of a T1 stream. This frame rate clocks out 24 frames of eight bits each second resulting in a bit rate of 1,536 Mbit/s. Another 8,000 bit/s framing pattern is added to produce a final T1 rate of 1.544 Mbit/s. The 64 kbit/s clock riding on this composite clock signal drives bit timing for each channel or frame. Since all 24 channels must be available to sample voice or clock data at 8,000 times eight bits, the 64 kbit/s clock signal coordinates this activity. When two clock signals combine to form a composite clock signal, bipolar violations are used to show where each signal is positioned. Figure 7.7 on page 190 shows how this composite clock is built.

The composite clock finds use primarily in DDS office equipment, but clocking in DDS extends all the way to each end user. This clock signal, delivered by the DDS receive wire pair, drives a user's data termination equipment (DTE) receive timing signal. It must also be used by a user's data communications equipment (DCE) to return the clock via loop timing on the DDS transmit wire pair. Connecting to DDS services requires a thorough understanding of these requirements.

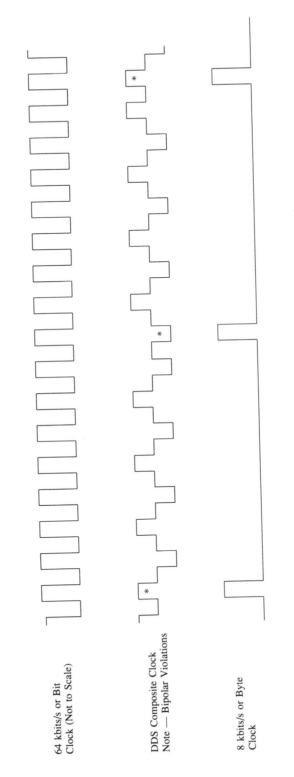

64 kbits/s or Bit
Clock (Not to Scale)

DDS Composite Clock
Note — Bipolar Violations

8 kbits/s or Byte
Clock

*Bipolar Violations (BPV) Occur at 8 kbits/s Clock Points

FIGURE 7.7 DDS Composite Clock Signal.

Connecting to DDS Services

In the previous chapter, DDS data service units (DSU) and channel service units (CSU) were covered at length. Connection to DDS services usually requires installation of at least a CSU which will recover timing from the DDS circuit. If a combination DSU/CSU is installed to provide normal data communications interfaces, it will also derive timing from the DDS network. Most DSU/CSUs will come from their vendors set to accept clock from the incoming signal network pair. Many units, though, offer other timing options, including internal oscillators. Under what conditions would these be used?

When DSU/CSUs are used as limited distance data sets, as described in Chapter 6, all of the clocking options may be needed to complete circuits. If a pair is used to run a local circuit in the building or on the campus, one unit may be chosen as an internally timed master. The other will run in the normal manner, receiving timing from the network (the single in-house two-pair copper circuit). This would be normal practice on any modem or limited distance data set on an isolated single circuit. This practice would be followed whether the speed were 9.6 kbit/s or 1.544 Mbit/s. When the local circuit extends a carrier DDS circuit, timing options must change.

As a DDS circuit extender, our local DSU/CSU pair must change. The far-end, away from the DDS network, continues to loop time, but the near end must now be timed externally from the DDS network. Cross-over cabling, detailed in Chapter 6, carries timing from the network DSU/CSU to the external port on the near end in-house DSU/CSU. Additional examination of the example cross-connect cabling outlined in Figure 6.12 on page 162 will show the details of the timing connections. Figure 7.8 on page 192 reviews a common DDS extension, showing how timing is optioned in each DSU/CSU unit.

Error Behavior in DDS Systems

Since most current DDS quality objectives are 99.5% error-free seconds in a 24-hour period, errors should rarely occur. Yet the behavior of digital systems may cause some apparent problems which differ from those of analog modems. These uniquely digital behaviors are discussed later in this chapter under "Errors in T-Carrier Systems." As DDS signals run through carrier networks on T-Carrier facilities, the discussion also applies to DDS circuits. A brief preview is given here relating only to DDS services.

An error-free second is just what it sounds like, a second of transmission time with no errors. At 99.5% error-free seconds, we should expect an errored second no more often than every 7.2 minutes, assuming an even distribution of the errors. During that errored second, at 56 kbit/s, up to 56,000 bits could be lost. If there were eight bits in a byte and 1,000 bytes in a block, then up to seven blocks could be garbled. This all assumes that errored seconds evenly distribute and that the second is nearly completely errored. Fortunately, this is not how it works. In Chapters 3 and 5, we learned that DDS services are most often derived from T1 carriers and that these carriers are often, themselves, carried on higher speed T-Carriers. This multilevel multiplexing causes a rather different error behavior to appear at the end of a 56 kbit/s circuit.

If a higher level T-Carrier experiences a momentary fault, the fault ripples down to the DDS circuit. As the higher level multiplexers recover, so will the DDS circuits, but some small delay is added. Errors of this type usually last less than 100 milliseconds and can cause, in our example above, a loss of one data block. This error rate is less than

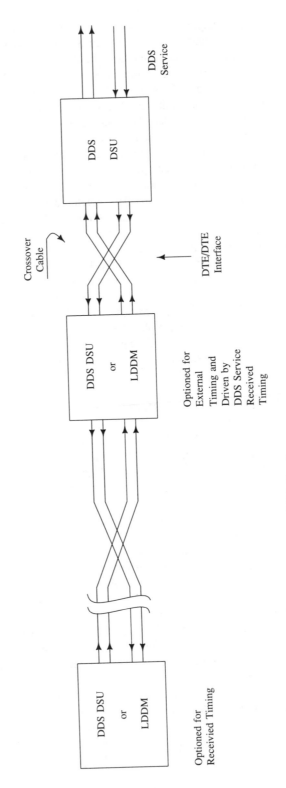

FIGURE 7.8. Timing Options in Interconnected DDS Services.

expected, and recovery is normal. Another type of error behavior, however, may cause unanticipated trouble. This is called burst error behavior.

Occasionally in digital systems, severe conditions cause errors in bursts lasting up to 2.5 seconds before recovery. In the example above, over 17 blocks of data could be lost. In some protocols, this could exceed an errored block or retries counter causing a communications controller or **front-end processor** (FEP) to declare a line out of service. When the DDS line clears, the FEP no longer tries to use it, and operator intervention is called. The operator, unable to find any problem, re-starts the FEP. This behavior can continue indefinitely, unless parameters in the FEP are changed to compensate for the differing error behavior of digital circuits.

Front-end Processor Tuning

While definite recommendations cannot be made due to the wide variations in equipment and programming in FEPs, some general approaches should be followed. In analog circuits, errors were usually evenly distributed; long lasting burstiness was rare. An analog line out for two seconds was usually out for several hours. With digital circuits, parameters and counters should be set to permit several seconds of outage without a line shut-down. This may involve retries or error counts, but a quick calculation, such as that done in the example above, will indicate ranges for these parameters. Vendor representatives can assist with calculations and parameter or counter settings. Prior to changing any parameters, error rates should be trapped and line restarts measured or counted. An old maxim prevails here: if it works, don't fix it. Only if the differing error behavior of digital circuits appears to cause problems, should a fix of this type be attempted.

T-Carrier Timing Methods

People using T1 circuits for the first time are surprised to find that most carrier T1 circuits do not provide timing. Indeed, many data planners and engineers still believe that timing on leased T1 systems "comes from the network." This is not the case. With some exceptions listed later, each user's data device must generate timing when attaching to T1 circuits; it must also match or exceed timing specifications of network or private T1 transmission equipment. This poses problems for new users, as timing generation and timing hierarchies are matters of some complexity. For isolated single point-to-point T1 connections, timing generation and recovery may be treated in ways similar to analog modem circuits. Simple point-to-point connections, however, have a way of growing into more convoluted networks; original timing solutions no longer work as T1 data networks grow.

Before detailing more complex timing needs, a few words must be said about simple T1 connections. Single point-to-point T1 circuit connections do not always quite follow rules learned on analog modems. That is, analog modems usually provide independent timing for each direction on a simple circuit. Since analog modems (data communications equipment or DCEs) usually control timing to attached data devices (data termination equipment or DTEs), each direction may run at a slightly different speed. Speed differences, in these cases, are small. For example, a 9,600 bit/s modem may run at 9,601 bit/s in one direction and 9,598 bit/s in the other direction. Small differences of this order cause no disruption to data transmission; most DTEs accept an amazingly wide range of timing. Similarly, some T1 digital devices will operate in this manner. D4 type voice channel banks may be optioned, or strapped, to run independent clocks in each direction. Channel banks used to carry 56 kbit/s data streams on private or isolated carrier circuits may be set and installed this way on point-to-point links.

Most devices intended to connect on T1 lines, though, require a single source of timing for both directions. **Data time division multiplexers** (TDM), discussed at length in Chapter 12, are among those generally designed to operate with a single source of timing. The reasons for this involve control and diagnostics. If diagnostic loopbacks are considered, this single timing source requirement becomes more evident. When problem determination requires that a data stream loop around at the far-end to return for comparison, it becomes more obvious that both directions must clock at the same rate. Single clock sourcing on point-to-point circuits means, simply, that one end takes charge of clocking; the other end recovers that clock to return data signals. Even D4 channel banks offer this possibility with an option called loop timing. Loop timing, by now, should be a familiar concept. For review, it means recovery of timing from incoming or received data streams, and use of that timing to clock out transmitted data streams in the return direction. One end acts as a master clock—the other end recovers clock and returns it. At T1's speeds of 1.544 Mbit/s, this requires more accurate circuitry to stay inside tighter limits imposed by T1. At these speeds jitter also becomes a more significant problem.

Independent T1 Timing and Recovery

T1 bit-stream transmission equipment, whether used for voice, video or data, holds tight limits on timing rate. The tight limits are not arbitrary, but are imposed by network equipment design limitations. Original T1 carrier devices carried bit streams over copper pairs offering wider limits on clocking rates. Newer digital technologies, whether used in carrier or private communications, require narrower limits to permit higher order multiplexing. Higher order multiplexing combines groups of T1s into T2s, T3s and higher T-Carriers. To accomplish this multiplexing successfully, tight tolerances for each T1 must be maintained. Higher order multiplexers carry the original clocking rates of each T1, but only within these imposed limits. If a T1 drifts outside of timing tolerance, bit errors on that T1 rapidly accumulate. Currently, a safe tolerance limit to use holds T1 bit stream rates to 1,544,000 Hz ± 50 Hz. Hertz (Hz) is used here to remind us that clock signals run continuously. It may also be expressed as bits per second (bit/s).

When individual T1 units connect to T1 transmission networks, holding safe clocking tolerances, error-free or near error-free operation will result. Devices designed to run on T1 connections usually include free-running clocks which meet or exceed stratum four accuracies of ± 50 Hz. Transmission networks accept this tolerance in T1 clock rates passing them through the network relatively unchanged. For instance, if a T1 device, such as a data T1 time division multiplexer (TDM), generates an internal clock rate of 1,544,003 bit/s, that rate will cross through a network, arriving at a far-end TDM at about 1,544,003 bit/s. At the other end, a receiving TDM recovers clock, using it for return direction transmissions. Thus a single T1 link may operate successfully on its own clock as long as that clock meets network tolerances. Most devices used in this fashion not only meet tolerance limits, but exceed them. Typically a device of this type will not vary more than several Hz (or bit/s) from a center or specified rate. When T1 devices must accept network timing, the situation alters only slightly.

Network Dependent T1 Timing

Remembering the far-end T1 device just described, T1 timing was recovered from incoming T1 network signals. This recovered timing was used to synchronize received data and to generate a transmit data stream. This T1 device did not know where timing originated, but merely accepted clock. This loop timing option exists in all T1 devices, permitting network originated timing. When a network must time devices at both ends of a link, both units are set to loop timing. The timing for both arrives from the network or T1 transmission equipment; end devices follow that timing. **Digital access and cross-connect systems** (DACS) are an example of network systems which insist on originating timing for connected end devices. Timing considerations in DACS configurations will be described in greater detail near the end of this chapter. Another case of network dependent timing concerns the type of T1 facility used.

While individual T1 circuits ordered from terrestrial carriers have an option, sometimes a requirement, to generate their own T1 clock sources, certain technologies mandate network timing. Digital satellite services, for instance, may carry all signals based on a network clock. MCI Communications CNS network service delivers clocking with satellite-carried T1 circuits; end equipment T1 devices must conform to this clock to permit error-free operation. Careful review with representatives from each supplying carrier will uncover timing options available or required for each user's end equipment. In addition, future plans for each link may dictate that carrier or network supplied timing be used from first installation. If a single circuit may grow into a network of many lines, or if backup T1 circuits using differing carriers or carrier technologies are possible, then network dependent timing may be a wise choice at initial installation. Most T1 devices, such as data TDMs may, of course, later be changed from independent timing to network dependent, but this will require bringing down circuits or devices while changes are made.

T-Carrier Hierarchy Timing

The higher levels of T-Carriers operate today with timing schemes which carry their own timing limits and carry T1s in a plesiochronous manner. That is, each T1 maintains its own rate within network limits; it is carried on the higher level T-Carrier without reference to any other T1 or higher level carrier. Many T1s may be grouped with each other through a common timing or clocking hierarchy, but each higher level T-Carrier runs on its own. While this may seem contradictory, a process called **bit** or **pulse stuffing** (**justification** in CCITT terminology) maintains order. Pulse stuffing accomplishes this blending of various timings by inserting incoming T1 streams into elastic buffers at their own rate, but removing them at a faster rate determined by the higher order T-Carrier. Clearly, if bits may be removed faster than they arrive, something will be missed, but pulse stuffing prevents this from happening.

Elastic buffers for pulse stuffing operate as follows. Imagine an eight-bit first-in first-out (FIFO) buffer with arriving T1 bits entering at 1,544,000 bit/s. Imagine a multiplexer or muldem which removes bits at 1,544,100 bit/s. The elastic buffer will quickly run out of incoming bits to remove. To prevent this, the buffer is tested continuously—adding or stuffing bits to the removed stream when the buffer is close to depletion. Each stuffed bit's position is noted by control circuitry; this control information is sent to the far-end demultiplexer so that extra bits may be removed before they are delivered back to a T1 stream. Now imagine that our incoming T1 stream speeds up to 1,544,050. Fewer stuff bits will be needed to meet the removal rate. If an incoming T1 rate decreases to 1,543,950, more stuff bits will be used. Digital multiplexers, used to combine several T1s into T2s, operate in this manner. When bit positions are counted in a T2, only 6,176,000 bit/s (4 times 1,544,000 bit/s) would be needed to carry four T1s, but T2's actual rate of 6,312,000 leaves room for T2 framing and stuffing bits. Since there must be room if all T1s are stuffed at their fastest allowable rate, T2's rate is 136,000 bit/s faster than would seem to be needed. Remember also that T2 framing must be added, primarily to find each T1 and its stuff bits for demultiplexing.

Demultiplexing removes stuffed bits following another process. This process also recovers the approximate timing rate of an original T1 delivered to an original multiplexer. In demultiplexing, T2 frame patterns show where each T1's bits are located; they are placed in individual elastic buffers with stuff bits removed. Now the multiplexer must clock out each T1 at some rate. This rate is determined by attempting to maintain the output elastic buffer's pointer at about its center. If this buffer begins to expand, clocking used to send T1 bits onward runs a little faster, thus depleting the buffer a little faster. If the buffer begins to deplete itself, clocking runs a little slower filling the buffer a little. These movements of output clocks are smoothed by allowing elastic buffers to shrink or expand. Since, on average, each T1's bits are removed to keep a buffer at about its center, an outgoing T1 will be timed, on average, at the rate T1 bits arrived at the other end. Thus a T1 arriving at a T1 to T2 multiplexer will keep its original or plesiochronous timing rate through the multiplexer. This process continues as higher level T-Carrier digital multiplexers come into play.

As each multiplexer raises groups of T1s to higher levels, original T1 timing from each T1 is maintained. This process thus adds bits at each level to keep track of T1 locations and to identify stuffed bits or pulses. This helps to explain why each level in the T-Carrier hierarchy differs from its expected rate. Figure 7.9 shows several levels in the North American digital hierarchy. The columns in Figure 7.9 identify a level number, its rate, the number of lower levels carried and overhead bits used for framing and bit stuffing. Similar relationships exist for the CCITT hierarchy, and relationships may be found in CCITT's "G-series" recommendations on digital networks.

The table shows how each level of a T-Carrier hierarchy relates. In this hierarchy, four T1s become a T2; seven T2s become a T3, and so on. With this approach, bits from each T1 imbed deeper into a faster stream; the hierarchy must be descended to find an individual T1 again. This means that, if a T1 multiplexes to T2 and T2 multiplexes to T3, then each step must be reversed to find the bits from an original T1.

SYNTRAN

Another approach would permit T1s and even 64 kbit/s DS-0 channels to be easily identified in a T3 stream. The proposal, called **synchronous transmission** or **SYNTRAN**, would reformat the T3-carrier. SYNTRAN, intended to be carried by existing T3 transmission equipment, offers two options or modes to co-exist on the same SYNTRAN T3 level bit stream. The first, bit synchronous, permits identification of individual T1 (or DS-1) streams directly from a T3 level without passing through a T2 level. This would reduce the need for complete two stage demultiplexing (T3 to T2 and T2 to T1) where only a few T1s were required from a main T3 stream. The second mode, byte synchronous, allows breakout of individual DS-0 channels from a T3 level.

Digital Level	Signal Type	Rate in Mbits/s	Number of Channels	of the Type	Number of kbits of Overhead
0	DS-0	0.064	1 →	DS-0	—
1	DS-1	1.544	24 →	DS-0	8
2	DS-2	6.312	4 →	DS-1	136
3	DS-3	44.736	7 → or 28 →	DS-2 DS-1	552

FIGURE 7.9. North American T-Carrier Timing and Relationships.

Since SYNTRAN runs synchronously without T1 bit stuffing, all T1s (and SYN-TRAN T3) must operate from the same clock source. Current proposals show synchronization from either external T1s or recovered T3s from another SYNTRAN unit. The proposals recommend that all bit signals in SYNTRAN trace their clock to a single stratum one source. While SYNTRAN proposes to run on T3 level transmission facilities, current M13 multiplexers would be incompatible. Current multiplexers require passing through a T2 level between T1 and T3. While current T3 level facilities can carry SYNTRAN, multiplexers at the ends of the facilities can not be mixed. There exists, however, another method to interconnect differing high-speed equipment.

SONET

The rapid deployment of fiber optical cable, fully described in Chapter 10, has lead to another approach for multiplexing higher digital levels. As T-carriers allowed communications between differing networks or between users and networks at electrical interfaces, an optical interface was needed for the fiber. This set of concepts and interfaces is called the **synchronous optical network** (SONET). SONET establishes new sets of speeds beginning at 51.84Mbit/s. Called synchronous transport signals, these SONET levels take new level numbers as: STS-n. The lowest level becomes the "super-carrier" for existing DS-0s, DS-1s and DS-3s whether they come from North American hierarchical levels or SYNTRAN. Higher rates of SONET transport signals take individual bytes from the lowest level, STS-1, and interleave then in the higher carriers. Only certain levels are permitted; currently "n" may be 1, 3, 9, 12, 18, 24, 36 or 48. If STS-1 is taken as 51.84 Mbit/s, STS-48 becomes 2.4 gigabit/s. Higher speeds fit easily into the scheme and permit conversion to optical signals which will continue to meet the upper limit of fiber technology.

After the STS-n level is set in the electronics, a conversion is made to optical level signals. The signals take the name OC-n and run at exactly the speed of the electrical signal. As all signals have exact speed relationships to all other levels, problems of frame slips are vastly reduced. As in (and including) SYNTRAN, all carriers are synchronous. This additionally enables the original objective: interconnection between networks and interconnection between users and networks at an optical interface. This really means differing equipment and differing organizations at each end of a fiber cable. To assure proper coordination, SONET standards include extra bandwidth for maintenance and operations communications channels.

As both SONET and SYNTRAN require all T1s to synchronize to the same clock, T1s would no longer maintain their ability to run plesiochronously. Under both proposals, bit stuffing and removal would no longer be needed. A very desirable side effect of this proposal would be a significant reduction in jitter resulting from stuff bit removal.

Jitter in T-Carrier Timing

Jitter, discussed earlier in this chapter, results from many sources—such as demultiplexing and bit stuffing. The removal of stuff bits may cause jitter as a removal clock adjusts, simulating original timing of the T1 bit stream. Sources of T1 jitter include those found in any bit-serial digital system: temperature effects on carrier equipment, equipment drifts from original specification, impulse noise, and so on. To cope with jitter in complex T1 networks, jitter limits are needed. Figure 7.10 on page 199 is an example

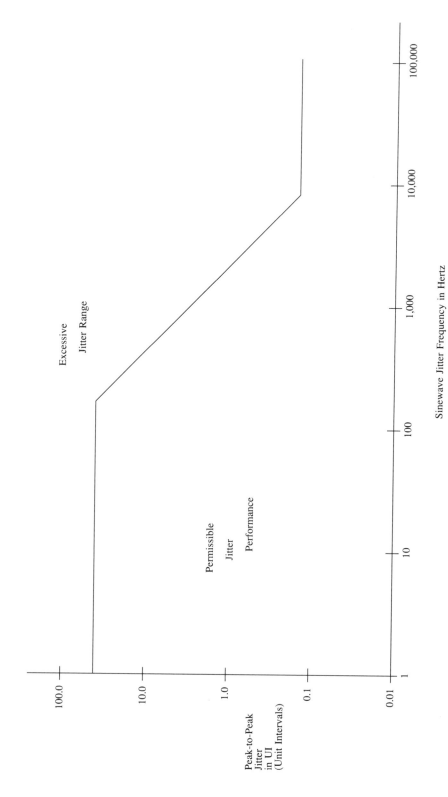

FIGURE 7.10. Example Jitter Mask for T1 Signals.

jitter mask or plot of jitter in unit intervals (UI) versus jitter frequency. The frequency here is not the frequency of a digital signal or bit stream, but the frequency of jitter itself. That is, if a data signal wobbles regularly at a jitter frequency of 1,000 Hz, then a jitter mask suggests limiting jitter to about three unit intervals. Actual jitter masks for specific services and equipment should be consulted to determine requirements for real installations. Jitter masks often differ depending on equipment function. For instance, clock recovery circuits need to accept larger amounts of jitter; devices inputting to a network should generate lower amounts of jitter.

Timing and signal jitter form one basis for errors in digital data transmission, but there are many more. Error behavior in digital systems differs significantly from errors in previous analog data communications. Data transmission error behavior directly affects a user's data equipment; it must be understood to provide optimum operation between the two.

Errors in T-Carrier Systems

Error behavior in an analog modem world follows several predictable courses, and computer industry data communications equipment handles it well. With high-speed digital data transmission systems, however, new types of error behaviors occur. In analog data communications, errors happen to individual bits. Noise on analog circuits introduce these bit errors, at most, to a few bits in sequence. While noise bursts may group errors when lines begin to fail, errors are usually distributed somewhat evenly in time. Communications line protocols check blocks or frames of data with parity and **cyclic redundancy checks** (CRC). When blocks of data do not check, block retransmission is attempted. On long analog circuits, bit error rates typically range from one in ten-thousand to one in a million. This may be expressed as a **bit error rate** (BER) ranging from one times 10^{-4} to one times 10^{-6}. Communications programming in front-end processors and communications control units handles this type of distributed error rate well.

With errors in this range, blocks of data need only be retransmitted when a block fails to pass error checking. For example, if data is blocked at 1,000 bytes of eight bits per byte with data moving at 9,600 bits per second, a BER of one times 10^{-6} causes only about one in 125 blocks to be retransmitted. This level of retransmission stays well within the capabilities of most data communications programming and equipment. The time to detect and retransmit errored blocks is typically less than two seconds, and the probability of second-time errors is very small. Raising transmission speeds to 56 kbit/s maintains the rate of errored blocks, but reduces retransmit time to below 0.3 seconds. No further action will be taken by a front-end processor (FEP) at this error rate. If, however, repeated retransmissions result in errored blocks, an FEP's programming may be set to signal operators of a circuit or modem failure. These considerations set the stage for a review of error differences in high-speed digital communications.

Digital transmission errors happen far less frequently, but usually affect more than a few bits. Digital error behavior is characterized by its burstiness; that is, when errors rarely occur, they come in a form of bursts of errors lasting from several tens of milliseconds to several seconds. This can be understood by remembering the multistage multiplexing of T1s as they pass through a digital network. T1s combine to form T2s; T2s combine to form T3s and so on. If a T3 circuit, carrying up to 28 T1s, experiences a momentary fault, reframing time for each multiplex stage may consume many hundreds of milliseconds before each T1 again runs error free. After error-free operation returns to a T1, data devices attached to it must again find their framing before re-establishing individual data circuits. D3 and D4 type digital voice channel banks usually hold their voice circuits active for about 2.5 seconds before disconnecting. Consider what may happen to data circuits from the paragraph above when two seconds of errors occur.

In two seconds, on a 56 kbit/s data circuit, an FEP will attempt to retransmit an errored block over 14 times. If an error threshold of five or even 10 bad blocks has been set in programming, our FEP may stop data transmission and notify an operator. When an operator checks the circuit, all will have returned to normal; our operator will restart data transmission while wondering what happened. If FEP parameters for error retransmission are reset to accommodate digital system error behavior, communications will begin again automatically. A recent notification by AT&T Communications to vendors of T1 data equipment alerts vendors to this type of errors. AT&T Publication 62411 recommends that user's equipment be set to cope with error bursts of up to 2.5 seconds.

If network timing for several data devices arrives on a T1, this burstiness should be considered; alternate or secondary sources of timing should take over when error bursts happen. Caution must be followed, of course, as two timing sources should not be designed to arrive on facilities which may suffer error behavior at the same time. This risk increases when all timing comes from the carrier network or some other central source, such as a DACS.

DACS and CCR Considerations

Digital access cross-connect systems (DACS) allow user DS-1 (T1) signals to have individual DS-0 channels reassigned among many T1s connected to a DACS. Since this cross-connection implies movement of many bit streams without error, all connected T1s must follow clocking from the DACS device. The DACS itself may derive timing from another source, but each connected T1 line will carry timing to devices attached to it. **Customer-controlled reconfiguration** (CCR) and similar services often use DACS type devices to permit reconfiguration of individual DS-0 digital circuits in a network. DACS units in AT&T's national network usually time at a stratum three level and supply timing to their connected T1 devices, which should hold stratum four specifications. These attached devices are set to loop time, returning this timing synchronized to the DACS.

If attached digital units attempt to use another source of timing, elastic buffers at the DACS may be unable to lock to an incoming bit stream and data will be lost. Situations exist, though, where several timing sources may need be used when interconnecting several digital networks.

Interconnecting Timing Systems

Few telecommunications networks enjoy the luxury of total containment. That is, all networks sooner or later may need to interconnect between private and public sections. In analog networks, this meant complying with public network analog levels and standards. If sound levels missed a little, and calls or circuits were a bit loud or soft, things worked until the levels were adjusted. In a high-speed digital world, standards and levels must still be met, but a new dimension must be considered—timing. Network timing controls when bit values are true. A little difference in timing accumulates with amazing swiftness, causing catastrophic errors. Timing synchronization between network sections becomes the critical factor, without which nothing works. How digital networks interconnect timing signals now holds our attention.

Perhaps the simplest example concerns connections of a private T1 circuit with a public network T1 DACS. The carrier DACS network supplies timing from its central clock system and delivers that timing to both ends of a circuit. Where a user chooses to interconnect a single T1 circuit with digital devices to privately owned facilities, timing connections must be correct. The margin for error in timing connection design and installation is small. A free running digital line driver works well without outside reference , but may not approach the clock accuracies of a carrier network. As a local point-to-point circuit, local devices operate without error. When interconnected with network T1 devices, errors begin to appear; they cannot be found by separating the two parts for testing. When separated, both parts work, usually without error. Only when interconnected do significant errors occur, for no apparent reason at all. When technical designers, used to analog data devices and interconnects, first face this digital interconnect problem, it appears baffling and insoluble.

While perhaps baffling, it is not insoluble. Understanding of timing relationships and connections can reduce timing errors to zero, or near zero. This simple example is fixed quickly because the private timing source comes from a single device. If that device, say a local area data set, runs on its own internal clock, data streams from a carrier network are sampled at the wrong time. Changing this interconnected device to external timing, supplying timing externally from the network, locks this end to a network clock. The far-end must then be set to loop time to return network timing back to the interconnection. If all elastic buffers are set wide enough, normal error-free operation should begin. This simple case, however, only begins to explore and solve more complex problems which lie ahead.

Private Network Timing

As users turn increasingly to digital voice and data systems for local or private operation, digital interconnection with other networks becomes attractive. While many private digital networks either do not interconnect or connect via analog facilities, cost and quality concerns drive users to investigate digital interconnection. Private digital voice PBX networks may find needs to connect to carrier digital voice circuits without passing through analog voice trunks. Private digital data TDM networks may need to accept a carrier DDS circuit for distribution. This becomes the moment when timing interconnection issues must be faced. When combined voice/data switching and transmission equipment is considered for needed business operations, timing interconnection should be planned well ahead of installations.

Private digital networks, whether voice or data, usually start with the first installed device providing timing for all other connected devices. The first digital PBX becomes the clock source for other connected PBXs. The initial data TDM forms a hub or point in a private network to synchronize timing. Expansion of these facilities adds complexity to timing designs; secondary sources should be identified and implemented. Early identification of network timing sources and alternate fallback sources may save many hours of later redesign.

Timing Sources and Fallbacks

Choices for timing in private systems are many. The easiest, of course, comes from accepting a stratum clock signal from a carrier. A DDS 56 kbit/s signal ordered from a **local exchange carrier** (LEC) traces its accuracy to the BSRF in Hillsboro, to LORAN-C or to a carrier's private clock system. This source may be used to lock units in a private network directly or can drive a master clock. Where a private digital network takes clock in this manner, it will stay locked as long as the local DDS circuit maintains connection to the timing hierarchy. Planning a clocking strategy involves contingencies for the failure of this local circuit. Several local circuits may be ordered to permit a fallback when one circuit fails. A caution must be mentioned; if two or more DDS carrier circuits back each other up, they should arrive at the private network facility through separate (diverse) paths, both physically and logically. Physical diversity extends over a range from separate cable entrances to a building, to cable routings to different telephone offices. Logical diversity ranges to discussions with carriers to identify telephone office sourcing of clocks through differing paths to the stratum one reference.

Another possible source for clocking derives from on-site satellite receivers traceable to sources such as MCI Communications CNS service or other digital satellite services. The satellite carrier's digital signals then drive local equipment or local master clocks. These satellite digital clock sources should be discussed with the carriers, and assistance should be requested regarding accuracy and reliability. As satellite services may be occasionally interrupted by extremely heavy rains or solar effects, alternate local or carrier sources should be considered for fallback usage.

A third possibility exists from local reception of LORAN-C (where practical) and its traceability to the U. S. Naval Observatory clock. LORAN-C radio reception involves installation of a whip-type antenna with equipment to receive and derive the timing signal. Clocks of this sort directly obtain the equivalent of stratum one clock signals. This level of accuracy comes as close to an on-site cesium-beam as possible, but may also suffer from radio interference. Clock equipment which can ride through short radio outages is now available.

Local station clocks become a fourth possibility. A **station clock** is another name for a local clock which can distribute its signals to other nearby digital equipment. A local station clock may synchronize a user's equipment and form a hub for the distribution of timing to a private network. Local station clocks come in a wide range of costs and accuracies. Where large numbers of digital data multiplexing or transmission units are installed in a single location, a station clock or building timing supply should be considered. Most station clocks offer both an accurate free-running clock source and the ability to lock to two or more external references. The external references may come from any of the first several alternatives described above. Choices of clocking sources and costs should be driven by an analysis of business or application needs, with the costs of outages calculated. While outages are rare and can be estimated from experience or from a vendor's performance objectives, the business costs of an outage may mandate a rather complex and expensive clocking system. As more and more business communications moves to digital methods, clocking costs should not be ignored, but should be compared to profits lost when communications fail due to timing outages.

Do communications fail when master clocking is lost? This depends on the complexity of the network. The single point-to-point link, mentioned often here, is rarely disrupted by loss of a central clock source. This simple link, though, usually expands to encompass several locations. Locations then begin to interconnect and discover that interconnected circuits fail when clocking fails. Now clocking becomes an issue, usually to be solved quickly. Private data networks also have a habit of growing and interconnecting with carrier digital services. Carriers discovered the critical nature of centralized and hierarchical timing many years ago. As more forms of communications move to high-speed digital facilities, carrier clocking networks gain greater accuracy and become more robust under stress. Private networks must follow to succeed. Digital interconnection, already well underway, will drive all networks towards a full understanding of timing interconnection.

Timing Interconnection Choices

Digital networks, growing beyond the bounds of a single geographic region, find that a universal timing solution can no longer be used. Timing islands, defined as equipment and circuit groups timed from different sources, need to connect to each other. If one island adopts the timing from another, islands merge to form larger islands. But, eventually, an island connects which cannot adopt timing and must run on its original master timing source. When this occurs, timing strategies come under very close scrutiny to find a workable solution. But before solutions come analyses and tests. Two islands timed from differing master clocks may work perfectly well if several conditions can be met. If each island traces its clock to a cesium-beam standard and interconnect elastic buffers handle maximum jitter and wander, timing related errors will not cause significant errors. Only when an island loses master reference will problems begin. If the timing island's clock drifts only slowly from the last know reference, elastic buffers may continue to cope. If master reference returns, the island's clock will pull-in again and normal operation will return before significant errors occur. Proper clock fallback designs and elastic buffer sizings can prevent catastrophic interconnect failures.

Clocking fallback strategies in private networks should follow rules designed many years ago by the carriers. Figure 7.5 on page 187 and Figure 7.6 on page 188, earlier in this chapter, showed timing distribution methods (and errors) for timing. Timing design concepts shown in these illustrations should be followed in any digital network. When islands exist, fallback clock sources should be installed between islands to pick up alternate timing from the non-failed side of an interconnect circuit. Fallback timing selections in large networks is not an easy task, but once begun, should yield significant improvements in network reliability. Caution against clocking loops, as shown in Figure 7.6 on page 188, must be exercised. Additional understanding of how fallback works in a given digital unit is needed. For example, if a unit switches from its first-choice timing source, what causes it to switch, and what to return, if anything? When are manual resets required? Can any combination of fallback clock selections cause loops? Once fallback timing designs are done, attention turns to interconnect elastic buffer sizing.

Jitter and Elastic Buffers

While not always accessible to the user, many digital communications units offer an ability to set the widths (or sizes) of elastic buffers. Where a user cannot, or chooses not to, change the sizing on these buffers, most equipment vendors will assist in determining and setting the right size for the buffers. These buffers come under a variety of names: **elastic buffers, elastic stores, phasors,** and so on, but almost all provide the same function.

Setting the size of the buffers to a small number (of bits) offers the fastest transit time for bit streams in and out of the buffer, but reduces jitter and wander tolerance. That is, a short four-bit buffer delays the bits only by an average of two bit times (remember that the buffer attempts to stay centered) but can handle less than ± 2 UI of jitter. A wide elastic buffer setting, such as 16 bits, delays the stream by about eight bit times, but can handle up to ± eight UI of jitter. If delay is more important and jitter is low, narrow buffers are better; if delay can be tolerated, wider buffers will cope with greater jitter. In circuit interconnections between networks or timing islands, remember that elastic buffer sizes may offer an additional tool to improve network timing and synchronization performance.

This concludes our somewhat complex discussions on timing and synchronization. We move now to several chapters describing the technical nature of carrier offerings in high-speed digital communications services.

CHAPTER 8

Common Carrier Digital Services

Chapter Overview

It is fitting that we begin our examination of present-day services with those of the long-distance companies, because the high-speed digital technology in use is to a great extent the legacy of the first long-distance company: the late, great Bell System. It is almost impossible to understate the role of the pre-divestiture AT&T and its research and development arm, Bell Telephone Laboratories, in the evolution of telecommunications technology in use throughout the world. Concepts, techniques, standards, and designs born at Bell Labs dominate the field and will probably continue to do so for many years.

At the beginning of 1984, the Bell System was dismembered and the United States was divided into regions called **local access and transport areas** (LATAs) shown in Figure 8.1 on page 207. Pieces of the Bell System (along with those of the independent companies) were classified into one or the other of two categories: inter-LATA and intra-LATA. The inter-LATA group are the long-distance telecommunications companies whose services are the primary subject of this chapter.

A major effect of the Bell System breakup was that, even if the voice or data customer stayed with AT&T, there were now at least two vendors to deal with: local and long-distance. In most cases, the **local exchange carrier** (LEC) (most often, one of the former 22 Bell Operating Companies) supplies the portion of a circuit (called an **access line**) between the customer premises and the long-distance carrier's nearest access point, called a **point of presence** (POP). The long-distance carrier provides a connection between the POPs nearest the desired termination points; the LECs provide access lines to the final end points between which service is desired. This arrangement, which can be compared to using taxicabs at both ends of an airline trip, is clearly more complex than dealing with one supplier for everything, and requires more sophistication on the part of the customer. This additional complexity is not only technical, but has legal and financial dimensions as well: the different companies involved may be regulated by different government agencies and use different rate structures.

AT&T Communications, MCI, and U.S. Sprint are the three largest long-distance common carriers in the United States. AT&T's network, shown in Figure 8.2 on page 208, consists of coaxial cable as well as microwave and fiber optic transmission facilities. The MCI and U.S. Sprint networks, shown in Figure 8.3 on page 209 and Figure 8.4 on page 210 respectively, are newer and consist of mainly of microwave and fiber. All three companies are deploying new facilities, mostly fiber, at a rapid rate.

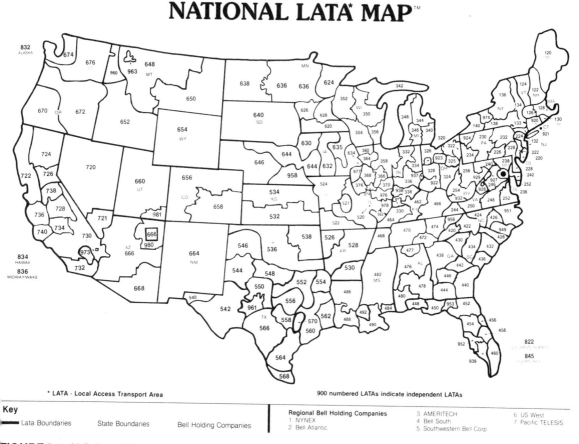

FIGURE 8.1. U.S. Local Access and Transport Areas. (Courtesy of CCMI/McGraw-Hill.)

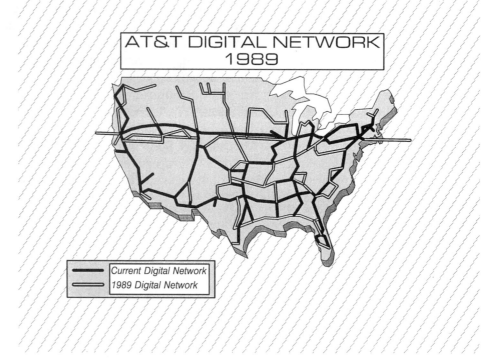

FIGURE 8.2. AT&T United States Transmission Facilities. (Map Courtesy of AT&T.)

Analog Services

The first data communications systems were adaptations of telephone technology based on analog transmission. Recall that an analog voice signal is continuously varying in nature, and that the standard 4,000 Hz analog telephone channel is designed to pass information in the frequency range of approximately 300 to 3,500 Hz (cycles per second). This range (called a **passband**) is sufficient to transmit human voices well, but is not suitable for transmission of binary data signals in their native form. The design of the long-distance telephone system prevents the direct transmission of such signals as dial pulses and digital data. Recall that transmission of a binary signal over a limited passband is accomplished by using it to alter another signal called a **carrier** which does fit within the passband of the channel; this technique is called **modulation.** The reverse process of detecting a binary signal from a modulated carrier is called **demodulation.** The theory and practice of modulation and demodulation were developed in great measure in response to the need to transmit telegraph signals and the signaling and supervisory (dialed digits, on/off hook) information for telephone calls over voice channels in large automatic telephone systems.

Analog transmission is subject to certain unavoidable impairments which accumulate as the length of the circuit and the number of repeaters along the path increases. These include various kinds of noise, distortion, delay (especially nonuniform delay which is frequency dependent), frequency shift, and random variations in gain and phase. All-digital

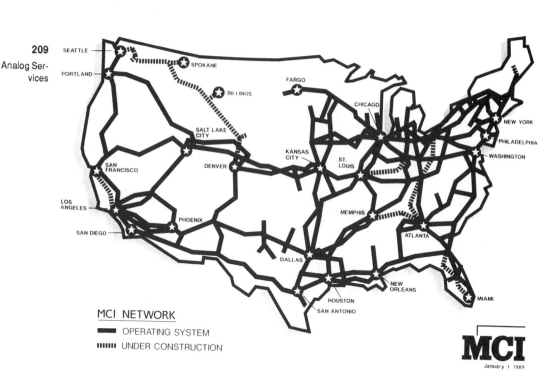

FIGURE 8.3. MCI United States Transmission Facilities. (Map Courtesy of MCI Telecommunications Corporation.)

transmission is inherently superior to analog because it is immune to many of these problems, but it is not available everywhere and many existing analog lines will not be replaced for some time. Because analog transmission is still very much with us, and because it offers a unique and useful advantage under certain circumstances, we would be remiss to ignore it here.

Fixed Analog Services

Channels supplied on a 24-hour (sometimes called **full period**) basis, or **leased lines**, between fixed locations are somewhat easier to understand and use than their switched counterparts. Because the transmission path never (or seldom) changes, automatic equipment to adapt to varying channel characteristics is not required. No provisions for switching or call supervision need be made; the connection is always "up."

VOICE GRADE LEASED LINES

The standard of the analog transmission business is the voice grade leased line, often referred to (for historical reasons which date back to Bell System tariffs) as a "type 3002" leased line. Available almost universally, this service is easy for a telecommunications company to provide because it is very similar to the voice trunk circuits that interconnect central offices.

Much confusion arises over some of the terminology used to describe the configuration of voice grade leased lines. The terms **full duplex** (meaning capable of transmission in

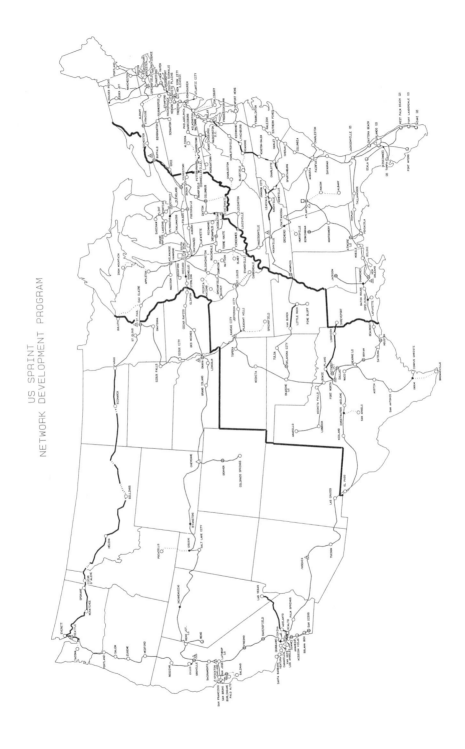

FIGURE 8.4. U.S. Sprint Transmission Facilities. (Map Courtesy of U.S. Sprint.)

two directions simultaneously) and **four-wire** (having separate wire pairs for sending and receiving) are often mistakenly used interchangeably. A **half duplex** line is capable of transmission in only one direction at a time. A **two-wire** line is one in which the same pair of wires is used for both transmission and reception. The most common configuration for analog leased lines is full duplex over four wires as shown in Figure 8.5 on page 212, but full duplex on two wires is possible (more commonly found with switched lines) and so is half duplex service on four wires.

Full duplex lines are often used with data terminal equipment that is capable only of half duplex operation in order to avoid the time (called **turnaround time**) required to change from receive mode to transmit mode. This delay, which can vary from a few to a few hundred milliseconds, is the time between the DTE's raising of the **request to send** (RTS) line to the modem and the modem's response with **clear to send** (CTS). Keeping request to send on, called **constant carrier** operation, can save a great deal of time when protocols such as binary synchronous communication (which involve numerous waits for responses) are used.

Voice grade lines which connect two points only are called **point-to-point.** Lines which interconnect more than two points are called **multipoint** lines. In a multipoint arrangement, one of the points (often called **drops,** leading to **multidrop** as a synonym for multipoint) is designated the **master station** (also called the **control station**) as shown in Figure 8.5 on page 212. The master station on a multipoint line "hears" transmissions from all the other stations by means of a device located within the network called a **bridge.** This device combines the transmit signals from all the **slave** (also called **tributary**) stations and presents it on the receive side of the link between the network and the master station. The slave stations do not "hear" each other; if they intercommunicate, it must be with the help of equipment on the customer side of the network interface. Normally, only one slave station transmits at a time, and only at the request of the master. In the opposite direction, the signal presented on the master station's transmit pair is broadcast to all slave stations.

The set of rules by which the master and slave stations interact without mutual interference is called a **protocol,** of which there are many variations. The protocol usually involves giving each station on a multipoint a unique code called an **address** by which it can identify transmissions for which it is the intended receiver. The master station controls the line via a combination of **polling** (requesting for any data which the slave may be ready to transmit) and **addressing** (sending data messages intended for the slave).

Multipoint lines have failure modes that are a direct result of the use of a bridge to combine signals from several stations. Noise on all of the tributary transmit facilities is added together and presented to the master station's receive pair; the total may exceed acceptable limits due to contributions along multiple paths. The multiple possible sources of noise and the addition of noise at the bridge can make troubleshooting difficult. Moreover, a failure at one of the stations in which one slave fails to stop transmitting at the proper time (called **streaming**) can prevent the master from receiving from any of the other slaves.

It is possible to compensate for some of the transmission impairments to which analog lines are subject. Many carriers offer a service called **conditioning** which selects signal paths and/or equipment which is adjusted to compensate for the undesirable characteristics of a particular line with the result that it meets a standard specification.

Type "C" Conditioning: This service offers several levels of compensation for **envelope delay** (signal delay that is frequency dependent) and **loss deviation** (attenuation that is frequency dependent) as shown in Figure 8.6 on page 213. Signal delay which is not

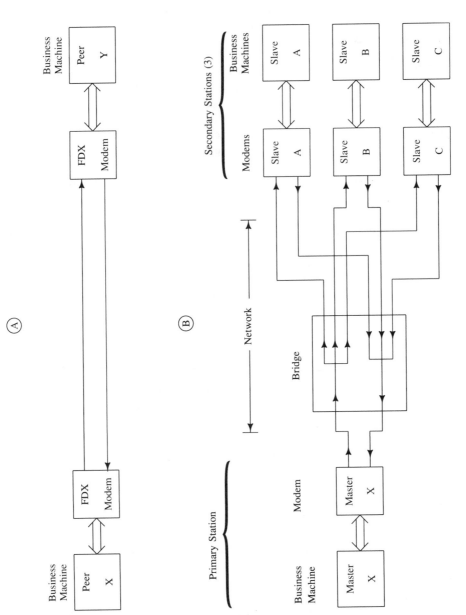

Note : Lines Represent Simplex Channels Which are Implemented
       as Twisted Pairs and/or DSO Bit Streams.

FIGURE 8.5. Analog Leased Line Configurations. (a) Point-to-point (b) Multipoint.

Type	Envelope Delay	Loss Deviation
C1	1.0 ms @ 1.0–2.4 KHz	−1 to +3 dBm @ 1.0–2.4 KHz −2 to +6 dBm @ 0.3–2.7 KHz
C2	0.5 ms @ 1.0–2.6 KHz 1.5 ms @ 0.6–2.6 KHz 3.0 ms @ 0.5–2.8 KHz	−1 to +3 dBm @ .5 to 2.8 KHz −2 to +6 dBm @ .3 to 3.0 KHz
C3	.08 ms @ 1.0–2.6 KHz .26 ms @ 0.6–2.6 KHz .50 ms @ 0.5–2.8 KHz	−0.5 to +1 dBm @ .5 to 2.8 KHz −0.8 to +2 dBm @ .3 to 3.0 KHz
C4	0.3 ms @ 1.0–2.6 KHz 0.5 ms @ 0.8–2.8 KHz 1.5 ms @ 0.6–3.0 KHz 3.0 ms @ 0.5–3.0 KHz	−2 to +3 dBm @ .5 to 3.0 KHz −2 to +6 dBm @ .3 to 3.2 KHz
C5	0.1 ms @ 1.0–2.6 KHz 0.3 ms @ 0.6–2.6 KHz 0.6 ms @ 0.5–2.8 KHz	−1.0 to +3.0 dBm @ .3 to 3.0 KHz −0.5 to +1.5 dBm @ .5 to 2.8 KHz
C6	2.0 ms @ 0.8–2.6 KHz	−2.0 to +6.0 dBm @ .3 to 3.0 KHz −1.0 to +3.0 dBm @ .5 to 2.8 KHz

FIGURE 8.6. Conditioning Standards for Envelope Delay and Loss Deviation.

uniform has the effect of distorting the modulated signal and causing **intersymbol interference**, a kind of spillover of the signal for one baud interval into that of the next. Loss
deviation, also called **frequency response**, is expressed in terms of signal power levels
using a logarithmic unit called a **decibel** (dB). Loss deviation for a particular frequency is
measured or specified with respect to that for a reference frequency such as 1,700 Hz,
which is in the approximate middle of the bandpass for a voice channel. In reading the
table, it should be noted that more positive numbers indicate greater loss.

Type "C" conditioning is implemented by adding equipment not unlike the equalizers used in a stereo system to a channel, usually at the receiving end. Special routes or
intermediate equipment for this service are usually not required.

Type "D" Conditioning: Often available in addition to that of the "C" standards,
this service guarantees a minimum ratio of signal to noise and maximum nonlinear (amplitude dependent) distortion (also called **harmonic distortion**). Harmonic distortion is the
nonlinear response of a channel to the amplitude of an input signal, and has the effect of
"flattening" the peaks of the modulated carrier. Unlike frequency-dependent attenuation
and delay, the effects of noise and harmonic distortion are irreversible, and the conditioning
service is implemented by choosing special equipment and routes. Signal-to-noise ratio is
expressed in decibels and is 28 dB for this service (where noise is measured using a
standard bandpass implemented by a "C-notch" filter). Harmonic distortion is specified in
terms of the amplitude of interfering signals at twice and three times the one in question
(i.e., harmonics) which would cause the specified flattening effect. For "D" conditioning,
these ratios are 35 dB for the second harmonic (double the reference) and 40 dB for the
third harmonic (triple the reference). "D1" conditioning is offered for point-to-point and
"D2" for multipoint channels.

Network Interface: The network interface for voice grade leased circuits is a four-
wire connector, most recently of the modular type but often the older four-prong Western

Electric model which was also used for telephones. Other connectors are also often used, especially where a large number of circuits are terminated in the same area. The customer is provided two pairs of wires with a full-duplex line, one pair for receiving (marked "T" and "R" for "tip" and "ring"—note the potential for confusion here) and the other for receiving (marked T_1 and R_1). The modem is connected to the line at this point, for which signal levels (at a frequency of 1,004 Hz) of +0 dBm for transmit and about −16 dBm for receive are common.

Leased analog circuits usually require local exchange carrier equipment on the customer premises, for which the customer is expected to provide space and power. This network circuit terminating equipment is used to compensate for transmission losses between the customer and the serving central office and, optionally, to perform conditioning, so that signals at the network interface meet the promised specifications. It also provides features to support testing, most commonly loopback in response to a command tone (commonly 2,713 Hz) on the station's receive pair. Loopback allows a rapid and convenient test for proper operation: the command is sent on the far-end or intermediate point's transmit pair, causing the disconnection of customer equipment at the far-end network interface and the connection of the receive pair to the transmit pair at that point. Tests for noise, frequency response, fading, and so on, may then be done. If these tests are successful from end to end, the line is probably not at fault and the customer equipment is suspect. If the tests fail, they may be repeated at various points along to isolate the source of trouble. When testing is complete, a second application of the command tone breaks the loopback and restores normal operation. The NCTE may include a timer which automatically releases the loopback after a preset interval, such as 15 minutes, to prevent long outages if the manual release is forgotten. The NCTE may also provide or permit flow of a sealing current, as described in Chapter 6.

WIDEBAND ANALOG LINES

Analog coaxial cable and microwave radio carrier systems such as those described in Chapter 2 divided their capacity according to a hierarchy of which the basic building block is a unit of 12 voice channels called a **group.** Since each voice channel is allocated four KHz of bandwidth, a group's total bandwidth is $12 \times 4 = 48$ KHz. The existence of group-wide bandwidth segments prompted the development of **group-band** or **wideband** modems for high-speed data and facsimile services. The first group-band modems, developed by Bell Laboratories, operated at 40,800 bits per second, corresponding to an efficiency of 0.85 bits per second per Hz of bandwidth. Today, modems are available which transmit with greater efficiency; 1.4 bits/s per Hz available with one model allows over 67,000 bits/s in the bandwidth of a single group.

The availability of group-sized segments of bandwidth in the network led to a similar packaging for tariff purposes, for a time. A Bell System tariff called **Telpak** once offered groups to large customers at attractive rates and with great flexibility. In some areas, it was possible to lease group band facilities with both group band modems and channel banks so that the bandwidth could be used for 12 telephone channels during the day and high-speed data at night.

Wideband transmission is still attractive in areas where long-distance telecommunications companies have analog carrier systems with available group band capacity and arrangements can be made to deliver it to the end user's premises (for example, with a DDS access circuit). However, as analog carrier systems are replaced with digital, wideband service will cease to exist as a technique, even if it survives as a tariff.

ANALOG TAILS IN DIGITAL NETWORKS

An analog line may be used for access to a digital network which has timing derived from a source (such as a private satellite system) not synchronized with public digital services. In cases where a public telecommunications company is the only way for a given location to gain access to the private network, an analog channel may be ordered from the public telecommunications company and the modem at the private network end set for external transmit timing. The off-network site modem recovers the private network clock from the received analog signal and then may be used for transmitting in synchronization with the private network. Such an arrangement is shown in Figure 8.7.

Switched Analog Services

The public switched voice network has been used for data transmission since early 1958, when AT&T first offered DATAPHONE® service through its Illinois, Michigan, and New York operating companies. Such usage has become very popular as long-distance rates and modem prices have decreased. While especially well suited to intermittent, low-volume applications, using the voice network for data is not without problems. These problems have also increased since the advent of competition in the inter-LATA message telephone business.

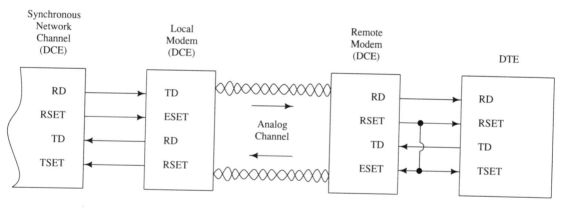

Abbreviations : RD   Received Data

RSET   Received Signal Element Timing (Receive Clock)

TD   Transmitted Data

TSET   Transmit Signal Element Timing (Transmit Clock)

ESET   External Signal Element Timing (External Clock)

Note : This Configuration is Sometimes Called "Loop Timing"

FIGURE 8.7. Analog Tail Circuit on a Private Digital Network.

As first described in Chapter 3, very few telephone calls today are transmitted in analog form from end to end. The deployment of digital facilities in the voice network has been so rapid and pervasive that an all-analog call of any distance would be rare indeed. It is true, however, that most residential and many business telephones at the present time are analog in design and so are the local loops that connect them to the central office. It is this characteristic that leads to the requirement for modems for data calls over the switched telephone network.

With the breakup of the Bell System, the consistent evolution of the U.S. voice telephone system under the technical leadership of the Bell Telephone Laboratories came to an end. Independent operating companies and long-distance carriers became free to adopt any technologies and standards they wished, as long as they satisfied their respective regulatory agencies. While the operation of the switched voice network for data transmission was never guaranteed, the common standards of the Bell System tended to promote customer expectations of adequacy. Connections which would be acceptable for voice communication are often inadequate for data transmission, while the reverse is rarely true.

Now that an inter-LATA call involves the services of at least two companies, the user experiencing transmission problems is faced with an even more difficult challenge in getting them resolved. Opposing this trend is the work of an organization called Bell Communications Research (or **Bellcore**), a consortium of local exchange carriers formed to share the costs and benefits of a common engineering and research organization. Bellcore is a descendant of Bell Laboratories and inherits the mission of managing inter-company connectivity and technical standards for its member companies; membership in Bellcore is voluntary and may change over time.

One characteristic of the voice network which has always complicated the lives of its data users is that the transmission path for any switched (data or voice) call is determined by the instantaneous distribution and magnitude of the load on the network, and can be predicted only on a statistical basis. Automatic routing within the network can cause the path between subscribers to vary from call to call. This can have the effect that data transmission may be error-free on one occasion and completely unusable the next. The only recourse in the case of an error-prone call is to disconnect and try again, perhaps after waiting long enough that chances are that network load has changed to some degree.

Another result of the optimization of the telephone network for human voice transmission is that analog call progress tones and error messages are poorly suited to reliable interpretation by machines. For example, a recorded announcement that a telephone number has been changed is useless to a modem, which may fail on automatic retry continuously until a human intervenes. Modern long-distance telephone companies, mindful of sharp competition, have little incentive to standardize on signals that are significant to both machines and humans.

Proliferation of modem technologies in an unregulated business environment tends to decrease the probability that two parties finding a need to communicate will have compatible equipment. Rapid development of voice coding techniques and decreasing costs for sophisticated signal processing electronics will tend to compound this problem.

In summary, we can expect the value of the voice telephone network for general-purpose data transmission to decrease as its components diverge in design with the only quality standard being a subjective "acceptable voice transmission." Applications using low-speeds or which are specialized in some way may resist this trend longer than others, but the homogeneity that long supported data transmission is disappearing rapidly. Fortunately, all-digital technology and global standards for its application are approaching to fill the gap. The most promising of these is the Integrated Services Digital Network described in Chapter 14.

Digital Services

The development of all-digital data transmission in the telecommunications business is the completion of a full circle in its technology. The early telegraph systems were digital, but were adapted to analog channels as the telephone displaced the telegraph. With the advent of the T1 carrier system in 1962, the advantages of digital transmission became available to both voice and data users. Systems to provide end-to-end digital data service were first developed by Bell Telephone Laboratories in the United States, and it is likely that their design will continue to influence the digital communications products and services of a more competitive era. Our examination of digital long-distance services will begin with those first offered by the Bell System.

Digital Data Service (DDS)

Digital data service brought the benefits of all-digital transmission on an end-to-end basis in December of 1974 to the cities of New York, Boston, Philadelphia, Washington, and Chicago. It offered speeds of 2,400, 4,800, 9,600, and 56,000 bits/s using facilities that were specially designed for data, rather than voice, transmission. During the following year, 19 "digital cities" were added, and availability of the service continues to grow. DDS was designed to offer the following advantages to the data customer:

- significantly improved circuit quality, with an objective of at least 99.5% error-free seconds (or about 43-errored seconds per day) over a monthly average for the 56 kbit/s service and better yet for the lower speeds;
- high availability, with an objective of at least 99.96% (corresponding to about 3.5 hours down time) per year;
- high-speed (56 kbit/s) transmission without the expense of group band modems;
- simpler, smaller, and more reliable terminating equipment;
- compatibility with existing business machines via the preservation of standard interfaces.

Functionally discrete from the voice network but physically integrated with it, DDS offered both point-to-point and multipoint service, and could be extended into areas not so served using analog channels. It was made possible by the availability of T1 circuits between the central offices of metropolitan areas and a digital addition to the long-haul microwave network called **data under voice** (DUV). The introduction of DDS was of special historical interest because it was evidence of significant confidence in the future growth of data transmission business on the part of the Bell System's planners.

DDS ARCHITECTURE

The facilities used to provide DDS on a long-distance basis may be divided into three parts, as shown in Figure 8.8 on page 218. These are:

1. the local distribution system, consisting of unloaded cable pairs between the customer and the serving central office;

2. the metropolitan area network which brings the DDS circuits from the serving offices to a common point, called a **hub office,** at which test, cross-connect, and administrative functions are provided;

3. the intercity network, most likely consisting of microwave and/or fiber long-haul transmission facilities.

Of these, the first two are normally the province of the local exchange carrier and the last, that of the long-distance (inter-LATA) carrier.

Local Distribution System: This portion of the DDS network consists of the local loops over which the service is delivered to the customer premises and of the terminating equipment at both ends. DDS is **full duplex, four wire,** using the terminology mentioned earlier. The pairs over which it is delivered are chosen or modified from the telephone loop cable plant so that no loading coils (which would severely attenuate the high-frequency components of the signal) are connected. In addition, bridged taps (branching connections of the type used to deliver the same service to two or more locations, such as an office and an answering service) are avoided, because of the unwanted signal reflections they would cause.

Figure 8.9 is a block diagram of an office channel unit (OCU), showing the manner in which the loop pairs are isolated using transformers from the rest of the central office equipment. Signal format in both directions is bipolar with alternate mark inversion, as described in Chapter 6. A sealing current is passed through both pairs in order to avoid buildup of resistance at unsoldered splices; this current may be reversed by the office

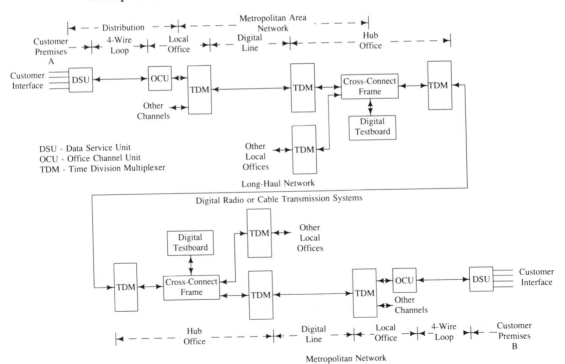

FIGURE 8.8. A point-to-point DDS Circuit. The boundaries of the three major parts of a long-distance DDS connection are shown. (Reprinted by permission. Copyright © 1975 AT&T.)

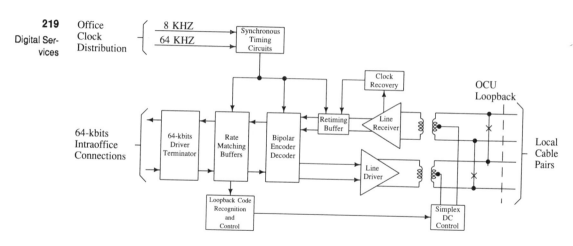

FIGURE 8.9. Block Diagram of an Office Channel Unit. (Reprinted with permission. Copyright 1975 AT&T.)

channel unit in order to force a channel loopback condition at the CSU. The OCU itself may be caused to provide a loopback to the network by a control pattern in the data stream.

At the customer end of the serving loops, the CSU (see Figure 8.10) or DSU (see Figure 8.11) reshapes and retimes the pulses received over the receive pair and delivers the customer's signal to the transmit pair.

Metropolitan Area Network: DDS circuits are converted into DS-0 channels at the local office (called the **end office**) serving the customer and multiplexed onto T1 facilities which feed, either directly or via intermediate offices, the area hub. This arrangement is shown in Figure 8.12 on page 221. At the end office, all circuits are converted to the DS-0 rate: 56 kbit/s become 64 kbit/s by the introduction of one control bit for each seven customer data bits, and lower service speeds are "geared" up to the DS-0 rate by both repetition (leading to an advantage in error rate because repeated data may be "voted upon" to identify bits in error) and by the addition of control bits. The T1 spans used for this purpose are typically fully duplicated and provided with **automatic protection switches**

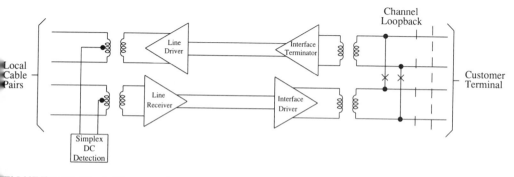

FIGURE 8.10. Block Diagram of a Channel Service Unit. (Reprinted with permission. Copyright 1975 AT&T.)

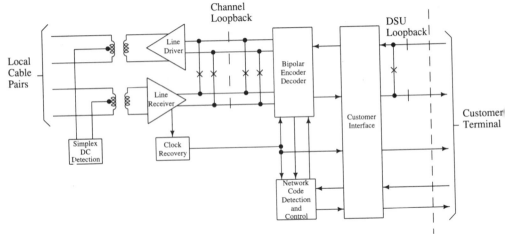

FIGURE 8.11. Block Diagram of a Data Service Unit. (Reprinted by permission. Copyright © 1975 AT&T.)

(APS) so that in the event of a failure, the backup T1 is switched in immediately. The T1 facilities used for DDS were specially designed for the application; the multiplexors at the ends of each span sacrificed one DS-0 channel (64kbit/s) of the normal 24 to a more robust design so that false indications of framing or the loss of same would be minimized.

The hub office is the cross connect point and maintenance center for the area it serves. Cross connections may be made to other circuits within the hub area, to other hubs within the LATA, or to inter-LATA carriers.

Intercity Network: In the original DDS service provided by AT&T, the intercity network was implemented using the Western Electric 1A Radio Digital System, which could be used with existing TD and TH radio systems. A technique already mentioned, called **data under voice** (DUV) provided digital channels in the low frequency part of the radio system's signal which was rarely used for voice. More recently, the medium of choice for long-distance transmission is optical fiber.

DDS INTERFACES

The availability of the data service unit, which has an interface to the business machine similar to a that of a modem, makes the substitution of DDS for analog service simple and, in most cases, trouble free. This has been the interface of choice for most DDS customers; however, we should not overlook the option of building part or all of the DSU into the data terminal equipment. If the DTE is certified as complying with the appropriate technical requirements of Part 68 of the Federal Communications Commission rules, the entire DSU may be part of the DTE. A compromise is an external CSU, with the rest of the function in the DTE, requiring only that the CSU be certified.

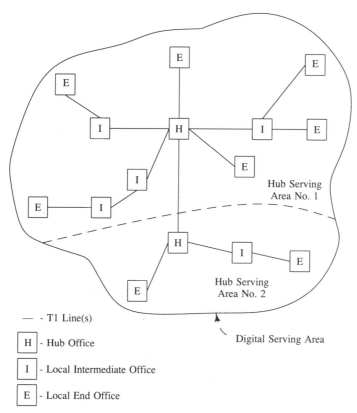

Hub Serving
Area No. 1

Hub Serving
Area No. 2

— - T1 Line(s)

H - Hub Office

I - Local Intermediate Office

E - Local End Office

Digital Serving Area

FIGURE 8.12. Example of DDS Metropolitan Network. (Reprinted with permission. Copyright © 1975 AT&T.)

MULTIPOINT DDS

DDS provides multipoint service in a manner that functions like multipoint analog service. The DDS component which performs the function similar to that of the analog bridge is called a **multipoint junction unit** (MJU). Located in a DDS hub office, the MJU combines the transmit signals of two or more circuit branches containing slave stations and forwards them on the receive side of the link to the master station. Operation follows these simple rules:

1. If the slave side of an MJU port is receiving control-idle codes, no data from that branch of the line is sent to the master;
2. If the slave side of any port of the MJU is in data mode and sends a space (0), a space is sent to the master station.

This design allows for both simulated control-idle and mark-hold operation. In the opposite direction, the MJU "fans out" the master station's transmit signal to the receive side of the slave station links. Typical MJUs are capable of accommodating five stations on a multipoint line; additional stations may be accommodated by connecting them in tandem.

Multipoint DDS lines are not affected by noise in the same way as their analog counterparts. Noise below the threshold of the OCU or of the MJU is not propagated into the DDS network and does not accumulate.

DDS MAINTENANCE FEATURES

Testing in DDS is accomplished primarily by monitoring the DS-0 circuit for control codes automatically inserted by equipment which detects a failure and by using loopbacks which may be activated remotely from a hub office at any of the following points on a circuit:

1. customer DSU;

2. customer CSU; and

3. end office OCU.

For multipoint lines, it is vital that the serving test center be able to activate a test path to one and only one station at a time. This is achieved with a device called a **multipoint signaling unit** (MSU) and special logic in the MJUs. The MSU selects the test path by transmitting control codes down the DS-0 channel to the MJU. Loopback testing is accomplished be automatically transmitting a pseudo-random bit stream along the selected path and checking the received against transmitted data.

The test features described here and in Chapter 6 may, with some carriers and in some areas, be available directly to the DDS customer. AT&T has provided customer access to an automatic test system via a standard dial-up asynchronous ASCII port which may be called by the DDS customer with a modem and personal computer or other ASCII terminal. After entering an authorization code and identifying the line, the customer may request any of the following tests:

- a complete test of a point-to-point circuit via CSU/DSU loopback in both directions;

- a similar test of one branch of a multipoint circuit, as above;

- a directed CSU or DSU test for one branch of a multipoint circuit;

- a directed CSU or DSU test toward either end of a point-to-point circuit;

- a simultaneous multiple test of up to 10 customer selected stations on a multipoint line;

- a simultaneous test of all stations on a multipoint line.

Tests may be scheduled for a later time or for regular repetition on a weekly, bimonthly, or monthly basis. Results of scheduled tests are saved and may be collected at the customer's convenience.

NEW OPTIONS FOR DDS SERVICE

DDS continues to evolve to meet the needs of customers. Recalling Chapter 6, we saw that the DSX-0 bytes included bits for both framing and control for the subrate services and for control only for 56kbit/s DDS. By altering the OCU and local loop designs slightly, two significant additions to DDS have been made possible. Both of them rely on extending

Primary	Secondary	Loop
2400	133 1/3	3200
4800	266 2/3	6400
9600	533 1/3	12800
56000	2666 2/3	72000

FIGURE 8.13. Transmission Rates with Secondary Channel (bits per second).

the byte-oriented network data format all the way to the customer premises, rather than only as far as the OCU.

Fixed DDS With Secondary Channel: Secondary channel is a feature by which an additional, logically independent, data channel is provided over the same facilities. Usually operating at a much lower speed than the main channel, these have long been common with analog services where they were implemented by inserting another (usually much more slowly) modulated carrier into the channel at a frequency carefully chosen not to interfere with the primary.

Equipment is now becoming available which "steals" the DSX-0 control bit part of the time to provide a secondary channel capability to DDS much like that provided with analog services. In order to do this, the DSX-0 byte structure is carried over the loop pairs, which are speeded up to carry the additional bits, as shown in Figure 8-13.

Operation of the secondary channel is completely independent of the primary; the secondary may be used while the primary is idle, and vice-versa. On multipoint lines, a tributary secondary may transmit to the master station while a different station is transmitting to the master on the primary channel.

Subrate Multiplexing: Another benefit of extending the network data format all the way to the customer is that, with the proper multiplexing equipment, the customer may use a (nominally) 56kbit/s DDS line to carry several slower channels which may be split apart at the DDS hub and fan out to separate destinations. This is equivalent to placing the subrate data multiplexor on the customer premises, and saves the expense of separate OCUs and loop pairs for each channel.

Switched DDS

Applications such as inter- and intra-enterprise batch data file transfer and digital video teleconferencing are perfectly suited to a switched service, where pricing is a function of usage and long haul facilities costs are shared by a number of users. AT&T was the first to design and offer such a service in May, 1985; it is called ACCUNET Switched 56®, and is available now and is planned for more than 80 U.S. cities. The original tariff called for pricing digital data calls with a minimum billing of 30 seconds and additional units of six seconds each.

ACCUNET Switched 56® is an all-digital, terrestrial, full duplex, long-distance data service which AT&T offers on a "premises-to-premises" basis. This means that the carrier will order and manage all services, including access lines, required to meet the customer's equipment at the exact locations desired. Alternatively, it may be reached via switched digital service provided by a local exchange carrier, where available.

This service is implemented using the existing digital switched telephone network and modified 4ESS® digital switches which are shared with voice traffic. The originating customer's access line or trunk is multiplexed onto a T1 with a special port in a D4-type channel bank. A special numbering plan (area code 700, numbers of the form 56x-xxxx) flags digital calls as they enter the toll network. The entry point switch consults the routing database via the CCIS network for the terminating switch and trunk and finds an all-digital path to that line. Handling within the digital network is similar to that of a voice call, as it is carried in 64 kbit/s DS-0 form with the same supervision and signaling.

Access to this service is called either "special", meaning via a leased 56 kbit/s DDS line or one channel of a T1 (on which other long-distance services may be carried), or "switched", in which a similar service provided by a local exchange carrier is used. The first such carrier to provide switched access to ACCUNET Switched 56® service was Northwestern Bell in 1986. More information on switched local services may be found in Chapter 9.

Special CSUs are required for switched DDS, because they must provide signaling and supervision functions that are not present with full-period services. These are available from several manufacturers and in several forms, including cabinet, rackmount, and printed circuit board for use inside a personal computer.

High-capacity Services

High-capacity, often abbreviated **Hi-cap,** is a telecommunications industry term for digital service at T1 rates and above. We should keep in mind that while such services may be new to marketing people and many of their customers, the rapid deployment of T-Carrier technology began in the early 1960s. This technology is well tested and its application is relatively straightforward; network designers and their managers should discount the aura of magic with which it is often presented.

High-capacity service is offered in various forms which differ in ways that affect quality, availability, and end-to-end delay. Understanding their differences will help the designer apply them in the most cost-effective ways.

Basic Terrestrial Services

The most basic high-capacity service is terrestrial T1. The term "terrestrial" indicates that the service is implemented totally with ground-based facilities (i.e., no satellite links are included in the channel's route). This distinction is important because terrestrial channels have much less delay than satellite channels, which are described in more detail below.

High-capacity terrestrial service may be used:

• To directly connect two customer premises; this is the simplest application from the carrier's viewpoint. Multiplexing, if used, is completely the end-user's responsibility and any multiplexing equipment is on customer premises, on the customer side of a CSU.

• To "bundle" a number of DS-0 services into a single T1 access line in order to gain economies of scale (sometimes called **integrated access**); here, the customer and the carrier each have compatible multiplexors, and the carrier rents the central office multiplexor to the customer.

• To gain access to another high-capacity service which is not directly available at a carrier's nearest point of presence; this usually involves only a cross-connection at a carrier's office without special equipment. Such channels could link a customer premises to a distant carrier POP or link offices of the same or different carriers.

Basic terrestrial T1 service is offered by the larger carriers under various names and with approximately the following service objectives:

• quality: 99.5% error-free seconds, measured over a 24-hour period; and
• availability: 97% over 12 months.

Current objectives or contractual commitments should be obtained as service is required, as they are subject to change.

Multiplexing High-capacity Services

Compatibility is the most important consideration in choosing multiplexing equipment used with high-capacity services. A basic choice is whether or not multiplexing will be completely a customer responsibility. If it is decided in advance that a network will use only customer-provided equipment on customer premises, the designer may choose multiplexing equipment which uses proprietary channelization. Such equipment may offer unique features and/or cost-performance advantages, but at the price of a reduced ability to use current or future carrier services based on standard channelization.

M24 is the generic name for a multiplexing scheme developed by AT&T which divides a T1 into 24 DS-0 64 Kbit/s channels with the D4 framing first described here in Chapter 3. Multiplexors adhering to the M24 standard are compatible with those in the AT&T offices used for integrated access and other services which use 24 DS-0 channels within a DS-1 aggregate.

M24 multiplexing is, in effect, an industry standard which should not be lightly disregarded. It is the basis for a number of important carrier services today and in the future.

DACS and Reconfiguration

A benefit of standardization on framing and channelization is that DS-0 channels may be automatically switched within the carrier network under customer control using a **digital access and cross-connect system** (DACS). A service option providing this function is called **customer controlled reconfiguration** (CCR), and is operated (indirectly) by the customer over a leased or switched connection between the DACS and an ASCII computer terminal on customer premises. CCR allows a customer to connect any DS-0 channel of a T1 (which could be carrying either voice or data) entering a DACS switch to any channel of any other T1 terminated on the same DACS. A recent AT&T DACS switch has a capacity of 128 T1s in its maximum configuration, allowing 1,524 cross-connections at the DS-0 level after saving 24 DS-0s for testing. Using this capability, a T1 customer might rearrange the use of its long-haul transmission network throughout the day as employees and customers arrive and depart and computers shift their attention between interactive and batch processing and back.

Switched High-capacity Services

When T1 service was first introduced, it was considerably more expensive than it is today. Customers not requiring full-period service were offered T1 on an hourly basis for applications such as emergency backup, traffic overflow, and video teleconferencing. Capacity could be reserved in advance and even could be had, when available, on demand. AT&T ACCUNET® Reserved T1.5® and U.S. Sprint's Meeting Channel® are current examples of switched high-capacity services.

Speeds Above T1

With carriers deploying T3 facilities throughout the U.S., it was only a matter of time before they were offered directly to customers, rather than piecemeal in the form of separate T1s. ACCUNET® T45 Service®, at 44.736 Mbit/s, was the first example of T3 service available on a retail basis from a major carrier. As fiber facilities are turned up along major routes, T3 service has become both more common and less expensive, where it is available. In areas not crossed by fiber routes, however, T3 service may never be offered.

Access to Long-distance Services

Access to inter-LATA carriers is the subject of considerable debate in regulatory circles, much of it centered on the issue of **local exchange carrier bypass.** If there is a massive migration of large business customers away from local carriers and toward, for example, direct microwave links to long-distance carriers, the financial effect on the local carriers could be severe. The resulting revenue loss in the presence of large fixed costs could bring increases in local business and residential telephone bills. Perhaps the best way to prevent this flight is for the local carriers to price access lines slightly below the costs of bypass, especially when the maintenance costs of private links are considered. In a regulated environment, however, no carrier may act unilaterally and such pricing is not necessarily assured. Careful consideration should be given to bypass decisions in an environment which will remain volatile for some time following the breakup of the Bell System.

Contamination

In the case of networks which contain *inter*state links, there may be a choice of applicable tariffs for links which are purely *intra*state but which carry (or could carry) voice or data traffic which crosses a state line. As the price difference between state-regulated and FCC-regulated tariffs is often substantial (with the FCC tariff usually cheaper), depending on the local carrier to apply the correct tariff may be an expensive mistake. Professional legal assistance should be sought when tariff applicability is an issue.

CHAPTER 9

Satellite Technology

Chapter Overview

The proliferation of artificial Earth satellites in the early 1960s made a revolutionary difference in the economics and connectivity of telecommunications, and this chapter describes their characteristics and use for data transmission. Beginning with the history of this technology, we will proceed to the characteristics of satellite systems and their components, followed by examination of several designs for sharing the capacity of a satellite channel. Finally, we will examine recent developments in the field and speculate on the near-term future of satellite data communications.

Satellite technology offers the advantages of microwave radio using relay stations with a line-of-sight path to a large portion of the Earth's surface. This combination results in a communications system with the following characteristics:

- the ability to broadcast transmissions to an unlimited number of receivers distributed over a very large area;
- costs which are almost entirely independent of distance and terrain;
- high bandwidth, due to the use of microwave carrier frequencies;
- independence from the world's telecommunications infrastructure; and
- comparatively large signal transmission time, due to the considerable distances involved.

Before the widespread deployment of fiber, most satellite applications focused primarily on high bandwidth, with some attention to the ability to place terminals almost anywhere. More recently, the latter advantage has become primary, with some attention to data broadcast applications.

This chapter is intended to provide an overview of the subject of satellite communications sufficient that the reader may understand and evaluate the offerings of satellite carriers.

History of Satellite Communications

The communications satellite was first proposed by the noted British writer Arthur C. Clarke in the October, 1945 issue of *Wireless World* magazine. Entitled "Extraterrestrial Relays," the article described how three equally spaced geostationary space platforms could be used to relay radio signals between any two points on Earth. Clarke also proposed providing electrical power from sunlight using solar cells, a technique prevalent today. At the time of Clarke's proposal, communications satellites were not practical because the technology to launch hardware into Earth orbit was not available.

The 1957 launching of the USSR's *Sputnik*, Earth's first artificial satellite, brought telecommunications into the space age. The worldwide reception of *Sputnik's* telemetry signals proved that radio communications with orbiting satellites was practical, and work began in earnest to adapt this technology to long-distance transmission. Progress was quite rapid in the early years of satellite communications, with the following events being important milestones along the way:

1960 The first passive communications satellite, *Echo*, was used to link stations on the ground. The receiver technology used in this experiment was a major advance at the time, with the received signal power being 10^{-18} less than the 10,000 watts transmitted.

1962 *Telstar,* the first communications satellite with an active repeater on board, was launched. *Telstar* first relayed television signals across the Atlantic on July 11, 1962. The brainchild of AT&T and Bell Laboratories, it was launched from Cape Canaveral on July 10 by a Thor-Delta rocket. It weighed about 176 pounds and occupied an orbit with a **period** (time to circle Earth) of 2.5 hours. *Telstar* (and most of its successors until 1978) used radio frequencies in the *C* band (4 and 6 Ghz), the same band used for much terrestrial microwave transmission.

The United States Congress passed the Communications Satellite Act of 1962, providing for the establishment of the Communications Satellite Corporation (COMSAT), a private "common carrier's carrier" to provide commercial services.

1963 World communications leaders met in an "Extraordinary Administrative Radio Conference" in Geneva to allocate frequencies for communications satellites.

Syncom II was the first successful communications satellite (*Syncom I* failed in orbit) to be launched into a geostationary orbit, making it appear to "hang in space" on a point over the Earth's equator.

1964 INTELSAT, a consortium of private and national telecommunications carriers, was formed. Representatives of 11 nations signed its charter, which provided for designing, developing, constructing, establishing, and maintaining a global satellite communications system.

Syncom III was the first geostationary communications satellite to carry a television broadcast over the Pacific, the Tokyo Olympic Games.

1965 COMSAT launched the first commercial communications satellite for use between Europe and North America, called *Early Bird* (also called *INTELSAT I*). *Early Bird* had an 18-month planned operational lifetime, but it performed with 100% reliability for four years, being retired in early 1969. *Early Bird* was recalled to service in June, 1969 to assist with communications for the *Apollo 11* space mission.

American Broadcasting Company (ABC) became the first U.S. television network to petition the Federal Communications Commission for authority to launch a satellite for use in distributing programs to affiliated stations.

1969 *INTELSAT 3F4* was launched, completing the global reach of INTELSAT's network.

1972 *Anik A1*, the first domestic (Canadian) communications satellite, was launched.

1974 *Westar I*, the first U.S. domestic communications satellite, was launched.

1975 Home Box Office, Inc. became the first company to broadcast premium television programs to cable customers via satellite.

1979 The U.S. Federal Communications Commission relaxed rules requiring licenses for all satellite Earth stations, opening the regulatory door to personal television receive-only (TVRO) installations.

1980 *SBS-1*, the first U.S. commercial communications satellite to use the higher frequency $K_u$band, became the first satellite designed as part of an all-digital transmission system.

1982 RCA's *Satcom V* became the first communications satellite with an all solid-state radio system.

SBS-3 was the first satellite launched by a U.S. Space Shuttle (the *Columbia*).

1983 The U.S. Federal Communications Commission halved the spacing requirement for satellites in equatorial orbit, from four degrees to two. This doubled the number of positions available for geostationary satellites.

1984 *Westar VI* and *Palapa B-2* become the first satellites recovered from space (by the Space Shuttle *Discovery*) after being launched into defective orbits.

In April of 1984, Solar Max was repaired in orbit by a Space Shuttle crew, demonstrating for the first time that space-based repairs were possible.

Today, Sir Arthur Clarke is better known for his prolific writing in fields other than telecommunications, but that article in *Wireless World* earned him the honor of having the collection of geostationary orbits named the Clarke Belt. Satellites have become an important part of the telecommunications business, carrying a significant fraction of long-distance (especially international) traffic.

Satellite communications technology has been adapted for purposes other than experimental and commercial telecommunications in the years since *Sputnik*. Soviet navigation satellites at altitudes of 400 and 11,800 miles, and their U.S. counterparts at 12,400 miles provide a precise position reference for all kinds of mobile vehicles; some of these satellites are equipped to receive and locate the source of radio distress calls. Numerous satellites are used to collect military, meteorological, and environmental information such as crop conditions and snowfall. Scientific satellites collect various kinds of information not available on Earth's surface, including astronomical phenomena which do not penetrate our atmosphere. All of these applications have benefitted greatly from advancements developed for communications purposes.

Progress in electronics technology has brought a revolution in satellite communications in recent years. The availability of smaller, cheaper, and more easily installed Earth
stations (called **very small aperture terminals**, or **VSAT**s, from the size of their antennas)
offers new options to the network designer who needs to link sites over a very wide area
and/or in "out of the way" locations.

Physics of Satellites

Using a satellite communications service doesn't require knowledge of astronomy, but
some astronomical physics is helpful in understanding the characteristics, limitations, and
economics of satellite-based systems. We will examine orbits and how they are achieved,
along with the physical factors that limit the lives of satellites in orbit.

Orbits

Like natural satellites, or moons (of which there are at least 54 in our solar system),
communications satellites revolve about a planet with a balance of forces in which the
attraction of gravity exactly matches the centrifugal force which would otherwise make it
fly off on a tangent to its elliptical or circular path. The path of the satellite about the planet
is called its **orbit**, which may be **polar** (intersected at opposite points by the planet's axis
of rotation), **equatorial** (about the planet's equator, at right angles to a polar orbit), or
inclined (in between polar and equatorial), as shown in Figure 9.1.

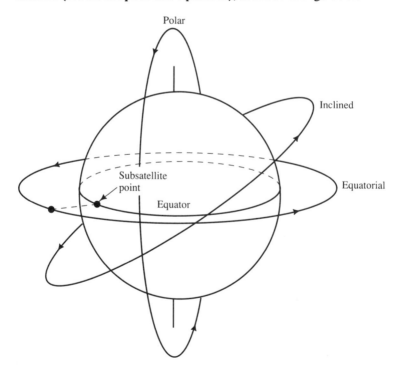

FIGURE 9.1. Polar, Equatorial, and Inclined Orbits.

Most satellites used for telecommunications occupy equatorial orbits at an altitude of 35,784 km (22,235 miles), which makes them appear to "hang" stationary above a point on the Earth's equator; such satellites are called **geostationary,** revolving about the Earth's axis in exactly the same time (called a **sidereal day**) as Earth: 23 hours, 59 minutes, and 4.09 seconds. The altitude of a geosynchronous satellite results in a propagation delay between the Earth and a satellite of about 250 milliseconds, or a round trip (Earth to satellite to Earth) of about a half second.

Figure 9.2 on page 232 shows U.S. domestic satellites in geostationary orbit, positioned over the area they serve. *Westar 1* was the first U.S. domestic satellite, launched in 1974 by Western Union and since retired. *Westar 3* is the oldest operating satellite (or "bird") of this series operating at this writing, in service since 1979 and designed for a 10-year operating life.

A geostationary satellite, like a microwave relay station hanging on a **skyhook,** is always "visible" (by radio) from approximately 40% of the surface of the Earth, corresponding to an equatorial distance of over 10,000 miles. An Earth station need not move its antenna to follow such a satellite, a considerable saving in complexity and cost over designs using inclined or polar orbits.

In reality, the Clarke belt is not an ideal circle; because satellites wander slightly, it is effectively a band around the Earth with a width and thickness measured in miles. The current degree of precision in station keeping, about 0.1°, would permit 1,800 geostationary satellites at a uniform separation of 0.2°; the effective limit on geostationary satellites is ability to share frequencies, rather than a shortage of places to put them.

Most communications satellites follow geostationary orbits, but the Soviet *Molniya* (Russian for "lightning") television relay series is a notable exception. Because much of the Russian population is so far North, the *Molniyas* use an elliptical orbit with an inclination of about 65° with respect to the Equator, a 40,000 km **apogee** (maximum altitude), and a 500 km **perigee** (minimum altitude). The apogee is in the northern hemisphere where a satellite appears almost stationary for several hours at a time; the perigee occurs near Antarctica, as shown in Figure 9.3 on page 233. Several satellites are used for 24-hour service, and antennas track them across the sky, switching when it provides a better signal.

Launching and Positioning

The launching of a satellite is an enterprise which requires immense technical and economic resources, with cooperation on a global scale. National governments have been key participants in launching all artificial satellites to date, and will probably continue in that role. Nations and national groups with satellite launching capability include the People's Republic of China, the European Space Agency (with major participation by the French company Arianespace), India, Japan, USSR, and the United States. More than 3,000 launches have put over 3,500 objects into space, with the U.S., the Soviet Union, and European Space Agency being major contributors to the total. Launching accounts for a large fraction of the cost of an in-orbit satellite; this is expected to be the case for some years to come.

U.S. LAUNCHING ORGANIZATIONS

In the United States, space activities are the responsibility of a nonmilitary organization called the National Aeronautics & Space Administration (NASA) and of the Air Force.

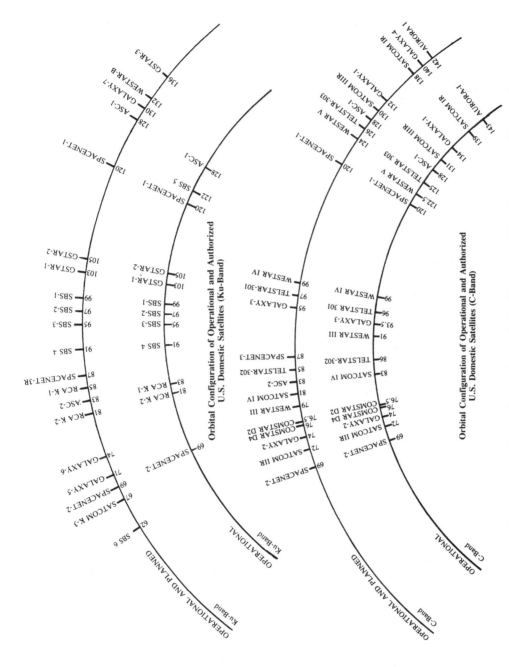

FIGURE 9.2. North American Domestic Satellites in Geostationary Orbit. (Courtesy of Satellite Systems Engineering, Bethesda, MD USA.)

232

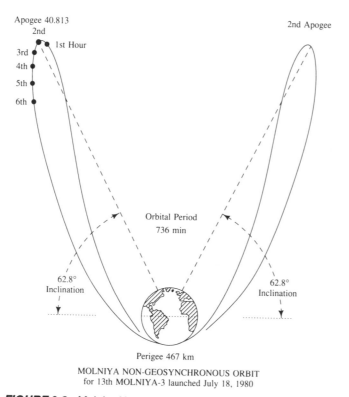

MOLNIYA NON-GEOSYNCHRONOUS ORBIT
for 13th MOLNIYA-3 launched July 18, 1980

FIGURE 9.3. *Molniya* Non-geosynchronous Orbit. (Courtesy of Quantum Publishing, Inc.)

The United States launches from three locations: NASA's Kennedy Space Center (space shuttle flights) and the Air Force's Cape Canaveral (unmanned rockets), effectively a single facility in Florida; Vandenburg Air Force Base in California (unmanned rockets); and NASA's Wallops Flight Facility in Virginia (unmanned rockets and satellites).

Launching *Early Bird* (*Intelsat I*)

The launching of *Intelsat I*, the first "production" geostationary communications satellite, is a good example of satellite deployment by rocket, and is illustrated in Figure 9.6 on page 236. *Intelsat I* was built by the Hughes Aircraft Company for COMSAT and carried aloft from Cape Kennedy in a three-stage NASA rocket called a Thrust Augmented Delta. Cape Kennedy's northern latitude made achieving geostationary orbit more complex than it would have been had the rocket left from a point on the Equator. The Delta's third stage aligned the satellite with its apogee motor in a forward position at an angle of 16.7° to the Equator, where commands from a control station in Andover, Maine started it spinning for stabilization. Twenty-six minutes and 32 seconds after liftoff it was separated from the Delta's third stage and coasted to its first apogee at 23,081 miles. Six revolutions later (63 hours and seven minutes after liftoff), the apogee motor was fired and the satellite moved to a near-circular orbit above the Equator at about 32° West longitude, drifting in an easterly direction at about 1.5° per day. On April 14, 1965, *Early Bird* was "parked" in its planned position at 28° W using on-board thrust motors.

Attitude Control

Once in orbital position, a satellite must be oriented with its antennas pointing in the right direction and kept that way, an activity called **attitude control.** The names given to the three kinds of motion to be controlled are **yaw, pitch,** and **roll,** as shown in Figure 9.4. A common stabilization method is spinning part of the satellite (for cylindrical satellites, usually the outer cylinder) to achieve a gyroscopic effect. This complicates the mechanical design considerably, however, as the antennas must remain stationary with respect to the Earth while part of the rest of the spacecraft spins. Antennas which are rotated to compensate for gyroscopic spinning are said to be **despun.**

Station Keeping

A satellite must carry equipment to compensate for weak forces which, if ignored, would eventually move it from its assigned orbit. These forces include the gravitational attraction of Earth (which isn't a perfect sphere), sun, and moon, and the pressure of solar radiation. Small gas jets, typically powered by tanks of hydrazine, are used to occasionally exert a small push in the right direction under ground control. This activity is called **station keeping,** and the fuel capacity of the satellite for this purpose is a major factor in determining its operating lifetime. Once the fuel is exhausted, the satellite drifts out of the sight of

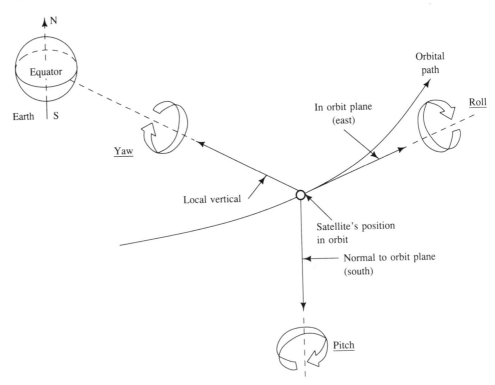

FIGURE 9.4. Motion Control: Yaw, Pitch, and Roll. (Reprinted from Martin: *Communications Satellite Systems,* courtesy of Prentice-Hall.)

fixed antennas on the ground, making it useless. The operating life may be extended by tracking the satellite with movable antennas, but this is only practical where the number of Earth stations is small.

Apparent Position

The position of a satellite in the Clarke Belt may be described completely by a single number, the longitude of the point below it on the Equator (called the **subsatellite point**). However, the direction in which an antenna on the Earth's surface must be pointed to "see" it depends on the antenna location. Two quantities called **azimuth** and **elevation** are used to describe the pointing of an antenna. Azimuth describes the East-West orientation of the antenna and elevation its angle to the ground, as shown in Figure 9.5.

Azimuth and elevation are measured in degrees; the 0° reference for azimuth is true North, and that for elevation is horizontal (parallel to a tangent on the Earth's circumference). Earth stations in the Northern hemisphere view geostationary satellites with an azimuth between 90° and 270° and an elevation between 0° and 90° (straight up from a point on the Equator). Those in the Southern hemisphere use azimuth values between 270° and 360°, with elevations between 90° and 180° The azimuth and elevation angles for locating any satellite in geostationary orbit may be calculated from its longitude; pointing the antenna requires only the two angles and knowledge of true North.

In practice, elevations of less than 5° (as would be required to view a geostationary satellite from close to the North Pole) are avoided, due to the excessive attenuation from the long path through the Earth's atmosphere and the chance of additional noise and interference from terrestrial sources.

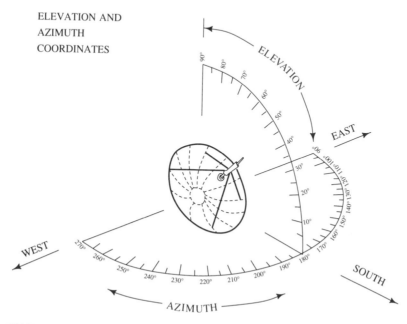

FIGURE 9.5. Elevation and Azimuth Coordinates. (Courtesy of Quantum Publishing, Inc.)

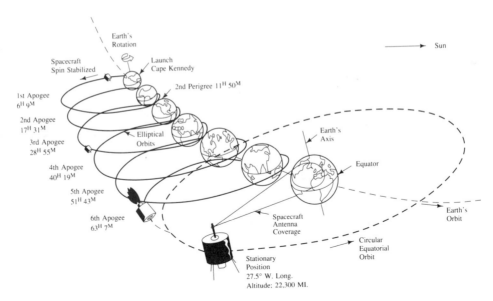

FIGURE 9.6. Launching and Positioning of *Intelsat 1*. (Courtesy of Hughes Aircraft Co.)

Periodic Phenomena

Artificial satellites are subject to certain effects which are results of their position relative to the Earth, sun, and moon.

ECLIPSES

Communications satellites are typically powered by converting sunlight directly into electricity using devices called **solar cells.** For up to 65 minutes at a time on 88 days of the year, a geostationary satellite's solar cells are cut off from the sun's rays by Earth. Less often, it falls within the moon's solar shadow, with the same effect. Interruptions in service are avoided by powering the satellite from batteries during these periods; the batteries are recharged by the solar cells.

SUN TRANSIT OUTAGES

In addition to light and heat, the sun radiates energy within the microwave portion of the electromagnetic spectrum; this is received as noise by an Earth station and is normally not a problem. However, for about 10 minutes on each of five days per year the sun is directly behind a geostationary satellite as seen from Earth, and the satellite's low power signal is drowned in solar noise. Until much more powerful satellites are launched, this effect can only be avoided by switching to another satellite in a different orbital position until the solar noise fades. A similar effect occurs when the moon is directly behind a satellite, but it is not nearly as severe.

Components Of Satellite Communications Systems

Satellite systems are traditionally divided into component groups called the **Earth seg-ment,** which includes all subsystems located on the ground, and the **space segment,** which includes all equipment aboard the spacecraft. Their design is not unlike that of a terrestrial microwave transmission system, except that (in present day commercial systems) there is only one repeater, and most systems provide for sharing the repeater among more than two terminals, making the terminals more complex. Figure 9.7 shows a block diagram of a typical Earth station used with transponders of the type shown in Figure 9.9 on page 242.

Earth Segment

Earth segment subsystems consist of both digital and radio components; the radio components are further distinguished by their operating frequency. The major components are clustered into indoor and outdoor groups interconnected by a cable called an **inter-fa-cility link** (IFL). The indoor group includes the port adapter subsystem, forward error-cor-rection logic, and modem; the outdoor portion is called the **radio frequency terminal** (RFT), which includes the antenna and components which must be near the antenna.

PORT ADAPTER SYSTEM

This portion of the Earth station contains the interface(s) to the user's data terminal equipment. Its function is to provide one or more standard data interfaces which operate in a manner compatible with the DTE; where there are multiple data ports, buffering and multiplexing functions are included. Because the DTE may or may not be directly con-nected, the data ports can be made configurable to present either a DCE (for nearby DTE) or DTE (for use with tail circuit modems and/or DSUs) interface. Data ports may be

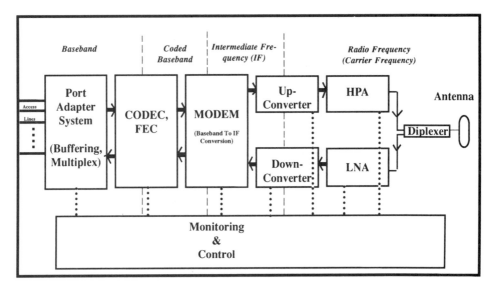

FIGURE 9.7. Block Diagram of a Typical Earth Station.

provided with RS-232, V.35, or RS-449 interfaces, and may be equipped with serial memories called **elastic buffers** for applications where the satellite system and the attached equipment (such as a DDS DSU) operate on separate clocks. With high-precision frequency standards such as atomic clocks and buffers of generous size, clock slips may be reduced to an insignificant number, but not totally eliminated.

The port adapter(s) of an Earth station may contain software to hide the effects of satellite propagation delay from the DTE, making the channel appear to operate more like a terrestrial line. Called **spoofing** or **delay compensation,** this technique requires that the port adapter be customized for the individual DTE protocol. It is often used with remote display control units for which a host system polls one or more cluster controllers to ask if any terminal input is ready. Much of the time, the response to such polling is negative, and the long propagation delay of a satellite link (over a half second) would make such operation insufferably slow.

Spoofing has the host-end port subsystem, acting as the remote controller, answer negatively to host system polling until data is actually received from the remote Earth station. The remote port adapter, pretending to be the host, polls the controller without any transmission over the satellite link until the controller responds with data. On the poll following reception of a data block via satellite, the host end port responds positively and forwards the data block to the host. Data in the host-to-terminal direction is immediately acknowledged when correctly received by the port, even though it will not reach the destination for some time. This rather elaborate masquerade game permits the host to proceed immediately with polling or data output for other stations on the (at least partially simulated) multidrop line. In this manner, satellite delay is not eliminated, but its effects are masked.

Data activity compression (DAC) is another function which may be implemented in the port adapter subsystem, most likely in large systems with many ports. This technique buffers a number of bits from a port and compares it with a reference bit pattern (such as all ones or the last bit pattern transmitted) and sends a special (short) message over the link when they are the same. The difference in length between this message and the buffered pattern represents transmission capacity which may be used for some other purpose. DAC is an adaptation of a similar technique used with voice communications systems which exploit the fact that usually only one person speaks at a time during a conversation. It is especially useful with ports which are used in a half duplex manner. The general subject of choosing an efficient representation for a baseband signal is called **source coding,** in order to distinguish it from coding for the purpose of detection and correction of errors in transmission.

Baseband signals from digital ports (assuming more than one port) are interleaved into a higher speed aggregate in the port adapter subsystem, just as with any multiplexer. This aggregate may include some bits used for synchronization and/or network management.

FORWARD ERROR CORRECTION

Most satellite systems provide for computing and inserting additional bits into the port adapter subsystem's output stream for the purpose of error detection and correction. It is common to include sufficient checking bits with the data so that the receiving terminal can automatically (i.e., without retransmission) correct for a burst of errors of some length. Called **forward error correction** (FEC), this technique is similar to that used with computer memories and can significantly improve the system error rate. The FEC device adds check bits to transmitted data and removes them from received data (following any correction required). If FEC device input is divided into groups of bits of length k and output is a (longer) sequence of bits of length n, then the coding process is said to have a **coding rate** $r = k/n$, and rates in the order of 2/3 are not uncommon, with resulting system error rates (after FEC) of 10^{-6} to 10^{-9}. One reason that FEC is important in satellite systems is that the propagation delay makes the cost of retransmission (in terms of response time) very high; the additional overhead of the FEC coding is considered a reasonable price to pay for eliminating a large number of retransmissions.

MODEM

As with terrestrial digital microwave systems a modulator and demodulator form the interface between the baseband binary data stream and a radio frequency signal. The modem's radio carrier frequency is usually an **intermediate frequency** (IF) such as 70 MHz, however, rather than one in the C or K_u band. Using an IF signal between the modem and the outdoor equipment lowers the cost of the interfacility link and permits it to be longer than would be possible at microwave frequencies. It also permits modems to be interchanged between C and K_u band systems. Note that the intermediate frequency is actually the center of a spectrum of frequencies as wide as the bandwidth of the total signal; using the entire bandwidth of a 36-MHz transponder and an intermediate frequency of 70 MHz would require an IF bandpass between $70 - 18 = 52$ and $70 + 18 = 88$ MHz. Conversion of the IF signal to the operating frequency of the transponder is handled within the RFT.

Systems for time-sharing the capacity of a transponder by multiple Earth stations make special requirements of modems. In particular, demodulators must be capable of detecting and synchronizing with a received signal in a very short time and modulators must turn on and off rapidly. Modems designed for this type of operation are called **burst modems.**

RFT

The RFT is at the antenna end of the IFL and includes up- and down-converters for the IF-microwave signal conversion, a **low-noise amplifier** (LNA) for receiving the signal gathered by the antenna, a **high power amplifier** (HPA) to increase the power of the upconverted modulator output, and the antenna itself.

The radio frequency energy collected by an antenna increases with its area, as does the narrowness of its transmitted beam. For these reasons, antennas are made as large as cost and other considerations (such as wind loading, zoning, and building codes) will permit. Increasing antenna size may permit economies elsewhere in the system and/or better performance.

While antennas up to 30 meters in diameter are not uncommon, the trend is toward smaller antennas as the cost-performance of other subsystems improves and higher power transponders become available. Antennas less than 1.8 meters in diameter and total terminal costs of under $15,000 are important factors in the growth of very small aperture terminal networks which permit organizations with widely separated sites to gain independence from the terrestrial telephone network and its limited choices in services, carriers, and prices.

Space Segment

The spacecraft containing the transponders and their antennas is a very complex package designed to extremely high standards of precision and reliability. Operating in the extremely hostile environment of space, it must shelter the transponders from micrometeorites, temperature extremes, and radiation while keeping the antennas accurately pointed at Earth, maintaining a stable position in orbit, and providing a continuous power supply.

Intelsat VI is a good example of current communications satellite technology, and is shown in Figure 9.8. The largest commercial spacecraft designed to date, it is almost 40 feet from end to end (with antennas deployed) and weighs 3,953 pounds. It is scheduled for launch in 1989 via *Ariane* rocket, and will have 50 transponders and use both C and K_u bands; total transmission capacity is 33,000 voice circuits and three television channels simultaneously. The solar power system for this satellite supplies 2,600 watts with nickel-hydrogen rechargeable batteries for use during solar eclipses.

Intelsat VI transponders are interconnected by both a static switch matrix and an electronic network which permits on-board switching of signals between up- and down-links in as little as four microseconds, permitting operation in a mode called **satellite switched time division multiple access** (SS-TDMA). SS-TDMA is a new degree of

FIGURE 9.8. Intelsat VI. (Courtesy of Hughes Aircraft Corp.)

sophistication in satellite on-board processing, a major step toward digital data switching in space.

Satellite Radio Transmission

The radio technology for use in satellite systems was borrowed directly from the microwave systems which served so well on the ground. Even though there were great obstacles to be overcome in adapting existing radio equipment for spaceflight, an immense advantage was to be gained: a geostationary satellite has line-of-sight access to almost half the area of the Earth. As fiber systems surpass satellite systems in capacity, it is the geographic coverage characteristic of satellites which will remain a unique advantage to the communications system designer.

Radio Services

International organizations and the U.S. Federal Communications Commission have classified satellite communications services, like other radio services, by type. **Fixed satellite service** (FSS) is transmission using geostationary satellites in a fixed point-to-fixed-point manner. Most of the data communications involving satellites has been of this type. **Direct broadcast satellite** service (DBS) is a point-to-multipoint service in which many stations are the intended recipients of the same signal, as with distribution of television network broadcasts (the major application for DBS).

Transponders

A communications satellite typically carries a number of radio receiver-transmitter pairs called **transponder**s, each of which is capable of amplifying and redirecting one or more radio signals toward Earth. Satellites with multiple transponders use frequency division and other techniques to avoid inter-transponder interference. The components of a simple transponder are shown in Figure 9.9 on page 242. This configuration, called a **bent pipe** because of the diagram's geometry, performs no processing on the uplink signal other than converting it to a different frequency (a process called **translation**) and amplifying it by 80 to 100 dB. The antenna presents the low-noise amplifier (LNA) with a very weak signal, in the order of a fraction of a microwatt. This signal is raised in power and some of the accompanying noise is filtered out. The LNA output is translated by mixing it with a stable reference frequency generated locally and filtering the result, which contains the two input signals along with both the sum and difference of their frequencies. The translated signal is then greatly increased in power by the **high power amplifier** (HPA) and fed to the transmitting antenna, which may be the same antenna used to receive the uplink signal.

The total transmission capacity of a satellite is determined by the number and bandwidth of its transponders; current designs include as many as 50 transponders, some of which may be reserved as spares. A bandwidth of 36 MHz per transponder is typical, with center frequencies spaced 40 MHz apart (four MHz is left unused to avoid interference between adjacent signals; the unused portions of the capacity are called **guard bands**). An advantage of the "bent pipe" design, in addition to its simplicity, is that it is independent of the modulation technique. Since the signal is not demodulated by the transponder, the only

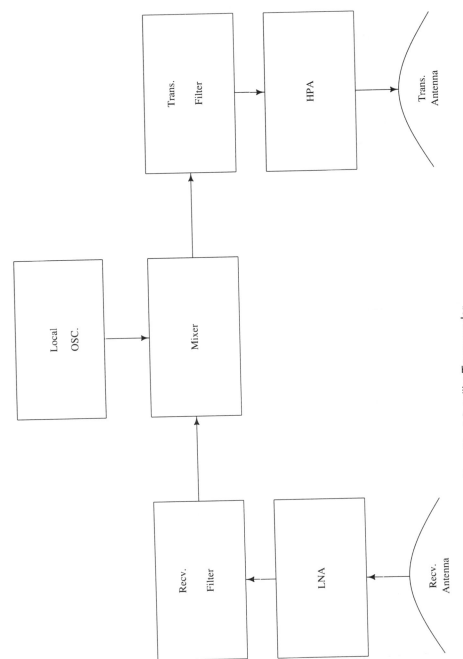

FIGURE 9.9. Block Diagram of a "Bent Pipe" Satellite Transponder.

limitation on it is that it not exceed the transponder's bandwidth—it could be a television program, many hundreds of frequency-division-multiplexed voice channels, or a digital data stream. Thirty-six MHz is a convenient choice for bandwidth because it will carry a color TV signal, thousands of FDM voice channels, or many megabits/second of digital data. The actual capacity of a transponder depends on the efficiency of the modems used and on other factors, but one example is *Westar IV*, for which Western Union claims a capacity of 7,200 (one way) voice channels, a single color TV signal, or 64 Mbit/s of simplex digital data on each of 24 *C*-band (36 MHz) transponders.

Frequency Bands

Microwave frequencies are especially well suited to satellite applications because of the large information-carrying capacity available at high radio frequencies and because the short wavelengths at these frequencies permits the design of small, very efficient antennas. Antenna size and efficiency are especially important for the satellite itself, because the payload capacity of current launch systems is small.

Frequencies for use by satellite communications systems are determined by a subgroup of the International Telecommunications Union called the **World Administrative Radio Conference** (WARC). Frequency bands allocated for nonmilitary point-to-point and broadcast applications are listed in Figure 9.10. Of these, the *C* and K_u bands are currently in heavy use. In order to avoid mutual interference of the signals to and from the satellite, different frequencies within a band are used for the path to (called the **uplink**) and from (**downlink**) the satellite. Note that the higher frequency is used for the uplink in all three bands.

THE *C* BAND

Often referred to as the 4/6 GHz band, the *C* band is also heavily used for terrestrial microwave radio. While a great deal of experience was available in designing equipment for use at these frequencies, interference between satellite and ground-based systems is a serious potential problem which affects the choice of sites for earth stations. *C* band transmissions are affected very little by weather, and equipment using this band has been manufactured for some time, so *C* band may be preferred for economic reasons where the absence of interference permits its use.

Name	Uplink (GHz)	Downlink (GHz)	Bandwidth
C	5.925–6.425	3.700–4.200	500 MHz
K_u	14.000–14.500	10.950–11.200 11.450–11.700	500 MHz
K_a	27.500–31.000	17.700–21.200	3.5 GHz

FIGURE 9.10. Satellite Frequency Bands for Fixed Applications.

THE K_u BAND

The K_u(12/14 GHz) band is not heavily used for terrestrial communications, so there is much more freedom in choosing Earth station sites. Also, the higher frequency permits smaller antennas than with the C band. There are disadvantages, however: signal loss due to rain is greater at these frequencies, and equipment may be more expensive. As electronics technology progresses, however, generally lower costs and higher power transponders tend to minimize these disadvantages. Today, the K_u band is the band of choice for many new systems, and recent satellites have had all-K_u or a mix of C and K_u transponders on board.

THE K_a BAND

Still a relatively untapped resource, the K_a offers both promise and challenge. At 20 and 30 GHz, antennas can be smaller, permitting more of them on board the spacecraft and lowering installation costs on the ground, where there is no K_a interference. In addition, the K_a bandwidth available is seven times that of either the C or K_u bands. However, atmospheric and rain-rate attenuation are considerably greater at the higher frequencies, effects which must be overcome by some combination of higher power and/or better receivers. K_a band operation can still be considered experimental at this writing.

Frequency Reuse

A number of techniques are available to use the same part of the radio spectrum for transmitting independent signals. This provides an economic advantage because portions of the transmission system may be shared.

POLARIZATION

Radio waves have an electrical and a magnetic component, and antennas may be designed to control the orientation of these components. Called **polarization,** this technique may be used to separate two signals on the same frequency, much like with light and the polarized eyeglasses used with 3D movies. Polarization may be **linear** (in which the signals are said to be at right angles: horizontal and vertical with respect to the receiving antenna) or **circular** (giving the appearance of rotating either clockwise or counterclockwise with respect to the receiver). Circular polarization has a slight advantage over linear because it is less affected by certain kinds of atmospheric distortion. While perfect separation is possible in theory, in practice signal isolation in the order of 30 dB is achieved. This is sufficient to double the information transmitted on a given frequency.

FOOTPRINT

The area "illuminated" on the Earth by a satellite antenna is called its **footprint,** and may range from something as small as the Hawaiian Islands to approximately 40% of the Earth's surface. Several antennas may be on board a single satellite; when footprints do not overlap, the same frequency may be used within each. Radiation patterns designed to favor a specific area are called **spot beams,** and the antennas that create them may be fixed or movable; the latter permits changing the area illuminated under control from the ground. Spot beams are practical on both the K_u and K_a bands, but antennas to produce them can be

WESTAR V
TYPICAL FOOTPRINT
EIRP CONTOURS (DBW) 122.5 W. LONGITUDE

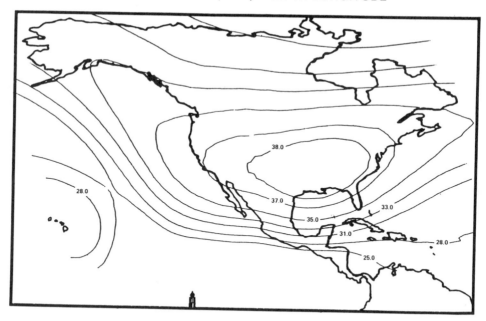

FIGURE 9.11. Footprint of *Westar V* Satellite. Essentially a contour map, the diagram shows the geographic distribution of the satellite's downlink power. The numbers indicate EIRP in dBW for the associated area. (Courtesy of Western Union.)

made smaller at higher frequencies. As K_a band-equipped satellites come into use, we can expect spot beams to be more numerous than they are today.

MULTIPLE CARRIERS PER TRANSPONDER

In applications where the full bandwidth of a transponder is not required, frequency division may be used *within* the bandpass of a single transponder. Adding carriers produces diminishing returns, however; operation at less than maximum power is necessary in order to prevent inter-carrier interference, and guard bands between carriers reduce the useful bandwidth available. Operating a satellite's HPA at reduced power for multiple-carrier applications is called **backoff,** and cost/benefit analysis of such tradeoffs is complex. As the geographical benefits of satellites begin to overshadow those related to capacity with the deployment of fiber, multiple carrier operation of transponders is expected to increase and may become a significant factor in satellite system design.

Factors Affecting Transmission

Major factors affecting satellite radio transmission are noise, signal power, and bandwidth. Noise can be minimized but not eliminated completely; its magnitude in comparison to that of the signal of interest is a basic consideration in communications system design. To a certain extent, bandwidth and signal power can be traded off in order to optimize the design of a particular system.

Shannon's Law relates the information carrying capacity of a channel to bandwidth, signal power, and noise power, as follows:

$$B = W \log_2(\frac{P_s}{P_n} + 1)$$

where B is the channel's information carrying capacity in bits/s, W is the channel bandwidth in Hz, P_s is the received signal power, and P_n is the power (or equivalent power) of the noise.

The signal to noise ratio P_s / P_n is an important figure of merit used throughout the field of telecommunications, to which Shannon's Law is fundamental.

NOISE

Noise, or random electromagnetic energy, is a characteristic of any system operating at a temperature above absolute zero (−273.1° C). It is a major consideration in the design of the receiving components of a satellite radio link, because power of the received signal (picowatts) is not large in comparison to that of the noise. Noise is received by the antenna from all directions, and is generated within all amplifiers. The error rate of any radio channel is related to the ratio of signal power to noise, and satellite links are typically operated with much lower signal to noise ratios than terrestrial microwave links.

Noise power is directly related to temperature (the measure of random energy in a system) and system bandwidth, as follows:

$$P_n = KTW$$

where T is the temperature of a system in degrees Kelvin, W is the bandwidth in Hz, and K is **Boltzmann's Constant,** 1.38×10^{-23} watts per degree Kelvin per Hz of bandwidth.

One figure of merit for a satellite receiver is its **equivalent noise temperature** $T°_{eq}$, the temperature at the antenna of an ideal receiver which would produce noise power equivalent to that measured on a real one. Noise temperature is commonly used to compare the performance of LNAs, even of consumer products such as satellite TV receivers.

Of special interest is **bit energy** $E_b = P_r T_b$, where T_b is the time to transmit one bit at the aggregate data rate. The ratio of bit energy to noise power E_b / P_n determines the system error rate and is useful because it expresses it in terms of radio frequency parameters alone, independent of modulation method.

Like death and taxes, noise and the probability of error will always be with us, and in satellite systems, forward error correction is the remedy of choice. Satellite error rates (after FEC) are typically comparable to those of terrestrial fiber, and better than those of terrestrial microwave.

BANDWIDTH

The radio system designer chooses the amount of bandwidth used to represent the transmitted signal(s) and any associated error correction information. To some extent, power and bandwidth may be interchanged, with the maximum bandwidth limited by the bandpass of the transponder. The minimum possible bandwidth (for a given signal to noise ratio) is a function of the signal's information content. One measure of bandwidth efficiency is the ratio of bandwidth (Hz) to data rate (bits/s), called the **bandwidth expansion factor.** For a 36 MHz C-band system, one to two bits per second per Hz of bandwidth is typical. Similar performance is available when narrower bandwidths are used with lower bit rates in order to pack several independent carriers within a single transponder, but at a cost in overall efficiency due to guard bands and other factors.

Bandwidth expansion is not limited to digital systems. A common analog example is the use of a full 36 MHz transponder to relay a standard six MHz television signal.

SIGNAL POWER

Signal power at a receiver's LNA input is a function of transmitted power, size and efficiency of both transmit and receive antennas, transponder altitude, and frequency. Since the effect of these factors is multiplicative, using decibels to account for power ratios simplifies link loss calculations because numbers which are truly factors are expressed in a way that requires only addition and subtraction. Power ratios are expressed in terms of decibels, 10 times the (base 10) logarithm of one power value divided by another. Absolute power is usually described in decibels referenced to one watt (dBW). Power ratios greater than one are positive in decibel notation; power losses (multiples of less than one) are negative.

System components which increase power are said to have **gain.** For amplifiers, the gain is the ratio of output to input power. Antennas are also considered components with gain, even though they are totally passive. For an antenna, the gain reference is a hypothetical omnidirectional point which is considered to have a gain of one. An antenna which collects 100 times as much power as the reference is said to have a gain of $10 \log_{10} (100/1)$ or 20 dB. **Effective isotropic radiated power** (EIRP) is defined as the power which would be required into an omnidirectional antenna to produce the same effect at the receiver as an antenna with a given gain, and is used as the power unit in footprint diagrams such as Figure 9.11 on page 245.

The two major sources of signal power loss in a satellite link are both related to distance. Free-space loss is a function only of total distance between transmitter and receiver, and is proportional to the square of the distance separating them. Atmospheric loss is proportional to the distance travelled through the Earth's atmosphere, and varies with frequency. The total loss in an uplink or downlink is in the order of 200 dB for C-band systems, and is somewhat greater for the K_u band. Figure 9.12 shows typical figures for losses and gains in a C-band link.

Characteristics of Satellite Transmission

In the early years of satellite communications, the principal advantages of the technology were high bandwidth and any-to-any connectivity independent of distance. Now that fiber systems are approaching and exceeding satellite transponders in bandwidth, the connectivity advantage is more of interest in areas where fiber is available. Satellite systems also differ from terrestrial ones with respect to delay and error distribution.

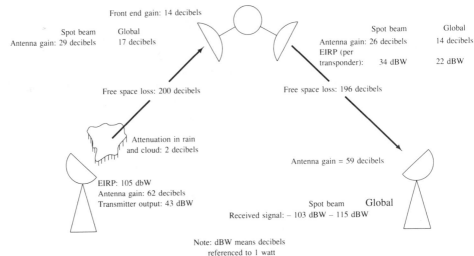

Transmitter output: 8 dBW per transponder

Front end gain: 14 decibels

Spot beam | Global
Antenna gain: 29 decibels | 17 decibels

Spot beam | Global
Antenna gain: 26 decibels | 14 decibels
EIRP (per
transponder): 34 dBW | 22 dBW

Free space loss: 200 decibels

Free space loss: 196 decibels

Attenuation in rain
and cloud: 2 decibels

Antenna gain = 59 decibels

EIRP: 105 dbW
Antenna gain: 62 decibels
Transmitter output: 43 dBW

Spot beam | Global
Received signal: – 103 dBW – 115 dBW

Note: dBW means decibels
referenced to 1 watt

FIGURE 9.12. Power Gains and Losses in a *C*-band Satellite Link. (Courtesy of Prentice-Hall.)

Connectivity

A satellite transponder is essentially a broadcasting repeater; all Earth stations pointed at and tuned to it (within its footprint) receive the signal(s) it is repeating. This characteristic may be exploited for bi-directional communications between any number of Earth stations without requiring a central communications hub. In addition, system costs are a linear function of the number of stations and largely independent of their geographical separation.

In order to appreciate this advantage, consider the number of links l required for any-to-any connectivity in a mesh network such as that of Figure 9.13. For any number of stations n,

$$l = \frac{n(n-1)}{2}$$

The geometric increase of l with n makes terrestrial mesh networks impractical for large numbers of nodes; for example, connecting each node to every other in a 100-node network would require 4,950 point-to-point links. Mesh connectivity is a basic characteristic of satellite systems, offering a significant advantage for applications such as interconnecting local area networks.

Star networks, such as terminals served by a central host computer, may also benefit from the use of satellites, especially where the terminals are numerous and/or widely separated. Use of a large antenna, high-power hub Earth station permits considerable economies in the design of VSAT terminals, described later. In addition, inter-terminal

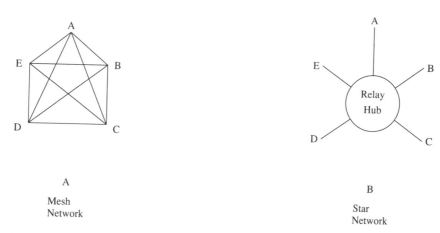

FIGURE 9.13. (a) Mesh and (b) Star Networks each of 5 Nodes.

communication is still possible using the central computer as a relay, but at the expense of doubling the propagation delay.

Earth stations may be located anywhere within the serving transponder's footprint, removing dependence on traditional common carriers and gaining freedom from the limitations they impose on where and how data services are available. The ability to quickly build private networks with this kind of independence (which has come to be called **carrier bypass**) is greatest with satellite technology, because Earth stations may be placed almost anywhere. As design improvements cause antennas to continue to shrink in size, this freedom can only increase.

Capacity

The number of bits per second which may be relayed through a satellite transponder is a complex function of the amount of bandwidth used, signal power, antenna size, the performance of the hardware selected, the acceptable error rate, and other factors. Systems which use the entire bandwidth of a transponder and antennas several meters in diameter typically deliver data capacities in the tens of megabits per second, corresponding to one to two bits per second of transponder bandwidth. For example, the first all-digital satellite system (SBS, now MCI) has a transmission rate of 48 Mbit/s using transponder bandwidth of 43 MHz, and Western Union advertises 64 Mbit/s for Westar transponders 36 MHz wide. The effective data rate may be considerably less, however, after subtracting the overhead for network management and forward error correction. Very small aperture terminals, with antenna diameters of 1.8 meters or less, offer transmission rates in the tens to hundreds of kilobits per second.

It is important to note that satellite system capacity is often described in terms of simplex (one-way) channels for data and half-circuits for voice. This is a result of their uplink-to-downlink repeater design and the fact that two-way transmission is accomplished only by sharing a one-way path.

Transmission Errors

Because much of the noise encountered in satellite radio systems is natural, rather than man-made, it has a more random and less bursty distribution than found in terrestrial systems. This characteristic may have an influence on the design of FEC hardware and on software specifically designed for use with satellite channels.

Weather conditions can cause increases in atmospheric attenuation which are manifested as an increased error rate or complete signal loss. These are sometimes overcome by temporarily increasing transmitting power, especially in K_u band systems.

Delay

The speed of light is normally not an important cause of delay in terrestrial communications systems, but the altitude of a geosynchronous satellite results in a delay of over 250 milliseconds between Earth station and transponder on the uplink and a similar amount on the downlink. For interactive applications such as data base inquiry/response, this results in adding half a second to the minimum response time, a significant amount. For this reason, tariffs for communications services (which usually ignore routing) may specify whether or not the carrier is permitted to use satellite transmission on a given link. Using two satellite links in tandem (called a **double hop**), such as might seem attractive between the West coast of the U.S. and Europe, is usually avoided.

Communications protocols which use polling (as with terrestrial multipoint lines) perform poorly or not at all over satellite channels. In applications where it is desired to keep existing equipment using polling, the spoofing technique mentioned above may be used with good results.

Applications which are essentially one-way in nature, such as file transfer, are not seriously affected by satellite delay when appropriate protocols are used. Large block sizes improve efficiency by increasing the amount of data which is acknowledged with a single message, and protocols which perform well with delay may be implemented inexpensively using microprocessors within communicating devices.

Security

Satellite systems offer unique challenges in the area of security due to the use of radio to cover large areas of the Earth, the hazards of launching, and the hostile environment of space. Many of these problems have straightforward technical solutions, but some hazards remain.

RELIABILITY

The reliability of satellites which successfully achieve orbit and have begun operation is extremely good; the major hazards are encountered in launching and positioning. Individual transponders may fail, and contracts for satellite services usually specify what arrangements (if any) are available for backup. Another contractual matter is the possibility of preemption of a working transponder by another customer whose transponder has failed; a carrier may offer classes of satellite service which differ based on the degree of risk to continued operation.

Satellites have been successfully repaired while in orbit, but the Clarke Belt is at a much higher altitude than that at which this amazing feat has been accomplished. Further development in aerospace technology must occur before in-orbit repair of geosynchronous satellites may be taken for granted.

AVAILABILITY

In addition to the possibility of failure, satellite systems are vulnerable to malicious interference, and the occurrence of such interference has been documented. The highly directional nature of microwave beams would make the source of a maliciously interfering signal very difficult to locate, leaving the possibility of long service interruptions. Such incidents are rare, but their possibility cannot be excluded.

PRIVACY

The footprint of a satellite antenna covers a wide area, within which anyone with the proper equipment may intercept the transmitted signal. In the past, the cost and availability of equipment has tended to limit the unauthorized reception of satellite signals, but that is no longer the case. Encryption of data transmitted via satellite links is an effective solution to this vulnerability, and advances in electronics have put the price of encryption hardware within the reach of most users of data transmission services.

Multiple Access to Satellite Capacity

A satellite transponder broadcasts the uplink signal(s) it receives downward to all Earth stations within the footprint of its antenna; the most basic use of this capability is one-way distribution such as of television signals. Many ways have been devised to share a transponder's capacity for communicating along multiple paths at the same time, some of them quite complex. They are all variations on the themes of time and frequency division, often in combination.

FREQUENCY DIVISION MULTIPLE ACCESS (FDMA)

The simplest multiple access scheme, and the earliest in use, is the same as used in terrestrial microwave systems: **frequency division.** Two or more Earth stations each originate an uplink carrier within the bandpass of the transponder on frequencies and with bandwidths chosen to avoid mutual interference. When each carrier bears a single signal, this is called **single channel per carrier** (SCPC) operation; however, a carrier is often an aggregate such as an analog group or supergroup of voice channels. A carrier may also bear a single or aggregate digital data stream. One carrier is required for each simplex path, so full duplex between two stations requires two carriers, the same between three stations requires six, four stations require 12, and so on with $(n^2 - n)$ carriers required for full-duplex links between all of n stations. Even if it is not required that each station have direct access to all of the rest, this approach consumes transponder bandwidth rapidly; not only does it lead to many carriers, but guard bands must be left between them. Another disadvantage of FDMA is that multiple carriers prevent operation of the transponder at full output power because of the inter-carrier interference that would result. This raises system costs by requiring larger antennas on the ground and/or more sophisticated electronics.

FDMA is simple and may be used with aggregates produced by older analog multiplex systems for telephone traffic. It grows less efficient with more stations sharing a transponder. In conjunction with analog carrier systems, it is of mainly historical interest; in more modern applications, it permits a number of VSAT networks to share a transponder.

CODE DIVISION MULTIPLE ACCESS (CDMA)

An outgrowth of military communications research, CDMA (sometimes called **spread spectrum**) is a variation on the theme of frequency division made possible by digital technology. CDMA offers unique advantages in privacy and resistance to interference, and is the basis for a unique C-band VSAT system originated by Equatorial Communications, Inc. (since merged into another company).

The CDMA technique uses a digital pseudo-random number generator to produce a series of codes which are used to control the carrier frequency of both the uplink transmitter and a synchronized downlink receiver, spreading the transmission of each bit over several discrete frequencies. Without both the proper equipment and knowledge of the particular pseudo-random sequence in use, the transmission, if detected at all, appears to be random noise. In addition, the transmission is relatively immune to man-made interference (accidental or otherwise) because the random effect works in reverse at the receiver to spread the effects of an interfering signal.

The equipment used in the Equatorial two-way VSAT system is shown in Figure 9.16 on page 257. The large bandwidth of the CDMA signal coupled with a modest data rate (9,600 bits/s receive, 1,200 bits/s transmit) allows the VSAT to use a small antenna and gives relative immunity from terrestrial C-band interference.

TIME DIVISION MULTIPLE ACCESS (TDMA)

TDMA is, conceptually, the timesharing of a transponder by multiple Earth stations. Because the transponder handles only a single carrier at a time, it can operate at full power. Not unlike computer timesharing, in a TDMA system each user (Earth station) receives exclusively the full power of the shared resource for a limited time, then waits while others take their turn. Because the shared resource is so powerful, each user receives (averaged over time) sufficient service. Each station receives, on the downlink, all the transmissions; those not addressed to the receiving station are simply ignored.

Timing in a TDMA system is extremely precise because the radio signal bursts must arrive in sequence at the transponder without overlap or long guard times (analogous to guard bands in FDMA) after being "launched" from separate sites over 22,000 miles away. The timing problem is like having a prearranged sequence of race cars (which travel only at one speed—the speed of light) arrive at the finish line, single file, bumper to bumper, in the right order after traveling only slightly less than the circumference of the Earth, but after leaving from widely separated points.

TDMA is a modern technique which owes much to digital technology, not only for multiplexing but for the control systems which allow operation at the fine edge between efficiency and chaos.

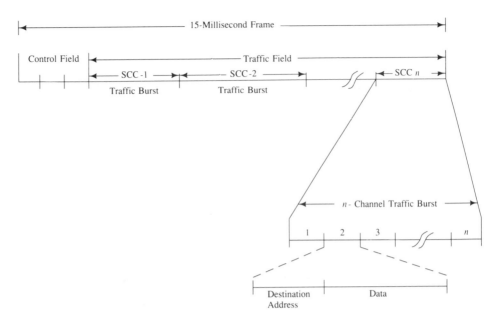

FIGURE 9.14. SBS TDMA-DA Time Slot. (Copyright 1983 International Business Machines Corporation. Reprinted with permission from *IBM Systems Journal*, Vol. 22, Nos. 1/2.)

Demand Assignment (DA)

Systems which allocate capacity as required by their users are said to be **demand assigned.** Capacity allocation may be relatively fixed (changed infrequently, perhaps with manual control) or adaptive to demand (as with how peak demand moves from one time zone to another with Earth's rotation). All of the transponder sharing systems described above may be used with varying degrees of demand-oriented flexibility; however, the TDMA system, with built-in digital control, may be the best candidate for adaptivity.

The Satellite Business Systems (now MCI) design is a good example of a high-capacity TDMA-DA system. Using a 48 Mbit/s aggregate via a 43 MHz transponder, the SBS system divides time into 15 millisecond units within which capacity is requested in one cycle and granted in a later one. This system allocates capacity for both voice (at 32 kbit/s) and data (in multiples of 32 kbit/s) upon request. Master timing is supplied by one Earth station called a **reference station**, which is equipped with a high precision frequency standard. Another station, similarly equipped, serves as a backup for the reference station. Figure 9.14 shows the division of a 15-ms time slot in the SBS system.

Economics of Satellite Communications Systems

Distance Independence

Copper, microwave, and fiber terrestrial communications systems are constructed in a linear manner and have costs which are a direct function of their length. In current satellite systems, there is only one repeater and the cost of a link is independent of geography within an equal-power area of the transponder antenna's footprint. Where the antenna's EIRP is lower, larger antennas may be required for the same error rate, but this is the only geographical cost factor.

The distance at which at which one communications medium becomes less costly than an alternative is called the **crossover point.** In the early days of satellite systems, when an integrated Bell System was the only competition and distance was the only major consideration in pricing, the crossover point was an important concept in marketing satellite services. The advent of competition in inter-LATA service, coupled with the effects of new technologies such as fiber, make evaluating satellite economics much more complex in recent years. Today, the crossover point is almost a meaningless concept and satellite systems are often favored for combinations of cost and strategic advantages such as:

- the ability to operate in areas where absence or deficiencies in terrestrial facilities would otherwise prevent it;
- lead times much shorter than for terrestrial facilities;
- need for large numbers of stations, especially where mesh connectivity is required; and
- ability to inexpensively link widely separated stations.

Earth Station Costs

The cost-performance of electronic components has been steadily improving, but that of fabricating, shipping, and installing large dish antennas has not fallen in a comparable way. High-performance Earth station costs remain in the hundreds of thousands of dollars, limiting their use to common carriers and the largest of private networks. VSAT networks, however, permit lower performance access to satellites at lower costs (typically under $15K per station), making possible applications which were previously out of reach. As fiber carriers take the high-bandwidth applications away from satellites in fiber-equipped areas, VSAT networks will become an increasingly important part of the satellite business.

Transponder Capacity Costs

Prices for transponder capacity tend to fluctuate, even though satellites in orbit have demonstrated long lives and excellent reliability. In addition to supply and demand, public confidence in aerospace technology affects transponder pricing to a considerable degree. Technical factors affecting transponder capacity pricing include bandwidth efficiency (a function of the number of radio carrier signals and their bandwidth) and the age of a particular satellite.

Trends in Satellite Communications Technology

New Spacecraft

Some trends in satellite system evolution are apparent upon examining the spacecraft in the *Intelsat* series, as shown in Figure 9.15.

Model		Weight (Lb.)	An-tennas	Primary Power	Trans-ponders	Design Life	Manu-facturer
I	(1965)	85	1	40 W	1 @ 25 MHz	1.5 Yr.	Hughes
II	(1967)	192	1	85 W	1 @ 125 MHZ	3 Yr.	Hughes
III	(1968)	322	1	120W	2 @ 225 MHz	5 Yr.	TRW
IV	(1971)	1300	6	460 W	12 @ 40 MHz	7 Yr.	Hughes
IVA	(1975)	1745	6	600 W	20 @ 40 MHz	7 Yr.	Hughes
V	(1979)	2200	6	1000 W	27 @ 40 MHz	7 Yr.	Ford
VI	(1989?)	3953	6	2600 W	50 @ 40 MHz	10 Yr.	Hughes

FIGURE 9.15. INTELSAT Series of satellites.

Succeeding models in this series have been more massive, more powerful, and have had more antennas and transponders; we can expect these trends to continue. In addition, the following are expected in the reasonably near future:

- *Space platforms:* In order to facilitate maintenance and conserve orbital positions, future communications systems in orbit may be designed to mount on a shared platform in space, with power, station keeping, and perhaps other subsystems in common.

- *Inter-satellite links:* Very long-distance links which now require two or more Earth-space-Earth "hops" may be replaced with an Earth-space-space-Earth configuration in which satellites intercommunicate directly. This would decrease propagation delay and require no intermediate Earth stations. Such links between satellites could be in either the radio or the light portion of the electromagnetic spectrum, and would not be subject to atmospheric attenuation or terrestrial interference.

- *New frequencies:* K_a and perhaps other frequencies higher than K_u will come into use.

- *On-board processing:* Orbiting hardware will become more sophisticated, perhaps to the point of digital circuit and packet switching between Earth stations and other satellites. The European Space Agency is already designing an orbiting digital exchange with a capacity of 16,000 circuits.

- *Greater lifetimes:* Launch costs will be recovered over longer times due to the introduction of components with less sensitivity to radiation, greater intrinsic reliability, and new designs (such as electric rocket motors for station keeping).

Teleports

Teleports are a recent phenomenon in the business of telecommunications, and access to satellites is an important part of their package of services. A **teleport** is a facility which provides its customers (which may be end users, carriers, or "carrier's carriers" like *Intelsat*) with access to all visible satellites and the capability to interconnect with local and regional terrestrial facilities, as well as with other teleports. A teleport may be compared to an airport: both provide shared access to a number of useful resources and services and are located on sites carefully selected for compatibility with and easy access to the surrounding area. A teleport might provide the following:

- Sites (typically 15 to 50 feet square) for customer antennas, located in an area selected for minimum interference from terrestrial microwave routes;
- Radio site and construction permit coordination;
- A concrete pad for mounting the customer's antenna;
- An equipment shelter, perhaps with heating, air conditioning, and fire protection, adjacent to each antenna;
- Metered uninterruptible electrical power;
- Cable duct from each antenna site to a common service building;
- A master electrical grounding system to minimize electrical noise;
- Space in a common service building for equipment to support interconnection with public and/or private networks;
- Office space in adjacent or nearby (digitally linked) buildings where the customer might locate data processing, switching, or customer service operations such as for airline reservations; and
- Engineering services to assist with equipment selection, installation, operation, and maintenance.

The first teleport was constructed on a 350-acre office park site on Staten Island in New York in 1982 by Western Union, the Port Authority of New York and New Jersey, and Merrill Lynch. About 70 teleports are in operation or development worldwide, some two thirds of them in North America.

Teleports are an interesting example of the old adage that the three keys to business success are: "Location, location, and location." One example is the Bay Area Teleport near San Francisco, with Earth stations located on 347 acres in a naturally shielded valley called Niles Canyon. Twenty-nine Atlantic (with 4° elevation clearance over local terrain), Pacific (18° elevation clearance), and U.S. domestic satellites are visible from this site. Common facilities at the satellite antenna complex link it to a large business park which is the hub of a regional digital microwave network of 20 nodes in ten California counties. Facilities such as this are well suited for use by carriers needing a convenient point of presence in a given area, as well as by businesses with high-capacity private networks and a desire to minimize their investment in network support facilities and personnel. Teleports make expensive and scarce facilities available to a larger community of users than would otherwise be possible, because capital investment and maintenance costs are shared.

VERY SMALL APERTURE TERMINALS

Progress in both digital and radio technology has made satellite communications possible at multiple levels of price/performance. Once the exclusive domain of international carriers, satellite services are now available for private networks formerly considered too small to be of interest. VSAT networks provide satellite-based connectivity at rates competitive with or better than those of terrestrial services which cover the same area; in some cases, they provide connectivity otherwise unavailable.

VSAT systems excel where numerous, independent stations need to receive and transmit important, but limited amounts of information. These include stockbrokers, insurance agents, and chains of retail stores for which item prices vary on a daily basis and recent sales figures are important for "just-in-time" buying at the wholesale level.

The future of satellite communications appears to be one in which major common carriers continue to apply the technology in bulk where terrestrial fiber is unavailable and in which more adaptive, specialized carriers apply VSAT designs to previously unrecognized niche markets. In the end, connectivity will reign as the most important advantage of satellite systems.

FIGURE 9.16. Very Small Aperture Terminal. (Courtesy of Contel ASC.)

CHAPTER 10

Fiber Optic Technology

Chapter Overview

This chapter introduces a technology which has had a truly revolutionary impact on the field of telecommunications since lightwave propagation in non-conducting waveguides was first proposed by Kao and Hockham in 1966. Optical fiber has displaced copper cable for new long haul transmission applications, and it has been predicted that by 1995 fiber will carry all long haul transmission in the United States. Fiber system costs have been decreasing at approximately 30% per year, making it only a matter of time before fiber is commonly used for short haul and local loop applications as well. Optical fiber offers unmatched advantages in bandwidth, distance, noise immunity, security, safety, and mechanical characteristics over metallic systems. We will examine the basis for these advantages, describe characteristics and components of fiber transmission systems, and conclude with some advancements which offer considerable promise for the future.

Principles of Fiber Optic Transmission

Electromagnetic radiation may propagate through free space, as in terrestrial or satellite radio systems, or it may be guided along a single physical path as with coaxial cable. Fiber optic transmission uses guided propagation of radiation at carrier frequencies on the order of millions of megahertz, corresponding to visible and infrared light. Because the frequency of an optical carrier is so high, its information carrying capacity when modulated is truly immense; systems operating in the **gigabit** (thousand megabit) per second range barely begin to exploit the capacity of the fiber optic medium.

Figure 10.1 shows the infrared and visible parts of the electromagnetic spectrum and their relationship to others used to carry signals; note that the frequency axis is logarithmic, with each division indicating a factor of 10. A unit of frequency called the **Terahertz** (THz) makes discussion lightwave frequencies more convenient; 1 Thz = 10^{12} Hz, or one million MHz. Typical optical carrier frequencies are on the order of 10 to 100 THz. For the human eye, frequency of light is perceived as color, with deep red corresponding to the

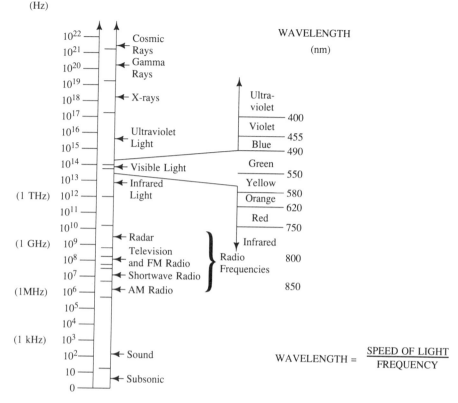

FIGURE 10.1. Electromagnetic Spectrum. The lightwave region is expanded for further detail. (Courtesy of AMP, Inc.)

lowest and violet corresponding to the highest visible frequencies. The infrared light commonly used in telecommunications systems is not visible to the human eye.

It is more common to refer to optical signals by wavelength (the distance spanned by one wave of the carrier signal) rather than by frequency. Such distances are quite small and are described by units like the **micron,** one-millionth of a meter, (often written as μm) and the **nanometer** (nm), one-thousandth of a μm. Figure 10.2 on page 260 contrasts the frequency-dependent attenuation of coaxial copper cable with the frequency-independent attenuation of fiber over the same range. For all practical purposes, loss in fiber is, for a given wavelength, a function only of cable length.

Historical Developments

Using light to carry information is an old idea; smoke signals, mirrors, semaphores, and flares have been used to send signals for many generations. Transmission of voice via light began in 1880 with Bell's Photophone, which used sound pressure to move a mirror and deflect a beam of sunlight aimed at the receiver. The receiver contained a selenium detector which controlled the electrical current through a telephone set. The Photophone

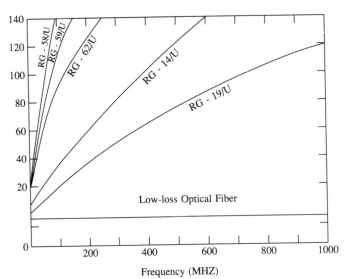

FIGURE 10.2. Loss vs. Frequency, Coaxial and Fiber Media. Fiber frequency response is flat over the useful range of frequencies for coaxial copper media. (Courtesy of AMP, Inc.)

succeeded in transmitting the human voice a distance of almost 700 feet; today, unguided lightwave data communication over distances of miles is both practical and economical.

Long-distance lightwave communications awaited the invention of low loss optical fiber in 1970, along with other modern developments in light emitters and detectors. The first fiber optic transmission system to go into service in the Bell System was installed by Illinois Bell in Chicago in 1977. The remarkably short time between concept and practical application has continued to be a characteristic of progress in the fiber transmission field. Capacity and distance between repeaters are important characteristics of fiber systems, and they tend to be inversely related. A useful "figure of merit" for a system is the product of these two, the unit of which is

$$\frac{bits}{s} \cdot km = \frac{bit \cdot km}{s}$$

Laboratory research has produced rapid advancements in both capacity and distance, approximately doubling their product every year, as may be seen from Figure 10.3, and today's technology is rated in units of $\frac{gigabit \cdot km}{s}$. This progress is mainly a result of learning to use longer wavelengths, where optical properties of glass fibers are more favorable for transmission.

Lightwave Propagation in Fiber Systems

The physical principles involved in fiber transmission are relatively simple. Fundamental to fiber optics is the phenomenon of **refraction,** or the change in direction of a ray

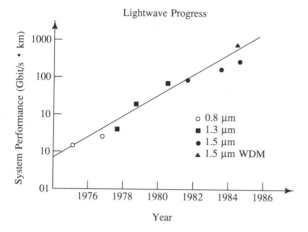

FIGURE 10.3. Lightwave Progress: 1975-1986. The product of bit rate and distance is used as a figure of merit. These are laboratory, rather than field, results. (Reprinted from Cohen, "Trends in US Broad-Band Fiber Optic Transmission Systems," *IEEE Journal On Selected Areas Of Communications*, July 1986, p. 491, ©1986 IEEE.)

when it passes from one medium into another such as from air to glass or vice versa. Refraction is a result of the fact that the speed of light varies depending on the medium in which it travels; $3 \bullet 10^8$ meters per second is the speed of light in a vacuum, but it is slower in other environments. A useful measure of this effect in any material is its **index of refraction,** *n*, given by

$$n = \frac{c}{v}$$

where *c* is the velocity of light in a vacuum and *v* is its velocity in the material in question. Since light is slower in any material than in a vacuum, this ratio has a value greater than one for all materials. Typical values for index of refraction are 1.0003 for air, 1.46 for fused quartz, and 1.5 for glass.

The angle of refraction for a ray depends on its frequency. White light is composed of many frequencies which may be separated using a prism, where refraction at the air-glass and glass-air boundaries causes rays of differing frequencies to be refracted at differing angles.

It is common in fiber system work to use wavelength, rather than frequency, when discussing lightwave signals. There is a simple relationship between the frequency of a lightwave signal and its wavelength λ (say: lambda):

$$\lambda = \frac{c}{f}$$

where *c* is the speed of light and *f* is the frequency of the lightwave signal. Attenuation in

Spectral Attenuation (typical fiber):

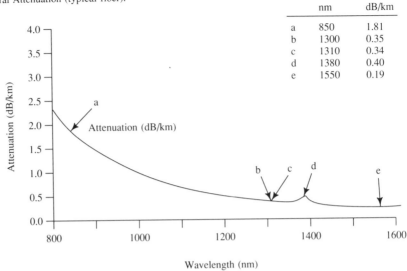

	nm	dB/km
a	850	1.81
b	1300	0.35
c	1310	0.34
d	1380	0.40
e	1550	0.19

FIGURE 10.4. Wavelength-dependent Attenuation in an Optical Fiber. Attenuation peaks are caused by absorption by metal and hydroxyl ion with increased wavelength is a result of Rayleigh scattering, which decreases with increased wavelength. (Courtesy of Siecor, Inc.)

fiber varies with the wavelength of the transmitted light, as shown in Figure 10.4; this is mainly due to absorption and scattering.

Absorption, the conversion of photons into heat, results from the presence of impurities in the fiber material; **hydroxyl ions,** for example, are responsible for a strong absorption peak between 900 and 1,000 μm. **Scattering** is misdirection of light resulting mainly from imperfections in manufacture and physical effects which occur when the light wavelength is close to the dimensions of molecules in the fiber. **Rayleigh scattering** dominates scattering loss at short wavelengths and is inversely proportional to the fourth power of the wavelength. It defines the theoretical lower limit for attenuation in fiber media. Low-loss areas in the optical spectrum for fiber materials are called **windows,** and exist at 725, 820, 875, 1,300, and 1,550 μm. **Long wavelengths** (1,100 to 1,550 μm) correspond to the part of the spectrum used by systems which offer the greatest distance-bandwidth product.

Fiber optic transmission depends on a physical process discovered in 1871 by John Tyndall called **total internal reflection.** This effect can occur when light passes through one medium to another whose index of refraction is lower. Light striking such an interface may pass through it at an angle or be reflected back (or both), depending on the angle at which it strikes the interface, as shown in Figure 10.5 on page 263. The angle between the incident ray and a line (called a **normal**) perpendicular to the interface at which total internal reflection occurs is called the **critical angle,** and it may be calculated where the indices of refraction of the two media are known using **Snell's Law:**

$$\sin \theta = \frac{n_2}{n_1}$$

or,

$$\theta = \sin^{-1}\frac{n_2}{n_1}$$

where θ is the critical angle, n_1 is the greater index of refraction, and n_2 is the lesser. Figure 10.5 shows how this effect is exploited in a fiber consisting of a central core surrounded by another material called the **cladding.** The cladding has a lower index of refraction than the core. Light entering the cable and striking the interface at an angle greater than the critical angle is trapped within the core, reflected back at every point where it strikes the interface between the two materials.

The geometry of the internal reflection shown in Figure 10.5 is characteristic of fibers in which there is a very sudden transition between core and cladding. Because the transition resembles a step function, these fibers are called **step-index** fibers. It is possible to manufacture a fiber with a more gradual transition between core and cladding, and these are

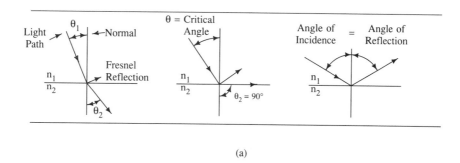

(a)

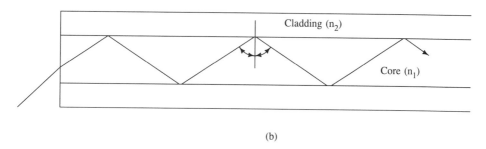

(b)

FIGURE 10.5. Total Internal Reflection. (a) Angles less than, equal to, and greater than critical (b) ray path in fiber. (Courtesy of AMP, Inc.)

called **graded-index** fibers. The gradual change in index of refraction results in a more arc-shaped path for rays trapped by total internal reflection, as shown in Figure 10.6.

MODES AND DISPERSION

A path along which a ray of light may travel in a fiber is called a **mode**. Fibers in which the diameter of the core is large in comparison to the wavelength of the transmitted light have many such paths and are called **multimode** fibers. Because the paths differ slightly in length, the travel times for several rays through a fiber will also differ, leading to an effect called **modal dispersion.** Modal dispersion limits the useful bandwidth of a fiber because it spreads out the energy of a transmitted pulse over a longer time at the receiving end. This effect, which increases the receiver's difficulty in distinguishing closely spaced signal elements, is measured in **nanoseconds** (10^{-9} second) of added pulse width per kilometer of fiber. Figure 10.6 compares the modal dispersion characteristics of the three basic types of fiber. Note that graded index multimode fiber exhibits considerably less modal dispersion than multimode step index; this results from the slightly higher speed of rays traveling where there is a lower index of refraction: the greater speed tends to compensate for the longer path of these rays, and their arrival time is closer to that of those travelling straight through the core.

Chromatic dispersion is a bandwidth limiting factor with effects similar to those of modal dispersion, and occurs in systems for which the transmitter emits light of more than a single color, or frequency. The angles of refraction differ for differing wavelengths of light, causing them to follow slightly different paths through the fiber. Since signal components of different wavelengths arrive at different times, the detector "sees" longer rise and fall times than it would with light of a single frequency. Chromatic dispersion is measured in units of picoseconds per nanometer of emitter bandwidth per kilometer of fiber, where a **picosecond** is 10^{-12} (one-million millionth) part of a second.

First used in production service by Continental Telephone of New York in September, 1983, **single-mode** or **monomode** fibers have a core of small diameter, in the order of five to 10 times the wavelength λ (typically less than 20 μm). The diameter of the core and

Types of Optical Fiber

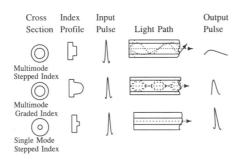

FIGURE 10.6. Characteristics of the Three Basic Types of Optical Fibers. (Reprinted from Nagel, "Optical Fiber—The Expanding Medium," *IEEE Communications Magazine,* April 1987, p. 34, ©1987 IEEE.)

the choice of refractive indices limit the light propagation to one mode and there is no modal dispersion; however, the very small core makes it difficult to couple light into a monomode fiber and to align two of them precisely for splicing. Monomode fibers are typically used with lasers (for higher coupling efficiency and low chromatic dispersion) over long spans.

NUMERICAL APERTURE

Numerical aperture (NA) is a measure of the ability of the end of a fiber to collect light, and is a function of the refractive indices of the core (n_1) and of the cladding (n_2):

$$NA = \sqrt{n_1^2 - n_2^2}$$

Because NA limits the amount of light that the fiber will accept from the light source, it is an important factor in determining the potential length of the span. A larger NA permits coupling more optical power into a fiber; however, it also means there is greater dispersion and hence less bandwidth. Good system design requires consideration of the NA of the fiber with respect to the radiation pattern of emitters and the light collection pattern of detectors. NA values range from 0.2 to 0.4 for commonly used fibers.

Fiber System Components

Components of a fiber system must be carefully matched if the desired performance is to be obtained. Emitters and detectors must be matched to each other and to a transmission window of the fiber, for example. Below are described major components of a fiber system: cable, transmitters, receivers, repeaters, splices, and connectors .

Cable

Optical fibers consist of a **core** as previously described (the innermost part) and a cladding of lesser refractive index. The core and cladding combination need not be large for practical communications applications; typical fibers are in the order of 125 μm in diameter

Characteristic	Silica	PCS	Plastic
Core Diameter, μm	< 10 - 100	125 - 600	350 - > 1000
Cladding diameter	125 - 200	250 - 900	400 - > 1000
Index Profile	Graded, Step	Step	Step
Numerical Aperture	0.2 - 0.3	0.3 - 0.4	0.4 - 0.55
Repeater Spacing	> 1 km	< 1 km	< 50 m

FIGURE 10.7. Typical Characteristics of Three Types of Fiber.

(about the diameter of a human hair) for silica (glass) and less than 2,200 μm for plastic coated silica (PCS) or all-plastic strands. The diameters of the core and cladding are often expressed in a shorthand way as a fraction such as 50/125. Figure 10.7 on page 265 shows typical characteristics of glass, PCS, and plastic fibers.

Each fiber in a cable is protected by a covering called a **buffer,** of which there are many types. In some cables, the fibers are each contained loosely in a tube of larger diameter, a design which isolates the fiber from strain and tends to resist excessive bending. Loose tube buffers are often filled with a gel in cables which are exposed to water; the gel fills space which might otherwise admit water and freeze, damaging the fiber. Another type of buffer is a plastic coating similar to the insulation on electrical conductors.

The cable's outer covering is called a **jacket** and provides a first line of defense against damage; the jacket often contains multiple fibers along with other material to add strength and rigidity. Steel is often used for a strength member where the cable's environment permits an electrical conductor, allowing considerable tension when cable is pulled through ducts and conduits. Steel strength members may also be used to carry power for repeaters where it is otherwise unavailable, as in submarine systems. Plastic strength members are used in environments where electrical conductivity is undesirable, such as where the cable is exposed to lightning. Figure 10.8 shows a typical fiber optic cable.

Transmitters

Two types of transmitters are commonly used as sources for fiber optic transmission, both of them semiconductor diodes (the dimensions of which are well matched to those of fiber). These are the **light emitting diode** (LED) and the **injection laser diode** (ILD), characteristics of which are compared in Figure 10.9.

FIGURE 10.8. A Typical Fiber Optic Cable. (Courtesy of Northern Telecom, Inc.)

Characteristic	Light Emitting Diode	Injection Laser Diode
Cost	Low	High
Output Power	Low	High
Spectral Width	Wide	Narrow
Directionality	Low	High
Reliability	Very Good	Good
Thermal Sensitivity	Low	High
Lifetime	> 100 Khours	< 1000 Khours

FIGURE 10.9. Relative Characteristics of Emitter Types.

Light emitting diodes are often chosen for short spans and low to medium speed applications, and offer long lifetimes with trouble-free operation. The more expensive laser diodes are typically used over long spans with monomode fibers. Factors which favor lasers for long spans include:

- higher output power;
- greater directionality for coupling more energy into the fiber; and
- narrow spectral width (leading to less chromatic dispersion).

Figure 10.10 compares the spectral width of a laser diode with that of a light emitting diode of the same peak wavelength.

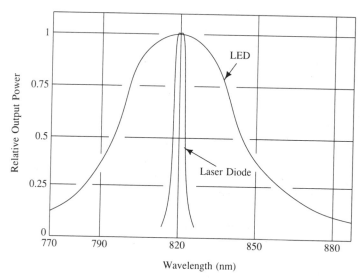

FIGURE 10.10. Spectral Widths of ILD and LED Emitters. (Courtesy of AMP, Inc.)

LEDs and ILDs differ considerably in a characteristic called **linearity,** which is the degree to which their output power matches the amount of current flowing through them. LEDs are much more linear than ILDs, which makes them the transmitter of choice for analog transmission on fiber. LEDs are typically modulated digitally by turning them on and off; laser diodes operate poorly in this mode, and are typically switched between two power levels, both of them greater than a threshold power, which permits high-speed operation.

Semiconductor lasers are much more sensitive to temperature than LEDs, and small changes in temperature can seriously affect operating characteristics such as threshold and lifetime. ILDs are often used in conjunction with thermoelectric cooling systems designed to keep them operating within a small temperature range.

Receivers

The receiver in today's fiber optic link consists of the detector and its associated electronics, and converts the lightwave to an electrical signal which may be easily repeated or demultiplexed into separate data streams at lower speeds. The detector converts received photons directly into an electrical current while introducing as little noise as possible; this scheme is called **direct detection. Responsivity** is a measure of the efficiency of a detector's conversion at a wavelength of interest, and is measured in microamperes of current per microwatt of received power. Detectors are typically semiconductor devices of various types:

- **PIN photodiodes** (the "PIN" is an abbreviation for the doping profile of its semiconductor material) convert light directly to an electric current, and are used with external amplification to provide a signal suitable for demultiplexing or repeating. An ideal photodiode produces one electron for every photon it receives from the fiber. The resulting current is too weak to be directly useful, hence the external amplification. Responsivity of PIN photodiodes is in the order of 0.45 to 0.65 $\mu A/\mu W$.

- **Avalanche photo diodes** (APDs) use a kind of "chain reaction" effect to produce the flow of multiple electrons for a single-received photon (an effect called **internal gain**), and, therefore, require less amplification than PIN photodiodes. The avalanche effect used to multiply the current resulting from a single received photon is inherently noisy, and requires a system design tradeoff of responsivity for noise.

- **Phototransistors** are similar to ordinary transistors except that they contain an opening so that the base of the transistor may be exposed to a lightwave signal. The current through the transistor is then controlled by the amount of incident light, rather than another (smaller) electric current. Phototransistors resemble APDs in that they exhibit internal gain, but are very slow in comparison to either PIN diodes or APDs.

- **Integrated preamplifier detectors** (IPD) are integrated circuits in which the detector and an amplifier circuit are combined on a common substrate.

Characteristics of special interest in detectors and their amplifiers are responsivity and noise, which directly affect the bit error rate and maximum span length. Amplification adds noise, so detectors which require less amplication are favored for fiber applications.

Coherent detection is a transmission technique which exploits unique characteristics of laser-generated light, processing the signal much as in modern radio receivers.

Lasers emit light which is **phase coherent** (i.e., all of the photons which leave the source do so in synchronism, like soldiers marching in step). In coherent lightwave systems, the source is modulated in amplitude, phase, or frequency. Coherent detection permits sensitivity and selectivity unmatched by the direct detection equipment common today, which will permit many high-capacity carrier signals (using wavelength division) over much longer links than is possible today.

Repeaters

As with metallic systems, it is necessary to regenerate optical signals where the length of the link exceeds the distance over which the components will support the desired error rate. Today, this is accomplished by converting the lightwave signal to an electrical one (just as if it were going into a demultiplexer), reshaping and retiming it, and using it to drive another transmitter. In the future, the intermediate electrical form of the signal may not be required; optical amplifiers with gains of 20 to 60 dB have been demonstrated in laboratory experiments, and may be commercially available before long.

Repeater spacing in fiber systems is much greater than in metallic systems, due primarily to advances in cable fabrication techniques. Practical systems with current technology are delivering 200 Mbit/s • Km/s with LED emitters and multimode fiber, 2,000 Mbit/s • Km/s with either 850 nm laser or 1,300 nm LED emitters and multimode fiber, and 10,000 Mbit/s • Km/s with 1,550 nm laser emitters used with monomode fiber. Commercially available systems with repeater spacing of 200 Km and capacity of 2 Gbit/s might reasonably be expected in the relatively near future. In low-speed systems, repeater spacing is determined mainly by the sensitivity of detectors; in high-speed systems, dispersion is the factor which limits repeater spacing.

Splices

Splicing is the permanent joining of two fibers, and splice losses in fiber systems are much more important than in metallic systems. Splicing may be required to achieve span lengths longer than the capacity of a cable spool, to join the parts of a span constructed from the end points, or to replace damaged fiber.

The ideal fiber splice would consist of two fibers with perfectly polished flat ends butted against each other in perfect alignment and with no intervening air. Small imperfections in polishing or positioning can make large differences in the loss through a splice, which is commonly in the order of 0.2 dB in field splices and has been as low as 0.05 dB in laboratory experiments. Service interruption due to construction near buried cable (commonly called **backhoe fade**) is sufficiently common that effective system design includes a loss budget for both planned splices and those required for repair.

The two most common splicing techniques are fusion and bonding. Both involve joining the fibers after they have been carefully aligned in a mounting fixture. **Fusion splicing** resembles welding in that after alignment the fiber ends are melted into each other, usually by an electric arc. After the ends are fused, the cable is removed from the fixture, which is part of the splicing machine. **Bonding** relies on an adhesive, usually epoxy, to hold the fibers in alignment inside the fixture, which remains as a part of the cable. Both techniques require careful preparation of the ends to be joined; they must be as flat and as highly polished as possible.

FIGURE 10.11. Biconical Fiber Optic Connector. The design relies on concentric cones for alignment. (Courtesy of OFTI, Inc.)

The best splices do not rely on mechanical alignment techniques which assume concentricity of the fiber core and cladding. For these, a light source illuminates the splice through one of the fibers and an optical power meter is attached to the other. Alignment is then adjusted for maximum transmission, often by rotating one of the fibers, before fusion or hardening of the epoxy. This optimization, often called **fine tuning,** is especially critical where single-mode fibers are employed.

Connectors

Fiber connectors may be thought of as impermanent splices. The same considerations apply as with splicing, except that the ends must be capable of separation and reconnection with the same or different mates, with very little change in transmission characteristics. Connectors are designed and produced with very small mechanical tolerances in order to deliver low-loss transmission after multiple matings. There are about 25 connector designs in use with little standardization other than of the *de facto* sort. Connector types include the Biconical (shown in Figure 10.11), originated by Bell Laboratories and capable of high repeatability; FSMA (shown in Figure 10.12), used where repeatability is not as important as cost; and the ST (shown in Figure 10.13 on page 272), a bayonet locking type which is easy to connect and remove.

Attenuation in Fiber Systems

Power loss in fiber systems takes place at the emitter-fiber interface, in the fiber itself, across splices and connectors, and at the interface between the fiber and the detector.

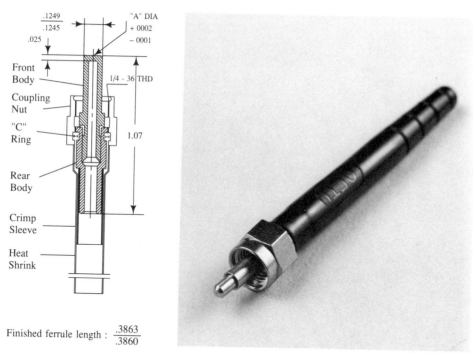

Finished ferrule length : $\dfrac{.3863}{.3860}$

FIGURE 10.12. FSMA Fiber Optic Connector. (Courtesy of OFTI, Inc.)

Absorption and scattering, described earlier, account for transmission loss within the fiber, and can be predicted quite accurately for a given wavelength as a function of distance using specifications from the manufacturer.

Reflection is responsible for much of the loss between the ends of the fiber and the emitter and detector. The fraction of light r lost at a single interface is given by the **Fresnel Formula:**

$$r = \left(\frac{n_1 - n}{n_1 + n}\right)^2$$

where n_1 is the refractive index of one side of the interface and n is the refractive index of the medium separating the components (usually air). Note that this formula is applied to each interface: emitter to air and air to fiber, for example. Reflection losses may be decreased by filling the gap with an index matching material, minimizing the difference between n_1 and n_2 .

Radiation may be lost from the fiber due to curvature, and is classified into two types. **Macrobending** is bending in which the radius of the curve is large with respect to the diameter of the fiber. Macrobending losses can result from improper installation or from pulling properly installed cable into short radius bends. It is easy to produce a macrobending loss of several dB by bending a fiber between the fingers of the hand, and instruments

FIGURE 10.13. ST Fiber Optic Connector. (Courtesy of OFTI, Inc.)

designed to tap a signal using this effect are sold. **Microbending** losses result from damage to the fiber geometry of size comparable to the fiber diameter. They may be caused by flaws in the cable fabrication or later, during storage, transportation, or installation. Considerable power is lost from the fiber when its radius of curvature R exceeds

$$R = \frac{r_c}{NA^2}$$

where r_c is the radius of the core. Cable specifications may contain different values for minimum bending radius during installation than for operation; the former is aimed at preventing damage, while the latter is required in order for the fiber to perform according to loss specifications.

Multiplexing in Lightwave Systems

Fiber optic transmission systems offer very large capacity with very low error rates, typically better than 10^{-9}. The most efficient way with current technology to exploit these characteristics is via a combination of digital and space division multiplexing. We have already noted that cables commonly carry several fibers, providing space division. Opti-

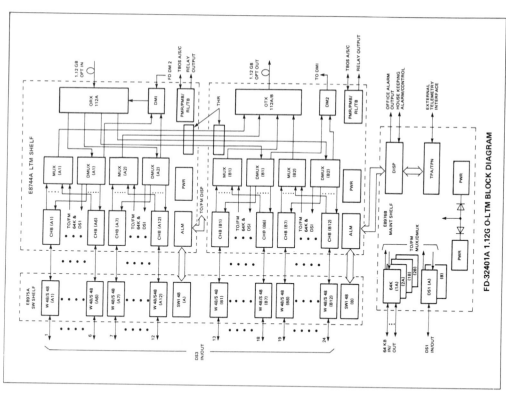

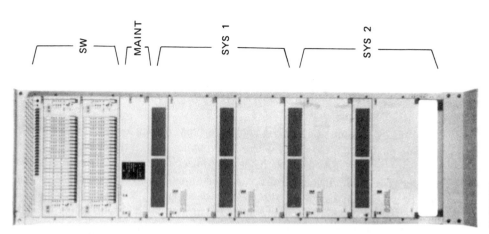

FIGURE 10.14. Terminal for a 1.114 Gbit/s Fiber System. (Courtesy of NEC, Inc.)

273

mum system design trades off the cost of fibers against the capacity of terminal equipment, taking into account the need for spares and to provide for growth. As fiber technology advances, it has become common to upgrade capacity simply by increasing the speed of terminal equipment, as the ultimate capacity of even the early fiber media has barely been touched.

Digital Multiplexing

The vast majority of fiber systems in use today are digital and employ time division multiplexing according to the digital hierarchy developed for T-Carrier systems. Digital techniques are well suited to fiber transmission with direct detection because of the simplicity in modulating the light sources: the binary signal is used to select which of two power levels at which the source operates. At the receiving end, the detector need only distinguish between the two signal levels reliably. Figure 10.14 on page 273 is a photograph of a commercially available fiber optic transmission terminal. Designed for use with 10/125 single mode fiber, the system has the following specifications:

- 1.114 gigabit aggregate capacity, packaged as 24 DS-3 digital streams (16,128 DS-0 channels);
- Repeater spacing of over 48 km (30 miles) at 1310 nm or 72 km (45 miles) at 1510 nm;
- Laser emitter with spectral width of 0.5 nm (1310 nm) or 0.3 (1550 nm);
- Avalanche photodetector receiver with −34 dBm sensitivity;
- Error rate of 10^{-11} for rated sensitivity;
- Automatic protection switching of 1 or 2 redundant DS-3 hardware modules.

Wavelength Division Multiplexing

Optical frequency division for long spans has not yet emerged from the laboratory, but shows great promise. Sometimes called **color multiplexing** or **wavelength-division multiplexing** (WDM), this technique places light of more than one wavelength on a fiber with separate emitters and detectors for each wavelength. Laboratory experiments have achieved 2,000 Gbits-km/s over 10 WDM channels in the region between 1,500 and 1,600 nm. Combined emitter and detector modules using WDM to provide a full duplex link on a single fiber are already commercially available for use over short distances.

Frequency Division with Analog Transmission

Analog transmission, although not widespread in long haul systems, is feasible using intensity modulation, especially where LED emitters are used. Frequency division multiplexing of the type described in Chapter 2 has been used in this environment; one system introduced in 1985 provides 20 analog carriers (multiplexed electronically) on a fiber pair, each of which may carry the 600 channels of an analog mastergroup or a standard TV signal. This type of design could be attractive in environments where fiber is available but a heavy investment in analog multiplexing equipment cannot be abandoned.

Advantages of the Fiber Medium

In addition to important technical advantages, the availability of a non-electrical transmission medium offers new and interesting advantages to telecommunications system designers. These include:

- *New freedom in right-of-way design*—Fiber cable, since it is not an electrical conductor, may be located near water or power lines or subjected to lightning without risk to personnel or to equipment.

- *Open-ended capacity*—A fiber's capacity may often be increased simply by changing out the end equipment. The high-cost fiber plant remains unchanged, but a greater return on investment results.

- *Increased security*—Because fibers, unlike metallic transmission lines, are not surrounded by electrical or magnetic fields, traditional methods of surreptitious snooping are not possible. Tapping a fiber cable requires physical contact with it and usually results in a temporary service interruption and/or noticeable power loss at the receiving end. While making an undetected tap is possible with a fiber cable, it is much more difficult than with copper conductors. In addition, the intruder has fewer easy access points to the cable because of the long-distance between repeaters and the equipment required to demultiplex the individual channels is bulky and expensive.

- *Noise Immunity*—Electrical and magnetic fields have no effect on fiber, so common sources of interference such as power lines and electric motors may be ignored.

- *Safety*—The inability to transmit an electrical current results in greater safety than with metallic systems because there is no hazard of electrical shock due to lightning or accidental contact with power lines. In addition, there is no chance of causing sparks which could ignite combustible materials.

Instruments Used with Fiber Systems

Many of the instruments used with electrical transmission systems have lightwave counterparts for use with fiber. These include signal sources, attenuators, power meters, and the **optical time-domain reflectometer** (OTDR). In addition, the critical importance of low-loss splices has resulted in the development of optical inspection equipment used to inspect the ends of fibers prior to splicing them.

Signal sources are used for the following purposes:

1. to inject light into a cable to be spliced, facilitating the best possible alignment of fiber cores;

2. to supply a precise power level for loss measurements; and

3. to illuminate one of several fibers in a group, for identification.

Optical attenuators are available in both fixed and variable forms, and provide a measured power loss. They may be used to test the signal power at which receivers fail or in cases where a short span results in excessive power for a receiver.

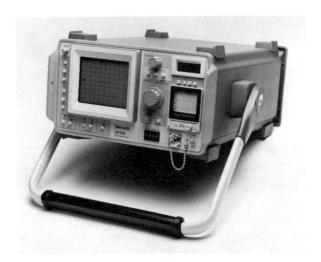

FIGURE 10.15. Optical Time Domain Reflectometer. (Courtesy of Tektronix, Inc.)

Power meters are special purpose receivers which indicate the optical power of a transmitted signal. When used with a calibrated source at the transmitting end, they make it possible to measure the loss over a fiber span.

The optical time domain reflectometer, shown in Figure 10.15, is a special purpose oscilloscope combined with an optical transmitter and receiver as shown in Figure 10.16. This device transmits a very short pulse of energy into the fiber and plots on a screen the reflected energy versus time. Knowledge of the speed of light through the fiber permits calculation of the distance to sources of reflection such as breaks, connectors, splices, and the end of the span. Accuracy of 0.1% of the span length (100 meters in a 100 Km span) is possible in measuring distance to a break if a reflectometer is used at both ends and the results averaged.

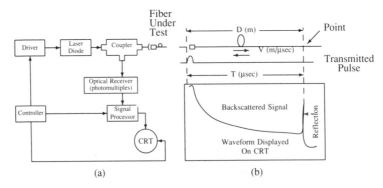

Time Distance Conversion Formula

FIGURE 10.16. Reflectometer Diagram. (Reprinted from Couturier *et al.*, Fiber Optic Placing, Splicing, Testing, And Cable Design, *IEEE Journal On Selected Areas In Communications*, August 1986, p. 659, © 1986 *IEEE*.)

Deployment of Fiber

Early fiber systems had a deployment similar to that of T-Carrier (i.e., for pair gain between telephone central offices in metropolitan areas). Fiber was especially welcome in areas where underground cable ducts and conduits were crowded. Medium and long-haul applications developed as the technology matured and confidence in it grew.

Long-haul Fiber

Competition in long-distance telephone business has resulted in creative and interesting acquisitions of right-of-way by carriers. The non-electrical nature of lightwave signals permits installing fiber cable almost anywhere. Use of railroad, highway, irrigation canal, pipeline, power line, bicycle path, and even storm sewer routes have been reported by carriers anxious to develop their networks cheaply and rapidly.

Not all the deployment of fiber has been by common carriers; in some cases, it is being installed by end users or cooperatives. **Condominium fiber** describes individual ownership of individual fiber strands and specifically associated repeater electronics, housings and so on, along with an undivided interest in the common system: right-of-way, manholes, poles, shelters, power systems, equipment housings, sheathing, jackets, conduits, and so on. Undivided interest means a partial ownership in the remaining whole without the ability to divide the whole. The owners divide their ownership interest by some mutually agreeable formula, but cannot take their part of the common system and act on it alone.

Dark fiber offers a kind of middle ground between turnkey service from a carrier and condominium fiber. A fiber owner may lease or sell individual fibers linking end points "dark" (i.e., without terminal equipment). The consumer supplies the terminal equipment of his choice, thereby "lighting up" the fiber which was "dark" when first acquired.

Feeder and Loop Applications

One modern trend in telephone loop plant engineering is the use of digital links to multiplexers located near customers or, in the case of large business customers, on their premises. Fiber is well suited to linking remote multiplexers to central offices, offering significant savings in material and labor. As fiber equipment costs continue to drop (to between $700 and $1,400 per subscriber, by some estimates), it is predicted that fiber will be extended to the loop ("last mile") environment as well. This may occur, at least for new construction, soon enough to significantly affect how the Integrated Services Digital Network functions described in Chapter 14 are delivered to consumers.

Fiber Submarine Cables

The availability of fiber has reversed the trend to larger submarine cables with shorter repeater spacing as system capacity increased. While a repeaterless trans-Atlantic or Pacific cable may never be realized, the savings due to using fiber for very long haul undersea applications are substantial. Several fiber submarine cables are planned in the near future; one already completed links Tuckerton, NJ in the United States with Penmarche, France and is called TAT-8. Spanning 3,600 nautical miles, the cable will have a capacity of 20,000 full duplex voice trunks (more than four times the capacity of its predecessor,

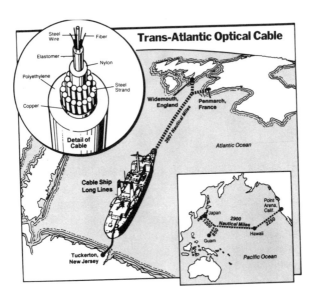

FIGURE 10.17. Two Fiber Submarine Cables. Cables for Atlantic and Pacific are shown. Both contain branching repeaters at one end. (Copyright © 1986 by The New York Times Company. Reprinted by permission.)

TAT-7) at a cost of $335 million. The cable is depicted in Figure 10.17 and has six fibers, of which two are used in each direction and two are spares. Repeaters (130 of them) are at 36 nautical mile intervals and are powered by copper conductors in the cable. The bit rate for each fiber is 296 Mbit/s, and the system operates at 1,300 nm. TAT-8 is the first submarine cable to use the **branching repeater**, a repeater with two terminals at the European end. This allows sharing the cable's capacity between terminals located in France and in Widemouth, England. A similar configuration is planned for a Pacific cable which will link both Guam and Japan with Point Arena, California.

The extremely high reliability requirements of the submarine environment, dictated by the enormous cost of making repairs, have motivated important advances in fiber technology. Among them are optical switches which allow substituting spare fibers between repeaters under remote control.

Fiber Futures

Frequently echoed predictions involving fiber are heard in both technical and economic circles. One economic forecast is that the very aggressive deployment of long-haul fiber will result in (at least short-term) overcapacity and a significant drop in long-distance transmission prices by carriers.

On the technical side, we may speculate that:

- Most of the new progress in fiber technology will be with emitters, detectors, and repeaters (the technology of the fiber medium itself is fairly mature).
- Optical signal processing will start to displace electronics in commercial lightwave systems; advanced techniques such as coherent detection may lead this trend.

- As the technology develops, repeater spacing will peak but fiber capacity will continue to increase.

Current equipment for transmitting information by optical means may be compared to the early days of radio, with Morse Code and on-off modulation. As the signal processing techniques perfected with radio transmission are applied to optics, the performance of lightwave systems will advance dramatically, making today's systems look as primitive as the early spark transmitters and crystal receivers.

CHAPTER 11

Private Digital Services

Chapter Overview

In a rapidly changing telecommunications climate, new opportunities arise for user-provided private digital transmission services. Frequent shifts in regulation and tariffs since divestiture have motivated users toward the benefits of installing and operating private systems for their own exclusive use. While user provided and operated systems have existed for many years in private radio communications and in telephone **private branch exchanges** (PBX), digital transmission systems for private use are still relatively new. Concluding our look at digital services, we turn now to an examination of some of these private services. As in previous chapters, we confine our view to concepts rather than actual equipment and systems. The concepts may be used to understand and compare current technologies in private digital systems and will remain valid as the technologies continue to change and improve. We examine the concepts of several kinds of private systems used to provide connectivity and "solve" the last-mile problem.

The last-mile problem becomes a focus for private systems as an opportunity to make direct connection to long-distance or **inter-exchange carrier** (IEC) services. This chapter describes the problem and offers suggestions on solutions which use private systems. Private digital services not only perform "bypass" tasks, but accomplish economies of scale in non-carrier connections. Private systems for campus and high-rise physical environments often permit novel linkages for differing parts of a user's environment. Physical space needs in a growing enterprise often result in a scattering to outlying buildings which must be connected. Private systems offer both rapid and cost effective connections back to central facilities. Digital systems may also yield an ability to share facilities between data, voice, video and image communications needs. Moving from the last-mile problem, we then look at the concepts of several private system technologies.

This chapter will first review private copper-cable systems in both baseband

and broadband types, showing how these systems can interconnect with other user facilities. Concepts of cable bandwidth and bit rate capability are reviewed by cable type and distance, and re-use of in-service cable to increase bandwidth and speed is also examined. As an alternative to new installations, existing but under-used twisted pair and coaxial cables are shown to be an inexpensive source of private media. Moving from copper cables to fiber, this chapter will look at the private use of optical cable systems. Now easily available and inexpensive, fiber systems have become a media of choice for many private applications. Earlier concerns about connectors and fiber repair have been largely overcome and private systems offer benefits beyond just cost and bandwidth. These benefits are reviewed and fiber optic systems are examined for both traditional communications and as computer channel extenders. Continuing in optics, the chapter then looks at free space optical communications.

Operating somewhat like microwave radio, free space optical systems usually do not require licensing and may be put into service very quickly. This aspect offers unique opportunities for disaster backup or recovery and for rapid deployment to serve new buildings. This chapter will look at both the concepts and the limitations of free space optical digital communications systems. Finally, this chapter will examine digital microwave radio systems for private use.

Unlike free space optical systems, microwave radio falls under the regulation of the United States government and must be in compliance with certain rules. While the rules are neither complex nor difficult, allowances must be made for both original license applications and regular renewals. The regulatory aspects of microwave radio are followed by a discussion of some technical concepts and some example system configurations. Beyond the engineering aspects of digital microwave radio systems, some practical operational matters receive our attention.

The Last-mile Problem

The last-mile problem in telecommunications arose when a single carrier could no longer provide end-to-end service. The expanded use of analog and digital carrier equipment to combine individual circuits also aggravated the problem. The location of the combining equipment caused some circuits to need extensions for the "last mile." The underlying problem results from needing end-to-end connections in a world where laws and economies dictate partial connections. Figure 11.1 on page 282 graphically illustrates the problem.

While end-to-end total service may still be available through a combination of vendors, users now must become involved. Many carriers and other vendors offer to "coordinate" the total service among carriers and vendors and usually do a very good job. Private systems may yield greater savings, but may require staffing and skills beyond the capabilities of the organization. However, when many circuits are involved, users owe it to themselves to at least examine alternatives. To aid in this examination, we will divide the last-mile problem into several different categories. These categories will then help us review several available technologies for private system consideration.

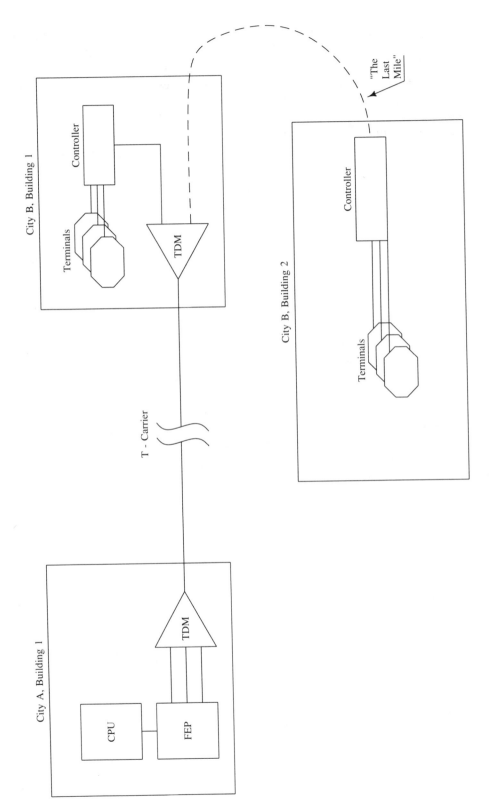

FIGURE 11.1. End-to-end Service and the "Last-mile" Problem.

Three fundamental categories or types of connections may be encountered in a last-mile problem. Most basic is the connection from a long-distance carrier's service **point-of-presence** (POP) to a user's point of need. The carrier's service point may be called a **central office**, a **serving office** or a **POP**, but one thing is usually certain: this service point does not bring the circuit the "last mile" to where we need it. The last mile may actually be 500 feet or twenty miles; the problem remains essentially the same.

The second fundamental type concerns local connections normally served by an exchange carrier. This type connects user buildings or campuses which are remote from each other, but are still inside the same **local access and transport area** (LATA). (LATA concepts and boundaries were previously discussed in Chapter 8.) When the local exchange carrier cannot offer the type of service needed, an examination of private systems will be in order. It may also be wise to compare private systems for other reasons, such as cost, diversity or security. A myth exists in communications that if a "public street" must be crossed, the connection must be done by the exchange carrier. The myth goes on to say that if a user does install a connection across the street, the user risks becoming a "common carrier." Later in the chapter this myth will be exposed as we examine "rights-of-way" issues.

The third type of last-mile connection to be examined covers property wholly under a user's control. A group of buildings in a campus environment, one or more high-rise buildings on a single property, or facilities grouped closely together may often be better served by a local private system. In this third case, the "rights-of-way" are assumed to be totally under the control of the user. However, while the user controls the right-of-way, local or national government jurisdictions may still require reviews, permits, and inspections.

As alternative technologies for private systems are covered in the following section, these three basic types of last-mile connections will form the structure. Private copper-cable technology will be first.

Private Cable Systems

Private digital systems began with copper cables for telegraph, telephone, and computer systems. A little history may help in understanding today's private cable systems. In the nineteenth century, communications vendors began this industry by supplying all equipment, wires, and connections. (Actually, Alexander Graham Bell's first telephones were rented to customers who put up their own wires, but this practice was short lived.) The telephone, telegraph, and teleprinter came to the customer as services, and the customer was generally not concerned with wiring or cabling. The early computer industry followed the practice by supplying all equipment and cabling between units. Again, the user was not concerned with cabling. As we moved into the last half of the twentieth century, however, the practice was challenged and began to change.

By the 1980s, distinctions arose giving names to sections of wiring once thought to be totally part of an integral system. United States federal courts and the Federal Communications Commission issued rulings declaring, among many other things, new definitions for services and service boundaries. The boundaries recognized user and customer rights to buy, install and maintain their own communications wiring and cabling. Users are now either responsible for telephone "inside wiring" or are slowly becoming responsible for wiring already in place. In the computer business, most cables between units in computer rooms continue to be supplied by the unit's vendors. Outside the computer rooms, however, cables of all kinds are now sold, installed, and/or maintained by a host of vendors. In the data communications field, these cables and their associated special connectivity equipment are often called **local area networks** or LANs. Many very good and current texts are available on the diverse and complex subject of LANs, and we will not attempt to repeat that information here. We will continue to follow our course of describing the fundamentals of high-speed digital communications.

Digital technologies, however, blur the distinctions between cables for voice telephony and cables for data communications. Once, technology restrictions kept analog voice telephone connections (and low-speed analog modems) on twisted copper wire pairs and computer connections on coaxial or expensive multipair cables. Now, ordinary copper cables find uses for both voice and high-speed data communications, and digital technologies permit speeds into the megabit range on ordinary twisted pair cables. Integrated Systems Digital Networks (ISDN) rely heavily on existing telephone twisted-pair copper cables for both basic (2B plus D or 160 kbit/s) and primary (23 B plus D or 1.544 Mbit/s) services.[1] Technology also expands the capacity of existing coaxial cables to carry speeds well beyond their original designs. Newer alternatives, such as the IBM wiring system, offer multiple media within the same cable to connect both voice and data. **Private branch exchange** (PBX) systems increasingly offer both voice and data connectivity over the same cables. With this brief overview behind us, we may now look at current copper cable systems technologies, cable types and their applications to private digital systems.

Outside of multipair computer channel cables, perhaps the three most common copper cabling systems in use today are twisted-pair telephone cables, coaxial cables used for data communications, and broadband coaxial cables most commonly used for analog video and local area networks. All three cable types adapt well to high-speed digital use and, in fact, are moving from analog use toward digital technologies. We move now to a closer look at high-speed digital concepts involving these cable types.

Digital Cable Systems

A fundamental property of all metallic cable systems concerns their ability to carry different frequencies. All metallic cables exhibit this property and differ only in degree. Figure 11.2 shows how analog frequencies move through cables without reduction in amplitude only up to a point. After that point, the ability of the cable to carry higher and higher frequencies degrades quickly. The point where degradation begins is often called the **knee.** That is, up to this frequency the cable offers little distortion or amplitude change to signals; above (higher in frequency) this knee, distortion and amplitude reductions become severe. When the term bandwidth is used, referring to cables, the meaning is usually from some very low frequency to the knee. If the knee is at, say, 1,000,000 hertz, the bandwidth will be stated at one megahertz.

The bandwidth of a cable controls the maximum bit rate that cable can support. Without involving complex concepts, simple "rules of thumb" can be set for bit rates on cables when this bandwidth or knee is known. Depending on the type of digital pulse and, of course, the length of the cable, the rule of thumb may be expressed as so many "bit/s per hertz." Expressed another way, if a cable's frequency knee (in hertz) is known, then we may estimate the

---

[1]ISDN recognizes several bit rates for D channels and several groupings of B and D channels. Chapter 14 will cover this material in greater depth. For the moment, we will use the common North American designations of ISDN.

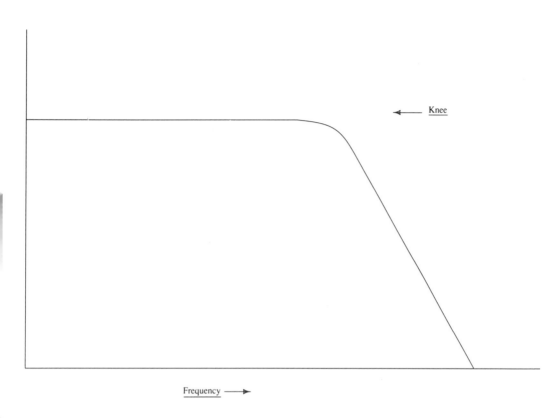

Knee

Frequency ⟶

FIGURE 11.2. Typical Metallic Cable Frequency Response Characteristic.

highest bit rate (in bit/s) that the cable will support. Knowing this frequency knee allows us to estimate what range of bit rates may be supported on a given cable system. Narrowing the range of bit/s per hertz, another variable is cost; that is, the cost of equipment at the ends of the cable. The frequency knee actually limits the maximum baud rate or the number of signaling elements per second. The number of bits contained in a signaling element varies based on the cost of the unit. The least expensive end units will support fewer bits per baud and, therefore, carry fewer bit/s per hertz. As higher cost is permitted at end units, they will support higher ratios and, therefore, faster bit rates on a given cable.

The confusion between bit/s and baud rate needs a little further explanation. Many people in the communications business use the terms interchangeably; the terms are not, however, totally interchangeable. **Baud rate** refers to the number of "signaling elements" sent down a line. **Signaling elements** are the actual changes in amplitude or other electrical characteristics of the originating signal. A long understood rule of communications is the **Nyquist Rate,** stating that the number of signaling elements sent per second should be limited to twice the available bandwidth. As an example, if the bandwidth available is 3,000 hertz, then no more than 6,000 baud can be sent. Violating this rate restriction causes a phenomenon called **inter-symbol interference,** which just means that: signaling elements run into each other. Now if each signaling element is a single bit, the baud rate and the bit/s are equal. But often, to gain greater efficiency in bit rate transmission, several or many bits may be combined into a single baud. It is this confusion of bit/s and baud that needs conquering to understand how many bit/s we can send over a cable.

If the maximum baud rate is limited to twice the bandwidth, then the number of bits per baud will determine the maximum bit rate. The number of bits per baud in the simplest and least expensive case is one. Therefore, the bit rate ranges upward from twice the bandwidth. As more exotic and expensive equipment multiplies the number of bits per baud, the ratio of bit/s per hertz rises. The multiplication itself, though, is limited by another communications rule: **Shannon's Capacity Formula.** The Shannon Formula, noted earlier in Chapter 3, refines the Nyquist Rate by considering noise which interferes with signals.

Shannon's Capacity Formula, with a reasonable amount of pure (statistical) noise considered, limits the ratio of bit/s per hertz to about 10 to one. That is, if the bandwidth of a cable (or any other real channel, for that matter) is one megahertz, then the maximum data rate will be less than 10 Mbit/s. If fact, to approach the Shannon limit requires rapidly increased complexity and expense in equipment. Most current equipment "tops out" at five to seven bit/s per hertz. For example, modems which send 19,200 bit/s over 3,300 hertz analog telephone channels operate at a ratio of 5.8 bit/s per hertz. With the differences between the bit rate (bit/s), the baud rate and bandwidth understood, we can look at several actual types of real cable. The first and most prevalent type is twisted-pair copper wire.

Digital on Twisted-pair Cable

Probably the most common communications wiring in the world is twisted-pair copper wire. This wire still runs through most business buildings and connects most residences for **plain old telephone service** (POTS). Typically the wires are either 22 or 24 gauge (a measure of the wire's diameter), which is quite small compared to ordinary electrical lamp cord (16 or 18 gauge). Because the wire was usually installed for ordinary analog telephone service, we associate the 4,000 hertz bandwidth of the telephone system with the wire. This bandwidth limit was originally imposed on the system by the carbon microphone and has endured through many years. Twisted-pair wire can run with much higher bandwidth, and this translates to very high bit rates.

Another factor limits the usable bandwidth of modern copper twisted-pair wiring. For wiring systems inside business buildings and in campus environments, the "old" analog wires may be able to carry megabit-speed digital signals. Certainly these pairs can carry 56 kbits/s digital data signals with ease. In many cases, the pairs will carry T1 signals at 1.544 Mbits/s using office repeaters which were designed to pass T-Carriers inside telephone exchange buildings. T1 office repeaters function much like T1 line repeaters already described in Chapter 5. High-speed **local area data distributors** (LADD) or digital "modems" also provide the necessary electronics to drive and receive T1 on ordinary twisted-pair. **Digital data service** (DDS) DSU/CSU units are often used on local twisted-pair in-house cable as an alternative to LADDS. It is always wise to verify the operation of both LADDs and DDS DSUs with their manufacturers prior to their use on local cable. Option changes may be needed and length limits will vary according to the wire gauge used. If the pairs used run in cables with normal analog voice lines or other digital circuits, users will want to verify that no crosstalk occurs between the pairs. Another alternative to carry local digital signals may be found in coaxial cable systems originally installed for computer terminals. To understand this application of coaxial, a differentiation between two basic types of coaxial cables must be made. These two types are baseband coaxial and broadband coaxial.

Baseband vs. Broadband: Concepts

Most everyone who has connected the small, round television cable to a TV is familiar with the fundamental nature of coaxial cable. Rather than twisting two conductors together to form twisted-pair, one conductor is placed inside a larger hollow conductor with insulation separating them. An outer insulation or jacket covers the two. Coaxial cables permit higher bandwidths than twisted-pair, carrying signals well into the hundreds of megahertz. While most people generally understand this because of cable television, baseband and broadband concepts may be new. **Baseband** and **broadband** concepts are not limited to coaxial cable, but cable can illustrate the concepts neatly. If the original terms had been one-band and lots-a-bands, we would need less space to explain the differences. For this indeed is the difference.

If a cable's entire useable bandwidth is taken by one signal, we will call it baseband. By comparison, each channel of a stereo (left and right channels) occupies the full bandwidth of our hearing from the lowest notes to the highest overtones. Thus a stereo channel could be called baseband. A stereo FM receiver, however, may bring us many channels from the FM radio band which we select by tuning the receiver to the station of our choice. Here, the FM band of radio transmission (88 to 108 megahertz) gives an example of broadband using the total bandwidth to carry many different signals. As a further example, the whole radio spectrum of many gigahertz is divided by agreement into many bands, each containing many stations. A broadband cable performs in the same way.

The television cable mentioned above carries channels 2 through 13 and perhaps many more, each separated by specific frequency band assignment. The agreement specifying the band assignments must be known in advance so that receiving equipment can select the desired channel of information. Once the channel or band is selected, any information contained in that band will be carried. The width of the assigned band then becomes our working bandwidth, and Nyquist's and Shannon's Rules for information transport can be applied. Illustrating this further, if a (very inexpensive) coaxial cable has a total bandwidth of 10 megahertz, then we may expect to carry upwards of 50 to 100 megabits/s. A more expensive coaxial cable will carry 300 to 400 megahertz and be capable of several gigabit/s with the correct end equipment. We can divide this more expensive cable into bands of 10 megahertz and each band can carry the same in broadband as our less expensive cable. The equipment attaching to the cable must be more complex as it must first select a channel or band and then bring that information back to baseband to use it. This is the function of a channel tuner on a television set.

Unlike the tuner on a TV set, broadband cable need not assign equal bandwidths to each band on the cable; this demonstrates the application flexibility of broadband coaxial cable. Cable television coaxial cable, or 75 ohm cable after its characteristic impedance, will usually support over 300 megahertz of total cable bandwidth. This bandwidth may then be allocated in some very interesting ways. Some may be assigned to normal television channels for security monitoring, education broadcast or television; others may be assigned to data communications applications including high-speed digital transmission. Cable television illustrates another fundamental concept in cable systems: directionality.

Signal Direction in Cable Systems

Cable television systems are, for the most part, **broadcast simplex systems.** That is, the signal flows outward from a center point to many receiving points. This make the flow broadcast, one to many, and simplex, one direction only. Broadcast simplex needs only one cable. Analog telephone systems also use only one cable—a single-twisted copper pair to achieve full duplex (both directions at the same time) communications. This single-twisted pair cable confuses people on signal direction as the pair can carry signals simultaneously in both directions. Analog telephone pairs carry both directions through some elegant but simple engineering involving hybrid coils. Hybrid coils are beyond the scope of this text, but this same simplicity is not easily applied to digital systems. Most cable systems devote a pair or a coaxial cable to each direction of communications. In both twisted-pair and coaxial cable digital communications systems, the signal flows in one direction per cable; two cables are needed for bi-directional or full duplex communications.

An exception to one pair, or coax, per direction may be found in contention or allocation baseband cable systems. In these single-cable systems, signals flow one way at a time upon demand or upon a time or position allocation method. Many schemes are available to either allocate sending times to stations or to resolve conflicts in contention systems. For more information on these single-cable contention systems, readers should look to texts on local area networks (LANs). There, allocation systems such as token-passing or contention systems such as **carrier sense multiple access** (CSMA) are fully described. Here, we shall limit discussions to one pair, or coax, per direction. Indeed, this approach is the most commonly used outside local area networks for digital communications by broadband or baseband cable systems. Prior to examining broadband digital applications we will look at baseband.

Digital on Baseband Coaxial Cable

Even the least expensive coaxial cable will usually support 10 megahertz over distances of several thousand feet. With 10 megahertz of usable bandwidth, simple electronics will send 10 megabits/s. With slightly more complex techniques, such as bipolar coding or alternate mark inversion (already described in Chapter 5), data speeds may be doubled. Extending the electronics to multiple bits per baud, speeds up to 50 megabits (T-3 carriers) may be handled for short distances. As the greatest expense in providing data services by cable is the construction of tunnels, ducts, or poles for the cables, additional expense for end electronics may be justified to reclaim old, low bandwidth cables. If old cables exist, this method's costs are almost always significantly lower than new construction or the pulling of new cable. Many DSU and LADD makers will adapt equipment, originally intended for twisted-pair, to coaxial cable if asked. The key question they will (or should) ask is: for what characteristic impedance?

Characteristic impedance should not be an intimidating term, but it certainly sounds like one. We are familiar with this engineering term, but no one told us we were. If we read the manuals for our stereo amplifiers carefully, we will be told what "impedance" speakers we need to connect to our amplifiers. **Impedance** is a term for resistance which includes the effects of other factors which vary with frequency or bandwidth. Characteristic impedance is a lot like the impedance of those speakers connected to our stereos; it is the natural impedance which "matches" the electronics used to drive and receive signals. Cables usually carry markings which either indicate the impedance or give a cable type from which the impedance can be found. Once this figure is known, LADD or DSU maker may be able to provide digital drivers to use the old cable. New cable, of course, may be used the same way, but should be installed knowing the impedance, application, and end equipment. Baseband use of cables dedicates the cable to a single signal. That signal may already be shared in some way such as time division multiplexing, to be detailed in the next chapter. If sharing of the cable by differing applications and types of equipment is desired, broadband cable should be considered.

Digital on Broadband Coaxial Cable

If the concept of placing narrow bandwidth analog signals on broader bandwidth cable is understood, placing digital signals on a portion of a cable's total bandwidth becomes easier to handle. This piece of the total, the assigned and usable bandwidth, will then follow all the rules set for individual twisted-pair, baseband cable or, for that matter, any inherently analog transmission medium. The key question to ask for a broadband cable is: "what is the portion?" That is, how big is the bandwidth assigned and available to a particular digital signal. Another factor enters again with broadband cable: the reverse direction signal.

As previously mentioned, most transmission media carry the forward signal direction on one facility, such as a cable, and the reverse direction on another. (A simple sub-case allows signals to use alternate directions in time—the classical half-duplex mode of operation.) In broadband cables, bandwidth is divided among applications and may also be divided by direction. Stated another way, a portion of the total bandwidth can be given to the forward direction signals and another piece of the cable's bandwidth assigned to reverse signals. While this frequency division technique can be accomplished with twisted-pair, it is rarely done due to the inherently lower available bandwidth. If it is done on a baseband coaxial cable, the cable automatically becomes a frequency shared or broadband cable. Directional frequency division on broadband cables occurs most frequently in systems using **head-ends,** a term derived from **Community Antenna Television** (CATV) systems.

CATV systems use multiple antennas and satellite earth station receivers to bring distant television signals down to an electronics facility. There, amplifiers and channel frequency translators place the on-air TV signals on different cable channels. The equipment which originally performed these tasks was known as the head-end of the CATV system. When later local area networks (LAN) began using broadband cables for data and video distribution, the terminology continued. A typical broadband system of this type is shown in Figure 11.3 on page 290.

Figure 11.3 depicts one type of frequency division called a **mid-split system.** It is mid-split because the total available bandwidth of the cable is divided or split at about the bandwidth center allowing half the total for each direction. While this seems intuitively obvious as the best way to divide the resource, both high- and low-split cable systems find application when other than pure point-to-point fixed circuit applications are encountered. High- and low-split systems differ only in the amount of bandwidth assigned to each direction in a head-end or active cable system. It may be called **active** as electronics is present to amplify, modify, or translate the signals. An additional variation in this active type system has developed around a device called a **frequency-agile modem.** Imagine the devices attaching to the cable system in Figure 11.3 without an assigned frequency.

A device at the head-end "listens" to a shared inward channel awaiting requests from the frequency agile devices. Upon a request, the assigning unit selects an available band and communicates the information to the requesting device (or devices if some form of session is requested). The devices then electronically switch to the assigned frequency and begin activities. Upon completion, the devices notify the assigner and the band is returned to the available pool. This process requires additional units at the head-end, but grants a

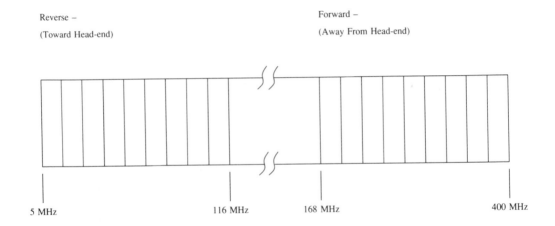

Reverse –

(Toward Head-end)

Forward –

(Away From Head-end)

5 MHz 116 MHz 168 MHz 400 MHz

Frequency Spectrum in MHz

FIGURE 11.3. Bandwidth Allocation in a Broadband Cable System.

large degree of flexibility to the overall system. There are also passive systems or broad-band cables with no head-ends or active common electronics.

One such broadband cable system uses two parallel cables to do the full job, but in a passive way. The two cable passive system, diagramed in Figure 11.4 shows how the cable is looped at one end, thus always having a forward and a reverse direction at all points. This means, of course, that attaching equipment must hook to both cables for full duplex operation.

While many other applications of baseband twisted-pair and coaxial cables and broadband coaxial cables exist and may be imagined, the concepts described here should yield the fundamental operational ideas. Extrapolating these concepts will permit newer or different copper cable systems to be more easily understood. From here we move on to a much newer transmission medium: fiber optic systems for private digital systems.

Private Fiber Systems

Fiber optic technology and applications were thoroughly covered in Chapter 10; here we will apply those concepts briefly to private systems use. All of the advantages ascribed to fiber in the previous chapter apply to private fiber optic systems, although some limitations do apply. While attaching connectors to fiber strands has become significantly easier, it still does not match attachment to copper cables. Improvements continue at a rapid pace, but "connectorization" will remain more complex for at least the next few years. Until connections can be made with tools as simple as pocket knives, fiber will not achieve the ease of installation possessed by copper. This really does not detract from fiber's usefulness, only its ubiquity. When fiber connector kits can be purchased in local hardware stores for reasonable prices, fiber will have achieved parity with copper.

Another fact about fiber: all current communications processing equipment continues to function on electrical signals. At each point where fiber optic cables meet electronic

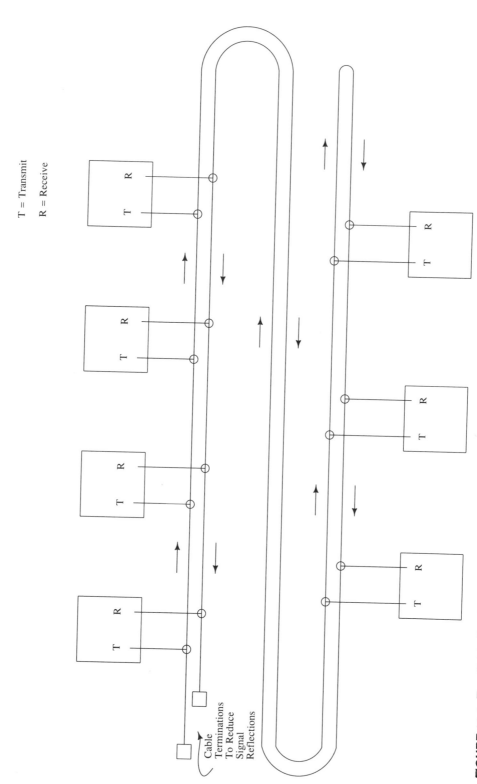

T = Transmit

R = Receive

Cable
Terminations
To Reduce
Signal
Reflections

FIGURE 11.4. Two Cable Passive Broadband Cable System.

units, conversion must be performed using the opto-electronic devices detailed in Chapter 10. While conversion devices for short-distance fibers and lower (under 10 megabits/s) speeds are now less expensive than electrical modems, conversion must still be done at each "drop" on the fiber. Many manufacturers overcome this problem by incorporating conversion devices within their application products. Examples of this combination will be given just ahead in the section on computer channel extenders. The greater difficulty of connecting fiber strands and converting optical to electrical signals remains probably the only point where fiber is not superior to copper for communications transmission. With these two limitations noted, we will explore briefly the uses of fiber in private digital systems.

A number of texts and articles currently examine fiber uses in local area networks (LANs). Although many LAN systems run well into the megabit range, we will leave their examination to others and concentrate our focus on T-Carrier, computer channel extenders, and data interface extenders as examples of private fiber optic systems.

T-Carrier Fiber Systems

Much of the equipment described in Chapter 10 for use by common carriers is made by commercial manufacturers and is available for private system T-Carrier use. As current single and multimode fiber cables are capable of bits speeds well into the hundreds of megabits, fibers installed to carry T1s may be upgraded to T2 or T3 using commercial M12 or M13 muldems and adding fiber conversion equipment. In fact, most manufacturers offering T-Carrier muldems offer fiber interfaces as optional parts of their equipment. This type of upgrade may, of course, also be an original installation for T1, T2 , T3 or higher speed private T-Carrier transmission systems.

Fiber Optic Computer Channel Extenders

A significant application of fiber optics in private communications systems has been found in the extension of computer channels. For those not familiar with computer channels, we will outline an example using IBM channels. Originally developed by IBM for its System/360s in the early 1960s, these channels have continued to connect almost all host support and peripheral devices. Typically, channel cables come as a set of two cables each about an inch in diameter and terminating in large rectangular blocks sometimes called **serpentines.** These two cables, called **bus** and **tag** after their functions, are re-powered at each connected unit and are finally terminated at the last unit in a series of units on that channel. Distances between units usually cannot exceed several hundred feet, limiting the total distance of a channel. As large host computer peripheral equipment can occupy significant floor space, computer rooms have begun to occupy several adjacent floors to contain channel cable distances. Typically the hosts and channel originating units take the middle floor with computer **direct access storage drives** (DASD) on a floor above; communications and support equipment takes the floor below. This three-dimensional "glass house" became a way to keep channel cable runs within their specified distance limits.

As fiber optic cable prices fell rapidly in the early 1980s, an opportunity arose to use fiber to extend the distance of the channel. IBM announced its first fiber optic channel extender (IBM's 3044) to push channel distances from several hundred feet to several thousand. An earlier channel extender (IBM's 2944) used many twisted-pair copper cables.

Both permitted much greater expansion in computer room distance limits, but more importantly, the 3044 took advantage of the lower cost and smaller size of fiber optics to allow channel attached devices to be located away from the computer room. The first application of these devices was usually to place channel-attached terminal control units closer to the user's terminals. With coaxial cables connecting terminals to control units, each fiber optic pair could substitute for dozens of coaxial cables. Figure 11.5 shows the rear of an IBM 3044 Channel Extender. The larger cable is a channel cable. Smaller cable is the fiber used to extend the channel. At the far-end, another 3044 reconverts the optical signal to normal bus and tag channel connections.

The computer channel extender application as previously dicussed also shows how the optic to electronic conversion can be packaged inside the application (channel extender) unit. Similar devices now exist to extend many forms of electronic communications over private fiber systems. The simplest is the **fiber optic modem** or data interface extender.

Fiber Optic Data Interface Extenders

Devices similar to the computer channel extender but somewhat less complex are the so-called **fiber optic modems.** While they are not really modems in the classic analog sense, they do perform all the functions of a modem, DSU or local area data distributor (LADD) unit. Offering digital data interfaces such as EIA-530 or V.35 on one side and fiber connectors on the other, they do interface conversion and electronic to optic signal conversion in a single package. When these devices carry less than megabit-speed data streams, one could argue that the fiber is under-utilized. This argument, however, could also easily apply to twisted-pairs used for analog voice telephone service or coax used for low-speed data. The use of fiber contributes several advantages which may not be achieved with copper. Already detailed in Chapter 10 are the advantages of light weight and freedom from induced electrical or magnetic interference. One advantage is not as obvious, opto-isolation of the ends.

Opto-electronic isolators or opto-isolators have been used for many years in sensitive electronic equipment to prevent noise on electrical grounds or common signals from one area of a unit from entering another area. These small and inexpensive units are really extremely short optical links which isolate electrical connections between their two sides. Actually two back-to-back optic-to-electronic convertors, they can be imagined as fiber optic systems without the fiber. Their isolation advantages carry through to fiber optic systems by eliminating potential data errors in noisy environments due to common mode

FIGURE 11.5. IBM 3044 Fiber Optic Channel Extender. (Photo Courtesy of IBM.)

interference. Common mode noise is introduced on balanced signals such as EIA-530 or V.35 when a large ground potential difference exists between the two sides of the interface. In fiber optic data interface extenders, this common mode noise isolation comes as a side benefit from using fiber. This isolation effect also helps explain the often error-free performance of fiber optic data interface systems.

Fiber optic system applications in communications will continue their rapid expansion as fiber prices continue to fall. End equipment will aid this spread as it continues to benefit from ever increasing integration in electronics. Primary applications will, however, continue to be in very high-speed digital communications. Where rights-of-way are available to string fiber cables, they will remain the transmission medium of choice for many years. Where natural or legal barriers prevent the laying of cable, non-cable private systems will continue to offer digital interconnection. The most common of these is, of course, digital microwave radio. We will give a brief review of digital radio shortly. First, a less well-known medium, **free-space optical transmission,** will be outlined.

Free-space Optical Systems

While fiber optic systems have received much coverage in texts and from the trade press, little about free-space optical can be found. It is perhaps because of the medium's somewhat limited application. When compared to digital microwave radio of fiber optics, free-space optics cannot match either in most applications. However, in several key areas, free-space optical should be considered. First, a brief review of the techniques and methods of free-space optical communications.

As its name implies, free-space uses only the air as its actual transmission medium. Usually housed in breadbox-sized units easily carried by one person, free-space units have an optical transmitter and an optical receiver. Looking slightly like car headlights because of their lenses, the units are intended for roof top or window mounting. The light transmitter of one unit beams signals to the receiver of the other unit and vice-versa, forming a full duplex communications path at and above T1 speeds. Power and signal cables connect the boxes to indoor units which provide a range of normal data interfaces and the control electronics for the roof-top units. With their small size and weight, the units may be set up quickly on industrial tripods and be in service in hours. This speed can be matched by very small microwave radios, but free-space optical has a significant advantage over radio.

Opportunities

Radio transmissions of all kinds are regulated by governments, and governments take time to issue needed licenses for radio transmitters. Free-space optical units are not regulated in the same way. Although the lasers used in some units receive safety classifications, the completed boxes do not require government permission to transmit. (Some local authorities may place special requirements on any new "structures" or "antennas," but operational licensing is not required.) This permits free-space optical units installation speeds unmatched by any other transmission devices. When existing communications paths are interrupted for long periods or when new paths must be created in a hurry, free-space units can provide service. On either tripods or already prepared mounts, communications may be established in a matter of hours. Once permanent paths are ready, the free-space units may continue as an alternate path or be stored for the next urgent requirement. Of course, the units have a few limits which must be understood prior to their application.

Limitations

The first limit is obvious—the units must be in visual contact. That is, there must be a clear and unobstructed path for the light to travel from unit to unit. As the transmission is actually light, even tree limbs may interfere. This clear path becomes the most important criteria when considering free-space optical communications. The second is distance, as the units do not carry as far as microwave radio. Depending on the power and type of the light emitter, free-space units will rarely find application over a few miles. This distance limit may also be affected by path alignment relative to the sun. In certain alignments, the sun may briefly "blind" the receiver of a unit for a few moments. Like sun-transit outage in satellites, this will happen for only a few days a year when the sun rises or sets just behind one unit and aligns exactly with the other unit over the path. If this time period (sunrise or sunset) is not critical or if the installation does not align with the sun, the problem is non-existent. As in microwave radio, weather must be considered.

Shortly we will review the effects of weather on microwave radio; weather also may affect free-space light communications. As weather affects both, the concept of loss budget or fade margin can be applied to both. Loss budget exists in nearly all forms of communications transmission. It is simply a calculation of the system's capability under the best conditions to the expected capability under the worst predicted conditions. Loss budget usually subtracts the minimum acceptable receiver signal level from the minimum expected transmitter output power. The difference is the budget which may be spent or saved in the overall transmission system. For example, larger lenses or parabolic (dish) antennas will increase the signal power and add to the loss budget. Weather conditions will eat into the budget. For each optical (or radio) path the budget should be sufficiently large to accommodate losses due to weather. In free-space optic communications, anything which reduces, deflects or disperses the transmitted light will cause loss.

Other than direct sunlight (or other strong artificial light sources) fog is perhaps the most difficult to deal with. The dispersion of light signals in fog is well known by anyone who has driven a car in intense fog. The effects on free-space optics is roughly the same. In those areas of the world which do not experience dense fogs, this is not a consideration. Other weather effects, such as snow, may be problems in one area but not another. The loss budget must allow for all but the most unusual and unexpected weather variations. Manufacturers of free-space optical communications systems should be consulted to determine what types of units are most appropriate to an individual application and climate. These vendors maintain information of weather patterns and can usually supply recommendations on paths, mountings, and loss budgets. Similar information also figures in the planning of digital microwave radio systems.

Private Microwave Radio

Once only the province of common carriers, private digital microwave radio came into its own in the late 1970s. Authorized in the United States by the Federal Communications Commission, private digital radio drew on manufacturers used to supplying the common carriers. Frequency assignments for private systems are different from those given to the carriers but the technology remains nearly identical. In the early 1980s, new radio systems were introduced to take advantage of higher frequency bands most usable for short distance paths. While some older terminology exists, such as C band (approximately six gigahertz) and K_u band (approximately 12 gigahertz), we shall use only the actual frequency bands in megahertz to outline available bands for private microwave systems. Concepts remain constant between the various bands; differences exist in ranges and capabilities. The concept of government regulation applies to all bands.

Regulatory Aspects

All forms of radio emissions in the United States are regulated by the Federal Communications Commission and private microwave radio is included. In practice, this means that applications to construct and operate private radio systems must be filed with the FCC along with certain attachments. The forms are short and uncomplicated, but most users will want assistance with the attachments. Unless antenna towers are high enough or are close enough to flight paths to require lighting, the only application attachments needed are a **path survey** and **evidence of frequency coordination.** The path survey is just that and is usually conducted by an experienced surveyor who will identify all aspects of the proposed path of the radio signals. Because of their parabolic antennas, microwave signals are highly directional; they are also subject to path impairments such as reflections. Path surveyors will identify the possible impairments and recommend "best choice" paths.

Like path surveys, evidence of frequency coordination may be done by the vendor of the microwave radio equipment or by the user. Most often, however, a specialist will be contacted for each. Frequency coordination is more complex than it sounds. Not only are the frequencies to be used examined against others existing or planned in the vicinity, but various combinations of the frequencies are examined. These combinations may interfere with other licensed services and frequency coordination firms use various computer programs to assess the combinations. Once the results of the path survey and the frequency coordinations are in, the license application may be completed and sent to the FCC. The FCC, after review, will usually issue a **construction permit** allowing installation. If no other impediments are uncovered, an actual operating license is issued and the system may begin production transmission. Manufacturers of microwave radio equipment should be contacted to assist in these license processes, but users will always take the final responsibility for both the license and the operation of the radios.

Microwave Radio Concepts

Although both free-space optical communications and microwave radio share line-of-sight path requirements, microwave paths may generally be longer. In addition, microwave paths may contain repeaters, either passive or active. Path impairments are fewer and loss budgets may be higher. A review of the basic concepts of microwave may help explain these assertions. We begin with the path considerations.

Microwave path lengths depend on the loss budget and the budget may be increased by using larger "dish antennas." Microwave radio differs from other types of radio largely in its very short wavelength, thus the word "microwave." These very short wavelengths, typically between 10 and 50 centimeters, permit the use of antenna reflectors which "focus"

FIGURE 11.6. Private Microwave Antenna Installation.

the radiation and thus intensify its power in a given direction. This is exactly the same principle used in a flashlight reflector to obtain a narrow, intense beam.

In microwave radio the larger the "dish," the greater the intensification or antenna gain. At higher frequencies, wavelengths become shorter (wavelength is inversely proportional to frequency) and antennas can be smaller for the same gain. Loss budget (and path length) are made greater by higher power radios and larger antennas. Path losses will reduce the budget and the path length.

Under normal conditions, path loss may be calculated knowing just length and frequency. This loss subtracts from the total budget and the remainder yields the power which may be given up to weather and other path impairments. A typical microwave path calculation is shown in Figure 11.7 on page 298.

After all path losses are subtracted from all path gains, the remainder is usually called the **fade margin**; that is, the amount of additional loss which can be tolerated through fading. This fade margin will permit operation of the microwave radio link during most heavy rain storms. Rain absorbs microwave energy and thus increases the path loss; this loss is proportional to rain rate, not rain amount. A steady rain over several days may cause flooding problems but will not affect a microwave path with sufficient fade margin, but a brief thunderstorm may interrupt the path if the rain rate is high. Radio transmission handbooks show maps and tables of probable rain rates for different areas of the world and these will guide microwave installers on proper fade margins. Companies selling and installing microwave radio systems will be among the best authorities on rain and fade margins for all types of microwave paths.

6 GHz, 1 Watt Transmitter Power Output	0 dBW
Waveguide Loss to Antenna	-3.0 dB
3 Foot Parabolic Antenna Gain	+32.6 dB
20 Mile Path Loss	-138.2 dB
3 Foot Parabolic Antenna Gain	+32.6 dB
Waveguide Loss to Antenna	-3.0 dB
Incoming Signal to Receiver	-79.0 dBW
Receiver Signal Threshold	-121.0 dBW
Fade Margin (Incoming – Threshold)	42.0 dB
(Equates to Approx. Availability)	99.99 %

FIGURE 11.7. Typical Microwave Path Calculation.

Point-to-point Microwave

The simplest and most usual private microwave systems link one building or campus with another where a line-of-sight path exists. This point-to-point microwave presents the fewest problems and will almost always be the least expensive to procure and install. If one point can easily be seen from the other, the path can usually be planned easily. Where trees, hills, buildings or distances over about 10 miles interfere, the path may be more complex or difficult. Where only long distances must be overcome, larger size dish antennas may be sufficient. Where hills, forests or buildings must be bypassed, structural steel towers may be needed for the radios to "see" over the obstructions. The towers may affix to solidly constructed buildings or may need poured concrete foundations of their own. Large dish antennas and high towers may require approval of local government planning bodies, and they should be contacted quite early in the process to assure that the necessary permits can and will be issued. Depending on local weather conditions, the dish antenna may need to be covered by a **radome,** a lightweight fiberglass cover protecting the sensitive heart of the antenna called the **feed horn.**

Figure 11.6 on page 297 shows a microwave antenna without a covering radome; the thin structure coming from the center of the antenna dish is the feedhorn. Waveguides, or hollow metal tubes sized for the microwave frequency range, bring microwave energy from the transmitting radio to the feedhorn where the horn "sprays" the energy evenly back against the dish. In the reverse direction, the feedhorn "collects" incoming microwave energy and sends it down the waveguide to the receivers. As transmitters and receivers operate at sufficiently different frequencies, the same dishes, feedhorns and waveguides work for both transmitting and receiving. The horn is located at the focus of the parabolic dish and the dish reflects the energy as a focused straight beam toward the next antenna. Where ice storms can load down the feedhorn and distort it from the parabolic focus point, radomes cover and protect the feedhorn. Very little energy loss is associated with the radomes and many times they will be used to provide basic protection for the feed horn. These fundamental constructions are used by almost all types of microwave installations, whether point-to-point or those requiring several different path sections with reflectors or repeaters.

Microwave Reflectors and Repeaters

Where direct line-of-sight is not possible between the points of interest, several other methods may be used. Where a single building or nearby obstruction blocks an otherwise simple path, a reflector is often suggested by path surveyors. The reflector is a straightforward flat microwave mirror usually located very close to one end of the path. Proximity to the end is desirable to avoid losses from a distant "mirror" or reflector. Reflectors may also be used at the tops of buildings or towers with the antennas located at ground level. Most often, reflectors are flat rectangular structures mounted and secured like antennas. The mountings permit slight variations in directional angles to align the energy along the correct path. The alignment process at installation measures received signal strength at one end of a path while path component antennas and reflectors are adjusted for maximum (and predicted) signal. While reflectors increase path loss, they yield a lower loss than passive repeaters.

Another passive approach to clearing line-of-sight obstructions is the passive repeater. Here, two antennas are mounted back-to-back but arranged to re-point the signal to miss an obstruction. Passive repeaters should also be located relatively close to one end of the path; loss encountered in a passive repeater is significantly greater than a reflector. This is because the received signal from one antenna becomes the transmitted signal from the other. Where a nearby hill or tower offers a direct line-of-sight to both ends of a path, the passive repeater allows the path to be constructed without active components.

Figure 11.8 on page 300 shows how the two interconnected passive antennas on the tower "bend" the microwave beam to reach around the hill. Passive repeaters perform this task well when loss budgets permit. If path loss budgets cannot tolerate passive repeaters, then active repeaters must be considered as the next step. Active components, such as transmitters and receivers require power and such power must be available at all times when the path is operating. This usually means battery power for the active repeater to permit operation during power outages. For longer outages or remote repeater stations, automatic starting power generators may be needed. Passive repeater stations may require only simple facilities, such as protection fences and bottled nitrogen to keep positive dry gas pressure in the waveguides. Active repeater stations will usually need batteries, generators, remote monitoring systems and equipment buildings in addition to the actual repeater

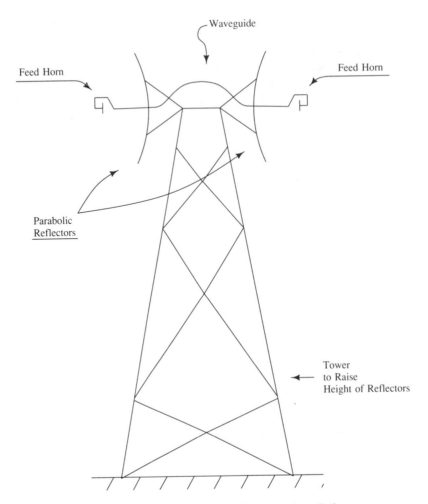

Waveguide

Feed Horn

Feed Horn

Parabolic
Reflectors

Tower
to Raise
Height of Reflectors

FIGURE 11.8. Typical Passive Microwave Repeater Installation.

transmitters and receivers. Remotely controllable spare equipment may also be desirable if outages severely impact the business using the private microwave system.

While this brief overview of private digital services and systems has not touched on all possible private technologies and systems, we hope to have introduced some basic concepts. This chapter completes our review of high-speed digital services and technologies. We move now to time division multiplexing technology which offers a digital speed bridge between the faster T-Carriers and the (now) slower data communications rates.

CHAPTER 12

Time Division Multiplexers

Chapter Overview

While megabit-speed digital communications carriers form the major focus in this book, most computer data communications equipment continues to run at speeds of 56 kbit/s and below. In prior chapters, we inspected services and techniques to furnish circuits at speeds of 1.544 Mbit/s and higher. We must now describe bridging devices to allow lower speed data devices access to these higher speed carriers. Many approaches exist to form the bridges, but we shall concentrate on **time division multiplexers** (TDMs). TDMs build speed bridges between very fast digital carriers and lower speed data communications connections or ports. Time division multiplexers take traditional data port speeds from communications front-ends or controllers and match them to high-speed digital communications carriers. With few exceptions, the base of knowledge and experience built upon analog modems and circuits applies directly to TDMs. Communications hardware and software continue their role and traditional DTE/DCE interfaces remain in place. This chapter, devoted entirely to TDMs, will relate the basics of data communications to these newer TDM techniques.

The chapter begins with TDM fundamentals and the origins of time division multiplexing. A technology and terminology section separates and explains terms from both telephony and data communications. While terminology descriptions tend to be dull material, much confusion occurs today in telecommunications terminology. As the once independent streams of telephones and computers converge, well understood words from one field may now hold very different meanings in the other field. The terminology section attempts to explain those differences. This section then introduces several new concepts in multiplexing and reminds us of concepts begun in Chapters 5, 6 and 7. The chapter divides TDMs into three broad groups:

- single-T1 TDMs;
- multiple-T1 TDMS; and
- network TDM systems.

These three broadly drawn classes illustrate fundamentally different types of TDM equipment and highlight the functions and features of each. As developments in time division multiplexers continue at a frenetic pace, no specific manufacturers or models will be described; the material would be obsolete before it was printed. Our intent is to explain fundamentals and concepts which will apply to both existing and future equipment. No attempt is made to draw conclusions of "better" or "worse," but guidance is developed to build user understanding. Systems designs, topologies and timing examples show sample applications of each generation. The chapter continues with a section on TDM voice/data integration techniques and voice digitization methods. We conclude with indications of TDM directions leading to Chapter 14 on Integrated Systems Digital Networks.

TDM Fundamentals

First widely introduced in the early 1980s, digital data TDMs have become indispensable tools to data communications professionals. While bridging the speed gap, these TDMs also offer features and functions not always found in older analog connections. But multiplexing did not start here. **Multiplexing,** or sending several messages over the same circuit, is nearly as old as electrical communications. The early telegraph systems of LeSage and Chappe, described in Chapter 1, multiplexed messages over single communications channels. Multiplexing, in its broadest sense, "shares" communications facilities between messages.

In modern terms, multiplexing several circuits together began with space division and frequency division multiplexing. One form of space division puts many wire pairs into a single multipair cable or facility. With each pair carrying its own channel, the space (within the cable) is divided and the multiple messages are carried simultaneously. Space division multiplexing takes many forms, but multipair cable is the simplest to explain. Frequency division multiplexing (FDM) began in the 1920s with AT&T's C-Carrier FDM system discussed in Chapter 2. Here, three individual telephone channels combined to share a single open-wire voice line. Later, a group of 12 voice channels combined in a "channel bank" to be sent over a single analog FDM facility. Frequency division multiplexing development continues to the present with coaxial cables, microwave radios and undersea cables carrying thousands of simultaneous calls on single communications facilities. By the 1960s, however, time division multiplexing (TDM) techniques became the area of the greatest development and potential for multiplexing. The first commercial digital carrier system, AT&T's T1 carrier, began service in the 1960s introducing voice digitization and digital time division multiplexing.

Origins of Digital TDM

Like its frequency division forerunner, time division multiplexing began by combining voice channels together for transmission over single facilities or cables. First, voice channel signals had to be converted to binary bits in a process called **digitization.** Analog voice signals simply could not be stored economically while awaiting their turn on a time-shared facility. By converting or digitizing analog channels to digital bits, the newly formed bits could be held until their time arrived. Waiting times in TDM are of short duration, but analog storage techniques are far more complex and costly than digital storage techniques. Thus the first TDM facilities depended on conversion of voice signals to bits for storage and transmission. These conversion devices continued to be called channel banks after their analog ancestors. While the **A-type** analog channel banks combined channels, the **D-type** channel banks also digitized individual voice signals before combining them.

The first digital channel banks, taking the name D1, digitized and combined 24 voice channels. The origin of the number 24 came from both practice and technology. Practice in the telephone system had already combined 12 channels into "groups" in earlier FDM carrier systems, and the concept of the "group" (of 12 channels) was imbedded in system practices. But digital transmission technology of the early 1960s permitted twice as many channels to be sent over wire pairs. The two concepts melded to produce **digroups.** Digroups, or double groups of 12 channels, produced both the number 24 for channels and the first commercial TDM digital stream at 1.544 Mbit/s.

The strange number of 1.544, as explained before in Chapter 3, derives from the digitization of 24 voice channels at a rate of 8,000 samples per second. As a reminder, this sampling rate is needed (using Nyquist's criteria) to fully sample a 4,000 hertz bandwidth voice channel. When 24 channels each produce 8,000 samples per second and each sample is eight bits (needed to define levels for each sample), 1,536,000 is the combined result. (Eight times 8,000 equals 64,000; 24 times 64,000 is 1,536,000.) When another bit is added to mark the boundary of a frame of 24 channels, and the boundary occurs 8,000 times per second, the result is 1.544 Mbit/s. All digital voice channel banks in the United States have been able to operate at 1.544 Mbit/s from the original D1 channel banks to the latest D5 units. Variations on channel banks were described in Chapter 3 and will not be repeated here, but concepts coming from channel banks will be examined in greater detail. We will spend an additional moment considering this channel bank process as it forms the foundation of almost all time division multiplexing. Figure 12.1 on page 304 outlines the functions performed in a D-type voice channel bank.

Each channel, when digitized in a voice channel bank, yields eight parallel value bits; that is, eight bits represent the value of a single sample of the voice signal. Using binary combinations, the eight bits can represent up to 256 possible values. These eight bits are stored, in parallel, until the time arrives to send them over the transmission line. At that time, the eight bits are sent serially (one at a time) to the other end where they are re-assembled to parallel form. From the parallel register (the digital storage), they convert back to an analog value. Converted analog values add together over time to produce a facsimile of the original voice channel. The digitization and re-conversion process of analog voice is described later in the chapter in the section on voice/data integration. Our interest here is the storage of digital bits in registers and the transmittal of them one at a time; for this is how TDM works for both voice and data.

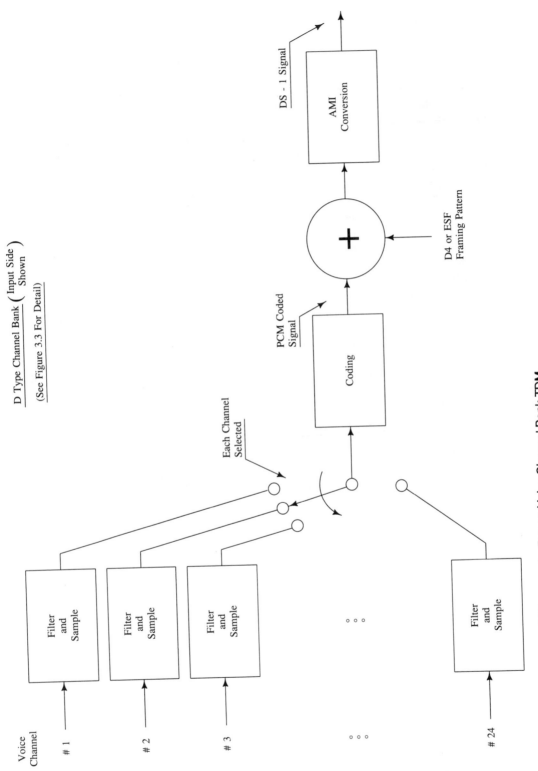

FIGURE 12.1. Functional Diagram of a D-type Voice Channel Bank TDM.

In data communications use, TDM units accumulate lower rate (such as 9,600 bit/s) incoming data bits from a DTE and hold them in registers until it is time to send them over a high-speed line. At the far-end, incoming bits from the high-speed line accumulate until removed by a far-end DTE at, say, 9,600 bit/s. Clearly, the incoming low-speed bit rate should equal the far-end removal bit rate or bits will be lost. (More will be said about TDM clocking and timing later in this chapter.) In voice channel banks, bits for each channel accumulate until time arrives to send. All eight bits (a **byte**) then leave, one at a time. This has become known as byte-oriented multiplexing and some data TDMs operate in this fashion. Another way of multiplexing, however, sends bits from each channel one at a time intermixed with bits from other channels in bit-oriented multiplexing. This design choice between bit- or byte-orientation becomes the first of many technology and terminology factors used to both understand and distinguish between data TDMs.

Continuing the story of TDM origins, once binary digits became the method of transmission for voice, their use for data communications formed a natural next step. This step was taken in the early 1970s when interface TDMs were built to handle data traffic. Early digital data services (DDS) used T1 carrier facilities, but instead of digitizing voice signals, took data bits directly and multiplexed them onto the high-speed T1 links. As digitized voice channels used 64,000 bit/s, a slightly lower speed was picked to handle what was then very fast data communications. By removing one of the eight voice channel sample bits, a speed of 7/8 of 64,000 bit/s could be easily carried. Thus was born 56,000 bit/s DDS. An early time division multiplexer used purely for data was designated T1DM by AT&T, but was almost always called a "tiddem." Other early multiplexers handled both voice and data, with the data at 56,000 bit/s or less. More traditional (at that time) speeds of 2,400, 4,800 and 9,600 bit/s were also offered by DDS by either dedicating a 64,000 bit/s T1DM channel to this slower data, or by combining slower channels in a technique called **sub-rate digital multiplexing** (SRDM). Each of these approaches will receive full treatment later in this chapter. As DDS began to use T1 carriers in the telephone system, time division techniques matured. With the availability of T1 circuits direct to user's computer rooms, manufacturers found a new and rapidly growing market for data TDMs.

Makers of voice channel banks saw the opportunity to move into the burgeoning data communications field, and makers of modems and lower speed data multiplexers joined them. In a very general sense, three kinds of manufacturers have entered the TDM business. First and second to market came the voice channel bank makers and the data modem manufacturers; the third group of manufacturers joined the market somewhat later with key people coming from packet networking backgrounds. While these backgrounds tend to blur somewhat today, each firm retains a flavor from its origins. These origins give valuable hints to the behavior and features of various TDMs. As we begin to examine each of the three general types of TDMs, these origin flavors may become more evident. But before we travel that road of examination and explanation, we must explore time division multiplexing technology and terminology.

Technology and Terminology

As telephone and data communications terminology have evolved separately, common words have sometimes come to mean different things. And, some confusion exists as to the boundary between telephone and data communications. Attempting to start from common ground, Figure 12.2 on page 306 outlines the domains of voice and data commu-

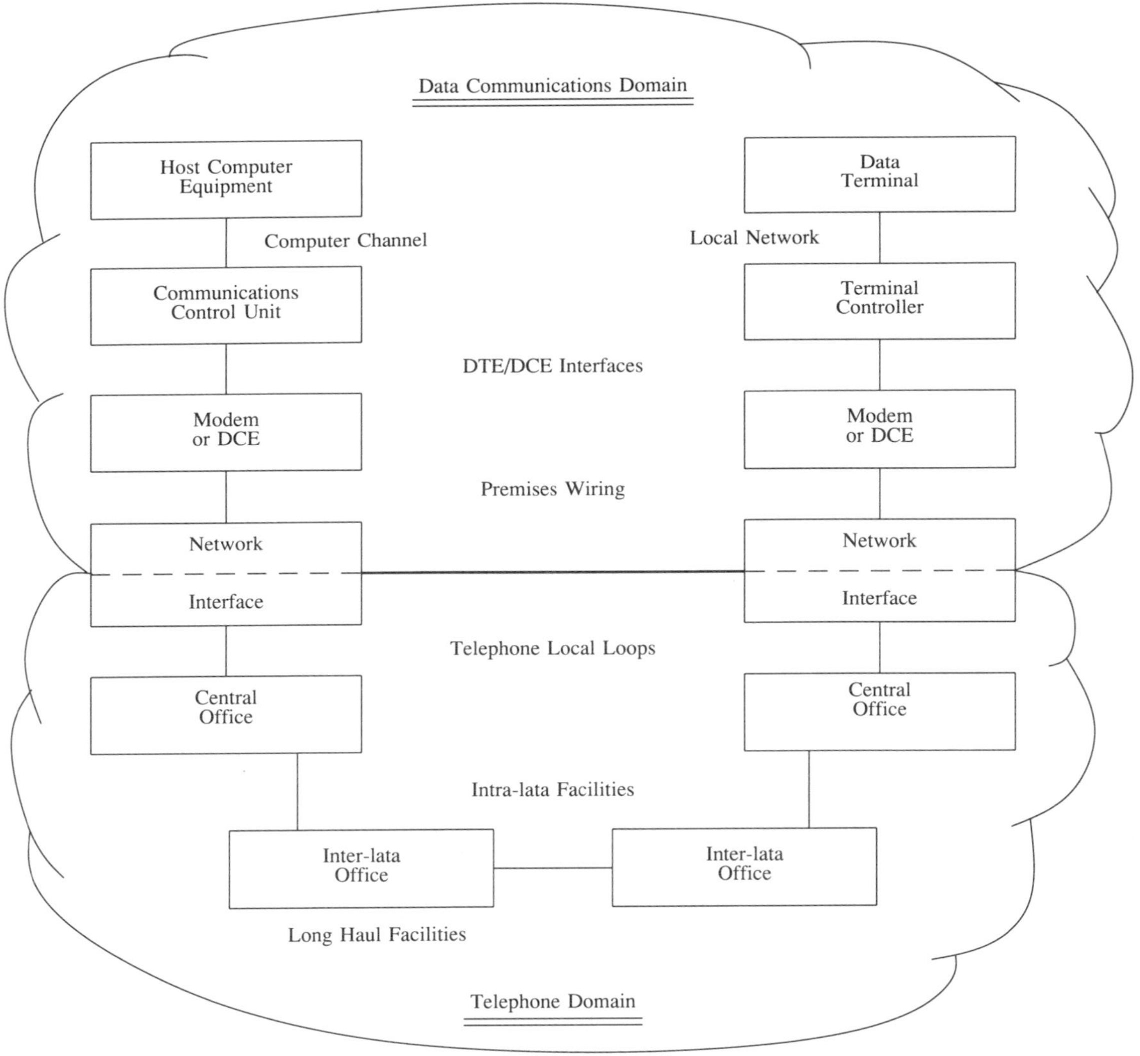

FIGURE 12.2. Telephone and Data Communications Domains.

nications as the authors understand them. Using this figure to show the boundary, we can then begin an examination of terminology from each field.

As the two fields move together in this digital era, a close examination of the terms is needed. To avoid further confusing our readers, we will attempt to compare terms from both fields and then use selected terms as we move forward. We start from a data communications and computer perspective. Figure 12.3 expands on some common terms used in both telephone and computer fields.

The terms will be used only as the underlined meanings indicate in Figure 12.3. That is, while a multiplexer may multiplex many circuits in a telephone meaning, we shall use multiplexer only in the data communications sense. Similarly, while DTE is used in both areas, we shall continue to use DTE as **data terminal equipment** in the data communications sense and always spell out **digital terminal equipment** from the telephone side. Also, computer channels which usually operate in parallel should not be confused with serial (one bit at a time) communications channels. Parallel computer channels will always be called computer channels or buses in the material which follows. The word channels (alone) will mean only individual circuits or signal streams from their telephone meaning.

DTE/DCE interfaces, first detailed in Chapter 4, become the dividing line for terminology. Time division multiplexers, as described in this chapter, exist only on the DCE side. They may be thought of as many sets of modem-like devices (DCEs) which take

Term	Usual Telephone Meaning	Usual Data Comm. Meaning
Channel	A real voice or data circuit in equipment.	A connection method from a computer to its attached supporting equipment.
Channel Bank	A device to share circuits or facilities among many voice channels.	Not used in data communications terminology.
Controller	Rarely used in telephone equipment terminology.	A communications device to control many data real or shared data circuits.
DCE	Data Circuit Terminating Equipment, a modem or data set; can now also include digital data devices, such as data DSUs or data TDMs.	Data Circuit Terminating Equipment, usually an analog modem or data set.
DTE	Digital Terminal Equipment, usually terminating a digital communications circuit.	Data Terminal Equipment, such as a data communications controller or data terminal.
Multiplexer	A device to multiplex high speed circuits to even higher speed circuits, also called a MULDEM, for MULtiplexer/DEMultiplexer.	A device to share common circuits or facilities among multiple data circuits; also, a communications controller.

FIGURE 12.3. Comparative Terms in Telephone and Data Communications.

separate digital signal streams from many DTEs and combine them for transmission across a high-speed carrier facility. In a moment, we will delve further into this combining or multiplexing process. First, a little more must be said about the differences in functions performed by communications controllers and multiplexers.

COMMUNICATIONS CONTROLLERS VS. MULTIPLEXERS

Those familiar with computer architectures will recognize that signals, in most computers, travel in parallel. Parallel **buses** or parallel computer channels carry information in bytes or words varying in width from eight bits to 32 bits or higher. Bits on these buses move together in time and in parallel on separate wires, recalling space division multiplexing. Communications architectures, however, move digital bits in serial fashion one after another. While bit rates vary according to available communications line speeds, in general the bits move serially. Another significant difference in the two architectures concerns error handling. In computer channel architectures, errors are environmentally designed out so that they do not (or very rarely) occur. When errors are detected on a computer channel, entire processes must usually be restarted. Error handling is minimal as an error is a rare event. Communications architectures have always considered errors rather differently. Communications channels, while as carefully designed as computer channels, cannot control their environment. Electrical storms, floods and wide temperature variations exist in their environment and all can cause errors. Communications architectures recognize errors as a way of life. A computer communications controller spans the two architectures and must operate in both environments.

Multiplexers operate mainly in a communications environment and perform very different functions. Replacing individual circuit connections, TDMs must buffer both bits from controllers and bits from high-speed lines. Multiplexers combine controller bits to form high-speed streams and manage the combining and de-combining process. In essence, they act as "retailers", taking bulk or high-speed services at wholesale costs and providing individual circuits at lower than individual circuit costs. An underlying assumption, of course, is that many circuits exist to be combined. Digital data service functions, described in Chapter 3, now move into the user's computer room or PBX room making each user a small (or perhaps large) digital "telephone company." Managing this telephone company service then falls to the user, and the TDM becomes a focus of this management. A multiplexer spans both low and high-speed serial communications channels. The multiplexer's low-speed serial channels usually connect at a DTE/DCE interface to a communications controller's serial channels.

The concept of serial channels now becomes key to understanding TDMs. Refining this concept further, a distinction must be made between the lower speed serial channels from the controller and the higher speed channel from the bulk transmission service. In the following material, channel-side refers to the DTE/DCE interface between the controller and the TDM's individual channels. As the main function of a TDM is combining or "aggregating," the high-speed bulk circuit side of a TDM will be called the aggregate-side. While aggregate-side serial channels may run at any speed, we will generally refer to aggregate-side communications channels running at T1 speeds or higher. Both sides of a TDM operate serially, but with significant speed differences, functions and behaviors. Aggregating and managing many channels from a controller (or several controllers) are two of a TDM's major tasks.

Converting parallel computer channels to serial communications channels and error handling are two of the major tasks usually assigned to a communications controller. Other functions given to a controller include bit recognition, byte or character formation and communications protocol handling. Here, we will touch only on parallel/serial channel conversion and (later in the chapter) on error handling behavior in both controllers and TDMs.

PARALLEL AND SERIAL CONVERSIONS

Controllers convert parallel bus or computer channel data to serial streams. TDMs convert serial low-speed data to serial high-speed data. Figure 12.4 diagrams both processes. While the Figure shows only conversion in one direction, remember that a reverse conversion must occur at a far-end. That is, parallel-to-serial conversion from a parallel computer bus to a communications channel at the near end must be undone, after transmission, by the far-end to provide the data to another controller parallel bus. Similarly, aggregation of many serial streams at a near end requires deaggregation or demultiplexing at the far end.

Parallel-to-serial conversion changes form while holding speed constant; serial-to-serial conversion retains form while changing speed. As Figure 12.4 indicates, the aggregate channel "spreads out" the channel-side bits to leave room for bits from other channels. In parallel-to-serial conversion, bits are removed one at a time until the parallel buffer is empty; another byte or word then shifts into the buffer for conversion. This process continues as long as a controller's parallel buffer has bytes or words to send. In synchronous data communications protocols (such as bisync, SDLC and HDLC), conversion continues with time-marking bit patterns originally intended to assure activity on the communications line. TDMs, unlike analog modems, do not always require this activity but pass on whatever is received in a **transparent** manner. Transparency, explained more fully later in this chapter, means total insensitivity of a channel to whatever bit patterns pass through. Most TDMs operate in total transparency mode ignoring both long "one" and "zero" strings and all bit pattern combinations. TDMs manage channel transparency by

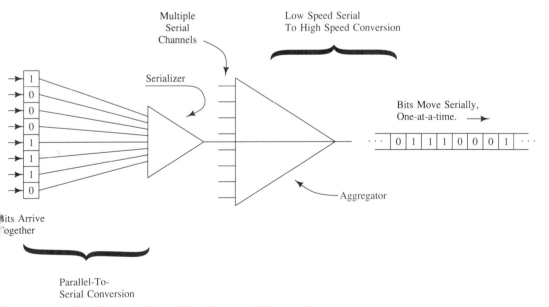

IGURE 12.4. Parallel-to-serial and Serial-to-serial Conversions.

many methods depending largely on multiplexer design. Design choices divide conceptually into the bit- and byte-oriented types mentioned earlier in the chapter.

Figure 12.4 on page 309 shows one method of TDM serial-to-serial conversion called
bit-oriented multiplexing where bits spread out on the aggregate channel. Another method
"bunches" a number of bits together in byte-oriented multiplexing. Bit versus byte multiplexing becomes another concept for our examination.

BIT VS. BYTE TERMINOLOGY

D-type channel banks have always used byte-oriented multiplexing. Early data-ori-
ented TDMs usually bit-oriented their multiplexing. As voice/data integration and Integrated Systems Digital Networks (ISDN) begin to roll out, byte multiplexing will become
the dominant method. But what is this method? Earlier we described channel banks
converting a single voice telephone channel to eight bits and doing this for 24 individual
channels. The aggregate channelization of these channel banks kept the eight bits from each
channel together on the aggregate. That is, when the time came for the bits from channel 1
to move out on the aggregate, all eight went together in sequence. Then the eight bits from
the next channel went together, and so on. Within the stream of the aggregate, each
channel's bits can always be found together and in the same position relative to the framing
bit position. Channel 1's bit are always the eight after the framing bit, channel 2's eight bits
always follow channel 1's and so on until the full 24 channels are sent and the process
repeats. Thus each byte of eight bits travels together and in the same relative position. This
is **byte-oriented multiplexing** and in D4 channelization is always very consistent. Bit-oriented multiplexing does not work at all this way.

In **bit-oriented multiplexing,** each channel's bits are sent individually without clear
relationships to the other bits from that channel. Bits are scattered throughout the aggregate
stream by a more complex method which is usually standard only to a manufacturer or a
product family from a single manufacturer. This is not, however, badness. Bit-oriented
multiplexing began as a method to improve the efficiency of multiplexing. In byte multiplexing, efficiency is high only if all channels run at the same rate. For example, D4
channelization assumes 24 channels of 64 kbit/s each. If, however, data channels are
needed at 2.4 kbit/s, 9.6 kbit/s and 56 kbit/s, byte-oriented multiplexing will use 64 kbit/s
channels for each. (Another method to preserve efficiency called **sub-rate digital multiplexing** will be shown shortly; it improves, but does not match the efficiency of bit-orientation). With microprocessor technology controlling the makeup of the aggregate, bit
multiplexers can allot only the bit rate needed to support a particular speed.

By assigning only needed bit rate, maximum packing of channels can occur. This
also means that if lower speed channels are needed, more than 24 channels can be handled.
Usually, TDMs operating in bit multiplex mode will use longer patterns for overall framing
than 193 bits. This greater length derives from the need for more complex frame location
and control patterns, sometimes called **frame synchronization words** (FSW). Complexity
is needed to assure validity of both channel data and control signal information. To prevent
the longer FSWs from consuming inordinate shares of the bandwidth, they are repeated less
often making the total pattern longer than 193 bits. Framing for the bit-oriented TDM frame
is usually longer than one bit position per 192 bits, but also retains the D4 framing needed
by some transmission equipment. Before describing the complexity of this dual framing
process, Figure 12.5 compares the two methods from channels to the aggregate.

As the figure shows, bits from bit multiplexing scatter according to the efficiency
dictated by the multiplex control processor. To describe framing in a bit multiplexer, we

311

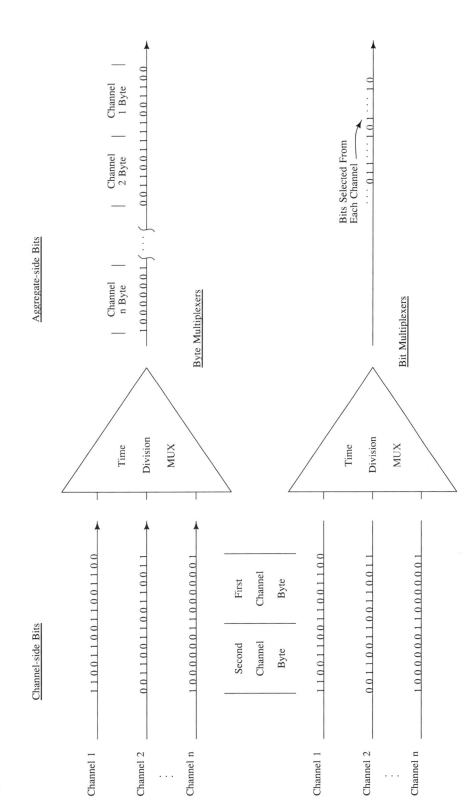

FIGURE 12.5. Bit Multiplexing vs. Byte Multiplexing.

must remember that most T1 and higher transmission equipment expects (and sometimes insists) on D4 type framing bit patterns. In a bit-oriented TDM this means two framing patterns must co-exist. To satisfy the transmission equipment, D4 framing patterns are superimposed on the longer bit-oriented frame bit sequences. This means that at the 193rd bit framing positions, a D4 pattern (or perhaps an ESF pattern) may be found. If the normal D4 channel positions are examined, however, no meaningful information appears. Bit-oriented TDM frame sequence are most often **proprietary**, that is, they are unique to a manufacturer or a product family. Channelization can only be demultiplexed by another product from the same family. The D4 framing pattern is only present to meet the requirements of carrier equipment and has no bearing on the highly efficient channelization. This does pose some problems for inter-equipment compatibility.

When TDMs operate in bit-orientation, only members of that product family can decode the frame sequences and demultiplex the channels. If other product families must inter-operate with them, very special arrangements must be made. Usually, no connection can be made at the aggregate side; channel connections using special cross-connect cables (see Chapter 6) are made between the two types of units. Newer TDMs to be described later in this chapter under network TDMs have an ability to accept D4 framed and channelized inputs on their channel side and produce bit-oriented aggregates. They do this by methods reminiscent of statistical multiplexing.

STATISTICAL MULTIPLEXERS

For many years another type of data multiplexer called **statistical multiplexers** or **stat muxes** have been used to "compress" data streams. Stat mux techniques have been applied for many years, primarily to very expensive circuits to share costs among several using devices or applications. Earlier TDMs did not offer this capability, but variations on the stat mux theme are again beginning to appear in the more exotic multiple-T1 TDMs and network TDM systems. Statistical multiplexers continue to be a valuable contributor to the efficient use of transmission facilities, and concepts used in stat muxes are reappearing in network TDMs. To understand this type of operation a brief review of stat muxes follows. Originally, stat muxes intended to capitalize on the "statistical" nature of serial data streams by compressing out repetitive or redundant bytes. Stat mux techniques are analogous to voice compression methods which combine the "silent" periods on many channels to reduce overall bandwidth. In voice communications, terms such as **time allocated speech interpolation** (TASI) and **voice activated compression** (VAC) compare conceptually to stat muxing in data.

Stat muxes assume that during some periods in each individual data stream, bits are used to merely mark time. These periods are filled with continuous marking ("one" bits) in asynchronous protocols, continuous SYN characters in bisync and continuous FLAGS in HDLC or SDLC. This marking of time occurs while people are reading screens or thinking or keying slowly or for other reasons such as job queues. Statistically, this will usually not occur at the same times on several independent data streams; the stat mux examines each data stream to see what can be safely cut out. The unit does this by knowing exactly the protocol, speed, and character set of each line. The stat mux then finds the time marking patterns and compresses them with commands to the far-end stat mux to "simulate" the correct time marking condition until told otherwise by the near end. To do this, the near end must buffer a number of characters or frames of each data stream and must provide the clocking to each connected DTE.

By clocking and buffering, the stat mux can pack, for instance, several 9.6 kbit/s streams in a single 9.6 kbit/s circuit. If each data stream becomes active at the same time, the stat mux must simulate transmission holding or slowing commands to the attached DTEs. Clearly this means that the stat mux must be programmed to know exactly all the characters and codes of each connected device. By knowing and operating on data streams based on their content, stat muxes become highly non-transparent. Another way of describing this non-transparency implies that no change may be made to the DTE or its programs without also involving the stat mux programs. Transparency thus becomes a key issue in these devices and in the newer TDMs; transparency is also a key issue in ISDN.

DATA TRANSPARENCY

Data transparency simply means the ability of a communications line, device or system to accept any length or combination of serial bits. If any pattern or combination of bits causes the systems to take any control action or to make any error, then the system is not transparent. In Chapter 5, it was noted that T1 carrier systems limit the number of consecutive "zero" bits to maintain timing. This limit restricts transparency. To further the understanding of transparency in TDMs, code and protocol transparency need to be reviewed. In Chapter 1, the concept of codes and protocols first appeared. To examine transparency, this concept needs some expansion. In a communications bit stream, information content and control content must be identified and separated. This is the function of both codes and protocols, but it is often confusing and difficult to sort out which does what. To understand transparency in digital communications, the relationships between control, information, code and protocol must be known.

In the earliest methods, such as Morse Code, protocol and code were combined and interpreted by the person receiving the information. Many dot and dash patterns were reserved to indicate actions to be taken and became the control parts of the messages. Anything which was not a reserved pattern or code was part of the information. Many users of telegraphy enciphered their messages to protect their information; control information used by the telegraph operators had to be unique. Expressed another way, dot and dash patterns had to be created which did not represent any known letter, number or punctuation mark. These special characters were reserved for use only by the telegraphers to control the communications system. This practice of reserved codes or characters survives today in start/stop and binary synchronous protocols. Usually called **byte-** or **character-oriented protocols,** each must reserve special codes to carry control information. Thus, in byte-oriented protocols the code must be known first! Without knowing the entire code, special control characters cannot be reserved.

These reserved characters or bit patterns must not inadvertently appear in the information part of a message or false control actions will be taken. This means that the information part of the message is non-transparent. That is, information bit patterns which look like control bit patterns must somehow be avoided. Whatever method is used to avoid the problem causes the incoming bit stream to be examined for false control characters. The system is thus not transparent to the incoming bit stream. In byte-oriented protocols, the usual method is the selection of yet another special control character. Sometimes called a DLE, or **data link escape,** the character is inserted ahead of any false control bytes found in the incoming stream. At the next station, a DLE means "ignore the next character for control purposes." (A little thought will reveal that a false DLE in the incoming stream may be treated like any other false control character.) One problem remains—all information bit streams must contain exactly the right number of bits to form the code's characters. So it becomes quite difficult for byte- or character-oriented protocols to achieve full transparency. Bit-oriented protocols, such as SDLC and HDLC, operate by another method and more easily reach transparency.

SDLC and HDLC, usually called bit-oriented protocols, separate control and information into different parts of their messages. By this separation, any bit pattern of any length is permitted in the information part without impact to system control or error. The different parts must, however, still be separated. This separation is controlled by the transmitting station which forms a composite of information and control. Since this **station** (or **unit** or **chip**) knows whether control or information is being sent, it provides the separations with special bit patterns usually called **flags**. The sending station controls all appearances of flags and does not permit anything else to look like a flag. At the receiving station, flags may be assumed to be legitimate and the separations may be easily found. Both SDLC and HDLC use structures called frames bounded by these flags. Figure 12.6 illustrates a typical frame showing the placement of the flags.

Flag	Address	Control	Information	Check	Flag

FIGURE 12.6. Typical SDLC or HDLC Frame Structure.

The last flag of one frame may also be the first flag of the next frame. Non-information fields in the typical frame usually follow the pattern shown above with an address byte or bytes followed by a control byte or bytes. Following the free-form information field, an error control pattern precedes the next flag. Each frame may contain an information field which can literally contain any combination of bits. That is, no pre-established code or character set is needed. All bits in the frame, subject to the protocol, may contain any combination of bits, except a flag. Flags are the only reserved bit pattern, and all separations and field definitions depend on correct flag generation and recognition. False flags, then, remain the only problem and these are prevented by the sending station.

In most bit-oriented protocols, flags take the form:

$$......0\ 1\ 1\ 1\ 1\ 1\ 1\ 0......$$

that is, six "ones" bounded by two "zeros." False flags would be any string of eight such bits not generated by the sending station. The usual method of false flag removal begins by noting whether the sending station is in flag generating mode or not. If not, the outgoing bit stream is continuously examined for five (not six) continuous "one" bits. If five "one" bits are found, the next bit to be sent is held temporarily and a "zero" is sent instead. Then, the bit which was held is sent. It does not matter if the held bit was a "one" or a "zero;" it is held and a "zero" bit substituted. By this method, the only flags received at the far-end should be real and true flags. But what about the false "zeros?" The protection of flags by **zero bit insertion,** (ZBI) has created a problem for the receiving station: **zero bit removal.**

Receiving stations must take responsibility for zero bit removal. This begins by counting continuous "one" bits. When five consecutive "ones" are found, the next two bits must be examined. A simple truth table indicates whether a flag is coming in or an inserted zero should be removed. Figure 12.7 shows the four possibilities. By including the "zero"

Last 6 Bits	Next 2 Bits	Flag ?	Decision
0 1 1 1 1 1	0 0	No	Remove Zero
0 1 1 1 1 1	0 1	No	Remove Zero
0 1 1 1 1 1	1 0	Yes	End of Frame
0 1 1 1 1 1	1 1	Error	Error Recovery

FIGURE 12.7. HDLC/SDLC Zero Bit Removal Decisions.

bit before the five consecutive "ones," the pattern may examined for both ZBI removal or the presence of a flag.

The last condition in the table should not occur in either a regular data stream or a flag—it is simply an error, and error recovery actions must be taken.

Completing the transparency of bit-oriented protocols, the final signal may be inverted for transmission over a line. The unipolar pulses on the line are called **non-return-to-zero—inverted** (NRZI). This puts "ones" on the line when "zeros" occur in the signal and vice versa. Notice that ZBI ensures a minimum number of signal "zeros" and thus a minimum number of "ones" on the NRZI line and an all "zeros" signal becomes an all "ones" pattern. Both cases provide a 14.3% "ones" density for all-flags patterns and a minimum 16.7% for any non-flag data.

This elegant combination of flags, ZBI and NRZI thus permits complete transparency in a data stream. Transparency, then, involves both code and protocol and some general statements can be made about how they relate. If the code must be known before setting the protocol, then transparency will be more difficult to achieve. If the protocol alone is set first and can carry both coded and non-coded information, then communications transparency comes more easily. We are now ready to examine concepts directly related to the time division multiplexing of data streams.

Multiplexing Data Streams

Now that technology and terminology have been outlined, an examination of digital multiplexing begins. Before delving into TDM detail, we need to recall why we multiplex at all. The answer lies in what may be a fundamental property of (human?) nature. Things procured in large quantities are less expensive (per unit) than things procured individually. "I can get it for you wholesale" has entered our speech and reflects underlying economic fact: bulk acquisition results in lower unit prices. As already described, multiplexing is then a method of using very high-speed (and lower unit cost) bulk facilities for lower speed circuit connections. Whether a multiplexer combines several 9.6 kbit/s circuits to a 56 kbit/s DDS circuit, or combines larger groups of lower speed circuits to T1 or T3-carriers, principles remain the same. A simple multiplexer is a serial-to-serial data converter used to obtain economies in circuit cost.

Serial-to-serial conversion oversimplifies the multiplexing of several or many individual digital streams. While it remains serial-to-serial, aggregating the many streams involves accepting each stream, buffering, speed shifting, combining, sending, receiving, de-combining, speed reducing, buffering, and delivering. In addition, each stream or TDM channel and the overall TDM process must be controlled. Compatibilities must be maintained with both connected data terminal equipment (DTE) and with the digital network. The serial-to-serial convertor potentially becomes a complex sub-system in its own right. It is that complex sub-system we now review.

Figure 12.8 outlines the major elements of digital time division multiplexers. The major elements of this diagram will occupy our focus as we detail the fundamental operations of TDMs.

Figure 12.8 shows the complete bi-directional operation of a typical TDM. As operation in both directions is usually identical, we shall trace one direction only; the reverse direction will generally conform. Later, as we discuss TDM control, several interactions between the directions will be outlined. The sections describing three basic types of TDMs will also highlight more significant differences in control and multi-directional operation.

TDM CHANNELS AND BUFFERS

We begin at the connected DTE (channel-side) and work inward toward the combining and framing of the aggregate-side digital signal. Each channel connection of a data TDM appears to the DTE (and its cable) as a normal DCE. Channel-side, the TDM provides an individual DTE/DCE connector so that no mechanical or electrical difference complicates the attachment of the DTE. TDM manufacturers offer a wide variety of DTE/DCE interfaces; many of the higher speed interfaces were described in Chapter 4. The TDM channel-side interface intends to conform with each DTE requirement whether it be EIA-232, V.35, RS-449, EIA-530 or others. Most TDM manufacturers design their equipment to make various interface adapters field-interchangeable, so that users may mix and match interfaces in the same unit over time. Whatever interface is offered or needed, it usually conforms to several DTE/DCE fundamentals.

These fundamentals imply that whatever interface is selected, an appropriate connector and a minimum set of data, timing and control signals will be accepted and generated according to the appropriate standard. Also, the signals will be digital and serial. That is, each information bit will arrive (and depart) one at a time under the control of well-understood timing and control signals. (Chapter 4 outlined the basics of these interface signals.) The TDM channel will thus appear to the attached DTE as a "modem," accepting and responding to signals as would a modem. Any differences arise after the bits enter the TDM channel. As the TDM is busy sending bits from many individual channel-side connections, incoming bits must be stored or buffered temporarily to await their turn to leave on the aggregate-side. These channel-side buffers are usually small, in the order of four to 16 bits, and operate first-in, first-out (FIFO). Among other reasons, this buffering is necessary to permit the TDM to select bits from each channel at an irregular rate.

The irregular selection rate arises from the mix of channel-side speeds that the TDM must handle. Another way to explain this irregularity is shown in Figure 12.9 on page 318.

Channel-side buffers accept a DTE's bits and hold them for combining into the aggregate-side signal. In the reverse direction, buffers also permit a smoothing in time of an irregular arrival of the channel's bits from the aggregate. Incoming bits are clocked into the buffer by the **transmit data timing signal**, and outgoing bits are clocked out by the **receive data timing signal**. This operation is identical to the operation seen by a DTE in a modem connection. The buffers, of course, add delay to the bit stream with larger buffers adding larger delay. Rarely, however, do these delays assume importance. For example, two 16-bit buffers in a 56 kbit/s channel will hold an average of eight bits each and delay the signal by less than 0.3 milliseconds. This is considered small relative to other delays experienced in

317

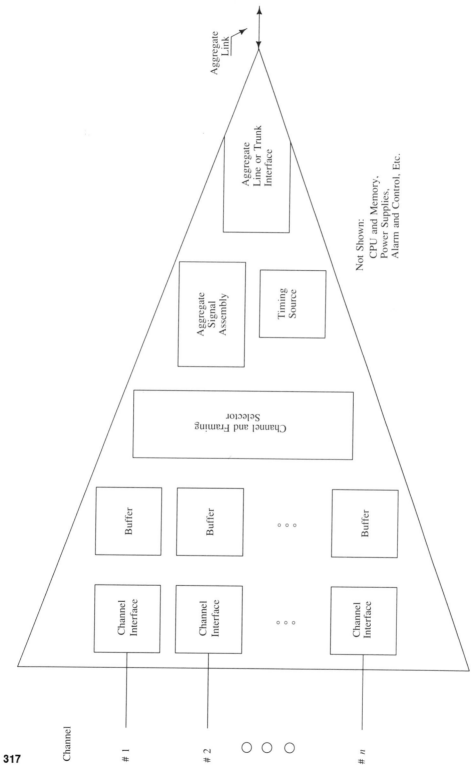

FIGURE 12.8. Major Elements of Time Division Multiplexers.

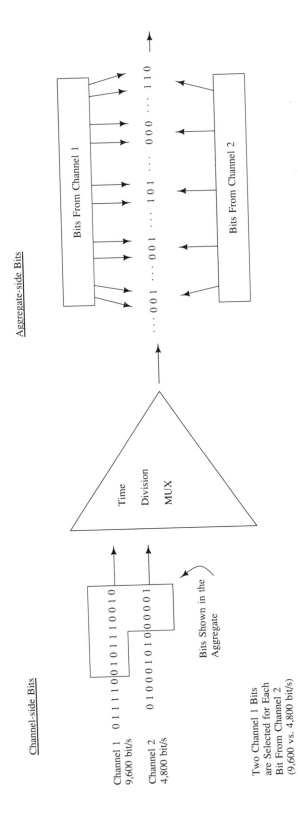

FIGURE 12.9. Channel Bit Distribution in an Aggregate-side Signal.

network transmission and computer communications control buffering. The major function, then, of channel-side buffers is to smooth out the "jerkiness" of the TDM's combining
process and permit two different clocks to work on the same bit stream. This is the essence
of serial-to-serial speed conversion. Two remaining interface items await discussion:
interface timing and interface control signals.

DTE interface timing on a TDM is most often controlled by the TDM's clock for
fairly obvious reasons. If a TDM is to control many individual channels, it should control
the rate of bit arrival and departure. If outside clock sources were used, channel-side buffers
might over or underflow. That is, even a small timing rate difference would eventually
accumulate to cause bit loss. Most TDM manufacturers require that channel-side timing be
taken from the TDM; where external timing must be used, special types of channel-side
electronics are offered to accommodate the possible time differences. These special electronics usually operate "isochronously" using bit-stuffing techniques similar to those
described for T-Carriers in Chapter 5 under North American Hierarchy Multiplexing. As
most DTE units accept clocking from the TDM channel, this more complex process is
rarely used. Channel-side interface control signal handling is not quite as simple.

TDM CHANNEL INTERFACE CONTROL SIGNALS

As described in Chapter 4, control signals in digital interfaces come from an analog
era and cause some confusion in a digital world. To alleviate this confusion, TDM
manufacturers offer several ways for handling these control signals. Some ways, however,
may cause additional confusion in their own way unless both sides of the interface are well
understood. Chapter 4 describes some adaptations for various interfaces and some methods
to "integrate" interfaces. These methods become particularly important in TDM interfaces
and require a firm and complete understanding of not only the TDM and its channel, but
also the connected DTE. Where data and timing signals may be integrated relatively
quickly, control signals may need significant study to integrate properly. This is due
primarily to the differing behavior of TDMs from their analog modem predecessors. An
example may help explain the problem.

Most computer communications controllers are designed to operate with modems
and analog communications facilities; indeed, most communications are probably still
running on analog local loops. Most TDMs are designed under the assumption that control
signals should appear "as if" they came from modems and analog facilities. The design
assumptions made when only analog modems are considered may cause difficulties in a
pure digital world. Our example concerns the behavior of two control signals and how they
may differ in two worlds. The two are **clear to send** (CTS) and **carrier detect** (CD). The
original function of these signals may be reviewed in Chapter 4, but in an analog modem,
these signals may reasonably be expected to change very slowly relative to data speeds. A
computer communications controller may assume that any unexpected change in these
signals reflects a significant problem in the communications path. So far, there is no
problem.

If the TDM is set to pass one or both of these control signals between TDM units over
the high-speed aggregate, a problem may arise. Analog communications facilities rarely
experience error bursts which interrupt the control signals; interruptions signify serious
troubles. The communications controller expect to take actions, such as shutting down lines
and notifying operators, when this occurs. In high-speed digital facilities, however, short
error bursts may be more frequent. If these digital error bursts interrupt CTS or CD even for

milliseconds, the communications controller may begin shut-down actions just as the digital line itself recovers. When the operator looks to correct the problem, no problem will be found, yet the non-problem may recur several times each day.

Preventing this complex type of interface interaction requires a thorough understanding of each unit in a communications chain. Another alternative involves setting a TDM or a DTE to "defeat" the action of many control signals. This also contains risks to diagnostic software and equipment which does not expect the "defeated" signals to be lying. As more and more complex equipment and software is interfaced, the problems may become even more severe. As an example, Figure 12.10 shows one possible way of setting (or strapping) control signals at the TDM channel-side connection.

This example should be used only to illustrate one method of handling control signals at an interface. Suggestions and corrections recommended by vendors involved should be solicited. While the authors cannot recommend any easy fixes, we can suggest that the methods of interface integration outlined in Chapter 4 be used as a guide.

Moving now from channel-side buffers and connections, the combining process of the TDM comes into view. Combining bits from many channels becomes useful only if the bits can be found again. Combining bits into recognizable patterns is the function of TDM framing and frame methods.

TDM FRAMING METHODS

A TDM frame is not unlike an SDLC or HDLC frame. Synchronous data link frames are defined by beginning and ending flag characters which contain exclusive bit patterns. TDM framing is made somewhat more complex by the distribution of the bits in "flag" pattern across the frame. As in synchronous data links, framing allows definition of sub-fields within the frame. In TDMs, framing sets borders used to locate channel bits or bytes. The key to TDM framing is frame alignment. Frame alignment simply means setting borders for an outgoing group (or frame) of channel bits and finding the borders again at the receiving end. Alignment is accomplished by adding a pattern of bits to the combined channel bits and locating those patterning bits in such a way as to form definitive, repeating and non-ambiguous borders. Once the rules for locating the framing bits are set, the receiving end uses one of several techniques to find the framing bit pattern.

Once the receiving TDM finds the framing bit pattern, channel bits may be easily located and distributed to their channels without risk of error. But finding a distributed frame pattern in a fast moving serial bit stream becomes a complex process. If transparency is permitted in the channels, then any combination of bits may appear in the aggregate bit stream. Accidental copies of a real frame pattern may appear to be the true frame border. Errors in locating framing patterns may cause channel bits to be de-combined to the wrong channels with resulting significant data errors. Framing bit pattern generating and locating thus becomes the magic by which serial channel bit streams can be combined into aggregates and then sorted out again to their individual (and correct) channels.

Early frame bit patterns were developed for the D-type telephone voice channel banks; these patterns remain the most commonly used today. As outlined earlier in the book, the D4 framing pattern contained in the 193rd bit position of each 193-bit frame has become a de-facto standard in North America. Data TDMs developed later by manufacturers experienced in analog modem and statistical multiplexers used more complicated framing patterns which were not compatible with D4 methods. The process now seems to be converging on a new variant of the D4 pattern called **extended superframe format**

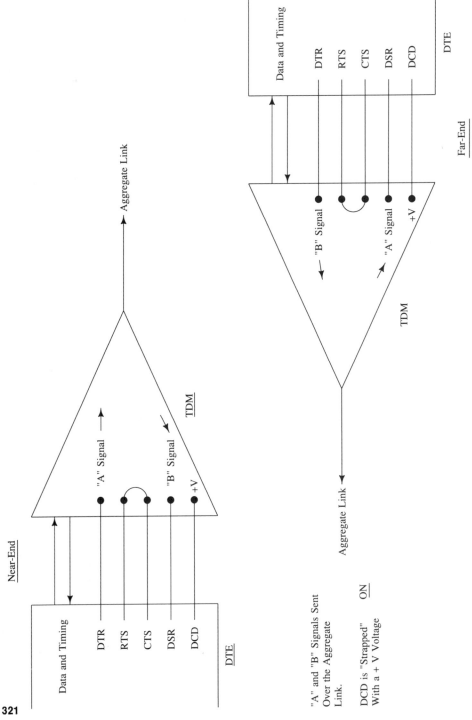

FIGURE 12.10. Example DTE/DCE Control Signal Strapping.

(ESF). The descriptions of ESF in Chapter 5 will not be repeated here, but ESF has provided a new method of frame alignment and that will be covered in the paragraphs which follow. First, we must understand the D4 framing concepts and methods used to locate or align the D4 frame on receipt at a far-end TDM.

Figure 12.11 shows the D4 frame pattern in a different manner from its portrayal in Chapter 5. In Chapter 5, the location of the 24 channels occupied our attention; here, the framing pattern is of greatest interest.

In Figure 12.11, notice the vertical pattern of bits at the right side of the block. This pattern,

$$1\ 0\ 0\ 0\ 1\ 1\ 0\ 1\ 1\ 1\ 0\ 0$$

represents the repeating framing (or **F bit**) pattern of all D4 framed devices. The very first AT&T digital channel band, the D1, used only alternating "ones" and "zeros" in the 193rd position, and this alternating pattern remains in the odd-numbered bits shown above. As some analog signals could also cause alternating patterns, framing was changed to the D2 type pattern. This D2 pattern remains unchanged today, but is usually called D3 or D4 after more modern channel banks. We will continue to use D4 for consistency. Individual F bits serve two functions, alternately locating frame borders and finding multiframes within the superframe.

Superframes, defined as 12 contiguous frames, were needed as telephone signaling

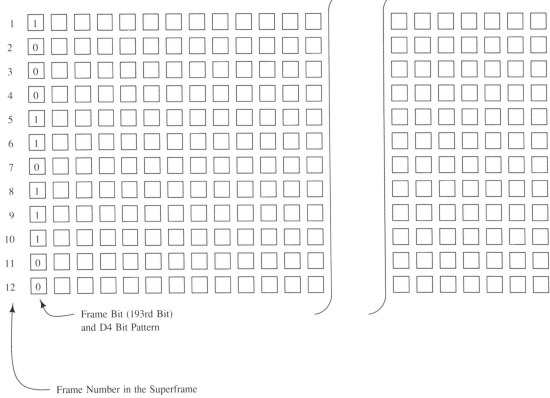

Frame Bit (193rd Bit)
and D4 Bit Pattern

Frame Number in the Superframe

FIGURE 12.11. D4 Channel Bank TDM Framing Bit Pattern

(on-hook, off-hook, and so on) information was carried by "robbing" the least significant information bits in the sixth and twelfth frames within the superframe. While this signaling information is still in common use, the identification of individual F bits has largely disappeared. The pattern shown in Figure 12.11 remains the consistent and fixed pattern for the 12 frames which make up the D4 superframe. The aggregating and sending TDM places these specific bits at the 193rd bit location of each frame for 12 frames and then begins again. No variations are permitted, as this is the only pattern available for use by the transmission network or receiving TDM to locate the individual channel bits or bytes. Placing the framing bit pattern is easier than finding it again in the network or at the receiving end.

Finding the frame pattern again is complicated by two factors: false frame patterns and transmission bit errors. We will outline the behavior of three different methods in the presence of both false patterns and bit errors. For the sake of simplicity, we will use the term **reframe** to describe the process of finding and verifying the real framing pattern. Reframing is the action to re-acquire the frame pattern when it has been lost for any reason, including the first ever acquisition of newly installed equipment. Shortly, we will describe the latest reframe method based on extended superframe format (ESF). First, the older serial and parallel methods are reviewed to appreciate the advantages of ESF reframing.

Serial reframe methods date back to the first channel banks used in early T1 carrier systems. The original D1 channel bank used an alternating "ones" and "zeros" frame pattern. Locating the frame pattern meant locking onto an arbitrary bit, counting forward 193 bits and examining the new bit. If the original bit was a "one" and the new bit was a "zero," the position was held and each new 193rd bit was tested for opposite value. If the alternating pattern continued after many repetitions, then the frame was considered found. If the pattern did not continue then the search position was advanced one bit and the process begun again. It was quickly discovered that certain digitized analog tones produced regularly alternating bits and caused **false framing.** The framing pattern was changed to D2 (older channel banks were converted and called D1D) and the frame pattern shown above was adopted. Now, the reframe mechanism looked for the pattern in the 193rd bit position; if it was not located, the mechanism shifted one bit ahead and looked again. This is an inexpensive and relatively easy reframe technique, but suffers from long reframe times.

This method of trying one bit, waiting for groups of 193 bits and testing the pattern is called serial reframing. The pattern would have to repeat at least three times, and preferably more, to assure that a real frame pattern had been found. Conceivably, it could take $193 \times 12 \times 3 \times 192$ (wrong positions) or over 1.3 million bits to locate and lock onto the frame pattern. At 1.544 Mbit/s, this amounts to 860 milliseconds. While this is a worst case, half of the number results in over 400 milliseconds as a nominal reframe time. Decisions now had to made about the loss of frame due to bit errors in the frame pattern.

After a frame pattern is located, it must be continuously verified to assure the proper location of channel information. If an error occurs in the frame pattern only once or twice (less than the number chosen to consider a frame found), then no action is taken. If the pattern fails a third time, then loss of frame must be declared and the reframe process must be started anew. As the framing pattern only uses one in every 193 bits, the error rate must be quite high for this to become necessary. Bursts of errors lasting more than three frames will, of course, also trigger reframing. The serial method is inexpensive due to a small amount of required electronics, but the method is the slowest to reframe. It is robust in tolerating high random bit error rates as several successive patterns must fail to lose frame and only one in 193 bits is used to form and locate the frame. If greater reframe speed is at issue, then the parallel method may be needed.

Parallel reframing consumes additional storage electronics by holding manÿ continuous frames in a parallel structure or matrix. The matrix is 193 bits wide and at least one frame deep. Electronic circuitry continually examines all 193 possible frame pattern positions and rejects all those not matching the required framing pattern. If no patterns match, the matrix may be shifted down one row and checked again. The checking may be done with high-speed electronics to scan all matrix columns and quickly reject columns not matching the framing pattern. As scanning happens quickly after the matrix is filled, the frame may be found in no more than $193 \times 12 \times 12$ or 27,792 bits. While scanning will usually take less than this maximum, parallel frame detection operates much faster than serial reframing. Even in the presence of bit errors, average reframe times will not usually exceed several frame times or about 10 milliseconds (193 bits $\times$ 12 $\times$ 6 divided by 1,544,000 bit/s). While parallel reframing is underway, however, channel assignments may not be made. The old framing reference is usually discarded when reframe begins. This may change with the advent of extended superframe format (ESF) framing and reframing.

ESF framing, described already in Chapter 5, extends the frame from 12 to 24 groups of 193 bits. In the extended pattern of 24 bits, six are used for actual framing, six for checking the validity of all the bits and 12 to form an independent channel for maintenance communications. While only six bits now form the frame pattern,

$$\ldots 0\ 0\ 1\ 0\ 1\ 1 \ldots$$

the validity checking (called CRC-6) allows the receiving electronics to check for bit errors and thus verify the frame. Parallel reframing may now be verified as the CRC-6 comes in for the preceding frame. The CRC-6 checks the entire frame including the frame pattern bits; correctness in the pattern is virtually assured. As the extended superframe now contains 24 frames, reframe time can be reduced to a (verified) 193 bits $\times 24 \times 2$ or 9,264 bits. This calculates to about six milliseconds, assuming that the CRC-6 checks correctly. As the CRC-6 checks all the bits in the frame, however, bit errors on the line may make reframe times longer than parallel methods, as any frame or non-frame bit error will cause failure of the cyclic redundancy check. Once reframe has been established, however, bits may continue to be assigned to their channels while reframe is attempted. Only when a reasonable number of superframes have failed CRC-6, is a loss of frame declared.

How reframing is actually accomplished in a particular unit is, of course, determined by the designer and manufacturer of the equipment. As the choice involves reframe time, electronics cost and robustness to bit errors, the choice is complex. This brief description of reframe methods does not suggest selection of equipment based on method, but is intended to help users understand how the units work. Also, the examples above concern only D4 or ESF framed serial T1 bit streams. Other proprietary methods, used in T1 data multiplexers and video codecs, will usually follow the concepts described here. With the serial bit stream now received and oriented by its frame pattern, one additional choice in multiplexing will complete our terminology map of time division multiplexing. That choice concerns how the original bits are distributed and recovered within the frames. Bit distribution within the frame is often called **channelization.**

TDM T1 CHANNELIZATION TYPES

Combination, transmission and recovery of information bits forms the main purpose of multiplexing. Channelization defines the distribution of these information bits within the transmission or aggregate frame. The orientations were earlier termed bit or byte multiplexing, depending on whether channel-side information bits are kept in groups (or bytes) during aggregate side transmission or are distributed in some other fashion bit-by-bit across the aggregate frame. The generic terms—bit- and byte-oriented multiplexing—help to define channelization differences, but do little to explain how channelization works. We prefer now to outline bit orientation by following two historic multiplexing paths, that of digital voice and that of the early data TDMs.

Using this approach, channelization will be easier to explain and understand as only two kinds of distribution techniques exist for our consideration. One kind, deriving from the historic path of digital voice, aligns the bits in eight-bit groups. The other kind, coming from the path of early data TDMs, usually does not. The first kind maintains an eight-bit or byte orientation begun in voice channel bank technology and AT&T's DATAPHONE® Digital Service. This type of bit alignment often goes by the name D4 channelization. D4-type channelization includes, of course, the CCITT and CEPT organizations of 30 channels within the first level of multiplexing. While not all byte multiplexing is exactly the same, there remains a strong influence of voice D4 channel organization. In most cases, D4 channelized units from different manufacturers maintain compatibility with each other.

The other non-D4 method is just that—not D4. By that we mean any proprietary channelization adopted by a single manufacturer. This is not a criticism of manufacturers who select non-D4 channelization. Indeed, there are significant advantages in efficiency and flexibility in non-D4 methods. However, at the time of this writing we know of no multi-manufacturer standards in T1 channelization other than the D4 (or CEPT) type. For this reason, we call these non-D4 methods—proprietary channelizations. As they are usually proprietary to individual manufacturers, little is available on their detailed makeup. We understand, however, that many involve bit oriented or non-byte oriented multiplexing. That is, bits originating from a single lower speed data, voice or video channel distribute throughout the frame in ways other than classical D4. To further complicate understanding, many of these proprietary channelizations also use proprietary framing methods. D4 channelization has already been examined in earlier chapters. Figure 12.12 on page 326 diagrams a comparison between D4 and a conceptual proprietary channelization and framing method.

Observe in Figure 12.12 that the proprietary frame exists in addition to the D4 frame. This is done to permit the signal to pass through a tariffed and regulated T1 network requiring the use of D4 framing methods. The D4 (or ESF) frame pattern allows the proprietary signal to meet all the requirements of a T1 network and yet take advantage of the efficiencies and flexibilities of a longer frame. This longer frame can permit more than 24 data channels and allows a wide range of data channel speeds to be packed together. It also simplifies the passage of interface control signals and supervisory information used by the TDMs. Interface control signal bits and supervisory bits are distributed to the best advantage of the TDM. Channel information bits are also distributed across the TDM frame to meet the best needs of the TDM. In some advanced multiple-T1 TDMs and most network TDMs, these bit locations may be re-assigned on the fly to accommodate changing network and channel loading conditions.

Note also that unless the proprietary frame length is an exact multiple of the 193 bit D4 frame, there will be an asynchronism or drift between the two frame patterns. While this causes no problem to the TDMs, it will not permit certain compatibilities.

DACS and TDM Compatibilities

In Chapter 5, the concepts of **digital access and cross-connect systems** (DACS) were reviewed. DACS-like systems operate primarily on T1 circuits which use D4 channel-

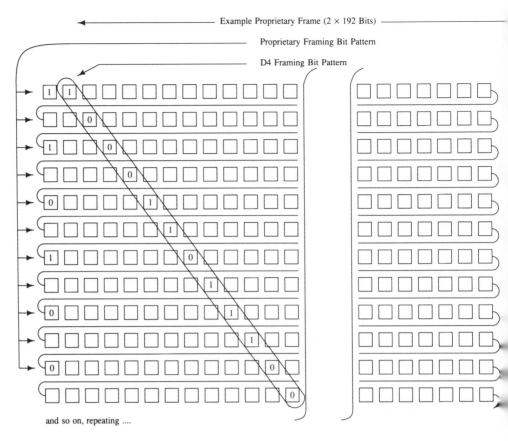

FIGURE 12.12. D4 and Proprietary Framing Comparison.

ization. Recall that DACS provide the ability to re-assign or switch 64 kbit/s eight bit channels from one T1 and place them in another channel position of another T1. The switching action is considered slow relative to electronic switching systems used in telephone networks and does not usually respond to switching signals carried in the bit stream (in-band). Special network features like AT&T's Customer Controlled Reconfiguration (CCR) use primarily DACS-type devices to permit re-assignment of channels (indirectly) from terminals located at the customers' premises. As the action of DACS-type switching is relatively slow, we will use the term re-assignment to denote the function of cross-connecting channels electronically. Other devices in high-speed digital networks also operate with T1 circuits and use D4 channelizations. Telephone switches for private (PBXs and CBXs) and public networks depend on the D4 (or ESF) framing and D4 channelization methods for inter-operability. Here the question of channelization compatibilities with TDMs arises.

If a data TDM uses D4 channelization techniques on its T1 aggregate side, each channel in the aggregate will be 64 kbit/s and the TDM will inter-operate with DACS type devices at the channel level. If, however, the data TDM uses proprietary channelization, the DACS must re-assign all 24 channels of the TDM's aggregate as a package. This will not damage the proprietary bit stream so long as a D4 framing pattern exists in the T1 stream.

The D4 frame pattern itself will be rebuilt by the DACS, but this does not damage the TDM's data stream, its proprietary framing or its channelization. The proprietary type TDM will not, however, be able to switch channels at the DACS. This compatibility either exists or does not exist between the TDM and the DACS at the TDM aggregate. Shortly, we will describe TDMs which offer DACS (or D4) compatibility on the channel side.

Discussions of the pros and cons of D4 channelization in data TDMs appear to be converging. The advent of ISDN and its 64 kbit/s channels seems to favor the use of D4 channelization. Remaining discussions now center on how to achieve the maximum efficiencies and flexibilities which proprietary channelizations gave. As ISDN approaches increasing degrees of reality and ubiquity, the 64 kbit/s channel will certainly be one of the key standards in data, as well as voice. Now it is time to look more closely at some examples of data TDM types.

TDM Generations and Capabilities

Earlier in the book, we described the origins of T-Carriers and digital channel banks used to convert analog voice signals to digital form. These channel banks were the first single-T1 time division multiplexers and were the ancestors of all TDMs. TDM concepts and terminology, already covered above, developed out of these early channel banks. When DATAPHONE® Digital Service was announced by AT&T, channel bank technology joined the data communications world and the first data TDMs were born. Until the early 1980s, TDMs emulating voice channel banks came in pairs and were the only type available. They were connected from one place to another, gaining the cost advantages of bulk high-speed carrier facilities. As the original channel banks had done, these TDMs connected only one point to another to form our simplest class of TDMs—the single-T1 TDM.

In the early 1980s, as T-Carrier use spread into private industry, needs developed beyond the simple point-to-point topologies, and another concept was borrowed from the telephone industry—**drop and insert.** A similar sounding concept, multidrop, had been in use for many years in data communications, but the two concepts differ markedly. Drop-and-insert concepts and applications will be covered more fully just ahead in the section on multiple-T1 TDMs. These TDMs joined their single-T1 forerunners as tools for data communications solutions. Multiple-T1 TDMs offered more complex network topologies, alternate paths for data and more efficient use of high-speed links, but at an added cost for more complex hardware. TDM technology was, however, just beginning its phenomenal expansion. Network TDM systems followed multiple-T1 TDMs quickly to make their own debut.

Network TDM systems built upon earlier digital telephone and transmission technology, but added a significant new dimension—intelligent (or software controlled) total network control. Developing largely out of techniques originally used in packet data networks, these **smart nodes** greatly extended the abilities of multiple-T1 units. Network TDM systems routed traffic, mixed voice, data and video, responded to load demands and managed the entire interconnected network. This latest generation of TDMs offered the greatest capabilities, but again, at an increased cost. This TDM class provides significant complexity along with its capabilities and is the most difficult to describe, understand and compare.

Clearly, these three broad groupings could have been cut along different lines.

Manufacturers constantly vie with each other to demonstrate product differences, and new features in one class reflect rapidly into newer features in all classes. We have selected this breakdown to follow our basic theme, that is, to explain "how it works." New offerings and new features on existing units spring daily from the pages of trade magazines and newspapers for all three classes. We shall not even contemplate describing individual offerings, but will attempt to outline the fundamental characteristics of each class. Hopefully, this approach will enable TDM users to understand the ranges of TDM capabilities and make informed judgments for their own environments. We begin with single-T1 TDMs.

Single-T1 TDMS

The earliest data TDMs came into service in the 1970s in military applications. By the late 1970s, time division multiplexing emerged as a way to pack many lower speed channels onto a 56 kbits/s digital data service channel. The conceptual jump to T1 came quite quickly, and by the early 1980s several manufacturers offered T1 data multiplexers. Unlike the statistical multiplexers already outlined, these TDMs offered full-time transparent data channels carved out of a higher speed digital aggregate. As industry and government users found that multiple data channels were running between two (or more) of their buildings or cities, the idea of saving line costs using T1 and TDMs became popular. Initial applications of single-T1 TDMs usually linked several large data or computing centers. These centers had installed data circuits for many applications, or had found the need to put in many low-speed lines to handle the data traffic.

When the costs of T1s and TDMs were compared to the multiple individual circuits, people in data communications saw that they could avoid significant expense by moving to TDMs. Figure 12.13 illustrates a typical installation of this type of TDM.

These early TDMs operated very like their voice predecessors, but did it in a fashion dedicated to data. As data communications had previously used modems, TDM makers made their TDM channels appear as modems at the DTE/DCE interface. From that point on, however, nearly everything operated differently.

Basic TDM Operations

Time division multiplexers operate on a relatively simple concept. Bits are accepted from outside devices (DTEs) and held briefly until their turn comes to be sent at high-speed to a far-end unit. At the far end, they are placed briefly in the proper buffer to be sent to another device (DTE). This operation may be thought of as two large rotary switches, one at each end of a high-speed line. The rotations are synchronized so that each switch is on the same contact number at the same time. Bits connected to contact number six (channel six) on one end will flow to contact six (channel six) at the other end. From the DTE's point of view, there is a permanent connection just as in a leased data circuit. The speed of the rotary switch, in our conceptual example, is fast enough so that no bits are ever lost. The TDM is most successful when the DTEs cannot tell the difference between the TDM and modems on a leased circuit.

As the early TDM manufacturers came mainly from the modem business, they did this quite well. Low-speed interfaces, such as EIA-232 and V.35 acted to the DTEs as though they were modems. Data signals at the interface acted as described in Chapter 4 and

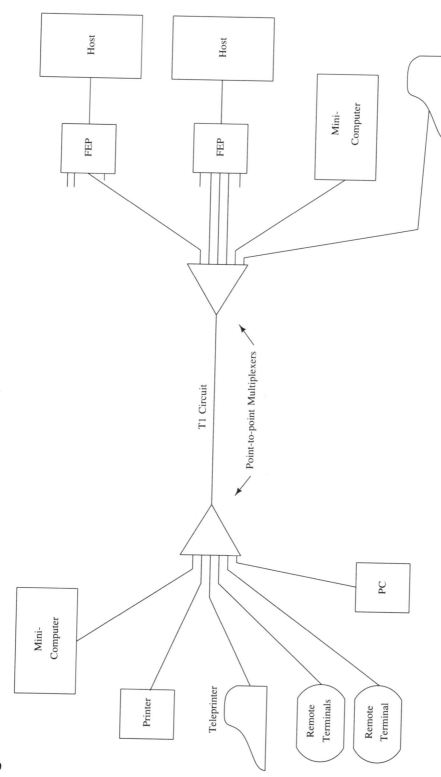

FIGURE 12.13. Typical Application of Point-to-point TDMs.

timing signals were supplied by the channel. Control signals like **carrier detect** (CD) were supplied, although no carrier in the analog sense was present. **Clear to send** (CTS) returned immediately from a **request to send** (RTS), as a full duplex channel was already open whether it was used or not. With minor exceptions, TDMs successfully connected DTE pairs which had run before on analog modems. Where interface control signals required special treatment, the TDM channel usually accommodated the needs by changing wires or straps (small moveable jumper wires used to select various options) on the individual channel cards.

The earliest TDMs followed voice channel bank practices and used individual cards for each connected data channel. The cards were assembled in a shelf or nest of cards along with **common cards**, again following channel bank practice. The common cards provided the electronics needed to sample each channel and combine the bits into the aggregate. Common cards also interfaced with the T1 carrier (actually with a T1 channel service unit). Several nests or shelves of cards were combined in either open frames, following telephone practices, or closed racks following electronic equipment practices. This use of a single channel card for a single data channel has eroded as **large scale integration's** (LSI) reduced costs have forced manufacturers to combine several channels on a single electronics card. The **cards-in-nests-in-racks approach** remains as the most popular for TDM packaging. Capabilities of single-T1 TDMs reflect their early directions as straightforward replacements for modems.

Capabilities

Although a wide range of capabilities exists in different TDMs and may be found in all three classes, we will describe fundamental TDM capabilities in the single-T1 group. As network complexity increases, additional capabilities become necessities, and we will detail the more advanced features with the more complex units. This does not mean, however, that the features may not be found on the less expensive and less complex units, as simple and inexpensive cars may still contain exotic sound systems. Voice features, by way of example, will be held until after we cover network TDM systems, although simple channel banks offer many of these features.

Channel Format

Although based in concept on voice channel banks, single-T1 TDM units often derive more than 24 channels from a T1 carrier. This class of data TDM may be divided quickly into channel banks which handle data, and units which offer more than 24 data channels. The distinction will usually be based solely on whether D4 channelization is maintained. In "pure" channel bank or D4 channelized units, each channel will occupy 64 kbit/s and there will be only 24 channels present in a T1 TDM. (D4 sub-rate multiplexing will be discussed shortly). Early T1 data TDMs took advantage of the tremendous bandwidth of T-Carriers by using only enough bandwidth for each data speed and thus gaining a greater number of channels. This more efficient use of the T1 resulted, however, in units which could only "talk" to each other. Their channelization was proprietary to themselves. As discussed in the previous section, their channelization was non-D4. Non-D4 channelization offered an opportunity to pack many more data channels into the aggregate.

If 1,344,000 bit/s are available from the 1,544,000 bit/s aggregate, the number of data channels possible may be easily calculated. The second column of Figure 12.14 shows how many data channels could be packed into such a T1 carrier. The figure of 1,344,000 bit/s is used to maintain enough extra or overhead bits to maintain the "ones" bit density T1 carrier requirement detailed in Chapter 5. Some T1 TDM units using complex packing techniques permit a greater number of channels than this and still meet the "ones" density requirements of the networks. The third column shows how many channels are possible when the maximum available speed of 1,536,000 bit/s (1,544,000 minus 8,000 framing bits) is used. In some cases the numbers have been rounded down to integer values. The table indicates the large numbers of data channels possible when D4 channelization is not used.

Notice the crossover number of 24 in Figure 12.14 at 56,000 bit/s. At this data speed the channel count equals that of a voice channel bank, although the channel bank sends 64,000 bit/s of digitized voice. The difference comes, of course, from the the reserved bits for "ones" density. In digitized voice, coding techniques assure that "ones" density will always be maintained. In data communications, the same assurances cannot be given; long "zeros" strings often occur in data transmission. Digital data services using channel bank technology actually take the data seven bits at a time and add an eighth bit to both indicate a data channel and meet the density needs of the network. Efficiency on the aggregate, however, is the major reason for departing from a standard D4 channel arrangement.

The numbers for speeds below 56,000 bit/s in Figure 12.14 clearly indicate the efficiencies possible with simple single-T1 TDMs which do not adhere to D4 channelization. Most data TDMs from the early 1980s used various techniques to pack the highest number of data channels into a T1. Some used bit-oriented approaches and some used byte-oriented techniques, but almost all of the "original" data TDMs used proprietary channelization methods. Each manufacturer developed a unique channelization, preventing data TDMs from different makers from being connected on the aggregate side.

Where TDMs followed D4 channelization, units from different manufacturers could sometimes be inter-connected over the aggregate. This was most often the case when D4-type channel banks added dataport cards to become data TDMs. Here the 24 available DS-0 channels followed the D4 channelization format for at least 56 kbit/s speeds. For higher speeds, 64 kbit/s DS-0 channels were **bundled** offering speeds in integral multiples

Data Channel Speed in bits per second	Maximum # of Channels at 1. 344 Mbit/s	Maximum No. of Channels at 1. 536 Mbit/s
2,400	560	640
4,800	280	320
9,600	140	160
19,200	70	80
56,000	24	27
128,000	10	12
256,000	5	6

FIGURE 12.14. Maximum Number of Data Channels in a T1 Carrier.

of 64 kbit/s, such as 128 kbit/s, 256 kbit/s or 768 kbit/s. For speeds below 56 kbit/s several methods of **sub-rate** multiplexing evolved. This remains an area for confusion by both users and manufacturers.

Standards now evolving will eventually permit limited interchange of sub-rate data speeds between multiplexers. Until each user can be assured by each manufacturer that complete compatibility to accepted standards exists, the rule for TDM selection remains the same as the old rule for analog modems: when in doubt, stay with the same maker and model when interconnecting. Mix units only after thorough testing and even then at your own peril. Problems arising after installation between units of different manufacturers lead to finger-pointing with the user as the only arbiter. More about coping with multivendor installations will be discussed in Chapter 13.

TDM Timing

Chapter 7 dealt extensively with timing and that material need not be repeated here, but several timing topics arise only because of TDMs and these require a few words of explanation. First, a source for timing the TDM units must be found. In Chapter 5, it was noted that few carrier T1s bring timing with them. Where timing comes with the T-Carrier, as in the case where the carrier passes the T1s through a DACS, the T1s will time the TDMs. The timing source most often used for single-T1 TDMs is the internal clock of one of the TDMs, which is designated the timing master. The other unit accepts timing from the incoming T1 aggregate and loop times. As a review, loop timing means accepting clock from the aggregate carrier signal and using it as the local source for both the outgoing aggregate signal timing and local channel timing. It is important to note that TDMs generally insist on being the timing source for all connected channel-side channels.

This requirement comes into being in the nature of time division multiplexing. As channel bits are selected to be sent over the high-speed aggregate, they must be delivered to the TDM channel at precisely the correct rate. That rate must be in exact frequency or bit rate synchronism with the TDM's channel bit selecting electronics, or bits will be lost. Although features exist on some TDMs to take channel data at approximately the correct rate, these "isochronous" channels usually cost more and use a greater than expected share of overall bandwidth. As most DTE devices willingly accept TDM (or modem) timing, this TDM times everything requirement causes few problems. The more complex question becomes deciding on a choice of stable clock for the master TDM.

If only two TDMs connect in an isolated point-to-point application, the internal clock of one will do the job nicely. (Multiple-T1 TDMs and network TDM systems need more complex timing arrangements and these will be covered shortly in the sections describing those unit types.) One situation complicates timing for all types of TDMs. When already clocked data signals connect to a TDM's channels, TDM system timing must be made to agree with the already clocked signal. This happens when **digital data service** (DDS) tail circuit signals must connect to a TDM's channels.

TDM Tail Circuits

Tail circuits occur when a data circuit aggregated on a TDM link must terminate somewhere other than at one of the TDMs. Such a circuit must be continued from the TDM location to its final termination with either analog modems or digital data services. With analog modems, timing is supplied to the modem at the TDM end of the tail circuit, and that TDM-derived timing continues to the circuit's remote termination. This works very well for analog tail circuits running at 9.6 kbit/s and below. For higher speed circuits where the digital media and digital **data service units** (DSU) exist outside a carrier's network, the DSUs may also be timed from the TDM. Where, however, the tail circuit must pass through a carrier's DDS network, either the circuit must connect isochronously through the TDMs, or the tail must time the TDM network.

This need to let the tail time the entire TDM network results from the synchronous nature of time division. Individual channel buffers will permit short-term variations in clocks but cannot tolerate fundamental differences in clock rates. As an example, if a 56 kbit/s channel's buffer is eight bits, then a clock difference of only 0.00007 bit/s will cause the buffer to over- or under-flow every second. Clearly the timing of the tail and the TDM must somehow be locked together. In most TDMs, timing may be derived from an internal clock, from aggregate loop timing or from an external source. Most often this external source will be capable of accepting 56 kbit/s to handle just this DDS tail circuit problem. The timing may arrive as a working 56 kbit/s data circuit or as an independent circuit used only to carry timing. In critical network hubs, several diverse timing signals may be brought in to maintain clocking if one should fail. Many TDMs (or station clocks) will offer hardware or software fallback methods to select a second (or third) clock source, should the primary fail.

Software Monitoring

While software control of TDM units is usually reserved for multiple-T1 TDMs and network TDM systems, some single-T1 TDMs offer software monitoring of key alarms and channel parameters. This monitor capability may be offered through an EIA-232 port to which a simple ASCII terminal may be connected. The port may also be used with dial-up modems to permit remote inquiry of the alarms and parameters. This monitor capability permits more rapid diagnosis of circuit or unit faults in the TDM. If ASCII terminals are connected at both ends of a single-T1 TDM system, the terminals may also be used to communicate between operators at the end points. This is the digital equivalent of a telephone function called the **order-wire**. Logging printers or personal computers can add historical record keeping or more complete analysis of alarms from the monitor ports of the single-T1 TDMs.

Single-T1 TDMs function mainly as cost reducers by aggregating many circuits onto lower unit cost bulk facilities such as T1 carriers. These TDMs do not differ in function greatly from groups of modems or DSUs, although software monitoring and redundancy of key components may add to overall reliability. However, with many circuits riding a single high-speed carrier, failure of the carrier can bring down many applications. If more than one T1 could connect to a TDM, new topologies could compensate for a single failing T1. By the mid-1980s, wide availability and dropping costs for T1s, generated another class of data TDMs—the multiple-T1 TDM.

Multiple-T1 TDMS

The D4 voice channel bank was probably the first multiple T1 TDM, but it did not take true advantage of all the possibilities. The D4 channel bank could be configured to use two T1s to handle 48 DS-0 voice channels (or data ports), but each channel was fixed to an individual T1. In this section we will go beyond that concept and investigate the multiple-T1 TDM as a device which could re-route channels when single T1 failures occurred. Early multiple-T1 TDMs supported between two and six T1 aggregates and should not be confused with later units which support more than ten T1s. These later units will be described just ahead in this chapter under network TDM systems. This distinction between multiple-T1 TDMs and network TDM systems has been done to highlight the evolution of TDM features and capabilities.

Two of the new data communications concepts which came together in the early multiple-T1 TDMs were **automatic alternate routing** (AAR) and **drop and insert** (D/I). Automatic alternate routing permits software in a TDM to re-assign bandwidth in an operating T1 link to compensate for a failing T1 link. Another way of looking at AAR is the re-connection of data channels from broken T1 links to working T1 links. Both concepts were borrowed from the telephone industry, but were adapted to data communications in multiple-T1 TDMs. We will shortly examine AAR more closely, but first we need to explain the concepts of drop and insert.

Drop and Insert

In its simplest form, drop and insert breaks a multichannel carrier at some point, removes (drops) some channels and places (inserts) some new channels on the carrier in place of the removed ones. Figure 12.15 shows this simple example in graphic form. Note that some channels go all the way from station A to station C, while some drop at B and some are inserted at B. Most often, one of two common methods are used to accomplish the D/I of channels. The first method demultiplexes all channels and makes them available for the drop. Those not actually dropped are combined with those to be inserted and are then remultiplexed to a new carrier. This method, while simple, is more expensive as all channels must be demultiplexed and remultiplexed.

A second, more complex, method selects from the carrier bit stream only those bits belonging to the channels to be dropped. Demultiplexing then operates only on those channel bits. Similarly, multiplexing occurs only for inserted channels; their bits are placed in the proper position on the carrier. Clearly, the bit positions must be known and easy to find, extract and replace. Channels passing directly through the TDM are not affected, except for buffer delay.

In Figure 12.15, two T1 lines exit the TDM as aggregates; this is perhaps the simplest of the multiple-T1 TDMs. As additional T1s are added to the aggregate side of the TDM, many more configurations become possible. These configurations offer more than just additional places to be added to a network of T1s for data communications. They permit new ways of handling individual failure of units and inter-unit linkages.

When the first multiple-T1 TDMs came to market, they brought more than just additional aggregates; they brought micro-processors and software control. Where earlier single-T1 TDMs had offered software monitoring of alarms and parameters, the multiple-T1 TDMs offered software control of parameters and channel routing. This was perhaps the most significant contribution of this class of TDM: software control and automatic alternate routing. Analog technology had required patch panels and multiple modems to accomplish the same function using operator intervention. Now the TDM itself had become smart enough to sense T1 link failure and re-route data traffic over still operating links. To fulfill this promise, point-to-point topologies gave way to network topologies of rings, meshes, and stars.

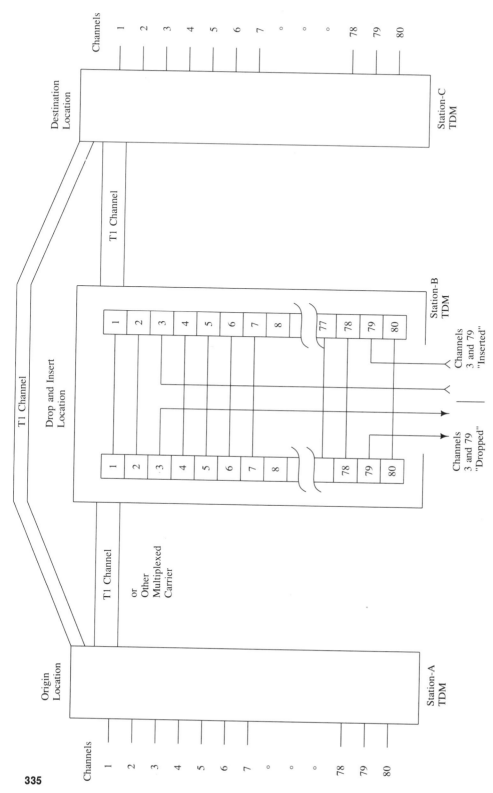

FIGURE 12.15. TDM Drop and Insert Example.

New Topologies

To understand the re-routing capabilities of the multiple-T1 TDMs, examples of network topologies must be presented. A significant branch of network study covers the intricate mathematics of network topology. We can present only the barest outlines of this here, but do so to highlight this important function of multiple-T1 TDMs. Figure 12.16 depicts the simplest form of several typical network topologies. Shown are the fundamental ring or loop configuration, the star or hub and the mesh. For each of these simple configurations, multiple-T1 TDMs offer possible alternate routing capabilities. In terms of robustness to link or unit failure, the mesh is strongest, followed by the ring. The star offers routes to alternate locations or end points but suffers from exposure at the hub. If the hub fails, the entire network fails.

The ring or loop remains operational if a single link or unit fails; traffic may be re-routed backwards around the loop avoiding the broken section or unit. A second failure, however, isolates the ring into two separate networks. Here the mesh becomes most resistant to multiple failures. As can be seen from Figure 12.16, single link failures do not isolate any unit, and single-unit failures, as in the ring, isolate only the failed unit. Multiple-link failures at worst isolate only single units, and multiple-unit failures do not necessarily break the network into smaller units. This assumes, of course, that the mesh network is "fully meshed," that is, all units (or **nodes**) connect in all possible ways to all other nodes. In reality, fully meshed networks are rare as their link costs become prohibitive. Partially meshed nodes in a mesh network, however, offer more alternate routes in the face of multiple link failures than ring networks, and most multiple-T1 TDMs offer the ability to operate in partially meshed networks. The additional costs of the multiple-T1 TDMs (compared to single-T1 TDMs) justify in their new capabilities, particularly, **automatic alternate routing.**

Automatic Alternate Routing

The most exciting new capability of multiple-T1 TDMs, at their initial announcement, was their ability to automatically re-route data channels from failed T1 links to good T1 links. There is, as always, a price for a new capability, and the price is lost channels. If two T1s can carry just so many channels when both are working, then one T1 can carry half as many when it is alone. The mechanism to decide which channels are not carried following a link failure is usually a priority scheme. Before any failures occur, all channels are assigned (by the user) one or more priority levels. If a link fails, those channels with the highest priority are assigned to the remaining link or links. Some units will interrupt existing traffic on the remaining links, and some will not. Some will interrupt all traffic and replace it with the highest priorities. Most often, these options can be set by the user at installation time through the software control system. A more comprehensive description of AAR will be found in the next section on network TDM systems.

Software Control

The most common feature of the multiple-T1 TDMs, as they became available in the mid-1980s, was their software control system. Almost without exception, multiple-T1 TDMs introduced in this period offered a software support and control system. In most units, the system was imbedded in micro-processors on-board the TDM unit with access

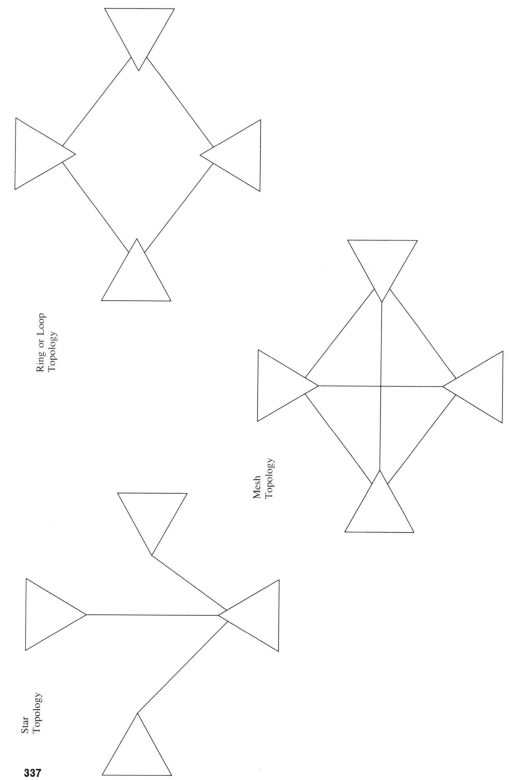

Ring or Loop
Topology

Mesh
Topology

Star
Topology

FIGURE 12.16. Example Topologies with Multiple-T1 TDMs.

through one or more EIA-232 ports. Some units also offered external control systems based on personal computers which communicated with the on-board micro-processors. The external systems were usually not required, but gave optional enhancements providing ease-of-use functions. Since the basic control of the TDM units came through commands issued at the EIA-232 interface, the optional external personal computers enhanced the system by giving sequences of commands. As many of the early on-board micro-processors were storage limited, the command sequences were somewhat terse. The external computers converted more easily understood English commands and choices from menus displayed on screens to the compact command language required by the TDMs.

Whether user-friendly or not, the software control offered by these multiple-T1 TDM units allowed users to accomplish tasks not previously possible. Channel routing could be specified from a card (or a port on a card) through a particular T1 to another unit or node in a remote city and from there onto a final destination. If the links connecting this primary path failed, an alternate route could be pre-specified to all the units in the system. This capability could be put in place for any or all data circuits, and priorities could be assigned to order the re-establishment of traffic after a failure. In multiple node systems, the control software could be accessed from any node and control could be exercised over any node. This degree of control from any to any has been termed **control visibility**.

Control Visibility

As more and more TDMs offered software control, questions of control visibility began to be asked. Control visibility meant two things to those who asked: what could be seen (and controlled) from one unit in the network of multiple-T1 TDMs, and what could be controlled (or monitored) from any point in the network. The first question involved the complexity of performing a control action on a distant node from an EIA-232 connected ASCII terminal or personal computer attached to a local unit. If distant remote control were possible, was the process (and the number of instructions or keystrokes) friendly or hostile? If not possible, what was needed to access the distant node? If a dial-up modem was provided at the distant node, what protection against unauthorized persons (hackers) was offered? Most of the multiple-T1 TDMs now offer comprehensive control consoles from any point in the network, but this greater simplicity came only after experience was gained in the practical use of the equipment and the software in real production situations. The second question of visibility varied to some degree between manufacturers.

Control of parameters in the TDM network of units was a relatively new offering in the mid-1980s. Previous modem systems had offered this type of remote control and diagnostic capability only with the addition of extra equipment which surrounded each node like a pair of electronic earmuffs. Now the multiple-T1 TDMs offered these functions plus several new ones to aid the user in monitoring the health and diagnosing the faults of the system. The older functions which carried through into the newer TDM types were the ability to loopback a circuit anywhere in the TDM network. This permitted operators to insert known test signals on possibly failing channel circuits and have the known data returned to them for analysis via the loopback at a distant circuit end. Additionally, operators could query the status of interface control signal leads at the distant DTE/DCE interface. This could permit diagnoses which, with earlier technology, would require a person to go to a distant site for a visual examination of the units. Several of the most interesting new functions were again borrowed from the telephone industry.

Testing by bridging a circuit dates back to the origins of the telephone industry, and usually required physical patch panels in the data communications business. With the software control capabilities of the multiple-T1 TDMs, a circuit could be bridged (or connected to another circuit without interruption) and examined from a remote point. If circuit interruption was deemed necessary, a built-in test generator could substitute for the real data and the total circuit could be examined from a single software control point. These test and diagnostic functions offered the best of practical and functional advantages of the combination of telephone and data communications technology. The range of exotic TDMs was, however, just beginning to emerge. The multiple-T1 TDM had been on the field less than two years before the network-TDM system arrived.

Network-TDM Systems

Several years elapsed between the introduction of single-T1 TDMs and the announcement of multiple-T1 TDMs. It seemed a much shorter time until the more complex network-TDM systems appeared. While it may be argued that only a fine line now separates multiple-T1 TDMs and network-TDM systems, the authors hold that significant differences once existed. These differences have become blurred as manufacturers compete with newer units, but the original differences educated us in significant ways. At their first announcements in the mid-1980s, these network-TDM systems confronted voice/data integration in an important way. The range of new concepts and features demonstrated a bold departure from previous approaches. The new systems came, for the most part, from start-up companies rather than established data communications companies. Many of the founders of these companies came from packet network backgrounds rather than modem design, and packet network concepts enlivened their systems.

Networking Capabilities

Perhaps the boldest departure in network-TDM systems is their ability to create and manage complex transmission networks based on channel bandwidth demands from either digital voice or digital data. In rings, meshes or stars of T1s, multiple nodes or TDM units pass control and status information continuously to respond to both channel demands and T1 link availabilities. Where the earlier multiple-T1 TDMs allowed the operators or external computers to set-up node status, link connections and circuit routing, newer systems can perform these tasks and then inform the operator. To examine these capabilities, we divide the functions into transmission management and capacity management. Together, these inter-connected abilities move the control of complex networks from the operators to distributed network-TDM systems software.

Transmission Management

The key justification for using T1 TDMs does not change with the arrival of network-TDM systems; it remains the effective use of lower unit cost bulk facilities. What network systems bring to the table is an even more efficient management of the bulk transmission facilities. In most network TDM systems, the T1 between nodes can be characterized by a number of parameters. Those parameters then become input to the capacity management process to be described next. Typical transmission parameters specified at installation time are whether a T1 link passes over terrestrial or satellite media, and whether link encryption is present. Satellite circuits possess an inherently greater end-to-end delay than terrestrial circuits and may be considered less suitable for interactive terminal sessions. On the other side, their usually very low error rate makes them more suitable for large block-size bulk data transmission. The encryption parameter is needed by some users to assure that highly sensitive voice or data traffic never passes "in the clear." In some TDMs, a relative T1 link "cost" number can be assigned to direct capacity management software to assure the most effective use of these higher actual cost links. Another parameter often used is a maximum node count for a circuit, preventing a circuit from traversing too many nodes.

In addition to installation-set parameters, transmission management usually includes link performance measurements which allow the TDM to assess the health of a particular link and its ability to handle traffic. Along with unit specific measurements, industry standard alarms and signals are received and, where necessary, generated by transmission management. The pattern of connection or network topology of links between nodes forms another parameter generated or used by capacity management.

Capacity Management

Once a TDM begins managing link or aggregate capacity, the line between statistical multiplexers and time division multiplexers blurs. Capacity management permits a TDM's control programs to "over-book" a particular link. When traffic demands build, priority schemes designate who will pass and who will wait. If alternate routes exist for denied traffic, all traffic will be handled; if no other routes exist, traffic will wait until the link can support the offered load. We have entered the domain of statistics; network-TDM systems decide via priority parameters or through other methods which offered traffic will be given a place on the link between TDMs. When multiple aggregates exist between network nodes, the TDM control system may route lower priority traffic over less desirable routes. Less desirable may mean complex routing through multiple nodes or via links which may contain more delay or possess lower transmission quality. Most often in TDM data communications, circuits have been held open whether they are in use or not. With capacity management, control signals such as **request to send** (RTS) will be used to actually request bandwidth on the managed link. If the link is too full to handle the offered traffic, **clear to send** (CTS) is not returned. When other data traffic lowers RTS or when a voice circuit "hangs up," link capacity is made available to the requesting circuit. This method of operation contains implications to data communication software outside the TDM.

Communication software designed to expect rapid (milliseconds) return of CTS from an RTS request may declare a circuit out of service if the wait for CTS becomes too long. Joint planning of both the network-TDM systems parameters and front-end software parameters is mandatory for many capacity management systems to work well in data communications applications. In mixed data/voice applications, priority may be given to data circuit requests, and voice requests receive either alternate routes or network all-trunks-busy (fast-busy) signals. These overload scenarios will generally occur only at peak traffic hours and these peaks vary depending upon the nature of the underlying business. Another benefit to the business from capacity management occurs during and after link failures.

Link failures act to combine the capabilities of transmission management and capacity management. In earlier multiple-T1 TDMs, **automatic alternate routing** (AAR) caused higher priority traffic to be rerouted over remaining good links. Some earlier units caused interruptions to all traffic while circuits were re-built on all affected links. In some cases, this meant that functioning circuits were broken and then re-established as part of AAR from failed links. Network-TDM systems combine transmission management to detect link failures and capacity management to re-route circuits. This combination, along with more advanced TDM software, permits the use of available bandwidth to reestablish circuits without breaking existing operational circuits. Remaining traffic from the broken link may then displace lower priority traffic, such as voice, by either breaking that traffic or waiting for capacity.

The displacement of existing, working circuits raises new complexities which, while new to data communications, have been studied for years in data base technology. The new complexities are analogous to reorganization in large databases. When many changes have been made over time to a data base, storage becomes disorganized and performance slows. At certain times the data base must be reorganized, that is, stopped and cleaned-up. In network-TDM systems, a similar disorganization may occur due to link failure and AAR. After a period, the failed links are repaired and a question arises of how to get back to the original design configuration. While many data base operations include reorganization at a specific time of the day, week or month, stopping a data communications network to reconfigure back to design level is generally a new concept. The alternative of letting the network configuration "wander" becomes an economic question. If failed and repaired links connect circuits with less delay and lower cost, then traffic should be placed back on them as soon after repair as possible. If they are held with open bandwidth waiting for a failure on a higher cost link, monies are wasted due to inefficient link utilization, and some of the efficiencies of the network-TDM system are lost over time.

Along with the economies of full link utilization, voice/data integration permits priority balancing during link failures. The nature of a business may permit nightly or weekly re-configurations to move back toward an original configuration. In addition, time-of-day switching may accomplish the re-balancing automatically. In these application areas, time-of-day switching of either priorities or management can balance requirements between data and voice and "reset" the network configuration.

Time-of-day switching, offered by many network-TDM systems, permits heavier voice loads during the normal business day and then allocates additional bandwidth to bulk data transmission during the off hours. Again, we return to the increasing statistical nature of the modern network-TDM system. The integration of voice and data, whether switched by time-of-day or not, has become a key ingredient of most network-TDM usage. Integration combines two fields which have remained separate since their conception, and the combination adds further confusion to both. **Voice/data integration** via network-TDM systems forms the base for better understanding and leads both groups toward greater understanding of each other's outlook and jargon.

Voice/Data Integration

Network-TDM systems are often called T1 resource managers. The resource they manage is, of course, the bulk T1 (or higher) facility. Nowhere does this appear more appealing than in the integration of voice and data communications. While data communications has been growing explosively in number of circuits and speeds, voice communications remains the dominant form of electronic communications. The balance may change in the next few years, but voice and data will each remain powerful forces in their own right. Network-TDM systems allow the combination of these two worlds through economic pressure. Long-distance voice communications is now almost completely digital in nature. While the voice bits look like data bits, a gentle clash exists between the people who work with voice and the people who work with data. Without detailing the clash between voice and data cultures, the network-TDM systems bring the cultures together to capture T-Carrier economies. Because of the clash, the merger needs the lubrication of common understanding to spread a common familiarity. To aid in this understanding, we introduce some digital voice communications terminology and techniques.

This brief tutorial cannot substitute for a complete review of voice digitization, signaling and switching. Our intent in the overview is a first exposure to "how things work" without detailing inner mechanics or the subtle variations of over one hundred years of voice communications development. Voice telecommunications, remember, has produced many of the very high-speed digital techniques now used so successfully by data communications. A more thorough study of voice network technology and technique is highly recommended.

To begin understanding in digital voice, we will start with the conversion of an analog voice signal to bits. There are more analog to digital techniques for voice than can be counted, but only two dominate in the majority of voice networks. **Pulse code modulation** (PCM), first described early in the book, and **adaptive differential pulse code modulation** (ADPCM) cover the majority of the world's digital voice networks. The two approaches will continue for some time to be the dominant techniques because they work well in both current technology and in ISDN. PCM converts a single, full-duplex voice channel to 64 kbit/s (64 K PCM) and ADPCM digitizes voice to 32 kbit/s (32 K ADPCM) in the generally accepted CCITT version. More complex and exotic techniques exist to convert a voice channel to rates as low as eight kbit/s, but these will rarely be found in national or international switched commercial voice networks. In specific point-to-point or private applications, low-bit-rate-voice approaches do their work quite well. We shall concentrate, however, only on 64 K PCM and 32 K ADPCM techniques as they are the "legal tender" of the world's voice networks.

Digital Voice—64 K PCM

As described before, 64 K PCM voice digitization started with the D-type channel bank families and remains virtually unchanged today. Every voice channel is sampled 8,000 times per second, which is the Nyquist rate for 4,000 hertz of voice channel bandwidth. Each sample, originally captured in **pulse amplitude modulation** (PAM), converts to a digitally coded value represented in eight bits. The eight bits tell whether the original signal was positive or negative and tell just how big the sample was. The relationships of the bit values and the samples are not linear, but are distorted in a precise way to maximize fidelity to the original voice signal. Expressed another way, a sample with a bit value of 128 is not exactly half the size of a sample with a value of 256. The relationship of the bit values is "weighted" to permit finer granularity to softer voice samples. The non-linear relationship accomplishes a process called **companding.** Two common techniques set the rules for companding for North America and for the CCITT, used throughout much of the rest of the world. Companding is more easily explained graphically and Figure 12.17 on page 344 illustrates the two methods.

Companding, also called **segmented quantization,** divides the analog signal by amplitude into segments. Each segment is defined by pre-agreement, and the bits tell where the sample falls in the segment. The names of the most popular companding methods derive from original articles in technical journals and are based on which "law" or mathematical approach is followed by the method. In 1957, an article in the *Bell System Technical Journal* described a companding method and used the Greek letter mu (μ) to describe how many bits were needed to place the sample in segments. The recommendation was 255 discrete values (plus zero) represented by eight binary bits. This companding method is sometimes called μ-**255,** but more often μ-**law companding.** The result was an AT&T method following the μ-law approach. In a 1960 *IEEE* proceedings article another "law" was suggested. This later became the A-law method standardized by the CCITT. As a result, North America uses μ-law and A-law is used elsewhere. Some differences do, indeed, exist. A-law, for example, can handle a slightly greater dynamic range and μ-law handles idle channel noise better. Both are really very satisfactory for use in digitized voice. They are not, however, fully compatible with each other.

As the figure demonstrates, the differences are small and the similarities great. Each exists as a method to code analog voice signals for digital transmission. These two ways form the basis of almost all digital voice in the world. But they consume perhaps too much bandwidth. A newer technique, namely 32 kbit/s **adaptive differential pulse code modulation** (ADPCM) cuts the bandwidth required for a voice channel in half.

Digital Voice Signaling

Voice network signaling is a somewhat foreign concept to most data communications people. In data communications, bits contain either addresses, control information or data. Codes and protocols set the meaning of the bits; once the codes and protocols are agreed upon, communications proceeds. Note that addresses, control information and data pass together, identified only by position (as in SDLC or HDLC) or by bit pattern (as in ASCII or bisync). In this sense, signaling (addresses and control) may occur at any time and are imbedded in the data stream. Approached in this sense, voice signaling is no different.

Voice signaling contains, just as in data, addresses and control information. Control includes both status information and control information. Status information is needed to start or complete a call, such as when a telephone is not in use (on-hook) or when a telephone handset is picked up (off-hook). Control information includes ringing and both instrument and network busy signaling. Voice addresses are telephone numbers, now coded worldwide as decimal strings. In North America, a typical address (telephone number) would be:

1-800-555-1234

That telephone number must somehow be carried by the digitized voice bits. In addition, control information must be carried by the same bit stream. Two mechanisms exist in digitized and companded voice bit streams to carry addresses and control information, but only one affects the actual bit stream. The complex tones we hear when we press the numbered buttons on a telephone carry those numbers through the network **inband.** With inband signaling, as first explained in Chapter 2, the address passes as a series of analog tones which are digitized just like the voice signal itself. Some busy signals also

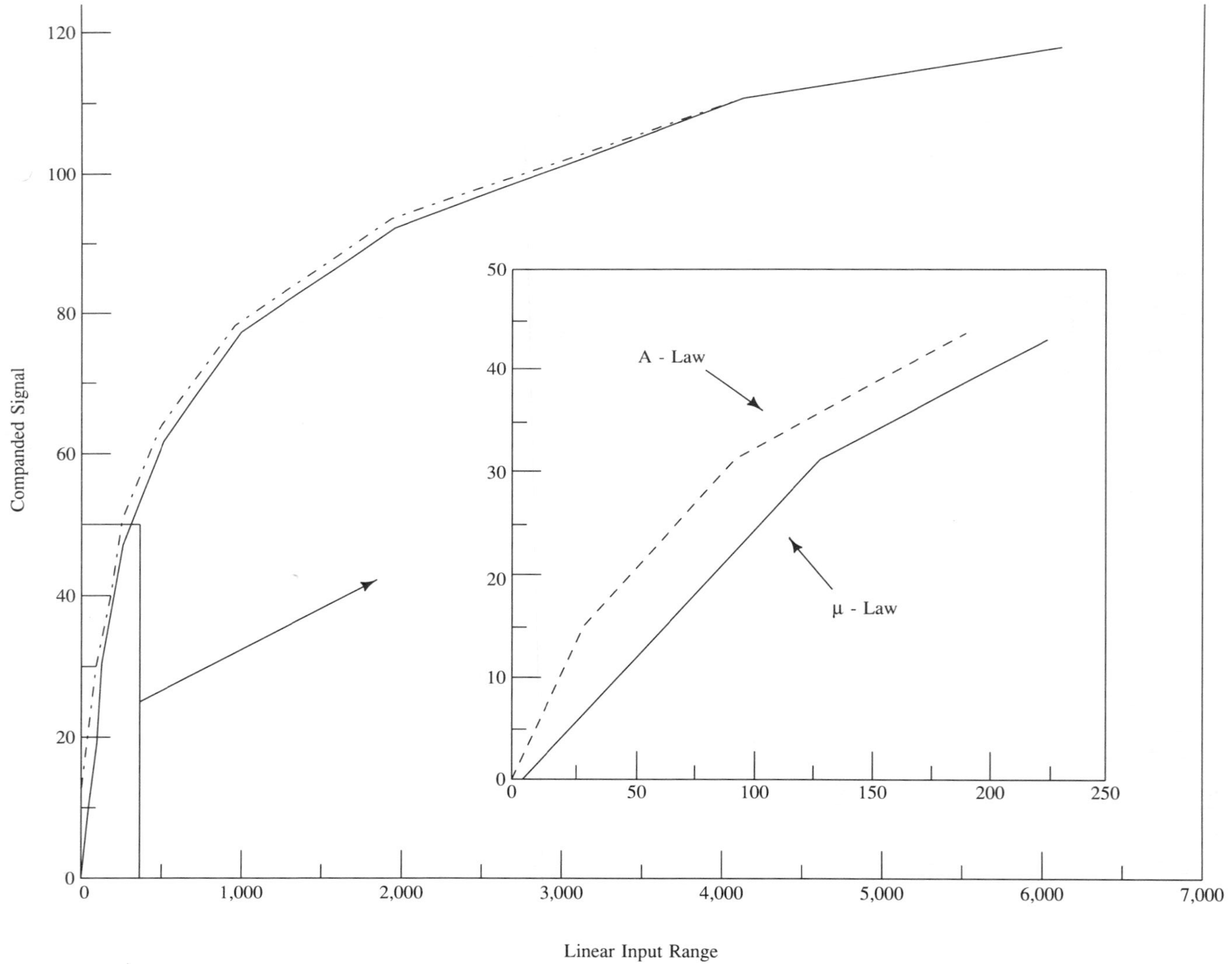

FIGURE 12.17. Digital Voice Companding—μ-Law vs. A-Law.

carry through the network inband. Once a call completes, that is, once we reach our party, the tone buttons have no effect on the network. Indeed, the same number buttons and tones often control some device attached to the telephone, such as a recording machine. We still need a control path which exists out-of-band. In μ-law voice digitizers (channel banks and digital PBXs), this out-of-band is done by "stealing" bits from the digitized voice signal.

In 64 K PCM, as previously described, one of the bits always represents the smallest change in sample amplitude and is called the **least significant bit** (LSB). As an occasional error in this bit is least likely to affect the quality of the voice signal after re-conversion to analog, the LSB is "stolen" or "robbed" in every sixth sample. The criminal sounding words stolen and robbed form a colorful metaphor for a mundane re-assignment of the bit's meaning. For each channel in a normal T1/D4 framed and channelized T1, the sixth LSB is re-named the "A" bit and the twelfth the "B" bit. (In T1/ESF places are reserved for "C" and "D" bits.) These bits actually form two independent data channels for control information. Each voice channel has these A-bit and B-bit channels to carry such things as on-hook to tell network elements when we hang up a phone instrument. It will surprise even some voice people to think of these two channels as 666.6 bit/s data channels, but that is indeed what they are. And they are assigned actual signaling use and meaning in the network at equipment installation time.

Once digitization, companding and signaling methods are set, agreement has been reached on what bits will be used to represent the sampled voice signal. The selection of digitization and companding methods really just sets the code and protocol agreement between sender and receiver for the voice signal. Agreement on the bits used to send signaling completes the definition of the bit stream for digital voice. At that point, the eight voice bits become very similar to eight data bits. Voice bits can pass through a transmission system just like their data cousins. There are several significant performance exceptions: error recovery and transmission delay.

Voice/Data Error Performance

In data communications, each bit within a message must be verified. The coded character "5" in a data message may be five people, five million dollars, five missiles or five cents. Extensive research and development has produced a wide range of methods to handle data error detection, correction, and recovery. In digital voice communications, errors are either unnoticed or ignored. As each eight-bit group in digital voice represents only one sample in 8,000 for a second in time, the group may be modified or even destroyed with no more effect than a hardly noticeable click on the line. At error rates which would all but destroy the most robust data communications code and protocol, voice communications merely sounds noisy and difficult to understand. If it becomes bad enough, another telephone call is placed and statistical routing in the switched telephone network usually grants a clearer call. This robust and redundant nature of digital voice defines one key difference from digital data. Another difference is delay.

If one frame of an SDLC or HDLC message arrives late or out-of-order, software will automatically correct the problem. If voice bit groups arrive late or out of order, the intelligibility of the voice signal suffers quickly. As the problem worsens, data continues to be relatively robust, but voice becomes nearly unusable. Voice communications depends on minimum or at least consistent delay and the bits must arrive steadily and in order. Data communications protocols support out-of-order arrivals and tolerate wide variations in transmission delay, although at a cost of reduced performance and throughput. Another application may yield mixed results, namely, **digital video.**

Video signals converted to digital form are usually further processed to "compress" the information. Digital video compression techniques continue to advance seemingly without limit. At this writing, clear, full-motion color video signals can be transmitted well below 256 kbit/s and reconstructed to analog video at the far-end. The performance of compressed digital video in the presence of bit or burst errors varies, of course, depending on the compression algorithms. If the digital video application conveys highly redundant information, such as video-conferencing between groups of people, burst error tolerance may be greater than resistance to bit errors. Burst errors lasting up to several seconds will cause a total reset of the picture compression and a flicker or roll of the picture. Bit errors, however, will impact the compression algorithms and may distort the picture. While digital voice and data robustness in the presence of various error behaviors is reasonably well known, additional work will need to be done to characterize digital video.

Whatever the error behavior, network-TDM systems make it possible to integrate and transmit digital voice, data and compressed digital video together in T-Carriers. This fundamental fact is already changing the way electronic communications is handled in government, education, and industry. Once separate parts of an organization must now cooperate in the planning and use of bulk facilities. Already, the channel side of many network-TDM systems will accept T1s from digital voice PBXs as channels. This impor-tant development leads directly to integration of voice and data and prepares the path toward ISDN.

Interconnection to Digital PBXs

The ability to connect T1s as channels on a network-TDM system immediately forces a reevaluation of data/voice separation. Figure 12.18 shows a network-TDM system col-lecting voice from digital PBXs and data from data communications facilities. The TDM combines bits from both and, most importantly, recovers unused bandwidth from voice and data sources. Note how unused channels from the digital PBX are used to provide data bandwidth. During a link failure, the TDM (or resource manager) carries critical voice or data traffic and **load-sheds** the rest. After link restoration, the TDM can either reconfigure again to re-balance or wait for external time or command to re-establish the original network configuration.

As Figure 12.18 depicts, digital electronic signals whether from voice, data or video sources may now be managed together on multiple T-Carriers. Network-TDM systems have now developed capabilities in units and systems which:

- maximize aggregate utilization;
- balance voice and data traffic;
- provide automatic alternate routes;
- offer time-of-day configurations;
- measure traffic and performance;
- collect call and data statistics; and
- connect data and voice management systems.

347

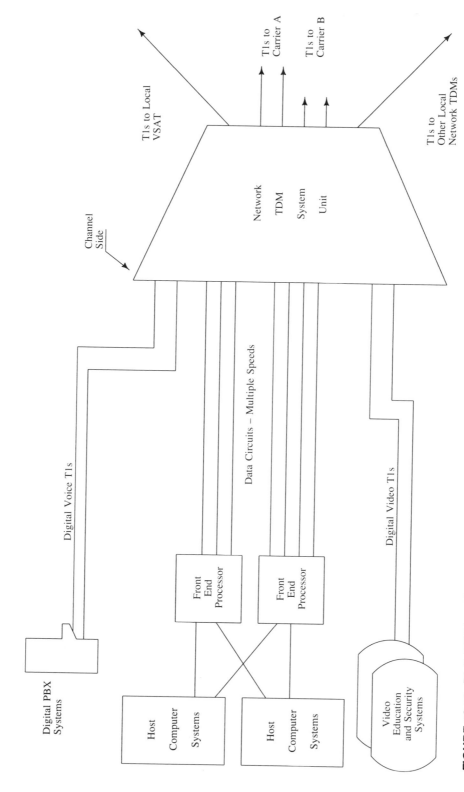

FIGURE 12.18. Digital PBX and Network-TDM System Interconnection.

These capabilities are not speculations of a brave new future, but exist as we write these words. Problems and inter-operability challenges remain, but fundamental voice/data/video integration into high-speed digital networks exists now. Future directions in both data and voice communications will be shaped by systems like those now being installed. Those directions, we believe, are now becoming clearer.

Future Directions In TDMs

When high-speed digital data TDMs arrived in a significant way in the early 1980s, they appeared to be unique niche-market devices created by bulk purchase economics. Years later, it becomes clearer that these complex systems will endure and will lead us toward the next major revolution in electronic communications—ISDN. Indeed, if current directions continue to play out, TDMs may be the bridges to a fully interconnected world of ISDN. To conclude this chapter, we will review some of those directions as they now appear. Three major items seem critical if we are to move to a fully integrated digital communications world. They are:

• converging standards and compliance;

• interconnected systems management; and

• relative technology independence.

A brief examination of each will conclude this chapter.

The early 1980s saw a plethora of incompatible technology developments, analog modems running over digital telephone facilities, personal computers unable to communicate efficiently with main frames and a myriad of unique high-speed data communications formats, protocols and speeds. This seemed the era of total independence and incompatibility. Then many factors began to force a reexamination of world-wide communications standards. The end of a slightly more forgiving analog era exposed the weaknesses in world inter-operability. Almost at once, standards bodies both old and new began to work toward common goals of inter-operability. Highly independent manufacturers began to join in efforts to promote standards and standardization. A few examples illustrate our point.

In the United States, the Corporation for Open Systems was formed to promote standards usable by all electronic computation and communications vendors, carriers and governments. The Exchange Carriers Standards Association created the highly visible T1 (for first telecommunications committee, not T-Carrier) standards committees. Internationally, the Plenary Assemblies of the CCITT have now yielded the foundations of a worldwide ISDN and have included prior worldwide and North American digital communications standards in a compatible fashion. The laying and operation of continental, international and trans-ocean fiber optic cables has hastened the cooperation between countries assuring the efficient use of these new facilities. The convergence toward a limited standards set for intra-LATA, inter-LATA and international is happening now. Of most interest to the field of high-speed digital communications, product and carrier services reflecting early versions of these standards are already coming to market. This will accomplish the first step toward true inter-operability. Network management, however, is yet to be standardized.

Promising at least network management coordination, a trend toward higher level control and management systems such as IBM's NetView® has begun. In the area of

interconnection, NetView/PC® offers a vehicle to pass information from the many dispa-
rate systems to a common monitor and control system. While significant work remains, the
direction of interconnection between network management systems must continue and
accelerate. We believe we see that happening now. The last direction, technology independence, has also begun to emerge.

While it is very dangerous to forecast a future relatively free of technology shock, we
believe that emerging high-speed digital communications technologies will be evolutionary. Developments will occur and surprise will come upon us, but they will merge into the
puzzle rather than throw the puzzle from the table. Certainly new and better ways will be
found and, we feel certain, they will adapt into and extend an existing structure. The
reasons for this belief revolve about two facts now in common view: an open-ended digital
transmission standards set and the spread of fiber optics. The North American and CEPT
T1s, T2s and T3s in this book form the beginning of an open-ended set. There appears no
fundamental limitation to extending this digital set (via SONET) upward into the hundreds
of gigabits/s. While this happens, the extension of at least T1 capability to the office and
residence is doable, if not yet fully justified. Here the power of fiber optics begins to replay
history.

When Bell and his contractors began to string copper wire at the end of the last
century, they could not conceive how far technology would push that copper. Wires which
once carried a single phone call now carry over a hundred calls. Fiber optics can and will
follow the same path of multiplication. Where equipment at the ends of fibers operates at
over 500 Megabits/s, it will go next to 2.4 Gigabits/s and continue its upward march. But as
copper before it, the changes will largely take place in the offices connected by the fiber.
The glass in the ground and on the poles will not change. As better, faster and less
expensive end equipment develops, it will migrate into the system. Increases in power and
speed will come by evolution, building on the base of fiber and standards already formed,
thus our belief that open-ended digital communications standards and fiber-optics will
permit the many-fold expansion. New and attractive applications of electronic communications will come upon us, but technology independence will handle them without major
disruption. Certainly the most imminent will be the deployment of Integrated Systems
Digital Networks.

After we cover the integration of multi-vendor and multi-carrier digital networks, we
will devote our last chapter to ISDN.

CHAPTER 13

Multivendor Integration

Chapter Overview

Once in this land of data communications, "choice" was nearly non-existent. Few technologies, fewer carriers and limited kinds of equipment formed the only features of a usable, if somewhat barren, terrain. Speeds were slow and options simple. Analog modems on analog telephone lines and teletypewriter services conveyed most data across the territory and, for many years, this sufficed. Then in the 1970s and early 1980s new winds carrying fresh rains forever altered the landscape. A downpour of technical and legal changes, hundreds of new vendors and millions of computers flooded the plains and valleys and a jungle of choice arose. Choice in carrier, choice in technology, choice in equipment and, most complex of all, choice in approach offered new opportunities. But new choices implied new responsibilities and those responsibilities began to challenge each communications user.

This chapter explores several paths in this new jungle and examines "choice" in a multivendor, multitechnology world. We begin with a problem we call **techno-centrism,** that is, every vendor's ability to focus their technologies, products and services at the center of a user's needs. Recognizing and controlling techno-centrism helps us find our way.

Next, a map of each of the major tasks or activities in a digital communications system is reviewed in the light of inter-system complexity. A study of the tasks involved in digital interconnection leads to the most important systems decision—**choice of approach.** Choice of approach really means the degree of delegation. Complete delegation of choice, which can also be called

turn-key vendoring, is compared to in-house and combined approaches. In a combined approach, some tasks may be vendored and some retained in-house. Other choices may now be examined, permitting us to understand both some concepts and practical aspects of voice/data/video integration. From here, integrated systems planning is introduced leading us to our closing chapter on Integrated Systems Digital Networks (ISDN).

Techno-centrism

If you have ever seen a world map printed outside the Americas, you will recognize that most countries place themselves as close to the center of the map as possible. This appears very strange to visitors from other countries, as things seem distorted and out of place. In an extreme example (to residents of the Northern Hemisphere), a new map from Australia and New Zealand shows the rest of the world "upside-down." This map, reproduced below, helps to illustrate the concepts of techno-centrism by startling us with known facts presented in a novel way. If you will turn the book upside-down to view Figure 13.1 you will see that the biggest change is in the viewing. Viewed normally, however, this figure demonstrates an unexpected way of looking at the world.

As the globe is roughly spherical, all world maps are really approximations to reality, correct, but open to challenge. So it is with interconnected digital communications systems.

A vendor or carrier describing an application of equipment, technology or service, will invariably place their offering in the center of both thought and diagram. When this offering is the only one in view, centering makes sense. When, however, multiple systems must interconnect to form a whole, techno-centrism must be questioned. While each system undoubtedly meets or exceeds a user's single need, an interconnected group of systems

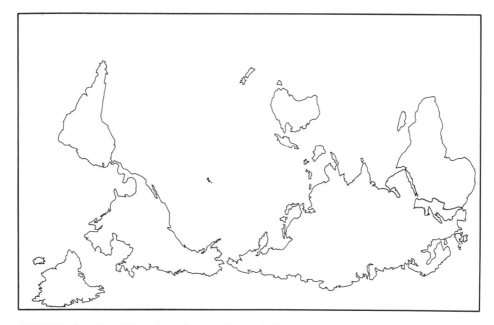

FIGURE 13.1. World Map from Another Point of View.

may fall short or even fail to operate at all. If each component or sub-system tries for center stage, the total system may be compromised. Techno-centrism becomes a problem, but it may also show us a path toward solving the problem.

Techno-centrism, as a solution, becomes a valuable tool by placing the fundamental user need at the center of our map and relegating each sub-system to its appropriate place. Then each component appears correctly positioned and interconnection design begins. In Chapter 4, the concept of interface integration was described and some suggestions were given on approaches on how to merge known, if slightly differing, interfaces. In systems interconnection, the problems are both more subtle and severe, but the same approaches may be followed. In a techno-centric sketch of a total requirement, each system's functions, connections, inputs and outputs may be detailed. Functions performed (and assumed from other systems) may be listed and compared. Compatibilities and gaps will begin to identify themselves and design corrections can be made.

At this point, however, users may wish to ask if the time, talent and desire exist in a group or organization to do these tasks. If skills exist or can be trained and the choice is made to do the tasks, the user embarks on becoming a systems integrator. This can also be called in-house vendoring or in-house systems engineering. An alternative used by many is turn-key vendoring, meaning that the complete design, procurement, supervision and control is placed in the hands of another party outside the organization. A third course takes elements from each and produces a combined method where many tasks are assigned to third parties while fundamental architecture and control remain inside the organization. Before choosing among the three, we must first outline these tasks that are required to integrate and operate digital communications systems. As we do this, we will keep techno-centrism in mind as both problem and solution.

Interconnecting Digital Systems

The first task of systems integration is perhaps the most difficult, that is, describing the job to be done by the system. That clear, unambiguous statement of total system function begins the integration task. An old saying illustrates the problem: "When you're up to your arms in alligators, it's hard to remember that your mission was to drain the swamp." The mission statement must come always first and foremost, in spite of each day's alligators, and mission statements may be hard to write. If the collection of equipment, software and services is totally new, writing the description may be easier. If, as is more usual, the new system augments or supplants an existing operating entity, mission statement complexity grows. In the latter case, a clear statement of what the current system actually does is needed, followed by a transition definition. The transition details how the new will bridge to the old, preferably without any significant disruption of the basic original function. Written descriptions of function can (and probably should) be augmented by layered diagrams showing both function and relationships.

Layered diagrams may be compared to construction drawings; the highest layer is the architect's rendering of the final structure complete with landscaping. Each successive layer shows greater and greater detail of smaller and smaller portions of the whole. The entire package eventually contains all information needed to build or alter the structure from the smallest detail to the overall appearance. In a similar way, layered systems integrations diagrams show the objective or mission of the system and then, in increasing detail, expand on the higher layer. As already discussed in Chapter 4 under interface integration, these diagrams need not be formal engineering drawings, but should be clear in meaning and easy to understand. At each level or layer the relationship to the top diagram must be shown so that both errors of omission and relationship can be avoided or at least reduced in number. A sample integration top diagram of a simple multivendor system is shown in Figure 13.2 on page 354.

In Figure 13.2 the vendor names, model types and interfaces are only shown as names without detail. On subsequent diagrams, each section and interface is exploded to indicate increasing detail. While individual vendor's systems now appear alone, they are no longer techno-centric. On their individual layers, the diagrams still relate clearly to the whole system and fit in their appropriate places. Additional advantages result from the systems statements and diagrams in later stages of each project. As each stage of the project is entered, the original objectives can be checked to assure we are still "draining the swamp." Project tasks, whether done in-house or assigned elsewhere, should be routinely compared to the original objectives. We would not claim that changes will not be necessary; we would claim that changes made while referring to the original job statements will be based on sounder judgements. Our very firm conclusion remains that clear statements of system intent and function must be the first and most important task of any system installation. The remaining integration tasks then build from this architecture.

Architectural Statements and Drawings

Statements of function and transition, along with the layered diagrams, form the architecture of the final system and begin to show the engineering and programming detail. These documents and diagrams should portray a clear and easy-to-understand idea of exactly how each vendor's parts will form a whole system. In addition, the user-desired functions should be easy to see. This architectural statement will be a continuous reference for everyone involved with the project. With all parties working from a common reference, errors and misunderstandings should be reduced to a minimum. Tasks needed to build and complete the project can then be identified and assigned correctly. Typical tasks for a multivendor project follow. The tasks below illustrate one way of approaching the multivendor project. These tasks are not intended to encompass everything which ought to be done; even the sequence of tasks may vary. The tasks may be done by one person in a small organization or divided among departments in a large organization. The importance of the lists and ideas which follow is that they stimulate thought. Building an actual project will be tailored to the culture of a particular organization. Our message here is that integrated multivendor systems require discipline and careful planning to achieve success. We hope to show some elements of that discipline and planning.

Systems Design and Engineering

Systems design describes the total system, showing how all the parts will fit and function. Design details each unit or software item, its cost, its place in the whole and how it will relate to the other parts in function. It may be viewed as the first detail layer down from architecture. While architecture defines overall direction and the elements of final form, systems design works with a subset for a particular system of real elements. The elements should fit within the specified architecture and they become a realization of that architecture. Design yields lists of specifics, such as:

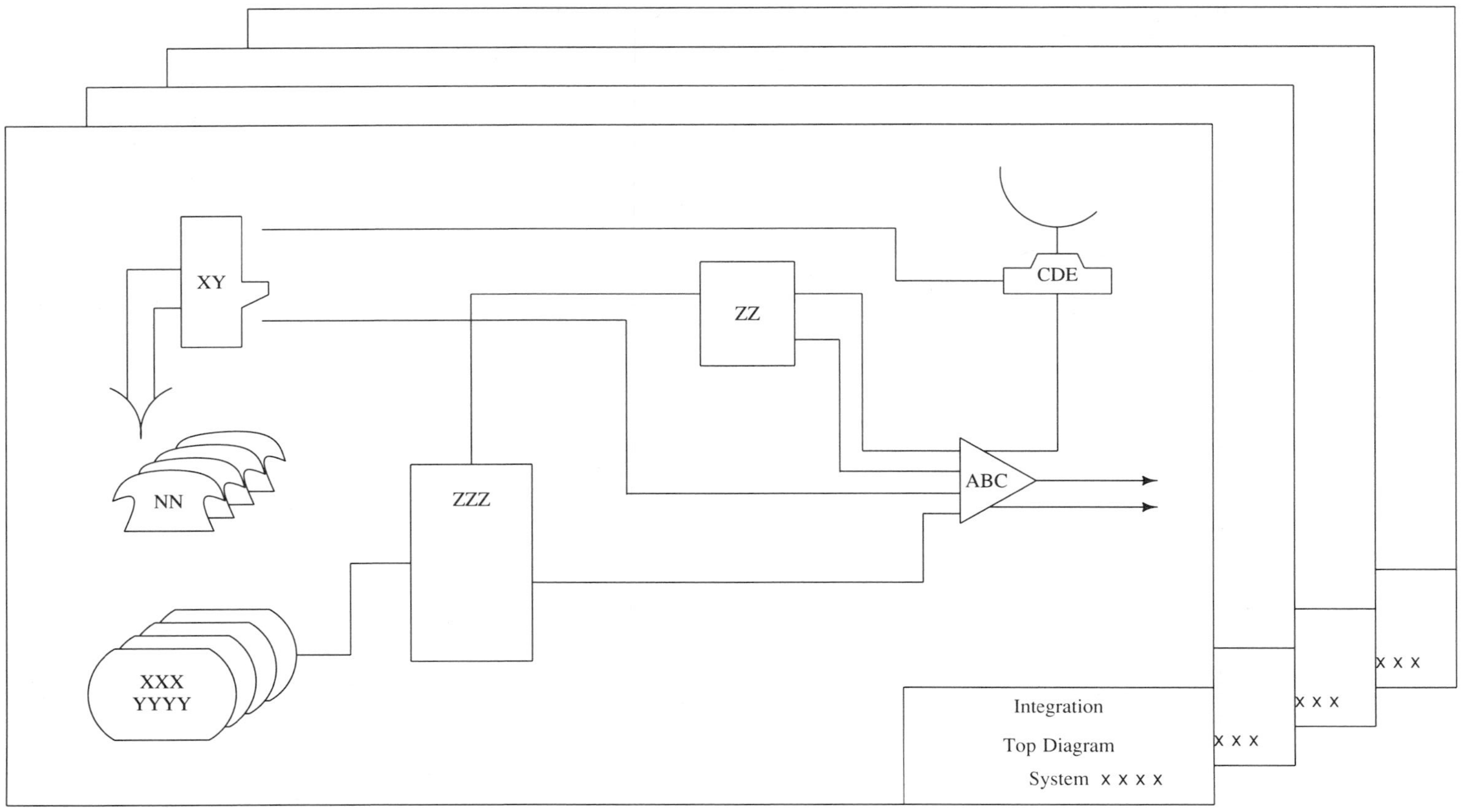

FIGURE 13.2. Illustration of Integration Top Diagram.

- integrated system objectives;
- total system intended functions;
- required hardware functions;
- estimated hardware unit costs;
- required software element functions
- estimated software element costs;
- hardware/software relationships (units);
- required unit functions;
- unit interconnections (sub-systems);
- required sub-system functions;
- required communications services (links);
- estimated communications link costs;
- sub-system and link management strategies;
- total system security strategies;
- sub-system failure alternatives;
- total system management strategy (network management);
- communications link outage alternatives
- disaster recover strategies;
- initial system implementation schedules;
- estimated total system usable life; and
- projected total system life-cycle costs.

This outline list illustrates the type and nature of systems design's output. The actual outputs, or deliverables, will vary with specific systems. This list is one guide to the type of output which may be needed. These deliverables begin the process of systems integration and provide input to engineering.

Integrated multivendor system designs, no matter how well planned, may not function well (or sometimes, function at all) unless the discipline of systems engineering is applied. Systems engineering goes beyond the design to examine unit and sub-system relationships under both normal and stressed operation scenarios. Systems engineering puts individual unit and sub-system specifications under a microscope, looking for incongruities. If one unit produces a signal, the next unit in the sub-system should expect the signal. Signals and information passing among units in the total system must mean the same thing, work at the correct electrical levels and tolerate variations from unit to unit. Unexpected events, conditions and possible failures will produce very unusual behavior in units and sub-systems. Unusual behavior must be contained and not bring down an entire system. While some events cannot be anticipated, the most usual and known can be predicted. Power failures, link outages and individual unit failure are common occurrences. Systems engineering asks what the result of each event will be and plans for systems recovery. Systems engineering prepares for the testing which will be needed to accept each part of the new system. Engineering details the steps to take for smooth transitions from old to new systems and worries about backing away from the transitions if things don't work. Finally, systems engineering must stand ready to support implementation, test and maintenance as the systems become reality.

In the information flow of a multivendor system project, engineering may prepare the following deliverables:

- unit procurement specifications;
- detailed software requirements;
- sub-system interface specifications;
- communications link specifications;
- unit acceptance test plans;
- sub-systems acceptance plans;
- total systems acceptance plans;
- old to new system transition strategies;
- element duplication or "flash-cut" plans;
- sub-system conversion and "back-out" plans
- network management detailed requirements;
- test equipment and software requirements;
- spare parts locating and stocking strategies; and
- failed parts repair and return plans.

In addition, engineering works closely with design to assure the technical validity of the project. The output of design and engineering flow to procurement for the actual purchase or lease of system elements.

Systems Procurement

Procurement of complex systems is the subject of several texts in its own right. We will not attempt to address the complexities of purchase or lease contracts and specifications here. This is an area requiring expertise in contracts and the assistance of lawyers. Procurement requires people skilled in that art, and no major multivendor project should be attempted without their assistance. People involved in complex projects can, however, ask some very relevant questions in the procurement process. Multivendor systems procurements add some complexities to the procurement process.

Normally, a purchase (or lease) may be based on specifications, and if specifications are met, the contract may be completed. In a multivendor environment, however, each unit, sub-system and link may meet specifications and yet the whole system works poorly or not at all. Procurement needs to work closely with systems engineering and design to establish safeguards. Continuous involvement of design and engineering in the procurement process with full and open technical communications helps; so do:

- full interface specifications;
- nested specifications;
- multivendor technical conferences; and
- pre-installation integration tests.

The next several paragraphs outline each of these suggested items.

Continuous, full, and open technical communications with frequent visits between user engineers and each vendor's engineers can promote clear understanding of needs, products and services. These visits and communications can aid even more if vendor engineers from different firms visit each other under the guidance of user engineers. This provides additional technical communications in behalf of the project. Technical agreements reached on these visits must, of course, be communicated through procurement to all parties and specifications brought up to date. Procurement should become the focus point for these communications and visits and should take the lead in assuring that specifications are kept current.

Full interface specifications detail what is expected at each interface from each vendor. Industry standard interfaces should be the basis for these full specifications, but should not be used alone. Each electrical, optical, radio or programming interface must be fully described and detailed. What it does, when and how often it does it, what response is needed and what happens in fault situations should be detailed. Tolerances and ranges should be described. If coded signals and protocols form part of the interface, all possible codes should be described, even the unexpected and illegal. Responses to all possibilities should be considered. Voltage ranges, jitter tolerances, timing faults, signal overloads, unconnected interface leads all become fair game for description. Experienced system integrators know that "meets RS-232" is not enough of a specification to bet a system on.

Nested specifications are described best in a diagram. Figure 13.3 on page 358 shows how the specification for the sub-system depends on the specification for the communications link. What this means to the procurement process is that the sub-system vendor must produce specified performance as long as the communications link meet specifications. If the communications link moves outside spec, the sub-system must behave in a predicted and specified way. In our simple illustration, "finger-pointing" between the sub-system and the link vendors is reduced. Negotiating for nested specifications is far easier prior to a procurement than negotiating a "fix" after the problem is found.

Multivendor technical conferences are common practice during bidding for a job or project. Rarely, after the various awards on a project, do all the vendors come together with the user at the same time. The user must bear the burden of communications. One suggestion for a greater flow of information and a reduced chance of miss-communications is a regular set of multivendor meetings. The user should be the host of these gatherings. At each meeting, a review of progress and detailed presentations of technical topics should be held. These should be working meetings with a free (as free as the contracts permit) flow of information. These meeting also smooth the road toward pre-installation integration testing.

Pre-installation integration testing becomes the first chance, prior to actual installation, for the user to merge various parts of the final system. Integrated testing should, of course, follow individual unit and sub-system testing. This may be done, subject to contracts, at a user facility, at one of the vendor's facilities or at a special base or laboratory. Choice of location is perhaps less important than the testing which occurs there. This series of tests will begin a demonstration of how well the various sub-systems function individually and then together. Integration testing connects the sub-systems in a near-final configuration and passes simulated data through the combination to detect faults or errors. It is an excellent time to begin stress testing, which will be outlined in the next section. If done on vendor's floors prior to shipment, the vendor may be able to more quickly identify and correct problems. At a minimum, the problems can be demonstrated to each vendor and

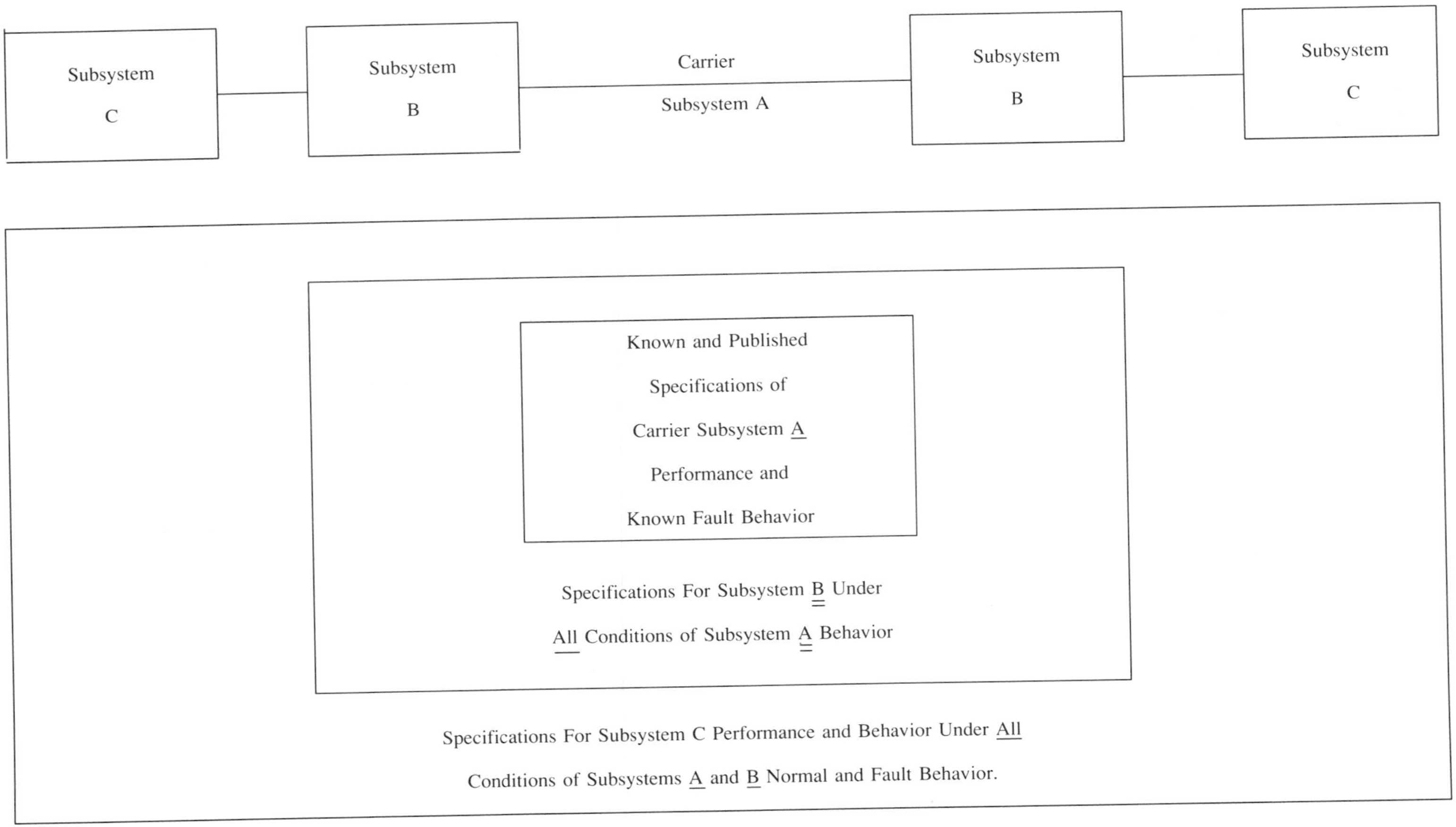

FIGURE 13.3. Nested Multivendor Specifications.

joint solutions proposed. Integration testing can prevent surprises at unit and systems acceptance test.

Unit and Systems Acceptance Test

There is no moment potentially more valuable in the life of any new system than acceptance test. Yet no value is squandered as often. This critical moment will determine how well any system will work well into its future. It will determine overall reliability and availability in service. Typically, and sadly, the moment is wasted. New units and systems are delivered, powered and checked "for smoke." Perhaps a normal signal is passed and some papers are signed. It may be days or months before we notice what we have wasted. Acceptance testing can pre-answer the repair-person's most critical question:

"Is it broke, or did it ever REALLY work?"

The answer will determine how easily repairs can be made and how long repairs can take. Records from thorough acceptance testing will guide technicians in knowing what is truly "broke" and what is not.

Acceptance testing offers significant opportunities which will never recur. At this moment everything should be working well, production pressures should be lower than after production begins, attention is focused and the vendors are ready. Final payments have usually not yet been made and everyone is eager to bring the units, sub-systems and total systems to full readiness. Now is the moment to determine the system's true and total health. Once this is done, the records of each test permit later reference when something fails or appears to fail. The total system, each sub-system and each unit will have been characterized under both normal conditions and under stress.

Stress testing sounds more complex than it really is. Stress testing need not involve altitude and temperature chambers in normal commercial systems; stress here means exercising the range of each critical parameter. This is best explained by example. The first example demonstrates how well a T1 transmission unit handles abnormal T1 inputs. Figure 13.4 on page 360 diagrams the test set-up.

In Figure 13.4, the unit under test is an M13 muldem which time division multiplexes 28 T1s into a single T3-carrier. Before connecting the M13 to a T3 transmission system, we can characterize the M13 and discover its limits. The limits will, hopefully, be greater than specification and we will then know how the unit will respond to future tests during maintenance. Several tests are suggested here, but many more may be desired. An assumption is made that current test equipment is available, recently calibrated and in the hands of experienced technicians. Acceptance testing records should contain not only information about the systems under test, but about the test equipment and personnel. Our suggested tests are:

- input voltage levels;
- input jitter capabilities;
- input frequency ranges;
- open input performance;
- input bit pattern behavior;

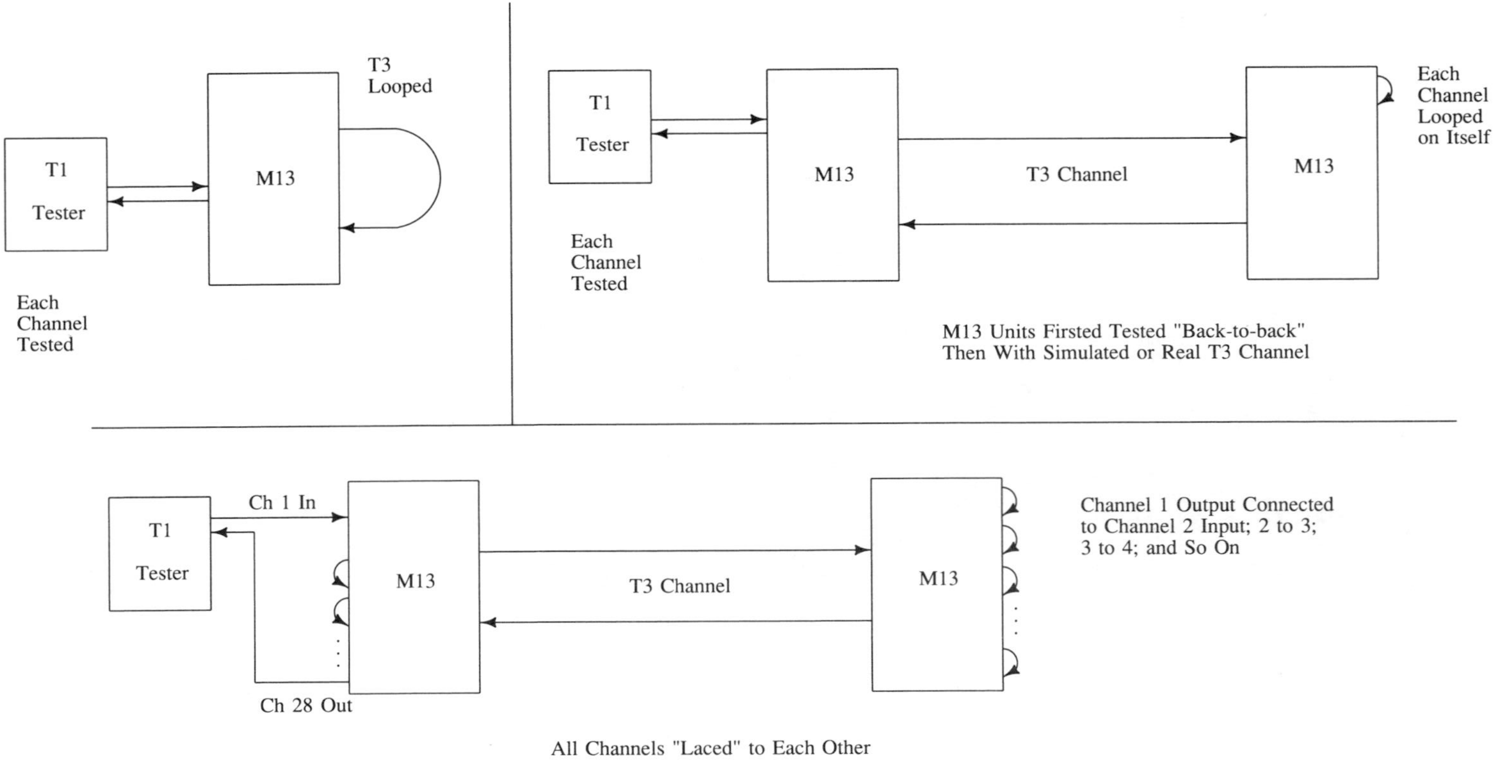

FIGURE 13.4. Unit Acceptance Test Illustration.

- output voltage ranges;
- output jitter level;
- loop jitter transfer;
- output bit patterns;
- channel removal re-insertion; and
- other miscellaneous tests.

Stress testing dictates that each channel's input signal level, jitter, and frequency should be generated at nominal, at specified limits, and well beyond limits to determine the actual failure point of that channel. That is, each channel should not only be tested individually, but should be stressed to and beyond its limits. Stress testing on outputs should include measurements under excess loading and recovery from direct short circuits. Other channels should be monitored during stress tests on one channel to determine any cross-channel effects. Other tests should determine that all controls and alarms operate predictably and correctly.

Testing times become even more valuable when they can be run for extended periods. Extended test periods can yield both significant results and greater confidence in test results. The results of each test should be kept and copies left with the unit for later review by maintenance personnel. The tests should be run for each and every T1 channel and for the T3 (and alternate T3, if it exists). Notice that the tests are recommended without the T3 facility being connected. This testing will characterize just the M13 unit at the near end. If the unit intended for the far-end can be shipped first to the near end, similar tests can be run without moving personnel or test equipment. While transmission facilities, such as T1s or T3s, are not usually considered units, tests similar to unit testing should also be run on the facilities without end units installed. In our example, the T3 testers can be turned to testing the facility after unit testing finishes.

Once unit and facility testing is completed, sub-system testing can begin with "known-working" units and facilities. Many of the same tests will be repeated during sub-systems testing to assure that the now-integrated units and facilities produce results not significantly different from unit tests. As each sub-system is added into the total system, new results and problems can be expected. It is exactly these problems which, when uncovered during pre-production testing, can cause significant down-time later if left undiscovered and uncorrected. Finally, the entire system can be tested using the same techniques from unit and sub-system tests. Results again are compared and new problems may still be uncovered. Test result documentation is saved, of course, to help answer questions during production problems. The test results, which form the basis of systems acceptance, may also be shared with the vendors of units, sub-systems and facilities. Both the test activities and results should become a formal part of the base of data kept about the system.

Systems Administration and Data Management

Post-acceptance operation of a new or revised system will entail administration of both the system and data about the system. These administration and data management activities will determine how well the system can be operated and maintained. Administration will include the maintenance of current data on:

- complete system descriptions;
- unit identifications;
- unit locations and connections;
- unit spares and locations;
- unit repair contacts and escalations;
- facility end points and identifications;
- facility repair contacts and escalations;
- systems user information and contacts;
- user service agreements and current problems;
- location security and power contacts;
- test equipment types and locations;
- test equipment calibration schedules;
- original acceptance test details;
- systems changes and change dates;
- disaster recovery plans;
- planned system changes;
- and so on.

As the list suggests, administration of a complex system is a system in itself, which must be backed up and audited at regular intervals. Most of the information will usually be automated and available to everyone involved with the system. Careful controls must be placed on the right to change or add to the data to prevent corruption of the database. Often, the data will reside in several systems and the data in the separate systems must be synchronized frequently. Each base must also be audited frequently for data integrity so that the people using the bases will not begin to substitute other methods.

A sure sign of weakness in database administration and difficulty in the use of databases is evident in the number of pencil-and-paper records used by operators and maintainers. These scraps of paper and marked-up listings on the walls of operations centers call for a review of data administration. Data about the system should be accurate, readily available and easy to use by all who need it. Anything less reduces the availability, reliability and usefulness of the system to its users. These databases of information about the system are needed most acutely by operation and maintenance people.

Operations and Maintenance

Once all other tasks are completed, operation and maintenance people take over to run the systems and keep them running. Most frequently, each new system adds to the responsibilities of operators and maintenance group or the O & M group, as they are sometimes called. If everyone before has done their jobs well, the operation and maintenance tasks can be done well. Flaws in earlier processes may, however, only come to light when production is up and running. Then the O & M people get the pressure and must take the heat when problems occur.

The heat and pressure become more intense in multivendor systems as vendors vie to show their sub-systems or units are not at fault. This is the dreaded and very real syndrome of "finger-pointing." As much as we would like to ignore the syndrome, it occurs and must be dealt with by operations and maintenance. There are no magic solutions in multivendor problem determination, but three concepts may help: overlapping diagnostic tools, problem segmentation and escalating support levels. We will describe each briefly, beginning with overlapping diagnostics.

Figure 13.5 demonstrates how individual sub-system diagnostic tools relate to overlapping diagnostics. Notice how overlapping diagnostics reach beyond the borders or demarcations of individual sub-systems. If diagnostics for sub-systems A, B and C each show no fault, overlapping systems diagnostics D and E can often isolate the trouble. In some cases, the fault may lie at the interface between systems, and the overlapping diagnostic will isolate the problem.

Another way of looking at overlapping diagnostics also describes problem segmentation. Referring again to Figure 13.5, end-to-end diagnostic F will verify that a fault exists in the total system; our task is now to isolate it to a failing sub-system or interface. We can start with overlapping diagnostic E. Assuming we wish to "segment" or divide and conquer the problem from the greater system down toward the least unit, we next run diagnostic D. This should isolate the problem either to the "segment" covered by one or the other of these diagnostics. Individual sub-system diagnostics A, B or C will then confirm the problem or suggest that the problem may lie at the interface between sub-systems. This repetitive reduction of possible faults effectively segments and isolates most "single" failures.

A more complex type of trouble may confuse the segmentation process: the multiple-problem problem. When several faults occur before diagnosis begins, or when a second or third fault happens while diagnosis is underway, problem isolation can become truly difficult. The same techniques of segmentation can be used, but multiple problems will yield confusing results. The real culprit becomes our own idea that a single fault is the source of difficulty. Whenever diagnostic results conflict, suspect a multiple fault problem. Notice here the importance of knowing that the system once worked correctly. If we are not sure of true acceptance test level operation, problem diagnosis can be very misleading. Here escalating support levels come into play.

When normal problem determination works, problems are isolated, units or facilities repaired and services restored. When multiple problems, finger-pointing or intermittent troubles happen, another line of defense is needed. More a procedure than a concept, escalating support levels automatically force higher levels of technical skill and greater management attention on unresolved problems as time elapses. In a typical scenario, a problem entering the O & M system is time stamped. If the problem is not cleared to everyone's satisfaction after a pre-determined amount of time, a more skilled or experienced technical person is assigned to the fault and first line management is made aware of the specific trouble. If the problem is still open at the next pre-specified elapsed time, a higher level of technical skill is brought in and second line management is alerted. This process continues until the very best technical skills are quickly and automatically brought into the problem and high levels of management are made aware of the problem's severity.

Escalating support levels will quickly involve the original designers and engineers who specified and accepted the system. This has two benefits: first, additional technical skill is brought to the problem and second, operational and maintenance information is fed back to those who engineer, specify and test new systems. This feedback improves not only

Unit and Subsystem Diagnostic Ranges

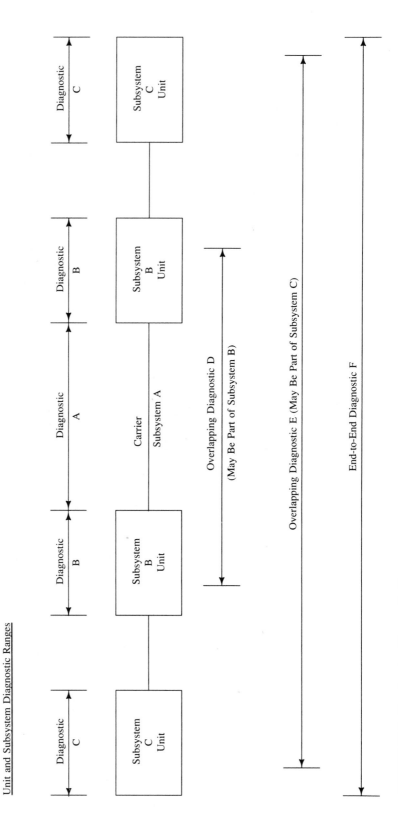

FIGURE 13.5. Overlapping Diagnostic Ranges.

current systems, but assures better designs and specifications in the future. The brief mention of these three O & M concepts is not intended to outline all the tasks involved in systems operation. These processes need the attention of experienced managers familiar with each organization's culture and operations.

Whole texts are devoted to the art and science of systems operation and maintenance. The decision of each buyer or user of a complex, multivendor digital data system must now revolve around the choices which introduced the chapter. These are the fundamental choices of intent. Each user must decide well in advance of the tasks outlined above whether the tasks are to be "made or bought."

In-House vs. Turn-key Vendoring

Two most obvious choices in digital systems design, procurement, acceptance, operations and maintenance are simply: do it or buy it. The choice, unfortunately, is rarely that easy. While experience, management style and existing capabilities will play a large role in the decision process, we offer several other considerations and suggestions. Each user must carefully examine both facts and desires and then judge the organization's capability to do the job. Probably the most critical capability will be the organization's desire and ability to attract, hire, train, and keep qualified people to do the tasks listed in the previous sections.

Staffing and Training

We believe that staffing and training is the most critical issue in a complex systems make or buy decision. Like maintenance, the issue may be segmented in deciding. If some, but not all, skills exist in the organization, a decision may be taken either to acquire or "farm out" the remaining task skills. For example, an experienced and well trained operations group may not be able to design a new digital system, but can be trained to acceptance test and operate it. Or perhaps a skilled set of designers can specify the new system but must rely on contracted O & M. The staffing and training challenge remains, however, unless all tasks are procured from outside the organization. Even here someone in the organization must be capable of judging the performance of the vended tasks and of the system itself. And that person must be trained. Where does one go for training in complex, multivendor high-speed digital systems? Surely, those who already know these tasks learned somewhere.

While no single training course or educational offering will prepare people for all the tasks in a complex system, many individual courses and seminars will help. First, of course, are the design and operations classes offered by each unit and sub-systems vendor. These classes will usually prepare designers and operators quite well on individual sub-systems. Similarly, carrier or independent seminar training can be obtained for digital carrier facilities such as DDS, T1 and T3. The applicability and quality of these offerings vary; consultation with others who have taken the courses or seminars can be a guide. Vendors, educators and seminar presenters should be contacted for references as a first approach. Professional contacts within each user business or interest area should be polled to identify the best candidates for training. Finally, of course, experience provides the most experienced personnel.

Whether this experience is brought in by careful hiring or acquired from knowledgeable consultants, experienced help should be sought. As a minimum, each major project should receive a "sanity test" from someone experienced in the area. In larger organizations these people may be found by asking professional contacts, vendors and carriers. In smaller organizations, qualified consultants should be sought. Two key "litmus" tests of the outside expert should always be: how closely the person's experience relates to the problem at hand and how independent the person is from all vendors and carriers. This outside expert may also guide the user toward a complete or partial solution of the make or buy decision.

A Partial Approach

A complete in-house solution is always preferable, but only if all the skills already exist in an organization. This is rarely the case. Yet a complete vendoring of a critical communications system also contains significant risks. The partial solution will usually yield the optimum results.

This partial approach will vary, but several cases can be described from minimum involvement to near complete in-house control. Since the complex, multivendor system can be assigned to a **prime** contractor or vendor, the minimum user involvement must be someone knowledgeable enough to assure performance of the prime. This infers a trained and experienced technical person who understands the needs of the organization and the function of the system. This person must then either have authority over the prime contractor to enforce the organization's requirements or report directly to someone who does. Good management practices require that the "one good person" approach be backed up in case of that person's vacation, illness, or resignation. Thus the minimum partial approach becomes two user organization people concentrating on multivendor systems with a prime vendor or contractor. The minimum approach also requires little in the way of expensive tools, test equipment, and administrative systems.

The next logical level of involvement adds organization people to perform the tasks described above. Which tasks will depend on the availability of trained people and the organization's culture. If design and specification are usually part of the culture, but O & M are not, then this pattern can be followed. The converse would vend design and engineering to consultants while holding O & M in-house. This partial approach begins to require expenditures for design tools, test equipment and systems to control and administer the communications systems. The key technical people from the previous minimum case must, of course, be maintained to oversee and control the vendored tasks. This partial level takes on limited portions of the work, but uses consultants and vendors for the rest. As organization involvement grows, the next partial approach level may vend only small parts of the needed tasks.

In a near-complete in-house approach, only a very few tasks will be assigned to vendors. Perhaps unit and sub-systems installation is given to the vendors supplying the equipment, facilities and software. Acceptance test and operations remains in-house. Now the base of skills within the organization has grown quite large and is capable of either accepting previously vended tasks or delegating tasks to vendors at times of heavy work loads. At this level of in-house involvement, the organization must be committed to significant expenditures in tools, test equipment, control and administrative systems and continuing training. This largest of the partial approaches clearly offers the most flexibility, but will probably cost the most. This cost provides the flexibility along with in-house control and the ability to closely manage the organization's communications systems. These choices must be consciously made by each organization in the clear light of operational and cost needs.

Data/Voice/Video Integration

The most complex of all multivendor integration also involves significant integration of previously separate user organization pieces. This is the integration of all voice, data communications and video systems. As the world begins implementation of Integrated Systems Digital Networks, this in-house integration will become more than desirable; it will become necessary. To preface our last chapter on ISDN we will examine some of the issues involved in integration and explore some of the benefits and constraints. Valid questions continue to be raised on whether (or at what level) integration should be considered. It is our view that once voice, data and video are converted to binary bit streams, integration of complete systems (or at least bit transport systems) should be examined. If operational and economic benefits can be shown, integration systems planning should be started.

Integrated System Planning

Planning integrated digital systems is not a simple process and we will only highlight this complex subject. Before outlining even parts of the process, a caution must be given. Considerable emotion can be generated by discussions about integration planning, as more than technology is being integrated. Philosophies, cultures, professions and personalities are involved. People can feel very threatened by challenges implied by the planning. This is but one of the non-technical and non-economic factors to be considered.

In the planning process, these other factors will play significant roles. As factors will differ widely between organizations, we can only alert systems planners of their existence. Our key alert is to be sensitive to all the people and all the operating departments who may be impacted by integration. With their active participation and cooperation, integration can succeed; without it, real and complex problems can and will develop.

Integration planning, like all good planning, must begin with fact gathering. For just the integration of voice and data circuits between major organizational locations, planners must know what goes where and how it is used. What, of course, details the type, speed, use and utilization of each circuit. Sample questions for each circuit might start with:

- Analog or digital?
- Switched or leased?
- Point-to-point or multidrop?
- Voice, data or mixed?
- Operational or spare?
- Speed (data) or type (voice)
- Equipment connected (each drop)?
- and so on.

It is not enough to know at which city, plant or campus the circuits terminate; the planner must know the:

- country, state and city;
- street address;

- building name or number;
- floor or level;
- room or floor coordinates; and
- column, wall, floor or ceiling.

Imagine yourself trying to locate four small wires in New York and you will quickly understand the need for this detail of information. Someone will have to install or move a circuit and someone else will have to find it. You could be that someone.

With the "what" and "where" established, use and utilization should be determined. Such questions should follow the lines of:

- What is the circuit's use?
- Who uses and controls the circuit?
- How critical is that use?
- What does the circuit cost today?
- Who pays that cost today?
- If the circuit fails, what happens?
- Can another facility be used temporarily?
- How many hours a day/week/month is the circuit used?
- What kind of information flows?
- and so on.

This seems like a tremendous amount of information to collect on each circuit, but often the process pays for itself. Any organization over a few years old will have unused or under-used circuits. The identification, and cancellation, of unused circuits will often pay back more than the information collection effort will cost. And, successful integration planning cannot proceed without this detailed information.

Next the planner begins to work with the organization's long range planners. Where are we going as an enterprise? What new places will we be in? What places will we leave? What new ventures are planned? What growth rates do we project? What will be the information needs of the organization next year, in five years? From this information and the current communications circuits picture, a planner (or planners) can begin to outline scenarios of growth and integration.

Each viable scenario can then be rough-costed to sort out the real possibilities. Finally, one or two paths will emerge. Note that "do nothing differently" should always be one of the alternatives to be examined. Another very limited scenario might consolidate separate circuits for cost reduction without major directional or organizational changes. Integration can, however, initiate major migrations from current communications systems, structures and ways of doing business.

Migration from Current Systems

Another immediate concern arises once decisions to change current systems are made. Current systems function well, serve the enterprise and can damage the organization if disrupted. Any plan for change must allow for smooth and non-disruptive movement from current systems operations. Steps should be small and each step must permit **back-out.** That is, if a change is made and results in unusual or degraded service, we must be able to return to a known previous working condition. After the problem with the change is found and corrected, we can again try the change; if it fails again (whether for the old fault or a new one), we must still be able to back out or return to known-working systems. There is no more serious commandment in communications than "Thou shalt keep thy back-out available." Another suggestion familiar to information systems and MIS people is the **roll system**. A roll system is an extra system used to roll from a previous system to a new one. The roll system may become the new one and the old system may be discontinued after the change. The roll system method also permits back-out through return to the old system. When roll systems are planned, old or previous systems should be kept operational after a successful change for at least a few days or weeks. This extends the time when back-out can be exercised if necessary. Roll systems can find applicability in digital communications systems change-outs. In communications changes, a roll system will most often be a parallel communications facility. In addition to providing back-out, all or part of the original system may be left in place for peak load or disaster backup scenarios.

While differences in philosophies were mentioned earlier as potential people concerns, real operational differences can result from these different philosophies when integrated services begin. An example of differences between voice operations systems and data information systems can cause friction in operational staffs. Voice systems for most private or commercial organizations meet their heaviest demands during the daylight hours. Problems which occur in the middle of the night can be dealt with early the next morning. Many commercial data communications facilities, however, must meet heavy overnight demands as well as daytime loads. Night may be when the databases are refreshed and synchronized. Night will be when the day's transactions are balanced and journaled. Plans which operate data facilities on voice rules or vice-versa may be headed for serious operational difficulties.

The next step then for integration planners will be to determine how current systems actually operate. This is best done in consultation with the current operations staffs (on all shifts). In addition to operators, communications service users should be consulted. Users can be polled to understand not only their current needs and perceptions, but what impacts the integrated systems may cause. This is also the time to identify new and, as yet, undiscovered user plans and needs.

While the list of tasks seems to grow longer with each suggestion, common sense and a concern for both users and operators will bring planners close to an optimum systems integration plan. The real message of our suggestions is that any systems plan be driven by an organization's planners (or their consulting surrogates) and not by individual vendors. Individual vendor's solutions may meet the needs very well, but the using organization must be an active and involved final judge.

System Location Planning

The "where" facts of existing circuits will tell planners where service is needed for the new integrated systems. The facts may also make location decisions quite complex. Few organizations have placed their voice, data, and video operations physically together. Yet the new integrated system may need to serve them all. This need to bring services together creates a new challenge in systems location planning.

Data communications planners have not usually been overly worried about where to locate communications equipment. In large raised-floor installations, the communications units were installed near the communications controllers or front-ends. Distance was controlled by DTE/DCE interface cable limits and was usually less than fifty or one hundred cable feet. Often the modems, data service units and multiplexers clustered together in the center of the front-ends for convenience of service. In smaller locations, communications terminate near cluster control units or right at data terminals.

In voice communications, the location of the telephone switch, either in the **private branch exchange** (PBX) or the **main distribution frame** (MDF) for central office switching, was determined by convenience. Voice local loops from the telephone instrument to the telephone switch may range from thousands of feet up to several miles. Telephone switches can be located conveniently to loop and cable connections in the building or campus. Similarly, video communications may be found near classrooms, video-conference centers, or security offices.

Planning locations for new integrated systems will always be easier than integrating existing and separated systems. Separated voice, data and video systems, however, may be connected using the very high-speed technologies we have been describing in previous chapters. If dispersed data, voice and video sources are converted to T1s, for instance, the T1s may be run like local voice loops with T1 CSUs. Network system type TDMs may then combine and balance traffic from these individual T1s and place the result on long haul T1 or higher carriers.

Several other concepts can also be used to bring existing systems logically together. Digital private branch exchanges now carry both voice and data terminal traffic on their local loops. These **computerized branch exchanges** (CBX) directly permit the interconnection of voice and data. New wiring systems, such as the IBM Cabling System, allow single wiring plants to bring voice and data to their respective systems.

The optimum solution for new construction, of course, would be to plan for co-location or physical proximity of voice switches with data centers and video distribution centers. Most new construction places plumbing, electrical and ventilation in central utility cores. Telecommunications planning for new construction should strive for the same goals. Physical proximity allows for not only effective cost and bandwidth sharing, but will permit greatly increased flexibilities to meet changing user needs. Major building remodeling projects also offer opportunities to redo telecommunications and plan for communications systems co-locations. Bringing systems closer together brings economy and flexibility, but it also brings some new exposures.

Diversity and Fallback Planning

Single, integrated and co-located communications systems also mean single points of failure. The classical "all the eggs in one basket" problem must be understood. Integrated digital systems planning includes planning for outages and disasters. Outage planning considers the ordinary (and expected) failure of units, programs and circuits. Disaster planning concerns the unlikely, but not impossible, destruction of whole segments of systems, buildings and sites. The general approach to outage planning is **diversity** and **redundancy** of units, systems, and circuits.

Diversity and redundancy may be as simple as buying a redundant unit or power supply. It may be as complex as arranging for completely separate cable ducts and circuit access from a building to two different carrier offices. Diversity planning is not complex, but it must be done very carefully. Redundant power supplies lose some of their effectiveness if they both operate from the same building power circuit. Diversely routed circuits lose some of their diversity value if they go thru any common points. Diversity planning really means looking for and eliminating common failure points in both systems and circuits.

Disaster planning anticipates systems operations following the destruction of key facilities. Typically, disaster planning for connections between systems ties to diversity planning to provide alternate circuit routes. For integrated systems, disaster planning must find alternate ways of doing business while the systems are rebuilt. If an integrated system can be over-simplified as consisting only of hubs and links, disaster planning must anticipate operations following the total loss of a hub or a critical link. Most often, duplicating integrated hubs in the network and setting up truly diverse links only begins the process. Records, operations methods, staff cross-training and regular disaster drills are equally important.

We have outlined in this chapter both the advantages and concerns in the integration of multivendor communications systems. We can now introduce our final chapter which will illustrate more clearly the directions of digital communications: Integrated Systems Digital Networks.

Moving to ISDN

Digitization of voice, data and video communications began in a serious way in the early 1960s. Every decade since has yielded significant improvements for each individual system, but significant integration of digital voice and digital data is only now occurring. That it is occurring in a coherent and organized way is a tribute to the planners of ISDN. In the next and final chapter, we bring together material from the entire book and detail the ultimate integrated multivendor telecommunications system: ISDN. We will describe where ISDN came from, what it is and does, and why it is so important to the future of all forms of telecommunications.

CHAPTER 14

Integrated Services Digital Networks

Chapter Overview

Our guidebook to high-speed communications moves now toward less explored territory. In preceding chapters, we related facts about an evolved and existing digital communications world. Here we venture toward a future whose facts still unfold. Outlines of those facts are becoming clearly visible and we will describe the outlines which suggest the future's facts. This future builds on all that has gone before in the evolution of digital communications and brings together the separated streams of voice and data communications. In the early 1980s, some new concepts merged with these separated streams to lead us toward the future. The result was named Integrated Services Digital Networks (ISDN). In this final chapter we shall introduce ISDN's concepts, terms, technologies and directions. A word of caution; ISDN unfolds as we write and details may change. We intend to build a foundation of basic understanding; evaluation of services and products in each year must rely on ISDN's evolving standards and developing practices.

ISDN became a commercial reality in early 1988 in the city of Saint Brieuc, France. From this administrative and market center in Brittany, ISDN began its spread throughout France. Germany, the United States and Japan introduced tariffs and services the same year and ISDN began its spread throughout the industrial world. This ever-widening ISDN conversion of the world's data and voice communications equipment, services, facilities and networks will continue well beyond the year 2000. What we see today, paraphrasing Churchill, is "the end of the beginning" of ISDN.

This final chapter will overview that beginning by attempting to answer the question: What is ISDN? Breaking apart the words, each is examined for its meaning. We introduce the integration of voice and data at several levels and suggest what **integrated** means to users and services. Next, both present and future **services** of ISDN are viewed, and we begin to understand the opportunities of new services. Then the ideas of separated and simultaneous **digital** signalling and services are outlined, building the real conceptual base for ISDN. Finally, ISDN will be seen as not one but many **networks,** with the interconnection of many smaller, similar networks with worldwide numbering and addressing systems. We return for comparison to the sequential concepts of analog switched voice systems, and their much more limited signalling and services. ISDN will be a world of all digital connectivity building on digital technology with all its advantages, but migration to ISDN will still involve the conversion and integration of many components.

This brings us to the components and channels of ISDN and their uses for existing voice, data and packet network services. Next, a small step leads us to the integration of applications for both business and residential customers and to some totally new services. We start with classical, separated applications and build toward an ever-wider scenario of integrated application directions leading to the year 2000 and beyond. ISDN's direction also comes from world standards, and the chapter briefly reviews standards bodies, carriers and countries and their contributions to standards. We cover the CCITT and world standards and then examine standards for North America, concluding the section with some ideas for planning digital systems in an ISDN era. To focus clearly on planning, we need to understand what changes with ISDN and what stays the same. We conclude the chapter with our views on the future of megabit digital communications considering a fiber optic and digital satellite world leading to a true global village.

What is ISDN?

In the early chapters of this book, we talked of digital communications coming first. Analog voice communications started well after digital telegraphy, but soon dominated the world's communications systems. The pendulum of technology has now begun its return trip as digital techniques regain their ascendancy. The name given to this movement even before its actual birth was Integrated Services Digital Networks (ISDN). To begin to describe what drives ISDN, some existing trends can be identified.

- Dramatic growth in commercial data communications.
- Explosive growth in personal computer communications needs.
- Widening demand for the quality of all-digital transmission.
- Continuing demand for increases in communication speed.
- Needs for applications which combine voice and data resources.

These demand trends march together with:

- Increasing voice digitization at the telephone instrument.
- Available worldwide digital integration standards and technology.

• All-digital transmission of voice and data leading to digital integration.

• Accelerating integration of business data/voice workstations.

These demand trends and supply availabilities have now converged within the world's telephone industries under the name ISDN. To understand ISDN, we can pull the words apart and look at each separately.

Integrated Voice and Data

Until recently, single business or residential communications lines have carried either voice or they have carried data. Some lines alternate between voice and data service, but almost never can one analog line be used for both voice and data at the same time. At work, on the road or at home, either two telephone lines must be used or one line must be shared in time. First, a voice call is setup, used and disconnected, then a data call is set-up and used. While either is in use, no other incoming or outgoing calls of either type can happen. When few data calls were needed, this caused little inconvenience. The commercial, academic and industrial world, however, now demands an ability to do both and do them at the same time. In a voice call, some data may be needed in real time; in a data terminal session, we may need to speak to someone. A simple solution for some is to install another telephone or data line. Globally, we cannot afford that; we need a way to integrate voice and data over the same line.

Integration of voice and data over digital lines promises to replace multiple (often under utilized) dedicated voice and data lines entering customer premises with one or a few lines which are ordered, used, maintained, and paid for in an economical and uniform way. The wires which once could carry only a single voice conversation (or a data call simulating voice with a modem) now carry digital bits. At the lowest level (called the **basic rate interface**, or BRI) of standard ISDN service, a single telephone line can carry two individual calls and another channel for signalling or data. With basic rate access, one D and two B channels move at the same time over the single telephone line. The B channels can each carry an independent voice or data call and the D channel continues to be available for data *and* signalling. Now the terminal user can place (or receive) a voice call in mid-session and the voice user can establish one (or more) data sessions without breaking the voice call. Here, indeed, is the opportunity for voice data integration. And that sounds intriguing, but how might it actually be used?

Envision two examples. In the first, an inside sales representative sits at a computer terminal equipped with an ISDN telephone. Customer calls arrive at the representative's desk accompanied (electronically) by the caller's telephone number, which is used as an index into the computer's customer file *before the call is answered*. The representative, with the customer's profile on the screen, answers the call greeting the customer by name. Since the customer is already identified, a significant amount of data entry for the transaction is eliminated, avoiding errors and saving time for both parties to the call. If transmission of text or graphic material is required, perhaps to assist the caller in choosing among products, an additional B channel call may be made to transmit it without interrupting the conversation. In a second example, an executive calls an information worker with an urgent request for data. The person receiving the call can set up a quick computer inquiry over the same access line without having to disconnect from the executive's call. The answer may be given verbally or, using ISDN's full capability, by sharing data screens with the executive. This allows interpersonal interaction about the voice question and response and may assure a better answer (and a more satisfied executive). Once multiple data and voice calls can happen at the same time over a single line, the possibilities become endless and new applications will flourish. The key becomes simultaneous integrated services.

Separated and Simultaneous Services

Services follow integration capabilities through the use of the multiple ISDN channels. Of course the first service will be **plain old telephone service** (POTS). Now however, even POTS takes on a new look; with two full channels possible over the same wires, another voice call can be made or received while the first call is still in process. Another party can be called with a question or added to the conversation. An incoming call can be quickly answered and then redirected, held or completed. Two independent calls may be made from different instruments on the same line at the same time and, if desired, merged into a conference call. POTS will never be the same again.

The second major ISDN service offering will be data communications. Both switched data calls and leased data lines will be handled by ISDN, but a specific target of ISDN's planners is telephone dial-up data communications. Dial-data calls will connect either from existing modems through **terminal adapters** (TA) or directly onto the digital ISDN lines. Leased line data will more likely connect directly through either TAs or new direct interfaces. Leased line data users may find that ISDN's projected fast call-connect times will lead them gradually toward switched data use. A big difference for both types of data users will be the greatly increased data speeds of ISDN. Most modems on switched analog lines now operate at 1.2 or 2.4 kbit/s. Under ISDN, office and residential telephone B channels will carry data connections at 64 kbit/s as opposed to a maximum of 19.2 kbit/s over switched analog voice-grade lines. Now the two B channels can connect simultaneously to a wide variety of both data and voice services, and there is still the D channel.

Over the D channel, call progress signalling (dialing, ringing, busy, and so on), continues while other data or voice calls stay connected. The D channel is a packet network type data channel and can handle signalling and many other lower speed data requests at virtually the same time. In the older analog telephony world only one action could happen at a time over the single voice line. Ringing or dialing or speaking locked each other out. One-at-a-time was the rule and the technology. ISDN separates the primitive functions of signalling from communications and adds a vast range of new capabilities. One prominent service feature will be **calling number identification**.

The Integrated Services Digital Network will have the capability to carry the identity of the originating telephone number along with the set-up and calling information. When the call arrives at its destination, this identity will be presented along with the request for an answer (ringing). The answering instrument can display the calling number: "213-555-4962," can interpret the number: "Your Mother is calling," or can take action on the number: "forward the boss's calls to 914-555-2885." And all this will be accomplished without noticeable delay due to the speed of the individual D channel. At the basic rate interface the D channel operates at 16 kbit/s; at the primary rate interface, the D channel speed rises to 64 kbit/s. A little later in the chapter the various uses of the D are outlined, but it should be remembered that the D channel alone operates faster than most modems today. All these B and D channel services depend on the digital connectivity basis of the ISDN communications line.

Digital Connectivity and Switching

To provide integration and simultaneous service features requires a digital network—digital connectivity end-to-end, digital switching and an internetwork signalling system. As we have already outlined, much of the world's long haul transmission has been converted to digital. Conversion to digital switching, most commonly the telephone exchange at the local carrier's central office, now nears completion. Most telephone switches now sold to public carriers and large private users are digital and will be capable of attaching ISDN add-ons. Signalling will conform to **Signalling System Number 7** (a CCITT designation), a fast packet data system superimposed on the telephone network to carry both current and ISDN trunk signalling. SS7, a descendent of the **common channel interoffice signalling** described in Chapter 2, has transaction and processing capabilities for the enhanced feature of ISDN. In SS7, **service control points** (SCP) store and process information and communicate through **signal transfer points** (STP). The communications continues, at 56 kbit/s (or 64 kbit/s) with local telephone switches which may be the actual **service switching points** (SSP) containing the **signalling point** (SP) features. The relationship may be more easily understood from Figure 14.1. Note that every major component in the network is duplicated for reliability.

Two additional significant areas, however, remain to be converted to digital: local telephone (access) wires and the telephone instruments themselves. An untold amount of investigation and engineering has resolved most of the problems with access telephone line conversion. Telephone access lines which are less than about 3.4 miles (18,000 feet) from their switches can be converted by removing any inductive (**loading**) coils placed there in the past to improve analog transmission. This includes most business, campus and high-rise access lines whether connected to private or public (carrier central office) switches.

Recall that the original design of the two wire telephone pair to the central office required voice bandwidths of about 4,000 hertz. ISDN asks the same two wire pair to operate into a range over ten times as great. While that sounds difficult, ISDN standards intend coverage of about 99% of the (non-loaded) local telephone access loops in North America. (In Europe, the ISDN interfaces will usually require four wires, making the problem somewhat easier.) Solutions for North America call for complex digital coding

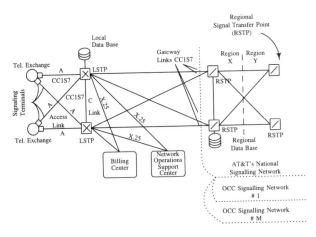

FIGURE 14.1. Signalling System 7 Network.

schemes and echo cancelling methods, but will provide for full duplex digital transmission rates of 160 kbit/s. This yields two 64 kbit/s B channels and one 16 kbit/s D channel for a total of 144 kbit/s. The remaining 16 kbit/s is used for framing, error checking and other overhead signalling. Conversion of access lines will entail removal of loading coils and equipment replacement at the central office. Those lines already connected to digital conversion units, such as SLC-96® subscriber loop carrier systems, require only equipment module replacement. Subscriber equipment replacement completes ISDN conversion.

As ISDN service conversions pick up speed, many types of direct ISDN end equipment will supplement the terminal adapters already on the market, ranging from simple ISDN voice telephones to complex, multi-function ISDN voice/data terminals. In the United States, customers will select from this variety much as they purchase (or lease) telephones, modems and terminals today. Businesses and other large organizations such as universities may elect to install complete private ISDN "islands" of their own for connection to the public ISDN, for ISDN is truly many interconnected networks.

Not One but Many Networks

A common ISDN misconception concerns just how many networks there are. Since ISDN is usually singular, people often believe that one great worldwide network is the object. While this is certainly not true, the result may (and should) appear to a casual user as one great network. Today's world telephone network provides a close parallel to explain how many ISDNs will exist and intercommunicate. A local telephone network, whether it serves a town or a building, is really a stand-alone network with limited connections to the outside world. Most private and many local telephone companies now require that a "9" or a "1" be dialed or touched first if a call is desired beyond the local area. Another (area) code is then entered if the call is to go beyond the borders of the local calling area, and an international prefix number is used if another country is desired. Anyone who frequently calls other countries knows how different calling number conventions are from country to country. Yet **international direct distance dialing** (IDDD) works and works well. This is not because there is one great world telephone network, but because national and international standards permit the individual networks to talk to each other. Thousands of independent ISD Networks will work exactly the same way—through national and international standards, but with new services, features and a new numbering plan.

Another change yet to come is the "Numbering Plan for the ISDN Era." This new world telephone numbering plan, now scheduled to go into effect on January 1, 1996, will move us from the current 12-digit plan to a 15-digit plan. In the United States and Canada little change will be seen as a subtle conversion is already underway. (In the U.S. and Canada, this change will permit area codes without a "0" or a "1" as the middle digit.) Those dialing international calls will see the change, as some international calls will require more digits.

In the world of analog IDDD, the main feature was an ability to address and connect to another voice telephone almost anywhere in the world. Transmission, addressing, and signalling standards came together across companies and countries to link the separated networks. That set of standards was formed in a set of concepts which are now yielding to the new concept of ISDN. Highlighting a few of the older concepts will help explain how ISDN differs. In analog voice telephony, events usually happen in sequence, rarely in parallel, for a single call. The sequence usually starts with a switch closure (off-hook) signalling a request for switch connection (dial-tone). When switch connection is granted, dial pulse digits or tones are expected by the switch. The digits then begin a sequence of switching actions to attempt connection with another telephone line. If that line can be found and is not busy, an incoming call signal (ring power) is sent out and a "ringing" sound is given to the originating telephone. If the called instrument closes its switch (off-hook), the ringing signals are stopped and a through voice connection is made. When either telephone switch is opened (on-hook), the connection is dropped to both instruments and all intervening switches. All this happens in strict sequence. For instance, digit tones or dial pulses are ignored during the voice part of the call and have no effect on the connection.

ISDN, with its usual minimum of two B communications and one D signalling and data channel can have many things happening at the same time. Clearly two independent voice or data calls can be in some state of progress while the D channel is *always* available for signalling. The D channel may be shared among many tasks because of its packet orientation. Incoming and outgoing signalling for both B channels can be interspersed with multiple data tasks. For instance, during two independent calls (voice or data), the D channel can indicate another incoming call and the caller's telephone number, carry on a running data transmission of news or financial quotes, monitor several fire and alarm systems and read the power meter for the local utility.

This, we hope, begins to answer the question: "What is ISDN?" Recapping the answer, ISDN begins with the complete digitization of all parts and pieces of telecommunications equipment, facilities, switching and transmission. Voice and data may then integrate through an interconnected world of many ISD Networks. ISDN changes the very nature of data and voice communications from single and sequential to multiple and simultaneous. While this is happening, all of today's current services are maintained; new service communications applications opportunities may then expand beyond our imagining.

Components of ISDN

International standards are the "glue" which binds the components of ISDN together into a system designed to answer the need for open architecture, universal digital access on demand, and improved speed and quality for both business and residential subscribers. A consistent and complete worldwide adoption of these standards, which were first conceived in 1972 by members of the CCITT, will permit the rapid availability of flexible end-to-end digital services to meet the commercial, governmental, and personal needs of an informa-tion-oriented population. Because the standards are *functional* in nature (they dictate *what* the components do, rather than *how*), they permit carriers and equipment vendors to pick and choose strategies and technologies best suited to their needs and those of their customers.

The major components of ISDN are the following:

• Services.
  A rich menu of worldwide services for human, machine, and human/machine interaction makes possible new communications applications and permits improvement in speed and cost/performance for those existing. Digital transmission combined with computer con-trol permit multiple simultaneous connections of various types and speeds via a single network interface on demand.

- Interfaces.

  Terminal, network, and internetwork interfaces specified at the mechanical, electrical, and procedural levels provide the means by which network subscribers request and receive services and by which networks cooperate in providing them.

- Facilities.

  Transmission and switching resources such as fiber lines, DACS systems, and packet switches are the infrastructure upon which ISDN offerings are built. These carry and route subscriber information and the intra- and inter-network messages which support facilities coordination.

The ISDN concept is the natural result of the gradual introduction of digital technology into information transmission (T-Carrier systems for interoffice voice trunks and DDS data circuits) and switching (stored program control and digital time/space division switches such as AT&T's #4ESS). The all-digital integration of transmission and switching, functions formerly so distinct that they had separate reporting structures on carrier organization charts, makes ISDNs possible.

Access Line Integration

It has been estimated that 40% of the investment in the world's telecommunications plant is in access lines linking customers to local switches and network hubs. Most of the access line investment is in the form of analog telephone subscriber loops consisting of one twisted pair per line, the longest of which are equipped with loading coils to counteract the effects of line capacitance. Digital access lines are mainly T1 (two pairs with repeaters at approximately 6,000 foot intervals) and DDS (two pair without repeaters). Any technology introduced for ISDN must make use of a large fraction of this investment, and do it without major change. An even better solution would diminish the number of loop plant pairs required, even as customer requirements grew.

One meaning of the word "integrated" in this chapter's title reflects the acceptance of this local access challenge. ISDN access lines provide multiple voice and/or data services over the same access lines, resulting in a decrease in twisted pair requirements over earlier systems. Conversion of a POTS line to basic ISDN service involves no outside plant changes other than removal of loading coils and some bridged taps (parallel-connected pairs) where they exist. It has been estimated that about 95% of the world's POTS loops are usable for ISDN service without change. The remainder may be reached via installing or converting remote subscriber line carrier systems such AT&T's SLC-96®, for which ISDN subscriber line modules are planned.

Transmission/Signalling Integration

Another meaning for "integrated" in this chapter's title is associated with the way the ISDN architecture multiplexes transmission and signalling data streams over access lines. In the ISDN world view, even the most basic access includes both user data and signalling information paths, and the signalling path is designed for messages between computer-controlled customer and network equipment. This kind of integration is evolved from the **common channel interoffice signalling** (CCIS) systems described in Chapter 2, and makes the subscriber's equipment an active participant in the operation of an intelligent network. Flexibility and efficiency are advantages of this arrangement, which provides for easy and economical introduction of new services.

B and D Channels and the DS-X Hierarchy

The basic unit of ISDN transmission capacity is the 64 kbit/s DS-0 channel. Called the **bearer**, or **B channel**, it is the same building block used with the PCM voice, DDS, and DACS systems described in the preceding chapters. This choice facilitates interchangeable use of channels for voice and data on existing transmission and switching facilities. ISDN bandwidth is supplied in DS-0 increments most commonly via access lines with either 2 or 23 (30 in European systems) DS-0 B channels. Bearer channels may be used either separately or in combination to produce multiples of the 64 kbit/s data rate.

One aspect of the ISDN subscriber access design which permits the **clear channel** DS-0 operation is the separation of signalling information from the data channel. Called **out of band signalling**, this technique was first used between voice network central offices to make more efficient use of trunks, provide faster call processing, and eliminate confusion of network and customer signals. Every ISDN access line provides a separate **D channel** over which messages between the network and the subscriber's equipment are passed. Because this channel is concerned with changes in the status or use of the associated B channels, the D channel is sometimes called the **delta channel**, after the Greek letter long used by engineers to indicate change. The D channel is also available for data transmission between subscribers using a technique called **packet switching**.

Access lines defined by ISDN standards are of two major types, as shown in Figure 14.2. The **basic-rate interface** (BRI) provides two 64 kbit/s bearer and one 16 kbit/s delta channel, a configuration called **2B + D** and intended for use by residential and small business subscribers. The **primary-rate interface** (PRI) offers 23 (30 in European systems) 64 kbit/s B and one 64 kbit/s D channel (**23B + D**) and is designed for customers requiring greater capacity than provided by the basic-rate interface.

Connections between ISDN hardware components follow a carefully architected conceptual model in which each of the interconnection points are named; Figure 14.3 is a diagram of this model. The interfaces are labeled with letters as follows:

- **U:** The U interface is between the carrier's access line and the NCTE at the customer premises, and is not, strictly speaking, a separate interface according to CCITT standards.

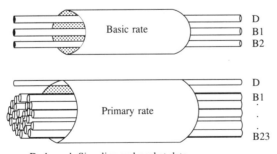

D channel: Signaling and packet data
B channel: Clear 64 kbit/s digital access

FIGURE 14.2. ISDN Access: Basic and Primary Rate Interfaces. Reprinted by permission. Copyright © 1986 AT&T.

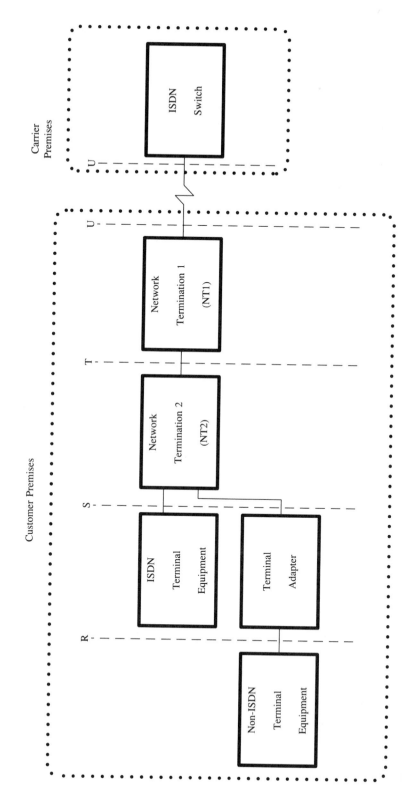

FIGURE 14.3. ISDN Interface Model.

It is a result of the telecommunications deregulation activity in the United States where NCTE is categorized as customer premises equipment. In other countries, it might be considered part of the network and not a concern of the subscriber. The U interface differs between basic and primary access designs. The NCTE is called NT1 (Network Terminal 1) and in the United States must be provided by the subscriber. The NT1 provides line termination and maintenance functions similar those of the CSU for a DDS line.

- **T:** The T interface (as are the others below) is the same for U.S. and other countries and represents a demarcation between the network and customer switching, concentrating, and/or multiplexing equipment designated NT2. The NT2 may be trivial (e.g., as with a single ISDN terminal on a basic rate access line) or may provide a number of S interfaces on the terminal side (as with a customer's switch).

- **S:** True ISDN terminals (designated TE1) connect directly to the S interface, which supports both data and signalling. Up to eight TE1s may share a single S interface, which is a two-pair "inside wire" passive bus up to 1 km (.62 mile) in length.

- **R:** The R interface is a result of the need to accommodate non-ISDN terminals with the help of a terminal adapter designated TA. R is, in a sense, generic: its characteristics depend on the device being adapted to the S interface and in a given instance might be POTS, EIA-232, V.35, and so on.

Multiplexing B and D Channels on Access Lines

The data rates and multiplexing method for B and D channels differ between the basic and primary rate interfaces. The basic rate interface provides a 16 kbit/s D channel to support two B channels on a single wire pair; the primary rate design is a variation on the T1 scheme with a 64 kbit/s D channel rate and requires two wire pairs.

BASIC RATE INTERFACE

The BRI was intended to replace the analog POTS loop and serve residences, small businesses, and workstations connected to ISDN switches on customer premises. In the case of the latter, the customer premises switch and its access lines are sometimes called a **subtended network** from the viewpoint of the ISDN carrier. Most likely, the access line(s) serving an ISDN customer switch would be primary rate interfaces, although any combination of PRI and BRI access lines is possible, in principle, on the network side of NT2 devices.

Specification of the U.S. 2B + D interface was delayed compared to those of other nations because of the need for multiple carriers within the U.S. to agree on it (in countries with a single carrier or PTT, the technical specifications could be determined unilaterally). Two designs were major candidates until shortly before this writing; now the adoption by the CCITT of **echo cancellation**, advanced by the **Exchange Carrier Standards Association** (ECSA), seems assured.

The electrical and physical characteristics of the ECSA 2B + D design for the digital subscriber line are described in ANSI Standard T1D1.3/87-003R8 (including a line coding for which it is also called: 2B1Q). Included in the specification are the line code, signal spectral composition, organization of data into frames, and functions of the operations channels (two kbit/s in each direction) used for maintenance commands such as test requests and loopback.

The echo cancellation process involves electrically subtracting the near-end signal and a replica of the echo of the near-end transmission from the total received signal, leaving the far-end signal for decoding. The process is designed to work with loop resistances of up to 1300 ohms, corresponding to a length of 18,000 feet and covering 99% of the North American unloaded local loops. It does not require that polarity of the tip and ring leads be preserved, and tolerates most kinds of bridged taps. Timing is supplied at the network end and loopback timing is used at the subscriber end.

A four-level pulse amplitude modulated line code called 2B1Q (two binary, one quaternary) is used at a rate of 80 kilobaud, giving 160 kbit/s in each direction. This capacity is allocated as follows: B channels, 128 kbit/s; D channel, 16 kbit/s; and overhead (including framing, checking, and operations channels), 16 kbit/s.

PRIMARY RATE ACCESS

Standard T1 multiplexing is used with either U.S. (24 channel) or European CEPT (30 channels) in which one of the 64 kbit/s channels is dedicated as a D channel. This choice permits an extremely easy transition for subscribers and CPE manufacturers already using T1.

Uses of the D Channel

The CCITT standard for packet networks provided the basis for sharing the D channel. Packet networks are well suited to intermittent, bursty data traffic; the standard provides for multiplexing a number of "virtual circuits" over a single link. The D channel data stream is shared between signaling and data transmission using a **link access protocol** called LAPD which is a variation on the LAPB (**link access protocol-balanced**) used with CCITT packet switching standard, X.25. LAPB, in turn, is a peer-to-peer variation on **synchronous data link control**. Packets (blocks) of either ISDN signaling information or user data to/from the carrier's packet network are blocked into HDLC frames and sent over the D channel; LAPD uses a code called the **protocol discriminator** to distinguish them, effectively creating a special virtual circuit for signalling information.

SIGNALING AND SUPERVISION

The ISDN standard defining the syntax and semantics of signaling messages between network and subscriber equipment for circuit mode operation is designated both I.451 and Q.931. It provides the means to establish, maintain, and terminate connections across an ISDN. These messages are the modern counterparts of the tone sequences and combinations used in analog telephone networks for call requests and progress messages. Q.931 messages include the following (S–> N indicates subscriber to network, N–> S indicates network to subscriber, and < – > indicates a message which can travel either way):

- Call establishment messages:
  —Alerting (<– >).
  This message is comparable to the ringback tone of the analog telephone network. The S–> N case arises when the network requests a connection through the subscriber's switch.

—Call proceeding (<–>).

This message indicates that a previously requested call establishment has begun and no further call requests will be accepted until the disposition of the call is determined.

—Connect (<–>), connect acknowledge (<–>).

Connect indicates the acceptance of a call by the called user. Connect Acknowledge indicates reception of Connect.

—Setup (<–>), Setup Acknowledge (<–>).

Setup requests call establishment; setup acknowledge confirms setup.

- Call Information Phase Messages.

—User Information (<–>).

This message may be used to transmit auxiliary data between the subscribers connected by a call.

—Suspend (S–> N), suspend acknowledge (N–> S), suspend reject (N–> S).

Suspend requests the (presumably temporary) discontinuance of a call in progress, an action which may affect charges for it. The network indicates confirmation with Suspend Acknowledge and denial with Suspend Reject.

—Resume (S–> N), resume acknowledge (N–> S), resume reject (N–> S).

Resume requests the resumption of a SUSPENDed call; resume acknowledge confirms resume and resume reject indicates failure.

- Call disestablishment messages.

—Detach (<–>), detach acknowledge (<–>).

Detach indicates that the sender has disconnected the B channel(s). Detach acknowledge indicates reception of detach and the equivalent disconnection at the opposite end. In both cases, the ability to identify the call in future messages is retained.

—Disconnect (<–>).

This message is an invitation to release both the B channel(s) and the ability to identify the call in the future.

—Release (<–>), release complete (<–>).

Release indicates that the sender has disconnected the B channel(s) and intends to do the same with the information identifying the call; the receiver should do the same and abort the identified call if it is in the process of being set up. Release complete confirms release.

- Miscellaneous messages.

—Cancel (S–> N), cancel acknowledge (N–> S), cancel reject (N–> S) cancel from the subscriber requests the network to discontinue use of a facility[1]; cancel acknowledge indicates acceptance of cancel; and cancel reject is used by the network to indicate failure of cancel.

—Congestion control (<–>) This message is sent to indicate the establishment or termination of flow control, a procedure which limits traffic in the case of resource shortage.

—Facility (S–> N), facility acknowledge (N–> S), facility reject (N–> S).

Facility is a request to the network for a facility; granting of the facility by the network and the beginning of its operation are confirmed by facility acknowledge and denial is indicated by facility reject.

—Information (<–>).

A kind of parenthetical message, information may add to something already transmitted

---

[1] In this context, a facility is a service option such as reverse billing, not a part of the physical plant.

in either direction, as with extension number for direct inward dialing or B channel negotiation.

—Register (<–>), register acknowledge (<–>), register reject (<–>).

Register from the subscriber requests registration of a network facility; when sent by the network to the subscriber it requests negotiation of agreement with a register request (perhaps originated by another subscriber). Register acknowledge confirms register or agreement to same and register reject denies it or agreement with it.

—Status (<–>).

This message may be sent at any time during a call by either the network or the subscriber to report conditions, expected or otherwise.

PACKET DATA NETWORK ACCESS AND TELEMETRY

ISDN D-channel design permits all of the packet network operations of CCITT X.25, long used for data communications and priced in a volume- (rather than distance- or time-) dependent manner. One example of such use of the D channel would be inquiring about a stock price while one B channel was in use for 64 kbit/s PCM voice call to a stockbroker and another used for transmitting video images of the voice call participants. X.25 is very economical for short data conversations such as data base inquiry/response.

Telemetry applications involve transmitting physical status information such as utility meter readings, temperature, flow, burglar and fire alarms, and so on. Where these transmissions are infrequent and short, the ISDN D channel provides an excellent access facility at very low incremental cost.

Uses Of The B Channel

Perhaps the most interesting application of ISDN is the displacement of leased lines by on-demand point-point digital connectivity with rapid call set-up and (unlike using analog telephone facilities for data) favorable error rates. ISDN supports the use of B channels by subscription with the carrier as leased facilities, and the need for full-time bandwidth will never disappear completely. However, many applications supporting leased facilities could do equally well with one or more B channels allocated as needed. As subscriber confidence builds in the availability and quality of on-demand ISDN bandwidth, leased lines will decrease in number. As inefficient leased lines are replaced with circuit switched connections, all subscribers will benefit from the facility sharing that will result.

Among the possible destinations for B channel calls are packet network carriers. Many packet network subscribers now using leased lines (called **dedicated access facilities**, or DAFs) will be able to replace them with ISDN circuit-switched connections which are activated (and paid for) on demand. The ability to create such access on demand will be a significant factor in their acceptance.

Application Integration

ISDNs will be the basis for integration along yet another dimension. In addition to consolidating access to multiple voice, data, and image services or reading and sending the administrative mail supporting all this telecommunication, ISDNs represent the beginning of a communications movement which will make it easy for individuals and business to interconnect in ways not previously possible: with integrated applications. Integrated applications represent a kind of interaction and cooperation both unknown and impossible before the wide acceptance of an abstraction called **open systems interconnection** (OSI). Until recently, correspondence between the OSI model for telecommunications and the real world was limited to the bottom three layers shown in Figure 14.4. Public packet networks offered the ability to exchange blocks of bytes for which the interpretation need be known only to the participants.

Business Communications

Forces pointing at business interaction above the network level of the OSI model include **electronic data interchange** (EDI) and intersystem electronic mail as facilitated by CCITT standard X.400. EDI is rapidly becoming a prompt and accurate way to exchange relatively standard documents such as purchase orders and invoices. X.400 is being integrated into private and commercial mail systems used worldwide. These interactions between network subscribers represent nothing less than a quantum leap in information technology, and are tentative and exploratory at this writing. Nevertheless, we can expect numerous social and economic benefits from the multilateral adoption of standards by which businesses interact faster, more accurately, and at lower cost.

Residential Services

Human nature being relatively more stable than information technology implies that personal telephone usage will not change much, at least when the caller and the called party connect on the first try. Digital transmission and signalling can be expected to offer useful alternatives, however, in the increasing number of cases where the first person-to-person try is unsuccessful. The ISDN network itself or one of its commercial subscribers may offer applications to the public called **teleservices**, including voice mail.

Another teleservice, still in its infancy, is computer conferencing; once it is better understood, application layer standards could appear to facilitate economical computer-mediated *text* communication between separate host systems or between autonomous work stations. Computer conferencing differs in connectivity from electronic mail, which is addressed one-to-one or one-to-few; it is essentially many-to-many and has traditionally relied on multi-user host systems to be practical. An ISDN teleservice standard for computer conferencing would facilitate the concentration of human intelligence at a level previously unknown.

Totally New Services

The ability to send megabits around the world at reasonable cost in time and money will encourage communications of kinds impossible to predict. Nevertheless, the potential for certain trends may be discerned.

One reasonable possibility is the common transmission of non-coded information such as pictures and music, perhaps in combination. The ability to identify the source of a data call by network address invites credit sales of popular music and associated graphics (album covers, video stills, and so on.) on demand or, at worst, overnight where sender and receiver are in proximate time zones.

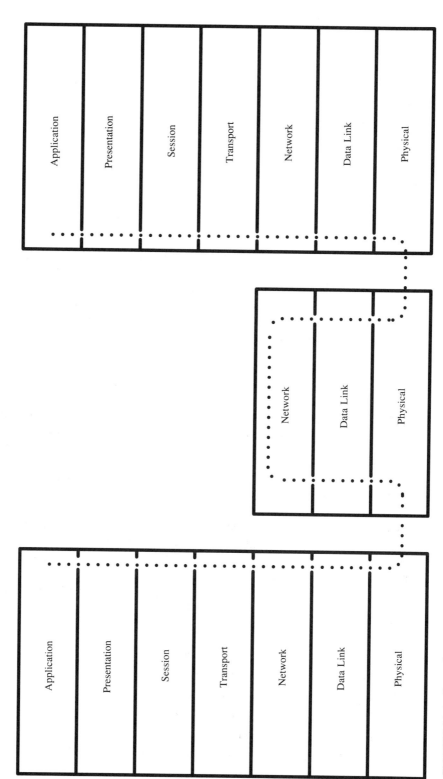

FIGURE 14.4. Open Systems Interconnection Layered Model. ISDNs will promote the use and expansion of upper layers.

ISDN Standards

While planning had been underway for many years under various names, 1984 was perhaps the true christening year for ISDN. That year, the International Telegraph and Telephone Consultative Committee (CCITT) approved a new series of recommendations specifically for ISDN. Called the "I-series" and published in the now famous 450 page Red Book, they formed the real basis on which ISDN began to be designed. The Blue Book, resulting from the 1988 CCITT Plenary Assembly in Melbourne, fills in many of the gaps from the original "I-series" recommendations. New standards and revisions will continue to amend those in force, but a strong base for real networks and real network interconnection is now in place. This standards effort is really worldwide and, because of its importance to ISDN, we pause to review it.

The CCITT and World Standards

The CCITT (its name in French comes in this order) is part of the International Telecommunications Union, a body of the United Nations. Nations are members and each nation contributes to the work effort in differing ways. In many countries, telecommunications is a government function and a postal, telephone and telegraph agency, or PTT, is the CCITT member. In the United States, although the Department of State is the official member, many organizations are involved in U.S. contributions and positions. The American National Standards Institute (ANSI) provides a key focus for many other bodies, including the Electronic Industries Association (EIA) and the Exchange Carrier Standards Association (ECSA). The latter, as one of the Accredited Standards Committee of ANSI, is the most active in ISDN matters and its T1D1 ISDN Technical Subcommittee provides the main U.S. focus group for ISDN. This group prepares technical reports and recommends standards relevant to ISDN which evolve to American National Standards from ANSI.

Prior to the break-up of American Telephone and Telegraph, AT&T exerted a major influence on U.S. Telecommunications standards. With divestiture, many more parties needed involvement. The Exchange Carrier Standards Association was incorporated in 1983 to represent the interests of local exchange common carriers. ECSA established the T1, or first telecommunications, committee to focus on "functions and characteristics associated with the interconnection and interoperability of telecommunications networks . . . ." (T1 here is the name of the committee and has no relationship to the first level digital T-Carrier T1.) Members of ECSA's T1 include not only exchange carriers, such as the seven regional bell operating companies, but interexchange carriers such as AT&T, U.S. Sprint, and MCI. Manufacturers, government agencies, telecommunications users and other organizations are members. Within standards committee T1, ECSA has established several technical subcommittees. these include:

- T1C1: customer premise equipment to carrier interfaces;
- T1D1: integrated services digital networks;
- T1M1: internetwork operations, administration, maintenance, provisioning;
- T1Q1: performance (within networks and at network interfaces);
- T1X1: carrier-to-carrier interfaces; and
- T1Y1: specialized subjects (such as video and advanced technologies).

The primary burden for ISDN standards falls on T1D1 and, because of deregulation, many standards structured by and for government-owned PTTs must differ in the U.S. An example is the two-wire U interface, technically called the: *Integrated Services Digital Network—Basic Access Interface for Use on Metallic Loops for Application on the Network Side of the NT*. This interface is not required by most national PTTs; the PTT supplies the customer premises equipment (CPE) and uses a four-wire T interface. In the U.S., CPE comes from many sources and a technical interface is needed due to political differences. ECSA's T1D1 Technical Subcommittee prepared the necessary interface standards to permit multiple sources of CPE to connect to U.S. ISD Networks. Similarly, T1D1 prepares U.S. technical reports and proposed standards for other ISDN related topics. This work then flows to the CCITT and, when reconciled with other national efforts, emerges as CCITT recommendations.

The path to accepted world standards is often slow and filled with strong argument. While ISDN has not been spared these trials, its progress has been amazingly steady. Credit must be given to the many individuals involved with this worldwide standardization for the conversion of the world's telephone systems. The growing number of operational private and public ISD Networks shows convergence of this massive standards effort. As ISDN accelerates, the next question becomes: what do we need to do to plan for ISDN?

Planning for ISDN

When new concepts and technologies loom just over the horizon, planning becomes much more difficult. With ISDN, some of that difficulty may be reduced as many of the fundamental changes will be evolutionary. Several factors make planning for the ISDN era easier and several make it more complex. In the next two sections we highlight some of each, but one factor is very unpredictable. The rate at which ISDN will arrive and the rate at which it must be accepted depends on non-technical factors. Service and equipment cost trends could accelerate or delay ISDN's rollout. The early availability of significant and attractive service features could speed the migration. The desirability of features and the productivity of their use will only be known after early use is well established. Speed of acceptance by businesses and individuals will be the final word. Earlier technology offerings give us clues but no certainties. The rapid acceptance of personal computers, compact discs, and videocassette recorders indicates readiness for a high rate of change. Not all new offerings, however, are swept up at that rate and planning become a readiness game. To help with that preparedness, we offer some thoughts about what changes and what remains the same in the ISDN era.

What Stays the Same

Many things already in place will remain and many will continue their expansion independent of ISDN. A review of these things may give rest to those concerned about rapid obsolescence of networks, facilities and equipment. The popularity of T-Carriers for both voice and data multiplexing and transmission acts as a precursor, as they are ISDN building blocks. In both North American and CEPT digital transmission hierarchies, the lowest level is equivalent to the B channel—64 kbit/s. At the first multiplexed level (1.544 or 2.048 Mbit/s) we have the **primary rate interface** of ISDN. The 24 channels of North American T1 give way to 23 B plus D. In the CEPT arrangement, 30 channels with a separate signalling channel are already 30 B plus D. Pulse code modulation methods of voice digitization remain and coexist with newer analog-to-digital coding methods, some which are much more efficient than the one first used for T1; standards provide for identifying voice coding and for converting between them (a process called **transcoding**).

In equipment areas, existing data interfaces of V.35 and EIA-232 will be met with **terminal adapters** (TA) which handle rate conversions (called **rate adaptation**) to B channel speeds. Most digital switches currently operate with T1 interfaces to digital networks and digital channel banks. Higher speed data devices already operate at 56 kbit/s or 64 kbit/s and T1 rates. Compressed video digital encoders run at rates compatible with ISDN's higher rate channels of H0 (384 kbit/s), H11 (1.536 Mbit/s) or H12 (1.920 Mbit/s). All these devices can exist in an ISDN world with little adaptation. In these intermediate years, equipment procurements will increasingly include provisions for ISDN adaptation and conversion.

During the rollout period, many claims may exist before their actual reality. This will be a most difficult period for planners trying to sort out both their ISDN conversion plans and true pace of price and equipment performance. As tariff and ISDN enhanced feature trends become increasingly attractive, change will become inescapable.

What Changes with ISDN

When the new features of ISDN become necessary or desirable, analog devices will be the first to go. Analog voice telephones and the data modems which emulate them must be converted. While TAs will be available to accommodate differences, eventually replacement will have to be considered. In the small business and residential environment, conversions may come on an instrument (or workstation) basis. Analog voice telephones and personal computer modems with TAs can co-exist on ISDN access lines with the newer ISDN devices. This process will allow a paced change. In larger establishments the conversion process will most likely be staged in larger steps. Replacement of telephone switches and instruments will often occur simultaneously. Data terminal and workstation changes need not happen at the same time. These conversions may take place in the host environment prior to or following the voice change.

Voice/data integration may be managed by changing out equipment or may be obtained by software changes and linkage between existing telephone switches and communications processors. Or voice/data integration may be delayed while only the tariff advantages of ISDN are realized. Planners at this stage in larger establishments may wish to return to Occam's Razor and slice apart the conversion into desirable and manageable steps. The ISDN era ushers in a new richness of choice; the future all-digital world of electronic communications has arrived.

The Future of Megabit Digital Communications

Connecting the Global Village

The arrival of ISDN completes our return to an all digital realm of telecommunications which began with the electric telegraph. The worldwide installation of fiber optic transmission accelerates, offering practically unlimited capacity to carry human and machine messages, whether they be voice, data, sound, or picture. As the fibers which now span continents and oceans spread to residences and small businesses, access to high-speed digital capabilities will become nearly universal. The new and enhanced applications of this access and capacity will change the economics of information-based products and services permanently. As well-traveled routes become saturated with fiber capacity, advances in electronics and in aerospace vehicles will bring similar capacity and economics via satellite to those off the beaten path.

These trends will combine in the very near future to help make the world a global village in the truest sense. The authors hope that you will agree that this is not only a worthy goal, but an adventure of the first order.

Glossary

Note. The glossary definitions below are meant to explain terms used in this text. There exist more formal definitions for many of these terms in standards documents and other more complete glossaries. Our aim here is understanding and explanation. For formal and exact definitions, the reader should refer to formal standards and glossaries such as those published by the EIA, CCITT and other standards bodies.

AAR. Automatic Alternate Routing (in a telephone switching system).

address. An indication of the location of the intended recipient or storage location for a message.

addressing. Transmission in which the location or identity of intended recipient(s) is indicated.

AMI. Alternate Mark Inversion (bipolar signal where "ones" alternate in voltage).

aggregate. A single bit stream combining many bit streams.

alphabet. The collection of symbols in a code.

alternating current. Periodically reversing electric current.

APD. Avalanche Photo Diode (used to receive fiber optic signals).

APS. Automatic Protection Switching (to switch to spare facilities).

ASCII. American Standard Code for Information Interchange.

analog. Characterized by a continuous (vs. discrete) range of values.

ANSI. American National Standards Institute.

assigned frequency. The frequency coinciding with the center of the radio frequency channel in which the station is authorized to work.

attenuation. Loss or diminution, usually of transmitted signal.

AWG. American Wire Gauge (size of electrical wires).

asynchronous. Without regular inter-symbol timing.

bandwidth. Range of all frequencies in an analog channel.

baseband. Original and unmodulated information frequency band.

baud. Unit of signal frequency.

BER. Bit Error Rate (ratio of errored bits to total bits).

binary. Characteristic of having only two states.

bipolar. Having both positive and negative voltage states with respect to a reference.

bit. Binary digit; two-valued information unit.

bit-interleaved. An orderly aggregate of multiple bit streams separated in time.

bit rate. Rate of transmission in binary (two-state) form per unit of time.

bit stuffing. Increasing a serial rate by adding fill bits.

blue box. Multifrequency signalling transmitter for in-band use, usually for fraudulent purposes.

BPV. Bipolar Violation (violation of AMI).

break. Long spacing condition to interrupt sender.

BRI. Basic Rate Interface (two B plus D) in ISDN.

busy-out. Setting a channel out-of-service, usually in a manner facilitating automatic selection of alternate channels.

bypass. Connection to a (communications common) carrier not using a local exchange carrier.

byte. A collection of bits, usually eight.

byte-interleaved. An orderly aggregate of multiple byte streams separated in time.

CATV. Community Antenna Television, now commonly known as cable TV.

CBX. Computerized Branch exchange, a computer operated PBX.

channelizaton. Organizing into channels.

carrier (signal or wave). In a frequency stabilized system, the sinusoidal component of a modulated wave; the output of a transmitter when the modulating wave is made zero; a wave generated at a point in the transmitting system and subsequently modulated by the signal; a wave generated locally at the receiving terminal which, when combined with the sidebands in a suitable detector, produces the modulating wave.

carrier frequency. The frequency of a carrier (signal or wave).

carrier system. A method of carrying several information channels.

CCIR. Consultative Committee on International Radio.

CCITT. Consultative Committee on International Telephone & Telegraphy.

CCR. Customer Controlled Reconfiguration (a feature permitting the user to control channel assignments within a T1 from a terminal without common carrier intervention).

central office. A landline termination center used for switching and interconnection of public message communications circuits.

channel bank. A device to place multiple channels on a digital or analog carrier.

channel slot. A position of a channel on a carrier.

character. An element in an alphabet.

circuit card. A unit of electronic hardware packaging, upon which components are mounted.

CLASS. Custom Local Area Signal Services (a set of software features for computer-controlled end offices which bring some of the advantages of Signaling System 7 (such as called party identification) to the customer).

clear channel. A channel without any format restrictions.

code. A method of representing signals.

CODEC. CODer/DECoder, a device to encode and decode signals.

common control. An arrangement by which a single control mechanism, such as a stored program computer, is shared over time by multiple connections.

common equipment. Equipment which is shared and not duplicated on a channel-by-channel basis.

communications common carrier. Any person engaged in rendering communications service for hire to the public.

companding. Non-linear reduction of a signal, usually compressing the larger signal values.

control-idle. A telegraphic or digital code used to indicate a ready but not busy condition.

CPE. Customer Premises Equipment (devices usually owned and operated by and at the telephone customer's location).

cross-bar. A switching system in which interconnections are established (either logically or physically) between channels separated in two dimensions.

CRC. Cyclic Redundancy Check (a group of bits created and checked to verify correctness of messages).

cross-connect. A place or time where channels (often DS-0 channels) are interconnected.

crosstalk. Interference between channels, often on an analog carrier system.

CSDC. Circuit-Switched Digital Capability (a service which provides switched digital connections between customers, typically at 56 kbits/s).

CSMA. Carrier Sense / Multiple Access (a contention method of placing information on a common medium).

CSU. Channel Service Unit (a telephone device facing the digital line).

CVSD. Continually Variable Slope Detection (a method of coding speech to digital).

DACS. Digital Access and Cross-Connect System (an electronic digital channel patching system).

dash. The longer of the two marking elements of Morse Code.

dataport. A digital data adapter in a voice channel bank or voice system.

dB. Abbreviation of decibel (a unit of logarithmic magnitude comparison).

DCE. Data Circuit Terminating Equipment, see Chapter 4.

DDD. Direct Distance Dialing.

DDS. Digital Data Services, such as DataPhone Digital Services® (a digital data communications service).

decibel. A logarithmic unit of magnitude comparison named after Alexander Graham Bell and abbreviated dB.

decode. Reverse the effect of coding, return to uncoded state.

demarcation. A connecting point separating responsibilities.

demodulation. The process of extracting intelligence from a modulated signal.

demultiplex. Reverse the aggregation effect of multiplexing, return channels to individual states.

digital electronic message service. A two-way domestic end-to-end fixed radio service using digital termination service for the exchange of digital information (may use point-to-point microwave, satellite, or other media).

digital modulation. The process by which one or more characteristics (frequency, phase, amplitude, or combinations thereof) are varied in accordance with a digital signal (e.g., one consisting of coded pulses or discrete states).

digital termination nodal station. A fixed to multipoint radio station in a digital termination system providing two-way communication with digital termination user stations.

digital termination user station. Any one of the fixed microwave radio stations located at users' premises, lying within the coverage area of a digital termination nodal station, and providing two-way digital communications with the digital termination nodal station.

digital termination system. A fixed point-to-multipoint radio system consisting of a digital termination nodal station(s) and associated digital termination user stations.

digroup. DIgital GROUP, an assembly of 24 channels into a digital aggregate.

direct broadcast satellite service. A radio communication service in which signals transmitted or retransmitted by space stations are intended for direct reception by the general public (includes both individual reception and community reception).

direct current. Electric current constant in direction.

distortion. Alteration of a signal in an undesirable way.

DLE. Data Link Escape (a bit sequence issued to ignore a following string as a control sequence).

dot. The shorter of the two marking elements of Morse Code.

double current. Telegraphy with current direction signalling.

downlink. The signal path from a satellite to the earth.

drop and insert. Access to a few of an aggregate's channels.

drop point. A location where service is rendered to a subscriber.

DSU. Data Service Unit (a digital telephone device facing the users terminal equipment).

DSX. Digital Signal Cross-connect (an electrical interface point).

DTE. Data Terminal Equipment (in this book, Digital Terminating Equipment is not abbreviated as DTE).

duplex. Bidirectional, either alternately (half-duplex) or continuously (full duplex).

DUV. Data Under Voice (a method of carrying data signals under frequency division multiplex voice carriers).

earth station. A station in the space service located either on the Earth's surface, including on board a ship, or on board an aircraft.

EBCDIC. Extended Binary Coded Decimal Interchange Code (a binary code to represent alphanumerics).

EDI. Electronic Document Interchange.

effective radiated power. The product of antenna power input and the antenna power gain (usually expressed in watts or dBW).

EIRP. Effective Isotropic Radiated Power (a measure of transmit power from an antenna).

element. The basic unit of a symbol.

ESF. Extended Superframe Format (an extended method of framing a T1 bit stream).

ESS. Electronic Switching System (a digital telephone switching family).

exchange. A unit of communications company or companies for the administration of communications service in a specified area, consisting of one or more central offices, together with the associated plant used in furnishing services in that area.

exchange area. The geographic area included within the bounds of an exchange.

equalizer. A device designed to compensate for predictable distortion.

facsimile. (FAX) A system of telecommunications for the transmission of fixed images with a view to their reception in a permanent form.

farad. Unit of electrical capacitance, named after Faraday.

FIFO. First-In, First-Out, usually bits or bytes in a buffer.

firmware. Software to run a device, usually implanted in chip sets.

fixed satellite service. A radio communication service between Earth stations at specified fixed points when one or more satellites are used.

flag. A unique delimiting symbol in digital frames.

frame. A delimited assembly of information.

framing. Setting information between delimiting symbols.

frequency. Rate of repetition or oscillation.

frequency division. Separation of signals by carrier frequency.

FSK. Frequency Shift Keying (a modulation method).

frequency translation. Alteration of carrier frequency by a fixed amount.

front end. An information computer controlling communications.

full duplex. Continuously bidirectional.

gain. Desirable increase.

geo-stationary. Apparently stationary relative to earth.

GMT. Greenwich Mean Time—world standard time, now Coordinated Universal Time (CUT).

grandfather. Accepted due to existence prior to regulation.

ground. Electrical connection to the earth or other reference point.

group. A collection of information channels (usually 12).

half-duplex. Bidirectional on an alternate basis.

henry. Unit of electrical inductance.

hertz. Unit of frequency, one cycle per second.

hierarchy. A ranked series of information levels.

HDLC. High-level Data Link Control (a bit-oriented protocol).

HPA. High Power Amplifier (in satellite transmitters).

IDDD. International Direct Distance Dialing.

IEC. Inter Exchange Carrier (a long-distance company).

IFL. Inter Facility Link (in satellite ground stations).

in-band. Signalling contained within an information bandwidth.

inside wiring. Wiring on customer premises side of a demarcation.

jitter. Short-term non-cumulative time variations in a digital signal.

keep-alive. Null-value bit stream to maintain connection.

LADT. Local Area Data Transport (a data transmission service added to local telephone loops, often used to provide access to the carrier's public packet switching service).

LAN. Local Area Network (an in-building or on-campus network).

LAPB. Link Access Procedure-Balanced (a protocol in packet networks).

LAPD. Link Access Procedure for the ISDN D channel.

LATA. Local Access and Transport Area (a geographical area of the local telephone company).

LBO. Line Build Out (a method of reducing signal for shorter lines).

LDM. Limited Distance Modem.

LEC. Local Exchange Carrier (a local telephone company).

LEDS. Light Emitting Diodes (to drive fiver optics).

LIFO. Last-In, First-Out (usually in bit or byte buffers).

line powered. Receiving operating power from a communications line.

LNA. Low Noise Amplifier (usually in satellite receivers).

loading. Local loop inductive coils compensating for capacitance.

local loop. Telephone office wiring to a customer premises.

loopback. Returning back the sending signal for testing.

loop-timed. Transmitting with timing derived from the received signal.

LORAN. LOng Range Aid to Navigation (a navigation radio system).

loss. An undesirable decrease (often in signal power).

LSB. Least Significant Bit (a bit coded with the lowest weight).

LSI. Large Scale Integration (in semiconductors or chips).

mark. "One" state for a binary channel.

marking. Condition of "one" state for a binary channel.

mastergroup. A collection of analog supergroups (usually 10).

MDF. Main Distribution Frame (a telephone wiring point).

measured service. A service for which charges are levied based on actual usuage (rather than availability).

microfarad. One millionth of a farad, q.v.

microwave. Radio frequencies at or above 890 MHz.

MJU. Multijunction Unit, to distribute multipoint DDS signals.

modem. Modulator-Demodulator.

modulation. Varying an electromagnetic phenomenon causing it to carry information.

MULDEM. MULtiplexer-DEMultiplexer, a T-Carrier multiplexer.

multidrop. Having more than two points of transmission and/or reception.

multiframe. Containing multiple digital frames.

multimode. Multiple optical transmission modes in a fiber.

multiplexing. Process combining channels to aggregates or groups.

multipoint. Having more than two points of transmission and/or reception.

multipoint distribution service. A one-way domestic public radio service on microwave frequencies from a fixed station transmitting (usually in an omnidirectional pattern) to multiple receiving facilities located at fixed points determined by subscribers.

MUX. Multiplexer (a combiner of channels).

NA. Numerical Aperture (used in fiber optics).

NCTE. Network Circuit Terminating Equipment (channel terminating telephone equipment at the customer premises belonging to the telco).

nest. An accommodation for a number of tenants, (often cards or units of electronic hardware).

non-coded data. Elements not comprising symbols (e.g., video).

NT1. Network Termination 1 (A reference point in the ISDN model, q.v.).

NT2. Network Termination 2 (A reference point in the ISDN model, q.v.).

null-modem. Connectors and wiring designed to simulate back-to-back DCEs between DTEs.

OCU. Office Channel Unit (unit at the telco end of a DDS circuit).

OOS. Out of Service (condition and code of a channel).

OSI. Open System Interconnection (a reference model for standards).

OTDR. Optical Time Domain Reflectometer (a test device for optical fibers).

out-of-band. Signalling sent outside an information bandwidth.

pair-gain. Number of channels multiplexed on a single pair.

PAM. Pulse Amplitude Modulation (a pulse height code for analog signals).

PANS. Pretty Amazing New Services.

parallel. Transmitted several units simultaneously.

passband. The operational frequency portion of a channel.

PBX. Private Branch Exchange (a users telephone switch).

PCM. Pulse Code Modulation (a pulse value code for analog signals).

point-to-point. Connecting two fixed points.

polling. Periodic interrogation for message traffic.

POP. Point of Presence (a telephone carrier's office).

POTS. Plain Old Telephone Service.

PRI. Primary Rate Interface (a T1 speed (23 B+D) ISDN interface).

private line service. A service whereby facilities for communication between two or more designated points are set aside for the exclusive use or availability for use of a particular customer and authorized users during a stated period of time.

protection. Automatically used spare transmission facilities.

protocol. Procedure or set of rules.

pseudo-ternary. Ternary in fact but binary in usage.

PTT. Postal Telegraph and Telephone, usually a government run telephone company.

public correspondence. Any telecommunication which the offices and stations, by reason of their being at the disposal of the public, must accept for transmission.

public message service. A service whereby facilities are offered to the public for communication between all points served by a carrier or interconnected carriers on a non-exclusive message-by-message basis, contemplating a separate connection for each occasion of use.

punched card. A paper data record, usually carrying between 540 and 960 bits and organized into rows and columns.

record communication. Any transmission of intelligence which is reduced to visual record form at the point of reception.

quantization. Reduction of a continuous signal to a time series of discrete approximations.

repeater station. A fixed station established for the automatic retransmission of communications received from one or more other stations and directed to a specific station.

register. Hardware used for temporary storage and/or accumulation, as of arithmetic results.

repeater. Device for extending transmission distance.

RF. Radio Frequency.

RFT. Radio Frequency Terminal (usually in satellite stations).

ringback. The ringing sound heard by the calling party.

RJ. Registered Jack (under Part 68 of the FCC Rules).

RJE. Remote Job Entry (usually in computer networks).

RJO. Remote Job Output (usually in computer networks).

robbing. Occasional stealing of information bits for signalling.

SAES. Small Aperture Earth Stations (small antenna satellite ground stations).

sampling. Observation and recording (often with the intent of quantization).

SCPC. Single Channel Per Carrier (non-multiplexed satellite signal channels).

SDLC. Synchronous Data Link Control (a bit oriented protocol).

SDRM. Sub-Rate Digital Multiplexing (usually for DDS speeds below 56 kbit/s data signals).

sealing current. A small direct current on signal wiring designed to preserve electrical continuity at interconnection points via an electrochemical process.

serial. Transmitted only one unit at a time.

signaling. Control information transmitted about information.

simplex. Unidirectional.

simplex current. Unidirectional current.

single current. Telegraphy with on-off signalling.

SONET. Synchronous Optical NETwork (a fiber optic interface standard).

space. "Zero" state for a binary channel.

space division. Signal separation by physical distance, as with open wire lines on a pole or wires in a cable.

spacing. Condition of "zero" state for a binary channel.

span. Length of transmission facility between terminals.

step-by-step. A control arrangement such as that of Strowger in which switching is sequential and synchronized to the originating terminal's signals, usually pulses.

stored program control. Control via software.

STP. Signal Transfer Point (a telephone signaling conversion point from tones to signal packets).

strap. An option switch in equipment (usually implelmented as a jumper or other movable bridge on a printed circuit card).

subrate. Usually DDS speeds below 56 kbit/s.

superframe. A repetitive pattern of 12 digital frames.

supergroup. A collection of analog groups, usually 5.

supervisory. Concerned with channel status, as with on/off hook in telephone systems.

symbol. Unit of information conveyed over a channel in a unit of time.

symbol rate. Modulation rate in bauds.

synchronous. A mode of transmission in which symbols are exchanged with fixed, rather than random, inter-symbol time separation.

SYNTRAN. SYNchronous TRANsmission, an alternate method for multiplexing lower to higher digital streams.

tariff. Price and technical document filed with regulatory agencies for new or revised service.

TASI. Time Assigned Speech Interpolation (a system for exploiting silences in human conversation where channels are scarce, as with older submarine cables).

T-CARRIER. Originally a 1,544 Mbit/s interoffice digital system, now generic for T1 and higher systems.

TDM. Time Division Multiplexer (a digital signal stream combiner).

TDMA. Time Division Multiplexer Access (a sharing method for transmission sharing, such as satellites).

telegraphy. A system of telecommunication for the transmission of written matter by the use of signal code.

telephony. A system of telecommunication for the transmission of speech or of other sounds.

teleprinter. Automatic telegraph receiver.

television. A system of telecommunication for the transmission of transient images of fixed or moving objects.

telex. A circuit- and, more recently, message-switched international telegraph service.

terminal adapter. A device which converts a non-ISDN terminal interface (e.g., that of a POTS telephone) to an ISDN S or T interface for use with an ISDN.

ternary. Having three states.

time division. Separation on a chronological basis.

tip and ring. Names for the two wires in a telephone local loop.

transponder. A frequency translating amplifier in a communications satellite.

trunk group. A collection of channels connecting exchanges.

TSI. Time Slot Interchange (moving channels in an aggregate).

turn-key. Furnished to customer functional (rather than design) specifications.

UI. Unit Interval (a digital pulse width for jitter measurements).

underflow. Over-depletion of bits in a buffer.

unipolar. Having only a single voltage state to ground.

uplink. Signal path from the earth to satellites.

UTC. Coordinated Universal Time (world standard time, formerly GMT, Greenwich Mean Time).

VSAT. Very Small Aperture Terminal (a small satellite earth station).

wander. A very slow change in rate, two slow to be jitter.

WARC. World Administrative Radio Congress (a UN body assigning radio and satellite usage and frequencies).

WDM. Wavelength Division Multiplexing (a sharing method in a fiber optic strand).

wideband. Bandwidth equal to many individual channels.

zero-substitution. Replacement of "zeros" by substitution "ones" in specific patterns.

wireline. Telephone companies who also operate cellular systems.

ZBI. Zero Bit Insertion (a data link control method to prevent false FLAG groups).

Index

T